DICTIONARY OF
COMMERCE AND MANAGEMENT

S.N.CHAND

ATLANTIC
PUBLISHERS & DISTRIBUTORS (P) LTD

Published by
ATLANTIC
PUBLISHERS & DISTRIBUTORS (P) LTD
7/22, Ansari Road, Darya Ganj, New Delhi-110002
Phones : +91-11-40775252, 40775214, 23273880, 23275880
Fax : +91-11-23285873
Web : www.atlanticbooks.com
E-mail : orders@atlanticbooks.com

Branch Office: Chennai
Phones : +91-44-48531784, 28291383
E-mail : chennai@atlanticbooks.com

Printed & bound in India by Atlantic Print Services

and practising managers, management consultants, professional accountants and the like. It would serve as an invaluable source of reference for anyone who comes into contact with the vocabulary of commerce and management.

Notwithstanding all the pains I have bestowed on its preparation, I am fully aware that some words might have escaped inclusion and despite all efforts made, some errors would have inadvertently crept in. I look forward for any notice of the same as well as penetrating comments and useful suggestions from readers in order to enhance the utility of the book. I shall be glad to incorporate them in the next edition of the book.

I have received great help from many people in the preparation of this book. I express my deep gratitude to all of them.

S.N. CHAND

Preface

There has been growing interest in the present generation of students to opt for Commerce and Management as their main subject and pursue their career in business or managerial field. The subject has a wide scope covering the trade and industry of the entire world. Globalisation and the expanding technology of networking has facilitated rapid international and interstate trade and commerce, thereby virtually compelling the concerned persons to keep up with today's changing business environment. Change is constant and the need to improve yesterday's practices always remains, otherwise one is sure to fall short of the mark. The same implies in respect to new terminology introduced in the subject. Students of all levels are faced with an almost bewildering array of terms, abbreviations and acronyms in books, magazines and newspapers, advertisements and their day-to-day conversation. Since each and every human activity in a way invariably reels around some kind of commercial activity, it is indispensable for all to remain acquainted with the terms related to commerce and management. Thus, it is with this view that the present dictionary has been compiled.

The *Dictionary of Commerce and Management* has been prepared with meticulous care, aiming at providing a fully updated, authoritative, and up-to-date coverage of words and concepts—both conventional and latest—with their comprehensive explanation. The book is organised for easy reference. Entries are arranged in letter-by-letter alphabetical order and every effort has been made to give the exact meaning as well as related relevant information in a jargon-free language and accessible style. This dictionary will help readers in countless ways to enhance their knowledge of the subject and improve their writing and speech and to enrich their vocabulary. It is primarily meant for students and teachers of Commerce & Management, executives, professional

A

ABACUS

The first mechanical calculator having beads for counting.

ABC ANALYSIS

(*i*) The abbreviation 'ABC' stands for *Always Better Control*. A technique of effective material control, materials are divided into three categories: 'A, 'B', and 'C'. Whereby the category 'A' of materials represents 5 to 10 per cent of the stores items which form 70 to 75 per cent of the stores value; the category 'B' of materials represents 20 to 25 per cent of stores items constituting 15 to 20 per cent of stores value; and the category 'C' of materials comprises 70 to 75 per cent of items but constitutes only 5 per cent of stores value.

(*ii*) The classification of inventory items, for control purposes, into three categories, according to unit costs and number of items kept on hand.

ABILITY

Actual power to perform any act; a resultant of environment and capacity.

ABILITY TESTS

It measure mainly mental (such as intelligence, mechanical, and clerical abilities or sensory capacities (such as vision and hearing). Except for measures of sensory capacities, the tests are usually the paper-and-pencil type.

ABSENCES PLANS

The objective might be to ensure that the work continues to get done when some workers are absent. Scheduling vacation time is an example of this form of planning.

ABORT

This is a program to terminate the running of a computer job or program because of some abend (It is a machine or programming error that occurs during execution and that cannot be resolved by normal routines.) and to return the control to the operating system so that operating system may warn the user by printing a message on screen and then get ready for executing a new command.

ABOVE THE LINE

A term applying to main media expenditure and its traditional accounting treatment. Now used for all costs of traditional media.

ABSENTEEISM

The official definition of absenteeism on the basis of which statistics in our country are combined and reported under the Factories Act, 1948 is as under: Absence is the failure of a worker to report for work when he is scheduled to work. A worker is to be considered as scheduled to work when the employer has work available for him and the worker is aware of it. A worker is to be treated as absent for purpose of these absenteeism statistics even when he does not turn up for work after obtaining prior permission.

ABSORPTION ACCOUNTING

An accounting system in which all costs (fixed or variable, direct or indirect) are "aborted" by the goods or services produced within the accounting period.

ACCELERATED DEPRECIATION

Depreciation of a fixed asset at a rate faster than with straight-line depreciation.

ACCELERATION CLAUSE

A selection of a contract that makes an entire debt become immediately due because of failure to pay on time because of some other failure.

ACCELERATION PRINCIPLE

The idea that a small change in consumer demand can lead to a major change in organisational demand.

ACCEPTABLE

A predetermined standard against which random samples of produced materials are compared in acceptance sampling.

ACCEPTABLE QUALITY LEVEL

A predetermined standard against which random samples of produced materials are compared in acceptance sampling.

ACCEPTANCE SAMPLING

(*i*) A statistical technique used in quality control that involves evaluating random samples from a group, or "lot," of produced materials to determine whether the lot meets acceptable quality levels.

(*ii*) The inspection of a portion of the output or input of a process to determine acceptability.

ACCEPTANCE THEORY OF AUTHORITY

A theory connected with the administrative management approach which argues that authority does not depend as much on "persons of authority" who give orders as on the willingness to comply of those who receive the orders.

ACCESS

It means to store data in a main memory or secondary storage devices or to retrieve data.

ACCESS TIME

The average amount of time required to retrieve an amount of bytes from the storage device. It is the time taken by the computer to read the data into the main memory from secondary storage device or write back from main memory to the secondary storage.

ACCESSION TAX

Tax levied on gifts and inherited property.

ACCIDENTS

An unexpected, unplanned event that may result in injury

is an accident. Mishaps that take place at work and may be caused by carelessness, by inadequate safety precautions, or by chance. Employees are generally entitled to record details of any injuries resulting from accidents in an accident books kept at the workplace and this may be used as evidence for insurance purposes. Some people are thought to be more accident prone than others for psychological reasons.

ACCOMMODATION

(*i*) The act of adjusting the lens of the eye to keep a sharply focused image on the retina.

(*ii*) A conflict-handling mode that focuses on solving conflicts by allowing the desires of the other party to prevail.

ACCOMMODATION STAGE OF SOCIALISATION

Socialisation activities undertaken or experienced after an individual takes a job or enters an organisation.

ACCOUNT DAY

The day on which pending accounts are to be settled between brokers and other persons. It is also called Setting Day or Pay Day or Settlement Day.

ACCOUNTABILITY

(*i*) Any means of ensuring that the person who is supposed to perform a task actually performs it and does so correctly.

(*ii*) Being answerable to others for some actions, *e.g.*, to a supervisor for completing a task or to a board of directors for company performance. Having responsibility and authority for seeing that something is carried out as expected, *e.g.*, that sales targets are met or that a budget has been properly spent.

ACCOUNTABILITY UNIT

A unit used in the accounting process for regulating fixed assets. It is selected as the basis of property accountability.

ACCOUNTANT

A professional who is responsible for the processing of financial data for score-keeping, attention-directing and problem-solving purposes.

ACCOUNTING

The establishment, maintenance, collection and analysis of financial records. It is used to provide data on the financial position of an organisation and any changes that have occurred, or may occur over time. This is one aspect of the profession (or art) of accountancy.

ACCOUNTING AND BOOK-KEEPING MACHINES

Accounting and Book-keeping machines may well be compared with typewriters used on a flat bed. These machines are used for:

(*a*) Posting in journals, cash books, ledgers, etc.;

(*b*) Preparation of cheques, payrolls cash received and payment sheets;

(*c*) Preparation of copies of ledger accounts along with posting; and

(*d*) Calculating and computing figures and drawing ledger or cash book balances, etc.

ACCOUNTING CYCLE

The repetitive processing of financial transactions during an accounting "cycle"—typically one month. The basic steps in the accounting cycle are:

(1) Entering transactions in one or more journals,

(2) Balancing the journals,

(3) Posting information from the journals to the general ledger,

(4) Posting information from the journals to the subsidiary ledger accounts,

(5) Recording and balancing the ledger accounts,

(6) Preparing financial statements, and

(7) Using the resulting information to improve operations.

ACCOUNTING EQUATION

A mathematical representation of the basic relationships between parts of a financial statement. For example, the accounting equation for the relationship among assets, liabilities, and fund balances (on a balance sheet) is:

$$A = L + FB.$$

Assets = Liabilities + Fund Bal.

ACCOUNTING ERROR

A mistake that occurs in the books of accounts during the process of recording classifying, summarising, posting, etc.

ACCOUNTING INFORMATION

It is one of the principal sources of data to support an operation research study. Accounting data, however, require careful interpretation and organisatian before they can be used safely and efficiently. Businessmen tend to forget that accounting costs are definitions derived in the light of fundamental accounting purpose, sometimes they tend to confuse accounting figures with "truth". Operations research, using the same raw data, may make other definitions which serve the special needs of the particular study. One of the great stumbling blocks in the organisation and implementation of an operation research study is the disentangling from accounting records of the costs appropriately defined and truly significant to the problem at hand.

ACCOUNTING PERIOD

A period of time of equal annual intervals for which books of accounts are prepared and on the closing date, are finalised.

ACCOUNTING PROFITS

Revenue earned during the accounting period minus expenses. It is also known as residual profits.

ACCOUNTING RATIO

Any ratio in analysing an organisation's financial condition. For example, a current ratio is the ratio of current assets to current liabilities.

ACCOUNTS PAYABLE

(*i*) Amounts owed to others for goods and services received and assets required.

(*ii*) Payments due from a business house for the purchase of goods or services.

A/C CREDIT

To invest with credit, sanction.

ACCUMULATED DEPRECIATION

That part of an asset's costs that have been depreciated (that is, for accounting purposes considered to have been consumed or used up).

ACCURACY OF COMPREHENSION

The exactness with which a person understands what he reads.

ACHIEVEMENT AGE (A.A.)

Level of ability, especially in school, measured in terms of the average for a given age group.

ACHIEVEMENT TEST

Tests designed to measure the level of knowledge and proficiency in certain skills already achieved by the applicants, *e.g.*, knowledge of English, Mathematics etc.

ACHIEVEMENT-ORIENTED

A leader behaviour identified in path-goal theory that involves setting challenging goals, expecting subordinates to perform at their highest level, and conveying high degree of confidence in subordinates.

ACID TEST RATIO

The accounting ratio used for analysis of financial statements, sometimes referred to as Quick Ratio or Liquidity Ratio. It measures the relationship between quick assets and current liabilities.

ACORN (A CLASSIFICATION OF RESIDENTIAL NEIGHBOURHOOD)

A geo-demographic database of residential locality types. Commercially available from CACI.

ACQUIRED-NEEDS THEORY

A content theory of motivation (developed by *David* C. *McClelland*) which argues that our needs are acquired or learned on the basis of our life experiences.

ACQUISITION

The purchase of all or part of one organisation by another, and a means of implementing growth strategies.

ACTION PLANNING

The establishment of performance objectives and standards for individuals.

ACTIVE LISTENING

The process in which a listener actively participates in attempting to grasp the facts and the feelings being expressed by the speaker.

ACTIVITY

A work component to be accomplished, represented by an arrow on a PERT network diagram.

ACTIVITY CHART

In both the manufacturing and the service industries, efficient accomplishment of objectives requires the use of teams. An activity chart can show the interaction of members of the group in performing a task. For example, in a hospital, the activities of a surgical team in performing an emergency operation must be carefully controlled. If any member of the team fails to act correctly at the right time, the results could be disastrous. An activity chart allows the actions of each team member in relation to those of other members to be graphically displayed.

ACTIVITIES

Are specified set of behaviours within a project. As we know that activities and events are the primarily elements of a PERT network.

ACUITY

Term used to describe someone's ability to discriminate fine detail in using one of the senses. Most often used of vision, though also used of hearing and other senses.

AD REFERENDUM

When applied to a contract, this term means that although that contract has been signed, certain matters have been left over for consideration when they actually arise.

AD VALOREM

A phrase used to indicate the value of something.

ADAPTATION

Originally a biological term used to describe physical or behavioural changes that increase an organism's chances of survival. Now used in psychology in two ways to describe responses to changes in physical environment, *e.g.*, where the eye adjusts to changes in the light or, where the changed expectations of the society demand some kind of social adaptation in people's behaviour, *e.g.*, the greatly increased number of women at work has led to covert rather than overt discrimination against them by men.

ADAPTER CARD

An adapter or interface card is a printed circuit board fitted with chips and other components.

ADDED VALUE

Increased with of a good or service, compared to the basic or expected product.

ADDING/LISTING MACHINES

Since adding is the most simple and most widely used computing operation and is also a basic operation in most calculating work, adding/ listing machines are commonly used in most business offices. Simple adding machines can be used for adding operation only, whereas listing machines enable the preparation of a printed record of the items added and of the totals simultaneously with the adding operation.

ADDRESS

An identification of the memory cells of storage device which identifies the cells uniquely.

ADDRESS BUS

This is a set of parallel wires which

is used to transmit the address to access the desired device such as main memory.

ADDRESS FORMAT

The address of any instruction can be stored in several manners. The way the address of instruction is stored is known as address format.

AD HOC COMMITTEES

Ad hoc committees are temporary bodies. These may be constituted formally to make recommendations on a particular matter.

ADJOURNING

(*i*) A stage of group development in which group members prepare for disengagement as the group nears successful completion of its goals.

(*ii*) The fifth and last stage of the team development process, is the stage in which the team finishes its job and prepares to disband.

ADJUSTING ENTRIES

Journal entries passed at the end of a trading period through the proper journal in the absence of any separate subsidiary books or journals to record any of the related transactions.

ADMINISTERED MARKETING SYSTEM

A type of VMS in which one player has control by way of influence and agreement but not through explicit ownership or contractual arrangement.

ADMINISTRATION

Means directing operations within the framework of policy laid down by higher managers or set by their predecessors.

ADMINISTRATIVE MANAGEMENT

An approach within classical management theory that focuses on principles that can be used by managers to coordinate the internal activities of organisations.

ADMINISTRATIVE ORGANISATIONS

An Administrative Organisation can be defined as an organisation in which jobs or functions to be carried out are clearly defined in order to achieve the target. The responsibilities and authorities at various levels of managerial positions are clearly defined.

ADMINISTRATION PROCESSES

Corporate culture may be affected by administrative processes. Firms that can develop direct links between performance and rewards tend to create cultures conducive to achievement. Communication systems that are free flowing tend to promote participation and creative atmospheres. The general attitudes that exists toward the tolerance of conflict and the handling of risk have considerable influence on team-work. They also affect the amount of innovation and creativity.

ADMINISTRATIVE PROTECTIONS

A type of trade barrier in the form of various rules and regulations that make it more difficult for foreign firms to conduct business in a particular country.

ADOPTION DEED

Any instrument other than a will that

(*a*) records an adoption, or

(*b*) confers or purports to confer an authority to adopt.

ADOPTION PROCESS

The mental and behavioural stages through which an individual passes before making a purchase or placing an order; awareness, interest, evaluation, and trial.

ADOPTION

Rate at which people accept and become users of a product. Often associated with the diffusion of innovation curve.

ADVANCES

Amounts of money prepaid in contemplation of goods, services, or other assets to be received at a later date. Advances are ordinarily made only to payees to whom an organisation has an obligation. A common example is the travel advance, which is an amount of money made available to an employee prior to the beginning of a trip, for costs the employee will incur.

ADVERSE IMPACT

The effect produced when a job selection rate for a protected group is less than 80 per cent of the rate for the majority group.

ADVERTISEMENT

A message from a person or an organisation to potential customers containing a specific message and in paid-for-media space. Sometimes shortened by practitioners to 'ad' and by the general public to 'advert'.

ADVERTISING AGENCIES

Companies that specialise in providing various levels of advertising services; some agencies focus on specific services or market segments, and others offer a complete range of services covering a wide range of markets.

ADVERTISING CAMPAIGN

A planned approach to communication over a defined period of time.

ADVERTISING MANAGERS

An employee of a firm who supervises the production of the firm's advertisements and decides which media will carry them.

ADVERTISING MEDIA

Communication channels such as radio, television, newspapers, magazines and posters.

ADVERTISING

An element of the marketing mix involving the use of paid media.

ADVERTORIAL

An advertisement written in an editorial style to attempt to give more credibility to the message.

ADVICE NOTE

A letter addressed by the seller of goods or freight.

ADVOCACY ADVERTISING

Non-product advertising that promotes a company's viewpoint on a particular issue of public concern.

AFFECT

The emotional segment of an attitude.

AFFIDAVIT

A declaration in writing made on oath before a person entitled to administer oaths—a commissioner for oaths, normally a solicitor. It is a criminal offence deliberately to make a false statement in an affidavit. Aftersales Service, a continuing service of maintenance repair, supply of information on possible uses and so on, provided to buyers of a product by the seller (or sometimes the manufacturer if the sale was made by a retailer).

AFFIRMATIVE ACTION

Any special activity undertaken by employers to increase equal employment opportunities for groups protected by federal equal employment opportunity laws and related regulations.

AFFIRMATIVE ACTION PLAN

A written, systematic plan that specifies goals and timetables for hiring, training, promoting, and retaining groups protected by federal equal employment laws and related regulations.

AFFIRMATIVE ACTION PROGRAMS

Are organisational programs whose basic purpose is to eliminate barriers against and increase employment opportunities for underutilised or disadvantaged individuals.

AFFORDABILITY

A test of the value or price of an offering from a customer viewpoint.

AFTER-SALES SERVICE

A continuing service of maintenance, repair, supply of information on possible uses and so on, provided to buyers of a product by the seller (or sometimes the manufacturer if the sale was made by a retailer).

AGENT

An individual or company acting in a sales capacity on behalf of a principal. An agent does not take ownership or handle the goods.

AGENTS AND BROKERS

Intermediaries who assist with the marketing of goods and services but who do not assume ownership of products; agents, unlike brokers, usually work long-term for producers.

AGGREGATE PRODUCTION PLANNING

A primary operating system used in operations management that is concerned with planning how to match supply with product or service demand over a time horizon of about 1 year.

AIDA MODEL

Acronym for awareness, interest desire and action, which represent the psychological steps a customer goes through on the way toward making a purchase.

AIDED RECALL

A post testing technique that shows specific ads to people who then answer various questions about them.

ALDERFER'S ERG THEORY

Is an explanation of human needs that divides them into three basic categories: existence needs, relatedness needs, and growth needs.

ALGORITHM

It is planned set of steps to be undertaken in a definite sequence so as to arrive at the solutions of a problem. Such steps can be carried out by a computer or dry run on paper.

ALLEVIATING

Breaking accumulated supplies into smaller units that are easier for later intermediaries and customers to handle.

ALLOTMENT

The acquisition, by one or more persons, of newly issued securities; commonly as a result of an administrative decision by which securities are allocated among applicants.

ALLOTMENT LETTER

A letter sent to the allottees accepting their offer to buy securities and containing details of how many and the terms of acceptance.

ALLOWANCES

Indirect reductions from list price in which part of the list price is effectively returned to the customers, such as with a rebate.

ALTERNATIVE WORK SCHEDULES

Schedules based on adjustments in the normal work schedule rather than in the job content or activities.

AMORAL MANAGEMENT

An approach to managerial ethics that is neither immoral nor moral but, rather, ignores or is oblivious to ethical considerations.

ANALYSE

To divide a complex whole into its constituents, analysis involves study and examination of something complex and the separation of its more simple components.

ANCHOR STORES

Large department stores or discount stores that serve as the main stores in planned shopping centre because of their strong customer appeal.

ANCHORAGE

Charges paid for anchoring in certain ports or harbours.

ANCHORING AND ADJUSTMENT

A decision-making bias that involves the tendency to be influenced by an initial figure, even when the information is largely irrelevant.

ANNUAL GENERAL MEETING

There is a legal requirement on all Registered Companies to hold a meeting of all members once a year, at which the directors present a report.

This includes an Income *Statement, Balance Sheet, Auditor's Report* and *Director's Report* and is usually published in one volume as the Annual Report of the company.

ANNUAL REPORT

A yearly financial statement prepared by the management of a company or any business entity as per the requirement of the Company Law. It is frequently summarised and translated into simple language for distribution among stock-holders and media.

ANNUAL RETURN

A return that a business house is obliged to make annually. Specifically, the details of membership and financial structure that each registered company must send to the Registrar of Companies who makes it available for public inspection.

ANNUITIES

A type of life insurance policy under which a fixed sum is payable by the insurer to the insured periodically after the insured attains a certain age.

ANTE-DATE

To give a document a date that is earlier than the actual date of writing the document.

ANTI-FREELOADER ARGUMENT

An argument that holds that since businesses benefit from a better society, they should bear part of the costs by actively working to bring about solutions to social problems.

ANTI-TRUST LAWS

Federal laws designed to make possible workable competition and to ensure that the competition is fair.

ANTITRUST LEGISLATION

Federal laws meant to promote competition in U.S. markets; the major antitrust laws are the Sherman Antitrust Act (1890), the Clayton Act (1914), and the Federal Trade Commission Act (1914).

APPLICATION

Any specific task performed by the computer such as processing the files of a company or writing the letter.

APPLICATION BANK

A form used widely as a selection method that contains a series of inquiries about such issues as an applicant's educational background, previous job experience, physical health, and other information that may be useful in assessing an individual's ability to perform a job.

APPLICATION PACKAGE

The set of programs or routines developed for some particular purpose such as Sales and Distributor package or Payroll Processing System.

APPLICATIONS SOFTWARE PACKAGES

Software programs available for

sale or lease from commercial sources.

APPRAISAL

A formal system of appraising a manager's performance periodically and in writing.

APPRENTICESHIP

The period of time spent, mostly at the workplace and usually on low wages, in learning the basic skills of a craft, trade or profession.

APPROVE

To accept as satisfactory. Approval implies that the things approved has the endorsement of the approving agency; however, approval may still require confirmation by somebody else. A manager approves plans subject to authorisation by the accountable executive.

APTITUDE

Readiness in learning; natural capacity or ability.

ARBITRAGE

Buying of foreign exchange, securities, etc., in one market for selling them in another with the .object of earning a profit.

ARITHMETIC OPERATOR

Operators are the symbols which are used to indicate the particular operation. For *e.g.*, '+/' is used for addition, '*' is used for Multiplication, '–' is used for Subtraction, '/' or '\' is used for division. Array Collection of two or more logically related elements of exactly same type which are identified by a single name. This is stored in consecutive locations of main memory.

ARREARS

Dues; outstanding amounts; money owed but not paid to a person who is legally entitled to receive the same.

ARTEL

A Russian word, which means, 'Cooperative Society of Workers'.

ARTIFICIAL INTELLIGENCE

A field of information technology aimed at developing computers that have humanlike capabilities, such as seeing, hearing, and thinking.

ARTWORK

The visual or graphic portion of an advertisement.

ASCII

American Standard Code for Information Interchange. This is the most widely recognised set.

ASCII CHARACTER

6 bit code for representing the alphanumeric of English language.

ASPIRATIONAL GROUP

In reference to an individual, group to which the individual would like to belong.

ASSEMBLY

The process of fabricating the IC's by which the IC is put into a package and is wired to the leads.

ASSEMBLY UNIT

A small program unit which could be integrated with different programs without modifications.

ASSEMBLY-LINE TECHNOLOGY

A form of manufacturing in which component parts are brought together and combined into a single unit of output. It is used to produce relatively standard products that have a mass market.

ASSESSEE

A person who is liable to pay any tax.

ASSESSMENT CENTRE

(*i*) A controlled environment used to predict the probable managerial success of individuals mainly on the basis of evaluations of their behaviours in a variety of simulated situations, thereby facilitating selection.

(*ii*) Refers a program in which participants engage in, and are evaluated on, a number of individual and group exercises constructed to stimulate important activities at the organisational levels to which they aspire.

ASSESSMENT

A procedure to identify ability carried out on individuals as part of the processes of recruitment and selection; a procedure carried out on property or profits to determine tax liability.

ASSET MANAGEMENT RATIOS

Financial ratios that measure how effectively an organisation manages its assets.

ASSET TURNOVER

The ratio of net sales to average assets for defined fiscal period. The ratio expresses financial activity in an analysis of return on investment.

ASSETS

Resources an organisation owns which are of economic benefit to it. These may be tangible (like machinery or property) or intangible (like goodwill).

ASSIST

To help by providing advice and service. Assistance involves providing aid without exercise of command authority. For example, the personnel manager assists the chairman.

ASSISTANT

Personal staff position.

ASSISTANT-TO

A staff aide to an executive. The assistant-to is not second in command and has no authority over other immediate subordinates of his chief, although he may represent his chief in matters of administrative detail.

ASSORTING

As the final step in the regrouping process, assorting creates the particular mix of goods required by target customers.

AT PAR

At nominal or face value. Thus, a share is issued at par when its selling price equals its face value.

ATMOSPHERE

A part of retail image that is created by a blend of sensory effects intended to create a specific shopping mood.

ATTENTION

A set, attitude or adjustment of the organism which makes it better able to respond to a given stimulus.

ATTESTED COPY

A copy of an original document verified to be true. Any document is required by law to be attested, as proof of its execution.

ATTITUDE

(*i*) Learned tendency to respond to objects, people, ideas, or products in a particular way.

(*ii*) A learned predisposition to respond in a consistently favourable or unfavourable manner with respect to a given object. There are many different attitude theories.

(*iii*) Is a predisposition to react to a situation, person, or concept with a particular response.

ATTRIBUTION

Is the process by which people interpret the behaviour of others by assigning to it motives or causes.

ATTRIBUTION ERROR

Is the tendency to overestimate internal causes of behaviour and underestimate external ones when judging other people's behaviour.

AUCTION HOUSES

Facilities designed to bring buyers and sellers together for the purpose of selling products to the highest bidder.

AUDIENCE

The person or persons who are receiving a transmitted message.

AUDIT

A process of detailed examination of a company's accounts to assess their accuracy.

AUDIT WORK (OF AN ACCOUNT)

Work comprising authentication of accounting statements.

AUDITOR

A professionally qualified person who examines and scrutinises various books of accounts.

AUDITOR'S REPORT

A legally-required report from independent and qualified auditors which must be attached to any Income Statement or Balance Sheet prepared by a Registered Company.

AUGMENTED PRODUCTS

The expected products plus all of their added value.

AUSTIC THINKING

Absorption in fantasy to the exclusion of interest in reality.

AUTHORISE

To give final approval. This implies final endorsement, such that no further approval is necessary. Thus, the chairman approves, and the Board of Directors authorises overall company objectives.

AUTHORISED DEPOSITORY

A person authorised by the Central Government to accept the custody of securities with related certificates of tide.

AUTHORITARIAN MANAGEMENT

A type of management which emphasises the discipline and control of people and sees little value in consulting them about the job—what you would expect from an authoritarian personality. It is usually contrasted with democratic management.

AUTHORITY

Formal power a person holds because of her position in the organisational hierarchy. The recognition of authority is necessary for organisational effectiveness and is a cost of organisational membership.

AUTOCAD

A software for working with detailed drawing on the monitor and print them out with the help of a plotter.

AUTOCRATIC

The behavioural style of leaders who tend to make unilateral decisions, dictate work methods, limit worker knowledge about goals to just the next step to be performed, and sometimes give feedback that is punitive.

AUTOMATE

To arrange a job so that part or all of the decision-making and control previously performed by humans is performed by machines.

AUTOMATION

Typical objectives of automation are increased human productivity, an expanded physical and mental capacity for workers, increased precision or accuracy, and reduced costs.

AUTONOMY

A core job characteristic involving the amount of discretion allowed in determining schedules and work methods for achieving the required output.

AVAILABILITY

(*i*) A decision-making bias that involves the tendency to judge the likelihood of an occurrence on the basis of the extent to which other like instances or occurrences can easily be recalled.

(*ii*) A test of the convenience of an offering from a customer viewpoint.

AVERAGE COLLECTION PERIOD

The result of dividing the average accounts receivable with net credit sales and multiplying the resultant by 365 days of the year. It indicates the average credit period actually granted during a year.

AVERAGE FIXED COST

The amount of fixed cost attributed to each unit produced; equal to total fixed costs divided by the number of units.

AVERAGE PAYMENT PERIOD

The average period that elapses between the purchase of goods on credit and the payment to creditors.

AVERAGE TOTAL COST (ATC)

The sum of average total and average variable costs; represents the average expenses required to make one unit.

AVERAGE VARIABLE COST (AVC)

The variable cost of producing a quantity of a good divided by the quantity produced.

AVOIDANCE

A conflict-handling mode that involves ignoring or suppressing a conflict in the hope that it will either go away or not become too disruptive.

B

BACK PAY

Wage/salary for work already done but for which proper payment has not been received. This differs from retrospective payment, which arises from an agreement to back date a new system or level of payment.

BACK UP

Making the additional copies of the files and data in secondary storage from the security and recovery point of view.

BACKED NOTE

An authority, endorsed by broker, the master of ship arranging the loading of goods for shipment.

BACKGROUND

The sum of ones experience, training, and education.

BACKHAUL

In rail and truck transportation, the practice of carrying a shipment by one its destination and then returning it, partly over the same route.

BACKLOG

The total of a business's unfilled orders at any one time.

BACKWARD INVENTION

Redesigning and producing a product for specific foreign markets after it is obsolete in industrialised countries.

BACKWARD PASS

In project network techniques the calculation of latest event times, or of latest start times of activities and earliest start times of activities.

BAD SECTOR

Defective sector on a magnetic disk which could neither be read nor written.

BAILEE

A person who is entrusted with the possession of goods and by a warehouse receipt, bill of lading, or other document of title, acknowledges such possession and contracts to deliver those goods.

BAILMENT

A transfer of possession of goods without the passing of title, as on consignment for safekeeping, repair, or sale.

BALANCE OF PAYMENTS

An international economic element that is an account of goods and services, capital loans, gold and other items entering and leaving a country, and a factor influencing the ability of an organisation to conduct international business in that country successfully.

BALANCE OF TRADE

A nation's total imports in relation to its total exports over a one-year period of time. In narrow sense, the difference between a country's exports and imports and, generally, the most critical determinant of a country's balance of payments.

BALANCE SHEET

A financial statement that depicts an organisation's assets and claims against those assets at a given point in time.

BALANCE TICKET

A kind of certificate required to sell only a part of a shareholder's shares. Normally a company issues one share certificate for all the shares purchased by one person.

BALANCED ACCOUNTS

A statement of accounts in which assets and liabilities have been balanced.

BALANCE-DUE

The quantity of material or parts ordered on a purchase order or requisitioned on a work order but not yet received.

BANDED PACK

A form of sales promotion in which consumer are offered two or more packages of a product, or a package of a product plus another product from the same manufacturer, attached together (usually by a band of tape printed with details of the offer), at a reduced price.

BANDING

A way of organising a salary structure where a series of different levels are first established into various jobs. These jobs are then classified by different levels, or by bank rather than fixing a different rate of pay for each job individually.

BANK CREDIT

A written promise by a bank that an organisation or person may borrow up to a specified amount.

BANK DRAFT

An order issued by a seller's bank against a purchaser's bank directing payment of money, usually through an intermediary bank. Bank drafts generally are negotiable and are similar to the cheques drawn against standard checking accounts except that they are drawn by one bank on its account in another bank.

BANK FLOAT

Efficient cash management involving the speedy conversion of payments into cash for use by a business concern.

BANK HOLIDAY

Any legal holiday or other special occasion when bank remain closed, usually but not always along with most other businesses.

BANK MONEY

Cheques and drafts used as a medium of exchange for money; and any bank deposits transacted by cheque. It is treated as a cash asset.

BANK NOTE

A kind of paper currency that is, in effect, the promissory note of a bank.

Such notes promise to pay the bearer on demand the amount stated on the face of the note. Bank notes are now issued by the Central Bank of every country.

BANK OVERDRAFT

Bank overdraft is granted when the customer has a current account in the bank. Under an overdraft arrangement, a depositor is allowed to draw by a cheque more than the deposited amount to his credit, but up to a specified limit. Interest is charged on the exact amount overdrawn by the customer. The rate of interest on it is always higher than that charged on the loans. This facility is given by banks on the security of some assets or on the personal security of the customer. It is a short period arrangement.

BANK PAPERS

Discountable commercial papers comprising *Bills of Exchange, Acceptance, Drafts* and *Other Commercial Papers* used in trade that may be discounted by commercial banks.

BANKING TIME OFF

A reward practice of allowing employees to build up time-off credits for such things as good performance or attendance. Employees then receive the time off in addition to regular vacation time granted by the organisation.

BANKRUPTCY

A defensive strategy in which an organisation that is unable to pay its debts can seek Court protection from creditors and from certain contract obligations while it attempts to regain financial stability.

BAR CODE

A set of vertical printed lines in binary coding that can be read into the computer with the help of light scanning.

BARGAIN

The process of achieving an agreement in which something is bought, sold, exchanged, or agreed upon between two or more parties.

BARRATRY

A wrongful act wilfully committed by the master or crew of a ship, which is prejudicial to the interest of the owner, or, as the case may be, the charterer, as per the rules for Construction of Marine Policy.

BARRIERS TO ENTRY

Competitive conditions that make it expensive, illegal, or otherwise difficult to enter a market as a competitor.

BASE PAY

Regular salary or wage excluding incentive pay, bonuses, fringe benefits, overtime pay, and all other extra-compensation.

BASIC WAGES

All emoluments earned by an employee while on duty or on leave with wages.

BASIC WORK-WEEK

The number of hours in a normal work-week. Premium payments

or compensatory time off must usually be made for time worked in excess of the basic work-week.

BASING-POINT PRICING

A form of delivered pricing that sets shipping charges based on delivery from one or more locations, even if the shipment never actually moved through those locations.

BATCH PROCESSING

An arrangement whereby data are accumulated and then processed as a group.

BATTERY

A collection of tests which have a similar purpose or are to be administered one after another at a single session.

BAYESIAN ANALYSIS

Statistical techniques which use and establish probability curves to help in decision-making by exploring potential outcomes of different options.

BAZAAR

Although associated with markets and oriental bazaars, the term has Western usage meaning a variety store like Woolworth. Also applied to grouping of trader under one roof, *e.g.* coin, stamp antique dealers.

BCG GROWTH-SHARE MATRIX

A portfolio approach involving a four cell matrix (developed by the *Boston Consulting Group*) that compares various businesses in an organisation's portfolio on the basis of relative market share and market growth rate.

BEARER CHEQUE

A negotiable instrument which banks honour on presentation for encashment. The payment of the amount encased is made to the person who presents the cheque to the bank.

BEHAVIOURALLY ANCHORED RATING SCALES (BARS)

Performance appraisal scales containing sets of specific behaviours that represent gradations of performance used as common reference points (or anchors) for rating employees on various job dimensions.

BEHAVIOUR

Anything that a person does, such as talking, walking, thinking, or daydreaming. The action that results from an attitude.

BEHAVIOURAL DISPLACEMENT

A condition which is a side effect of poorly designed and/or excessive controls in which individuals engage in behaviours that are encouraged by controls and related reward systems even though the behaviours are actually inconsistent with organisational goals.

BEHAVIOURAL SCIENCE

An approach that emphasises scientific research as the basis for developing theories about human behaviour in organisations that can be used to establish practical guidelines for managers.

BEHAVIOURAL SEGMENTATION

A way of dividing large markets into smaller groupings according to consumer behaviour.

BEHAVIOURAL VIEWPOINT

A perspective on management that emphasises the importance of attempting to understand the various factors that affect human behaviour in organisations.

BELIEF

A conviction concerning the existence or the characteristics of something.

BELONGINGNESS NEEDS

The needs in *Maslow's* hierarchy that involve the desire to affiliate with and be accepted by others.

BENCHMARKING

The process of identifying the best practices and approaches by comparing productivity in specific areas within one's own company with the productivity of other organisations both within and outside the country.

BENEFIT SEGMENTATION

A form of behavioural segmentation that divides the market according to benefits sought by consumers.

BENEFITS

Forms of compensation beyond wages for time worked, including various protection plans, services, pay for time not worked, and income supplements.

BID PRICE

A term associated with Unit Trust. Units are quoted at two prices: the *bid pricey* which is the sum that the management company will pay for units held by third parties; and the *offer price,* which is the figure at which they will sell. The offer price is higher than the bid price so that when people buy units they must, if they are not to lose on the investment, retain them until they have risen to a point above the bid price. For this reason unit trusts are seen as a longterm rather than a short-term investment.

BILL MARKET

A short-term credit market in the money market; also known as *Discount Market.*

BILL OF ENTRY

A bill of entry is a document prepared by the importer for the purpose of paying the custom duties. It is prepared in triplicate and contains full information regarding the goods due to arrive. The bill of entry forms are printed in three different colours—*blacky blue* and *violet.* The black form is used for goods imported from the outside, the blue form is used for goods to be used within the country and the violet form is used for goods means for re-export. On the basis of the information given in the bill of entry, the custom authorities calculate the amount of duty and charge the same from the importer.

BILL OF LADING

A list identifying all goods or property within a shipment, which serves as an inventory, provides directions for shipment, and acknowledges their transfer and receipt.

BILL OF MATERIALS (BOM)

An input to MRP system that consists of a listing of all components, including partially assembled pieces and basic parts, that make up on end product.

BILL OF PARCELS

An invoice or list of purchased items and their value.

BILL

A statement of items and charges made for services rendered, products purchased or rented, or accommodations used; also, a draft of a law for consideration by a legislative committee or Body.

BILLING MACHINES

Billing machines generally combine typewriters of roller type with calculators. Papers and carbon are feed into the machine and set automatically. The machines make calculations regarding discount, extensions, totals, etc., and are useful for the quick preparation of bills, invoices, credit notes and similar documents.

BIN CARD

A stores record; it records the quantity of materials received, issued and the balance-in-stock particulars.

BINARY FILE

File whose contents are in binary from *i.e.*, machine form.

BINGO CARD

Enquiry card bound into a magazine and containing matrix of number or letters which correlate with similar keys in advertisement or editorial items. Facilitates reader enquiries and is usually prepaid for return to publisher. May also be refer to as reader's enquiry card.

BLACK BOX

In concept, an apparatus whose input and output may be observed but whose inner workings are not known. The term is often used, however, in cases where a subsystem (in a computer-controlled system) is purchased from outside rather than designed by the designer of the system. In that case the designer does not care what goes on inside the box (although he probably knows): he is interested only in the output it will produce for a given input.

BLACK ECONOMY

The informal sector of the economy where work is done but no record of it is officially available and on which no tax is paid.

BLACK MONEY

Unaccounted, undisclosed money kept secretly, thereby escaping tax liability.

BLACKLIST

A list of people or organisations against whom some kind of discrimination will be practised, usually for political reasons.

BLANK CHEQUE

A cheque where no sum of money is stated The holder can fill in the amount himself. Blank cheques are often used in latter transactions where the price of the goods to be purchased is not known. The buyer may send a blank cheque but write, *e.g.*, not to exceed ₹.....' on it. The bank will need this instruction.

BLEND

In phonetics, a blend is the sound resulting from the combination of two or three consonants within a word without loss of identity of the sounds of the separate letters. For example, BL in BLUE is a blend.

BLINK-METER

Used in advertising research to measure the frequency of a person's blanking, so giving indications of interest or arousal.

BLOCKED CURRENCY

A currency that cannot be redeemed in the World Financial Marketplace.

BLUE CHIP

Shares of companies with a good track record and which offer high rates of dividend.

BLUE SKY RESEARCH

Long-term high-risk research which involves a high level of speculation (both financial and intellectual) but which might yield significant gains by opening up totally new field opportunity.

BODY COPY

Main copy in advertisement, as opposed to headlines or illustration.

BODY-SHOPPING

A term sometimes used of the practice whereby a consultancy supplies people to work on a temporary contract basis in place of regular staff in the public sector.

BONA FIDE OCCUPATIONAL QUALIFICATION (BFOQ)

A legitimate job qualification that necessitates an employer's selecting an individual in a certain sex, religion, national-origin, or age group.

BOND CREDITORS

A class of creditors who lend money on the security of assets. They represent creditorship securities.

BOND NOTE

A note giving the list of goods subject to export/import duty that are to be put under a bond.

BONDS

Debt certificates issued by a business constituting a lien against the physical assets of the enterprise.

BONUS ACCOUNT

A saving account that pays a higher than normal rate of interest.

BONUS PAYMENT

An incentive payment to salesmen for above the norm achievement; often *ex gratia* rather than contractual.

BONUS SHARE

Shares issued to existing shareholders without consideration on the capitalisation of reserves built up over a period of time.

BONUS STOCK

Common stock offered as a bonus. Either to the underwriter of the issue as additional incentive, or to buyers of bonds or preferred stock in the same company.

BONUS

Any payment in addition to regular or base wages. It may be in the form of a Christmas bonus or other annual allotment, or it may consist in higher rates paid for night-work, overtime hazardous work etc. Also used in connection with incentive wage systems to designate amounts earned in excess of base or guaranteed rates.

BOOK VALUE

The value of an asset or liability as recorded in the books of accounts.

BOOM

Rapid growth in market values and expansion of business facilities and activity.

BOOTY

The value of goods captured from the enemy during wartime.

BOULWARISM

In industrial relations, a position in which an employer maker an analysis of what it considers reasonable—in terms of wages, conditions etc., and then refuses to negotiate beyond this positions in collective bargaining. The term takes its name form a former vice-president of the General Electric Company in the USA.

BOUNDARY SPANNING

An approach to influencing the environment that involves creating roles within the organisation that interface with important elements in the environment.

BOUNDED RATIONALITY

A concept that suggests that the ability of managers to be perfectly rational in making decisions is limited by such factors as cognitive capacity and time constraints.

BOUNTY

The payment by the state of a specific sum per unit of an article—so much per unit produced or per unit imported/per unit exported. It differs from subsidy in that a subsidy is paid as a lump-sum or upon some other basis than that of commodity unit.

BOYCOTT

The refusal of a government or public groups and consumers to buy certain goods from another country. In other words, an action in which some group refuses to buy certain products. A government may enforce a boycott of the products of some other country.

BRAINSTORMING

The generation of ideas in a group through noncritical discussion.

BRAND

(*i*) A name or some other identifying feature that distinguishes one marketer's product; much competition is among brands. In other words, it refers in Marketing, a product or service sold under a particular name in order to differentiate it in the marketplace.

(*ii*) An article identified by a name, symbol, trade mark or characteristic which differentiates it from competitive offerings. In other words, the name, term, symbol, design, or a combination of them that identifies the goods or services of one seller or group of sellers and distinguishes them from those of their competitors.

BRAND EQUITY

Means the situation in which market share or profit margins are greater because of the goodwill associated with the brand.

BRAND EXTENSION

Assigning an existing brand name to a new product in the same product line or in a different product line.

BRAND IMAGE

Refers the complex of symbols and meanings associated with a brand.

BRAND LICENSING

A type of licensing arrangement in which one company sells others the right to use one or more of its brand name.

BRAND LOYALTY

A situation where consumers remain loyal to a particular brand of good or services even if it costs more than its competitors.

BRAND MARK

A unique symbol that is part of a brand.

BRAND NAME

The verbal part of the brand; the part that can be spoken.

BREACH OF WARRANTY

A violation of the guarantee or representation of the contract, performance, condition, quality, or endurance of a product of service. A breach of warranty does not necessarily entail fraudulent misrepresentation.

BREAK-EVEN ANALYSIS

A profit analysis technique that identifies the sales volume at which total cost is equal to total revenue; you'll make a profit if sales exceed this level and suffer a loss if they don't reach this level.

BREAK-EVEN POINT

The sales volume at which a company breaks even *i.e.,* no profit, no loss point.

BREAK-EVENT CHART

A chart on which two curves are plotted: the expected sales revenues from the production of various quantities of a product and the costs (fixed and variable) of producing those quantities. The curves intersect at the break-even point.

BROKEN LOT

Goods offered for sale in smaller than normal quality include damaged packaged goods where some contents have been lost or remove.

BROKER

A mercantile agent who makes contracts for the purchase or sale of property or goods.

BROKERAGE

Commission charged by a broker. Synonym for *Broking*.

BUDGET SURPLUS

The amount by which budget receipts exceed budget outlays for any given period.

BUDGET YEAR

The fiscal year for which a budget is being considered.

BUDGET

The financial statement of an organisation planned income and expenditure for a given length of time; the proposed income and expenditure of the British Government over the coming year as presented to Parliament by the Chancellor of the Exchequer; sometimes used in place of appropriation.

BUDGETING

The process of stating in quantitative terms, usually dollars, planned organisational activities for a given period of time.

BUFFER

Stock held to cover production or sales demand when unforeseen circumstances arise such as machines breaking down, suppliers unable to deliver etc.

BUFFERING

A method of adapting to environmental fluctuations that involves stock-piling either inputs into or outputs from a production or service process in order to cope with environmental fluctuations.

BUG

An error or fault in the software which causes a computer program to malfunction.

BUILT-IN OBSOLESCENCE

The deliberate design of a product so that it needs replacing after a certain length of time.

BULL

Refers to the state of the stock exchange market; a speculator who has bought shares in expectation of a rise in prices.

BUMPER STRIKE

Now largely outdated type of industrial action in which strikers are directly supported financially by similar workers in other factories.

BUMPING

The displacement of one worker by another with more seniority common in industries where labour contracts include rigid seniority rules. The team "backtracking" comes from the fact that a senior employee may move to a lower-level job causing the layoff of a junior employee.

BUNDLING

Combining products for promotional reasons, often at a discounted price.

BUNK

A place where a sole trader generally carries on his business.

BUREAU DE CHANGE

This is a shop or sometimes merely a counter where one type

of currency may be exchanged for another. It is primarily a service for tourists.

BUREAUCRATIC CONTROL

A managerial approach that relies on regulation through rules, policies, supervision, budgets, schedules, reward systems, and other administrative mechanisms aimed at ensuring that employees exhibit appropriate behaviours and meet performance standards.

BUREAUCRATIC MANAGEMENT

An approach within classical management theory that emphasises the need for organisations to operate in a rational manner rather than relying on the arbitrary whims of owners and managers.

BUREAUCRATIC THEORY

The theory developed by *Max Weber* that defines the characteristics of an organisation that maximise the stability and controllability of its members. The ideal bureaucracy is an organisation that contains all of these characteristics to a high degree.

BURGLARY INSURANCE

Basic protection against loss due to crime committed by outsiders rather than by employees of an organisation or authorised visitors. It applies only when there is physical evidence of forced entry coverage is provided for specific goods or property and damage incurred in the course of the burglary.

BUSINESS ADMINISTRATION

This term usually refers to the field of study concerned with the control, direction, or management of a business organisation.

BUSINESS ANALYSIS STAGE

The stage in new product development in which the new product is reviewed from all organisational perspectives to determine performance criteria and likely profitability.

BUSINESS CYCLE

A predictable economic fluctuation that gives rise to four stages: prosperity, recession, depression, and recovery.

BUSINESS GAME

Enactment by students or trainees of business situation based on presentation of skilful selected information followed by progressive decision-making leading to assessment of profitability and other crucial factors. Sometimes involves use of a computer often played competitively by teams particularly in management training. A judication can be human or computerised sometimes known as *Management Game*.

BUSINESS LIFE CYCLE

The progression of events in business formation that starts with the establishment of a new business and continues through growth, maturity, and decline.

BUSINESS PLAN

A document written by the prospective owner or entrepreneur

that details the nature of the business, the product or service, the customers, the competition, the production and marketing methods, the management, the financing, and other significant aspects of the proposed business venture.

BUSINESS-LEVEL STRATEGY

A type of strategy that concentrates on the best means of competing within a particular business while also supporting the corporate-level strategy.

BUSINESS-TO-BUSINESS MARKETING TRANSACTION

A transaction in which a product is sold for any use other than personal consumption. The buyer may be a manufacturer, a reseller, a government body, non-profit institution, or any organisation other than an ultimate consumer. The transaction occurs so an organisation may conduct its business.

BUY PHASE

One of the stages of the multistage process by which organisations make purchase decisions.

BUYER

A manager with responsibility for purchasing within a firm.

BUYER BEHAVIOUR

The way in which customers act, and the steps taken in the purchase decision process. In other words, the buying-centre role played by the organisational member with the formal authority to purchase the product.

BUYER CREDIT

A method of financing exports in which bank in the exporter's country loans money to foreign buyers for purchase from the exporter. Such a deal is usually set up on the exporter's initiative and the money is in practice paid direct to the exporter.

BUYER FOR EXPORT

Any customer or intermediary that buys a mix of products in the domestic market for sale in other markets.

BUYERS' MARKET

(*i*) Market situation in which excess manufacturing capacity and oversupply of a commodity puts buyer in strong negotiating position as the result of an imbalance between supply and demand particularly affects movement of prices for seasonal goods.

(*ii*) A market condition in which supply exceeds demand.

BUY-IN

A business arrangement by which an individual secures a financial or ownership interest in a partnership or organisation. The buy-in is often used by physicians to become members of group practices.

BUYING CENTRE ROLES

Roles assumed by various members of the buying centre, including initiator, influences decision-maker, gate-keeper, purchaser, and user.

BUYING CENTRE

The group of individuals involved in making a particular buying decision within an organisation.

BUYING GROUP

Group of associated buyers *e.g.* farmers retailers horticultural societies buying in bulk and selling at low price to members.

BUYING POWER INDEX (BPI)

A measure of various geographic regions' collective purchasing power, based on population, effective buying income, and retail sales.

BUYING POWER

The consumer's ability to purchase products.

BUYING SIGNALS

Indirect indication of a prospect's growing interest in the product being presented.

BUYING-IN

The practice of hiring expert help as required by an organisation rather than employing such experts on its staff.

BUZZ GROUP

A form of brainstorming group used in management problem-solving.

BUZZ WORD

Pejorative way of describing the frequent use of fashionable management terms by those who do not necessarily understand their full meaning.

BY-PRODUCT

Any product resulting from manufacturing or processing a firm's primary product.

C

CABLE TRANSFER

In foreign trade a bank draft transmitted by cable or telegraph instead of mail. The correspondent bank team notifies the payee to the remittance's arrival.

CACHE MEMORY

A small high speed memory which is placed between the processor and main memory.

CALCULATING MACHINES

Where calculations have to be made on a large scale, calculating machines are used. These contribute greatly to business efficiency by eliminating chances of error and relieving the office worker of much tiring mental work, thereby increasing the output of work. This in turn results in economy in office expenses by reducing staff requirements. Calculating machines can perform additions, subtractions, multiplications, divisions, calculations of interest, discount, exchange, etc.

CALL FREQUENCY

Frequency with which salesmen visit or contact customer distinguished from conventional journey cycle by customer categorising into group of varying priority.

CALL PREMIUM

The excess of face value of a callable bond.

CALL-OFF

A form of materials purchase in which a supplier is given a schedule of goods likely to be required over a future period say one year the actual number of goods are called off against that schedule in batches as and when needed by the producer.

CANNED APPROACH

An approach to selling that utilises a memorised presentation and doesn't take into account individual customer and selling situations.

CAPACITY

The total amount that is possible to produce with existing plant and equipment. (Sometimes it is slightly less than the true total. Therefore some companies may, for short periods, produce at more than 100 per cent of capacity.)

CAPACITY ARGUMENT

An argument which states that the private sector, because of its considerable economic and human resources, must make up for recent government cutbacks in social programs.

CAPACITY PLANNING

A primary operating system used in operations management that is concerned with determining the people, machines, and major physical resources, such as buildings, that will be necessary to meet the production objectives of the organisation.

CAPACITY REQUIREMENT PLANNING

A technique for determining what personnel and equipment are needed to meet short-term production objectives.

CAPACITY STRATEGY

Is an operational plan of action aimed at providing the organisation with the right facilities to produce the needed output at the right time.

CAPITAL

The money involved in a business enterprise which is invested in goods, equipment, buildings, stock, etc.

CAPITAL ACCOUNT

The section of the statement of a country's balance of payments that records all payments not in the current account. An account recording the contributions by partners to the capital in a partnership.

CAPITAL ASSET

Assets, including investments not held for sale, conversion or consumption in the normal course of business.

CAPITAL BUDGET

A statement of planned expenditures of funds for facilities and equipment.

CAPITAL CREDIT

The present acquisition of long-term productive facility such as land, buildings, and machinery against promises of enterprises to pay in the future.

CAPITAL EXPENDITURES BUDGET

A type of budget that involves a plan for the acquisition or divestiture of major fixed assets, such as land, buildings, or equipment.

CAPITAL FINANCING

The acquisition and use of funds for purchasing, improving and expanding capital assets such as buildings and non-disposable equipment contrasted with the financing of operations and maintenance.

CAPITAL GAINS

Gains accruing from the sale or exchange of capital assets.

CAPITAL GOODS

Goods, such as machine tools, which form part of capital investments—as distinct from consumer goods.

CAPITAL RESERVE

A reserve of a company or enterprise which is not available for distribution as dividend.

CAPITAL SUM (INSURANCE)

The maximum amount of money payable in a single sum for loss due to accident.

CAPITAL SURPLUS

Surplus created from capital gains realised by selling fixed assets at a price higher than their book value.

CAPITAL, WORKING

The different between current assets and current liabilities.

CAPITAL

In Accounting capital is the term for total financial assets of an organisation whether in the form of money, property goods or equipment. It represents the organisation stock of wealth as opposed to its income.

CAPITALISM

An economic system characterised by the private ownership of a society resources; by competition in the pursuit of financial gain; and by support for the ideal of a free market in goods and services.

CAPITALIST ECONOMY

An economy in which economic activity is governed by market forces and the means of production are privately owned by individuals.

CAPITALISATION

The term refers to the reserves of limited companies which, either because they are not legally distributable or because the company wishes them to become a permanent part of capital, are given capital status by being allocated to members as bonus shares to rank alongside existing shares.

CAPITALISE

To convert into capital; to compute the present value of a future flow of income to be realised from an asset.

CAPITALISED EXPENSE

An expense item usually charged to profit and loss that is added to the capital-asset account because it is related to a period of construction.

CAPITALISED VALUE

The capital equivalent of an annual payment. Capital values are determined by the rate of interest and the rent produced.

CAPITATION TAX

Fixed rate tax on every person in a class or geographic location.

CARD

A circuit board inserted to a computer (CPU) for additional features.

CARD INDEX

This system was invented by a French Scholar *Abbe Jean Rozier;* under this system information is typed or written by hand on cards of uniform sizes.

CAREER

A career, on the other hand, is an individual concept. An employee plans his career in any enterprise. A career is defined as a "sequence of work-related experiences in which a person participates during the span of his work life". A career can lend order and meaning to events and provide a relationship including work, in which a person is involved. A career is central to complete development of an individual's identity. It is important for an employee to plan a career, even if the employer provides little guidance or encouragement.

CAREER DEVELOPMENT

Career development refers to individual's engaging in the developmental activities required to attain career goals. Career planning and career development may be viewed from the perspective of the individual or the organisation.

CAREER PATHS

Sequence of jobs and/or positions associated with a specific career.

CAREER PLATEAUING

Is a period of little or no apparent progress in the growth of a career.

CAREER STAGES

Distinctly different yet related stages in the progression of a career.

CARRY OVER

The term refers to the postponement of a transaction from one settlement date to the next settlement date. In case of carry over the speculator has to pay *badla charge* to the other party.

CARRYING COST

An inventory cost comprised of the expenses associated with keeping an item on hand (such as storage, insurance, pilferage, breakage); also called holding cost.

CARTEL

A monopoly or confederation of companies in related business with the objective (among others) of controlling prices, markets, and inventories. A combination of two or more independent organisations which produce the same product, for the purposes of eliminating or restricting competition between them and preventing new competitors from entering the market. This is accomplished by fixing prices, level of production or market segmentation, *e.g.*, (OPEC) the Organisation of Petroleum Exporting Countries. A term implying bonding together of business houses producing similar type of goods with a view to associate to secure a monopoly of the market. A cartel is a voluntary agreement of capitalistic enterprises of the same branch for regulation of the sales market with a view to improving the profitability of its member's business by agreeing to limit competition among themselves.

CASCADE NETWORK

A form of Project Network diagram related to Critical Path Analysis.

CASH AND CARRY

An epithet applied to a manufacturer's or wholesaler's collection of goods for sale to the general public; cash and carry is kind of retailer's supermarket.

CASH BOOK

A journal in which only cash receipts, disbursements, or both are recorded.

CASH CREDIT

A popular method of borrowing money from banks by traders, agriculturists, industrialists, etc.

CASH DRAIN

By cash drain, *Prof. R.G. Hawtrey* meant the flow of currency into the hands of individuals, for their daily needs. This definition approximated Keynes's later transactions motive for holding cash balances.

CASH FLOW STATEMENT

It highlights the causes which changed the cash position between two balance sheet dates. A statement of a firm's actual or projected cash inflows and cash outflows measures at suitable intervals over a period.

CASH FLOW

The amount of cash flowing into and out of an organisation; the amount of cash required to finance operating expenses or further production over a given period of time.

CASH INFLOW

Cash coming into a business house from various sources. It indicates the financial position of a concern.

CASH PROFIT AND CASH LOSS

Cash profit is the net profit as increased by non-cash costs, such as depreciation amortisation etc. When the result of the computation is negative, it is known as *Cash Loss.*

CASH RESERVE RATIO (C.R.R.)

Under the Reserve Bank rules, every commercial bank required to keep a minimum proportion of cash reserve against the deposits.

CASH WITH ORDER

A requirement by a seller that any order for his goods must be accompanied by payment for them.

CASUAL

Describing an employee or a job that is irregular in some way, in that it is occasional, temporary, or part-time. Casual workers usually do not accrue seniority, and often they do not share in benefits such as pension plans.

CASUAL WORK

Work, or opportunity for employment, that occurs intermittently. (Also known as 'Dayworker'.)

CATALOGUE

List or register of names of products, objects, pictures etc., with their descriptions and, if possible, illustrations along with other relevant data such as instructions for use, etc., arranged methodically on the basis of some principle.

CAUSAL RESEARCH

Research that helps marketers identify a specific factor that causes an effect in the marketplace.

CEILING PRICE

The highest price obtainable or permissible in the sale of particular goods or services. It is the price to change above which is an offence.

CENSUS

A description of the characteristics of a population. A census differs from a survey in that all members of the population under consideration are included; a cumulative count of persons or things either wholly or by characteristics or class.

CENT

General used with per to mean per cent. A hundredth part of a rupee.

CENTRAL TENDENCY ERROR

The tendency to rate all ratees around an average score.

CENTRALISATION

A system of management in which major decisions are made at high levels of management. In other words, a vertical coordination method that addresses the extent to which power and authority are retained at the top organisational levels.

CENTRALISED DATA BANK FOR PUBLIC ENTERPRISES

PESB is maintaining about all public sector personnel, practically the personnel drawing ₹ 2500 per month or above. This bank maintains a list of suitable candidates for the top level managerial posts which may be drawn from various government departments, defence services, state Governments etc., and also persons from the private sector, particularly specialists in the industries concerned, willing to serve in the public sector. The bio-data of each personnel is duly maintained in the data bank.

CEREMONIAL

A system of rites performed in conjunction with a single occasion or event.

CERTIFICATE OF VALUE

A statement in a transfer or conveyance that the consideration being received is less than a certain amount so that conveyance duty is either not payable or is payable at a reduced rate.

CHAIN OF COMMAND

The unbroken line of authority that ultimately links each individual with the top organisational position through a managerial position at each successive layer in between.

CHAIN STORE

Sometimes, when a retail shop becomes popular, the retailer finds it profitable to open new branches in the city. All these branches deal in the same commodities and are chained together as they are one of a group of retail stores of essentially the same type, centrally owned and controlled. Chain stores may be defined as retail selling organisation with a number of branches which are centrally owned and controlled. All the branches are operated on very similar lines. The purchases are centrally made, and thus, economies in buying are secured. A chain store system represents centralised buying combined with decentralised selling. The chain store may be a 'Variety store' when it deals in a wide variety of goods, or it may be a specialised store when it specialises in a limited range of goods or it may be a fixed price chain store when the price of goods sold is fixed and varies between narrow limits.

CHAIRPERSON

The presiding officer of an organisation, committee, task force, or meeting. "Chairperson" (or "chair") generally has replaced the term "chairman".

CHAMBER OF COMMERCE

An association set up for the promotion of trade in an area. Chambers of commerce are voluntary organisation and business representatives.

CHANGE

Any alteration of the *Status Quo*. Or in narrow sense, moving from a known to an unknown.

CHANGE AGENT

An individual with a fresh perspective and a knowledge of the behavioural sciences who acts as a catalyst in helping the organisation approach old problems in new or innovative ways and thus plays a key role in OD interventions.

CHANGE SEQUENCE

The sequence of events that is needed to bring about change in an organisation.

CHANGING

Is the state in which individuals begin to experiment with performing new behaviour.

CHANGING AN ORGANISATION

Is the process of modifying an existing organisation to increase organisational effectiveness.

CHANNEL LEADER

A distribution channel member that is able to exert power and influence over other channel members. Also called the *Channel Captain*.

CHANNEL POWER

The extent to which a channel member is able to influence the behaviour of another channel member.

CHARISMA

A leadership factor that comprises the leader's ability to inspire pride, faith, and respect; to recognise what is really important; and to articulate effectively a sense of mission, or vision, that inspires followers.

CHARISMATIC LEADER

One whose ability to get others to follow him is a natural gift.

CHARISMATIC LEADERSHIP

The ability to influence followers based on a supernatural gift and powers that are attractive. Followers enjoy being with the charismatic leader because they feel inspired, correct, and important.

CHARTER

The document creating an organisation; a document establishing the accountabilities and functions of an organisation or a key position in an organisation; a document establishing the purpose, goals, functions, and authority of a program of work or service.

CHEAP

Low price relative to other prices for similar goods. Usually avoided in business, because it tends to be associated in the minds of consumers with inferior goods; alternatives used may be inexpensive, competitive, or covered by the use of the expression 'Sale price', or 'bargain'.

CHECK LIST

Comprehensive categorisation of actions to be taken in order to achieve a given effect with maximum efficiency.

CHEQUE

A bill of exchange drawn on a banker payable on demand, a common way of settling debts. Cheques may be open (bearer) or crossed. An open cheque is payable over the counter provided it is in order. A crossed cheque has to be paid into a bank account only.

CHEQUE-WRITING MACHINES

Cheque writing machines as used in big offices are required to issue numerous cheques regularly. Handwritten or typewritten cheques are exposed to possible frauds. The contents of the cheque may be willingly altered and the crossing lines may also be erased. The alterations and the erosion may go unnoticed by the bankers and then the wrong persons are likely to encash the bills. In order to prevent the tempering of cheques, big business houses use cheque writing machines. Cheque writing machines shared the contents into the vary texture of the cheque and then fill them with an indelible ink. Any alteration subsequently made with fraudulent intention is easily distinguished. Thus, the chances of frauds are minimised. Moreover, cheque-writing machines save time because large number of cheques can be written quickly with their help. Officers may also use cheque-signing machines.

CHEVISANCE

An agreement between a debtor and a creditor.

CHIEF EXECUTIVE

The individual position that has accountability for the overall management and operation of the enterprise as a whole. The Board of Directors, which is a committee, is superior in position to the chief executive.

CHOICE CRITERIA

The critical attributes a consumer uses to evaluate product alternatives.

CHRONOCYCLEGRAPH

A composite photograph of how a worker performs a job. Light bulbs which produce a pear-shaped flash of light at regular intervals are attached to each of the worker's hands. A long exposure photograph is taken which shows the path of the hands (and also the direction—from the shape of the flashes and speed—from the distance between successive flashes). This is superimposed on a conventional photograph of the worker so as to show the path of movement in relation to the layout of the workplace.

CHUNKING

The process of grouping items of information into units, or 'chunks' as an aid to memorising them.

CIRCULAR CHART

In this chart, top position are located in the centre of the concentric circle. Positions of successive echelons extend in all direction outward from the centre. Position of equal status lie at the same distance from the centre on the same concentric circle.

CIRCULATION

(*i*) The number of copies of a publication distributed among readers. This is often substantially less than the readership, because of the multiple uses of each copy.

(*ii*) In publishing, the number of copies of a single issue of a periodical (newspaper, magazine, journal, etc.) that are sold or distributed. This figure is particularly important to advertisers, who want to know the size of the audience they can reach through a particular publication.

CLAIMANT (INSURANCE)

An individual asserting eligibility as a beneficiary of an insurance policy or contract and who is presenting a demand for payment.

CLAN CONTROL

A managerial approach that relies on values, beliefs, traditions, corporate culture, shared norms, and informal relationships to regulate employee behaviours and facilitate the reaching of organisational goals.

CLASS CONFLICT

The conflict between the working class interest in high wages, and the employing class, interested in low wages.

CLASSICAL APPROACH TO MANAGEMENT

Is a management approach that emphasises organisational efficiency to increase organisational success.

CLASSICAL DESIGN THEORY

A design theory that emphasises the design of preplanned structure for doing work and minimises the importance of the social system. Evolved from scientific management, classical organisation, and bureaucratic theory.

CLASSICAL ORGANISING THEORY

Comprises the cumulative insights of early management writers on how organisational resources can best be used to enhance goal attainment.

CLASSICAL VIEWPOINT

A perspective on management that emphasises finding ways to manage work and organisations more efficiently.

CLEARING AGENT

Clearing agent is a person who gets the imported goods cleared from customs authorities on behalf of the importer. He attends to all the formalities and gets a commission for his work.

CLEARING BANKS

Commercial banks are members of the bankers' clearing house which facilities the settling of daily balances due between member banks arising from the cheque and cash transactions throughout the country, whether by the general public or individual banks.

CLEARING HOUSE

In the broad sense, a centre of organisation that collects, reviews and disseminates information on topics of interest to certain people and/or organisations.

CLIENT

The element of the task environment that includes those individuals and organisations that purchase an organisation's products and/or services.

CLOCK CARD

A card on which a particular employee's starting and finishing times are stamped by a device connected to a clock, each day or each shift. (Also known as a *Time Card.*)

CLOSED ECONOMY

An economy which has no economic relations with other countries is known as *Closed Economy.*

CLOSED MORTGAGE

A mortgage that cannot be paid off before maturity.

CLOSED SYSTEM

(*i*) A system that does little or no interacting with its environment and receives little feedback

(*ii*) An organisation or assemblage of things that neither affects nor is affected by outside events.

(*iii*) Is one that is not influenced by, and does not interact with, its environment.

CLOSE-OUT PROCESS

A special process used to sell off remaining inventories of a discontinued, out-of-style, or otherwise unattractive product.

CLOSING ENTRIES

Journal entries passed for transferring balances of ledger accounts to trading and profit and loss accounts, which close some ledger accounts.

CLOSING PRICE

It is the price at which shares are quoted at the close of any day's stock exchange dealings. The prices can be found in the daily official list of the Stock Exchange. Two prices are given for any share. This is because stock jobbers and brokers quote two prices: one for buying and one for selling.

CLOSING SIGNALS

Signals from the prospect revealing that he or she is ready to buy.

CLOSING STOCK

It is the value of the raw materials, semi-finished goods and finished goods at the end of the accounting year.

CLOSING THE SALE

Salesman technique in requesting his order from a buyer (and securing it).

CLOSING

The end of the accounting period when all books of accounts are closed to ascertain the financial results of a business during that period.

CLOSURE

An element of perception by which an observer mentally completes an incomplete stimulus.

CLUSTER SAMPLE

A probability sample resulting firm a process by which certain geographical areas are selected on a chance basis and then probability sampling techniques are used to select samples within these areas.

CLUSTER SAMPLING

A term used in market research for the practice of drawing a sample of informants from a geographically localized area (like a single street).

CMOS

Complementary Magnetic Oxide Semiconductor, a chip in micro-computers.

COACHING

Is leadership that instructs followers on how to meet the special organisational challenges they face.

COALESCING

The process of individuals or groups combining their resources to pursue common objectives.

COBOL

Common Business Oriented Language, *i.e.*, a programming language.

CODE OF CONDUCT

A statement establishing a company's or a professional organisation's guidelines with regard to ethical principles and acceptable behaviour.

CODE OF ETHICS

A document prepared for the purpose of guiding organisation members when they encounter an ethical dilemma. Or it is a formal statement that acts as a guide for making decisions and acting within an organisation.

CODER

One who creates the code for a computerised solution of a problem using some computer language.

CODING

Establishing meaningful categories for responses collected by means of surveys or other data collection forms so that the responses can be grouped into usable classifications.

CODING FRAME

Pattern of likely answers which can be coded on questionnaire (or afterwards from open-ended answers) so that individual answers may be aggregated into limited number of categories.

COERCION

The use of power to get people to do something they would not otherwise do. Typical of Authoritarian management.

COERCIVE POWER

Power that depends on the ability to punish others when they do not engage in desired behaviours.

COGNITION

(*i*) A general term which includes all the psychological processes by which people become aware of, and gain knowledge about the world.

(*ii*) This is basically what individuals know about themselves and their environment. Cognition implies a conscious process of acquiring knowledge. The perception, opinion, or belief segment of an argument.

COGNITIVE DISSONANCE

In terms of consumer behaviour, the negative feelings that may occur after a commitment to purchase has been made. It describes the tension that results from holding two conflicting ideas or beliefs at the same time.

COGNITIVE LEARNING

An approach theory that focuses on thought processes, assumes that human beings have a high capacity to act in a purposeful manner, and so to choose behaviors that will enable them to achieve long-run goals.

COGNITIVE PROCESS

The general term for the broad range of mental activities, such as perception. Learning, thinking, information processing, and reasoning, that involve the interpretation of stimuli and the organisation of thoughts and ideas.

COGNITIVE THEORIES

Theories that attempt to isolate the thinking patterns that we use in deciding whether or not to behave in a certain way.

COHESION

The degree to which some module performs one general function.

COHESIVENESS

The degree of attraction the group has for each of its members.

COINCIDENTAL METHOD

Interviewing technique to question listeners or viewers. Used in USA to measure audience figures by making telephone checks on what program people are watching or listening to. Not as effective in Britain where domestic telephones are less common.

COLD CALLING

A form of selling where the salesman approaches a prospective customer by telephone by post, or in person—with no prior contact being made.

COLLABORATE

To work together. Collaboration involves two or more people cooperating to produce a joint end product. It implies that no member of the group exercises command over the others. Collaboration implies equality in relationship. For example, the production control manager and the production superintendent collaborate to develop a production schedule.

COLLABORATION

A conflict-handling mode that strives to resolve conflicts by devising solutions that allow both parties to achieve their desired outcomes.

COLOPHON

Inscription a front to publication giving author's, publisher's, printer's names and other details regarding copyright, ISBN number.

COMBINATION

An association of trading companies that produce and sell similar types of commodities and compete with one another.

COMBINATION ORGANISATION

An organisational structure based on more than one of the following: geography, product type, type of customer, or marketing functions.

COMMAND

Giving of orders.

COMMAND GROUP

A formal group consisting of a manager and all the subordinates who report to that manager; also called a functional group.

COMMAND LANGUAGE

A language which is used to create or modify the programs.

COMMERCIAL AGENT

A person who manages the commercial affairs of another person or persons; also known as a *Mercantile Agent.*

COMMERCIAL BANK (JOINT STOCK BANK)

A form of bank which offers basic services for deposits and short-term loan to individuals and organisations. They do not generally offer the more specialised services of investment banks or merchant banks.

COMMERCIAL CREDIT

The debts or promises to pay of enterprises or businessmen incurred or given in the present acquisition of goods to be used in productive operations.

COMMISSION

A form of payment made to someone who obtains business for a firm—often a percentage of the value of that business.

COMMISSION AGENT

Agent paid on a commission basis for the business he obtains, the principal then dealing with the customer.

COMMITMENT

A sense of identification, involvement, and loyalty expressed by an employee toward the company.

COMMITMENT PRINCIPLE

Is a management guideline that advises managers to commit funds for planning only if they can anticipate, in the foreseeable future, a return on planning expenses as a result of the long-range planning analysis.

COMMITTEE

A group of people assigned to work together to do something not included in their regular jobs.

COMMODITY EXCHANGE

Also, board of trade, produce exchange. An organised market where traders buy and sell contracts for immediate or future delivery of certain commodities.

COMMODITY MARKET

The market in which commodities are bought and sold. The other types of market based on three subject of transaction are factor market, money market, capital market, bullion market, stock exchange etc.

COMMODITY PRODUCING SECTOR

This term is used to refer to the agricultural and industrial sector which produces material goods.

COMMON CARRIER

Carrier prepared to transport goods of any description for anyone willing to hire its services.

COMMON MARKET

Where two or more countries agree to form a customs union between themselves and a common external tariff against goods and commodities imported from other countries.

COMMON STOCK

Shares of ownership in a corporation that depend for their worth on the value of the corporation.

COMMUNICATION

(*i*) Flow of information from one point to another. The point from which the information is transmitted is source and to which the information is transmitted is receiver.

(*ii*) Is the process of sharing information with other individuals.

(*iii*) Passing on ideas, information, orders, or instructions in such a way that the recipient understands exactly what is meant.

(*iv*) The exchange of messages between people for the purpose of achieving common meanings.

COMMUNICATION CHANNELS

Patterns of organisational communication flow that represent potential established conducts through which managers and other organisation members can send and receive information.

COMMUNICATION GOALS

In the context of marketing, what the marketer wants the promotional message to accomplish: to gain attention, to be remembered.

COMMUNICATION MACROBARRIERS

Are factors hindering successful communication that relate primarily to the communication environment and the larger world in which communication takes place.

COMMUNICATION NETWORK

(*i*) The pattern of information flow among task group members.

(*ii*) The pathways through which messages between and among people in organisations flow.

COMMUNICATION, TWO-WAY

Communication not only from top management down through the chain of command but also the transmission of information, ideas, and feelings in the opposite direction.

COMMUNITY HEALTH SERVICES

Diagnostic, therapeutic, and preventive health services provided for individuals in the community.

COMPANIES (AMENDMENT) ACT, 1965

This was the third major amending Act based mainly on the recommendations of Shastri Committee. It amended fifty sections and added several new sections, viz., 68-A, 233-B, 250-A, 294-A, 394-A, 396-A, 511-A, 635-A, 637-B, and 640-B. Some of the more important changes introduced by this act are:

(*i*) By amending section 13, the Act provided that the objects clause in the memorandum of association of any company must be divided into two sub-clauses: (*a*) the main objects and (*b*) other objects,

(*ii*) By adding sub-section (1A) to section 108, restrictions on the period of currency of blank transfers were imposed, and

(*iii*) By amending section 410, Advisory Commission' attached to the 'Company Law Board' was to be replaced by an 'Advisory Committee'.

COMPANIES ACT—APPLICABILITY OF

The Companies Act, 1956 extends to the whole of India except that (1) As regards the State of Nagaland, it applies, subject to such modifications, if any, as the Central Government may, by notification in the Official Gazette, specify [Section 1(3)]; (2) As regards the Union Territory of Goa, Daman and Diu, such of the provisions of this Act shall not apply or shall apply only with such exceptions and modifications, for such periods or period with effect from the 26th January, 1963 or any subsequent date, to any existing company or any company registered under this Act on or after 26th January, 1963, as maybe specified by the Central Government by notification in the Official Gazette (Section 620-B); and (3) As regards the State of Jammu *8c* Kashmir, such of the provisions of this act shall not apply or shall apply only with such exception and modifications, with effect from the commencement of the Central Laws (Extension to Jammu *8c* Kashmir) Act, 1968 (*i.e.*, 15th August, 1966) or any subsequent date, to any existing company registered under this Act after 15th August, 1966, as maybe specified by the Central Government by notification in the Official Gazette (Section 620-C).

COMPANY

Broadly, any group of people voluntarily united for performing jointly any activity, business, or commercial enterprise. Synonymous with firms. Partnerships and corporations are also considered to be companies.

COMPANY DIRECTOR

The member of the board of directors appointed to run a company by its shareholders. A director may or may not be a shareholder himself.

COMPANY LAW BOARD

It is an administrative authority, set up in February, 1964, by the Central Government, in accordance with section 10E instituted by the Companies Amendment Act, 1963. According to section 10E, the Company Law Board is to exercise and discharge such powers and functions, conferred on the Central Government by or under the Company Act or any other law, as may be delegated to it by the Central Government. The Company Law Board is to consist of such number of members, not exceeding nine, as the Central Government may appoint by notification in the Official Gazette, and one of such members shall be appointed as its Chairman. The Board so controlled may, with the prior approval of the Central Government, by order in writing, form one or more Benches from among its members and authorise each such bench or the chairman or any of its other members or its principal officer to exercise and discharge such of its powers and functions as it may think fit. Every order made to act done in pursuance of such authority would be deemed to have been order or act of the Board section 19E (4B) inserted by the Companies Amendment Act, 1974.

COMPANY LEGISLATION IN INDIA

The origin of India's company law can be traced back to 1850, when the first Indian Companies Act providing for the registration of joint stock companies was passed on the lines of English Companies Act of 1844. In 1857 another act was passed on the lines of the English Companies Act of 1855, according to which the privilege of Limited Liability was extended to joint stock companies except Banking and Insurance companies. The Indian Companies Act of 1860, passed on the lines of English Companies Act of 1858, however, extended this privilege to banking and Insurance companies as well. The first comprehensive act, providing for the incorporation, regulation and winding up of companies, was passed in India in 1866, on the model of the English Companies Act of 1862. This Act was recast in 1882 to bring the Indian Companies Law in conformity with the various amendments made in the English Company Law up to that time. Further Amending Acts were passed in 1887, 1891, 1895 and 1910, till we had a consolidating Act, the Indian Companies Act,

1913, which brought our Law almost at par with the English Companies Act of 1908. This Act contained 288 sections and 4 Schedules. It was by this Act that the institution of private company was for the first time introduced in the Indian Company Law. Extensive amendments were made by the Indian Companies (Amendment) Act of 1936, which not only brought our Law at par with the English Companies Act of 1929, but which went a step further. This amending Act, for the first time, introduced various provisions relating to the powers and limitations of management agents and devoted a separate chapter for Banking Companies. In the light of experience gained in the working of company law, minor amendments in the Act were made almost every year from 1937 to 1946.

COMPANY SECRETARY

The term 'Secretary' has been derived from the Latin word 'Secretarius', which stands for a notary, scribe or confidential writer. In fact, the term has been used for a person who keeps the secrets of any venture, public or private. Presently the term 'Secretary' is used to signify an officer who is entrusted with confidential matters by his employer or who conducts correspondence, keeps records and transacts other business for a person or an organisation. Whenever the question of defining the secretary comes to our mind, immediately we get the picture of a person of integrity, intelligence and personality, moving with grace and discharging his duties to the administration shareholders, directors and the company law authorities, with unprecedented accuracy and efficiency.

COMPANY UNION

An employer version of a trade union within a single organisation. It does not have the independent status or power to represent the employees in any industrial relations matters.

COMPARABLE WORTH

The concept that requires the value for dissimilar jobs to be compared under some form of job evaluation and pay rates to be assigned according to their evaluated worth.

COMPARATIVE ADVANTAGE

The position a country occupies when it uses its resources to make the goods and services it can produce most efficiently. In theory, when each country produces according to its competitive advantage and trades with others to obtain products it cannot produce efficiently, everyone benefits.

COMPARATIVE ADVERTISING

A type of demonstration advertised is directly compared with a competing brand.

COMPARATIVE MANAGEMENT

Is the study of the management process in different countries to examine the potential of management action under different environmental conditions.

COMPARATIVE PARITY METHOD

A method of setting a promotional budgeting which the marketer tries to match competitors' expenditures.

COMPATIBILITY

Properties of some computers which makes them work in a similar way though they are different or manufactured by different manufacturers.

COMPENSATION

(*i*) All rewards individuals receive as a result of their employment.

(*ii*) Wages paid directly for time worked, as well as more indirect benefits that employees receive as part of their employment relationship with an organisation.

COMPENSATION MANAGEMENT

That face of management concerned with the selection, development, and direction of the programs that implement an organisation's financial reward system.

COMPENSATORY DAMAGES

Payment for an actual personnel or property loss suffered by a plaintiff, as opposed to punitive, or exemplary damages, which are intended to punish a defendant for wanton or reckless behaviour.

COMPETITION

(*i*) A conflict handling mode that involves attempting to win a conflict at the other party's expense.

(*ii*) The attempt to do better than others supplying goods and services in the same market. Fostering competition is one of the basic principles of capitalism, which was first formulated in the eighteenth century by Adam *Smith*.

COMPETITIVE ADVANTAGE

A significant edge over the competition in dealing with competitive forces.

COMPETITIVE ADVANTAGE OF NATIONS

The concept that environmental elements within a nation can foster innovation in certain industries, thereby increasing the prospects for the success of home-based companies operating internationally within those industries.

COMPETITIVE ADVANTAGE

(*i*) An element with a product offering that is particularly attractive to customers, and not offered by competitors.

(*ii*) Superiority to or favourable difference from competitors along some dimension important to the market.

COMPETITORS

The element of the task environment that includes other organisations that either offer or have a high potential of offering rival products or services.

COMPLACENCY

A condition preventing effective decision-making in which individuals either do not see the signs of danger or opportunity or ignore them.

COMPLETE AUDIT

A detailed audit of a specified class or classes of transactions for a specific period.

COMPLETE CERTAINTY CONDITION

Is the decision-making situation in which the decision-maker knows exactly what the results of an implemented alternative will be.

COMPLEXITY

A dimension of organisational structure that refers to the number of different jobs, units, and authority levels within an organisation.

COMPLIANCE

The act of following instructions, orders, or prescribed pattern of behaviour.

COMPLIANCE AGENCY

Generally, any government agency that administers laws or regulations.

COMPOUND INTEREST

Interest paid on a principal sum and the interest already collected by that sum *e.g.* ₹ 200 invested at 10 per cent simple interest for two years would increase by ₹ 20 in each year and would provide ₹ 240 at the end of two years. If however this amount is invested at 10 per cent compound interest, with interest added annually, it would earn ₹ 20 in the first year and 10 per cent of ₹ 220 *i.e.* ₹ 22 in the first year and at the end of two years, it would provide ₹ 242.

COMPRESSED WORKWEEK

An alternative work schedule whereby employees work four 10-hour days or some similar combination, rather than the usual five 8-hour days.

COMPROMISE

A conflict-handling mode that aims to solve conflict issues by having each party give up some desired outcomes in order to get other desired outcomes.

COMPULSORY WINDING UP

A winding up of a company ordered by a Court. (Also called 'Compulsory Liquidation'. Compare Voluntary Winding Up.)

COMPUTER

Is an electronic tool capable of accepting data, interpreting data, performing ordered operations on data, and reporting on the outcome of these operations. Computers are extremely helpful in generating information from raw data.

COMPUTER CRIME

Acts of misusing the computer system or criminal actions accomplished through the use of computers such as unauthorised use of computers system resources or destroy the data stored in the computer.

COMPUTER ENGINEERING

The branch of knowledge which deals with the study and designing of computer hardware system.

COMPUTER ETHICS

The set of principles which governs the legal professional, social and moral responsibilities of computer professionals and end-users.

COMPUTER FAMILY

All models based on a single design type architecture and which shares the same logical design and arrangement but have different capacities.

COMPUTER NETWORK

Is a system of two or more connected computers that allows computer users to communicate, co-operate, and share resources.

COMPUTER PROGRAM

A set of instructions to a computer, written in a computer language, that tells it to perform a particular task. The spelling of 'Program' is usually American, in recognition of the American predominance in this field.

COMPUTER TRAINING

A method of training in which the medium of instruction, with which the individual interacts, is the computer or computer terminal.

COMPUTER VIRUS

A small program, usually hidden inside another program, that replicates itself and surfaces at a predetermined time to cause disruption and possibly destruction.

COMPUTER-AIDED DESIGN (CAD)

Is a computerised technique for designing new products or modifying existing ones.

COMPUTER-BASED INFORMATION SYSTEMS (CBISS)

Information systems that involve the use of computer technology.

CONCEALED SURPLUS (OF LABOUR)

Manpower surplus concealed by labour hoarding.

CONCENTRATED MARKETING

Development of a marketing mix and direction of marketing efforts and resources to appeal to a single market segment.

CONCENTRATED REPETITION

An act repeated at one sitting, a short period of study. This term is opposed to *Distributed Repetition*.

CONCENTRATION

A growth strategy that—focuses on effecting the growth of a single product or service or a small number of closely related products or services.

CONCENTRIC DIVERSIFICATION

The development of businesses related to the firm's current businesses.

CONCEPTUAL SKILL

The ability to comprehend abstract or general ideas and apply them to specific situations.

CONCLUSION JUMPER

An impulsive individual who

arrives at a conclusion or opinion without sufficient evidence.

CONCURRENT CONTROL

A control type based on timing that involves the regulation of ongoing activities that are part of the transformation process to ensure that they conform to organisational standards.

CONFIGURATION CLUE

Overall form of a word which aids in its recognition.

CONFLICT

(*i*) Antagonism or opposition between or among persons.

(*ii*) A perceived difference between two or more parties that results in mutual opposition.

CONFRONTATION CONFLICT RESOLUTION

A strategy that focuses on conflict and attempts to resolve it through such procedures as rotating key group personnel, establishing superordinate goals, an improving communications.

CONFUCIAN DYNAMISM

The extent to which people believe in the importance of the values of persistence, status, thrift, and feeling shame and the unimportance of the values of personal stability, face saving, respect for tradition, and reciprocation of favours and gifts.

CONGLOMERATE DIVERSIFICATION

A business organisation, usually comprising a group of companies, with diverse and often unrelated financial interests but sometimes trading under the one name.

CONNOTATION

The significance suggested by a word apart from its explicit and recognised meaning.

CONSCIOUS GOALS

The main goals that a person is striving for and is aware of when directing behaviour.

CONSENSUS

Is agreement on a decision by all individuals involved in making that decision.

CONSERVATISM

Conservatism refers to the policy of choosing the procedure that leads to understatement, as against overstatement of resources and income. This implies:

(*i*) earlier larger charging of expenses but later smaller receipt of revenues, and

(*ii*) liabilities, and hence under-reporting of owner's (*i.e.*, residual) equity.

CONSIDERATION

Acts of the leader that show supportive concern for the followers in a group:

(*i*) The degree to which a leader builds mutual trust with subordinates, respects their ideas, and shows concern for their feelings.

(*ii*) The extent to which leader's relationships with subordinates are characterised by mutual trust and respect for employees' ideas and feelings.

CONSIDERATION BEHAVIOUR

Is leadership behaviour that reflects friendship, mutual trust, respect, and warmth in the relationship between leader and followers.

CONSIGNEE

An agent to whom goods are merchandised or sent for sale.

CONSIGNMENT NOTE

(*i*) The documentation accompanying an order when delivered, which lists details like quantity and nature of all goods in that consignment.

(*ii*) Document listing the goods that are supplied (by the consignor to the consignee) with a particular order.

CONSIGNMENT SELLING

Goods sent to distributors who take possession but title remains with manufacturer until consignment is paid for.

CONSIGNOR

A person who sends or consigns goods for sale to an agent.

CONSONANT

A speech sound formed by the obstruction of the breath stream as it passes through the mouth. Each of these letters is a consonant: b, c, d, f, g, h, j, k, l, m, n, q, r, s, t, v, w, x, y, z.

CONSORTIUM

(*i*) A group of companies engaged in a single venture.

(*ii*) A group of individuals and/or companies which join together to undertake a specific project.

CONSPICUOUS CONSUMPTION

Consumption for the sake of enhancing social prestige.

CONSTELLATION

A team assigned to work together in an effort to solve a problem.

CONSTITUTIONAL CAUSE

One which resides within the body and is not local.

CONSTRAINT

A prior limit on the solution that will be acceptable to a problem.

CONSULTANCY

The process by which specialist advice, opinion or other service is given to an organisation by individuals or groups outside its own staff; individuals or groups offering specialist services, advice or opinions on a professional basis.

CONSULTANT

Generally, a counsellor or business affairs who works with companies in professional—client relationship rather than as a regular employee, although some consultants work for a single company on a salaried basis.

CONSUMER ADVERTISING

Loosely relating to all advertising of goods or services to the mass markets of individuals or families. Used in contrast to industrial or capital goods advertising.

CONSUMER BEHAVIOUR

The activities people engage in when selecting, purchasing, and using products so as to satisfy needs and desires.

CONSUMER DURABLE

Consumer goods designed for long-term use, such as washing machines, refrigerators or hi-fi systems—as opposed to consumer disposable, designed for one-time or short-term use, such as food-stuffs.

CONSUMER GOODS

Products which are targeted at individuals in the general population, rather than at organisations.

CONSUMER INFORMATION PROCESSING (CIP) APPROACH

A model of consumer decision-making that focuses on the information processing aspect of decision-making. It looks at buyers as problem solvers who actively acquire the information they need.

CONSUMER INVOLVEMENT

(*i*) The extent to which an individual attaches interest and importance to a product and is willing to expend energy in making a decision about purchasing the product.

(*ii*) The extent to which an individual attaches interest and importance to a product and is willing to expend energy in making a decision about purchasing the product.

CONSUMER MARKET

(*i*) Market consisting of buyers who use the product to satisfy personal or household needs.

(*ii*) The market for consumer goods.

CONSUMER PANEL

A research method using a group of consumers who continuously report on their purchases over an extended period of time.

CONSUMER

(*i*) A person who uses goods and services that directly satisfy human needs and desires.

(*ii*) Someone who, or a firm that consumers specified goods *i.e.,* buys them but does not directly use them or manufacturing other goods or for resale at a profit. Someone who usually buys goods for consumption by himself or by members of his household and not for use in manufacturing other goods or for resale at a profit;

(*iii*) The final user of a product or a service.

CONSUMERISM

(*i*) A movement that looks after interests of the consumer in the market-place by trying to have the safety, quality and informational content of consumer goods and services improved. It can be traced back to the efforts of *Ralph Nader* in the early 1960s to publicise serious safety hazards in the manufacture of American cars.

(*ii*) A movement which aims to change the actions of organisations in favour of particular groups.

CONSUMPTION

The purchase and use of goods and services to satisfy needs and desires. The purchaser/user and individual or an institution.

CONTACT

Market research term for a person met in an interview though not necessarily providing enough information to be classified as an informant.

CONTACT CHART

A diagram showing various individuals in the organisation and the numbers of interactions they have with others.

CONTAINER

Large metal box in which goods are packed in bulk for shipment by road or rail to container port. Also means of containing or packing goods; *e.g.* bottle, jar, tube, carton, box, aerosol, etc.

CONTANGO

Interest paid by a buyer of stock to a seller on consideration of which the former is allowed to postpone further purchases.

CONTENT MOTIVATION THEORIES

Theories that focus on the factors within a person that energise, direct, sustain, and stop behaviour.

CONTENT THEORIES OF MOTIVATION

Are explanations of motivation that emphasise people's internal characteristics.

CONTERVAILING DUTY

A special form of import duty which is designed to counter the effects of export subsidies. This duty is in addition to any formal duties imposed on that type of goods.

CONTEST

In the contest of a wholesaler's or retailer's sales promotion, a means of motivating a sales force by offering bonuses or prizes for sales performance.

CONTEXT CLUE

A means of identifying a new reading word by anticipation of the meaning or through the words and ideas adjacent to the new word.

CONTINGENCY APPROACH TO MANAGEMENT

Is a management approach that emphasises that what managers do in practice depends on a given set of circumstances—a situation. This approach to management states that there is no one best way to manage in every situation but that managers must find different ways that fit different situations.

CONTINGENCY DESIGN THEORY

An approach to organisation design that states that the effective structure depends on factors in the situation, including technology, environmental uncertainty, and strategic choice.

CONTINGENCY PLANNING

(*i*) The development of alternative plans for use in the event that environmental conditions evolve differently than anticipated, rendering original plans unwise or unfeasible.

(*ii*) The development of plans to be placed in effect if certain events occur.

(*iii*) The attempt to anticipate emergencies or unexpected difficulties that might arise in the future.

(*iv*) The process of developing a series of alternative plans for achieving an objective. Different alternative plans may be implemented according to future events, opportunities, or barriers.

CONTINGENCY THEORY

A viewpoint that argues that appropriate managerial action depends on the particular parameters of the situation.

CONTINGENCY THEORY OF LEADERSHIP

Is a leadership concept that hypothesises that, in any given leadership situation, success is determined primarily by (1) the degree to which the task being performed by the followers is structured, (2) the degree of position power possessed by the leader, and (3) the type of relationship that exists between the leader and the followers.

CONTINGENT DEBT

A debt payable only on the occurrence or non-occurrence of one or more future events.

CONTINGENT LIABILITY

A liability which has not been recognised as such by any entity, but becomes so only on the occurrence of a certain future event. An example of such a liability could be one which may arise out of a pending law suit.

CONTINGENT PROFIT

A profit whose realisation is dependent upon the occurrence of a certain event.

CONTINUOUS INNOVATION

A new product characterised by minor alterations or improvements on existing products and little change in consumption.

CONTINUOUS PROCESS

A method of production that enable the uninterrupted flow of materials and parts into a processing operation and of completed end products out of the operation.

CONTINUOUS REINFORCEMENT

A schedule that is designed to reinforce behaviour every time the behaviour exhibited is correct.

CONTINUOUS RESEARCH

Research that is conducted regularly over an extended period of time, used to monitor trends in the marketplace.

CONTINUOUS PROCESS PRODUCTION

A type of technology in which products are liquids, solids, or gases that are made through a continuous process.

CONTRACT GUARANTEE

General term covering performance, repayment and tender guarantees.

CONTRACT MANUFACTURING

In international marketing, an agreement by which a company allows a foreign producer to manufacture its product according to its specifications; typically, the company then handles foreign sales of the product.

CONTRACT OF EMPLOYMENT

A legal agreement given to employee which sets out the terms and conditions of his employment—such as the period of notice required by employee and employer etc.

CONTRACT RESEARCH

Research (especially scientific or technological) carried out by an organisation, the results of which are to be used by another organisation which commissioned the research.

CONTRACT

A formal binding agreement between two or more parties, presenting pledges of tasks, acts, processes, products, or resources to be provided by one party in exchange for a consideration (money or other goods) from another party.

CONTRACTOR

An organisation or person who takes on work from another organisation but generally retains control over his or her own work. Usually, contract work must meet negotiated standards and be done within a specific period of time. Other stipulation also govern the work.

CONTRACTUAL VERTICAL MARKETING SYSTEM

A vertical marketing system in which channel coordination and leadership are laid out in a contractual agreement.

CONTRIBUTION

The technique of marginal costing; also called 'marginal contribution', 'marginal income', 'marginal revenue', 'marginal balance' and 'profit pick-up'.

CONTROL

(*i*) Control in terms of accounting, control refers to the process of checking actual financial performance against planned performance; in general, the power to direct an organisation.

(*ii*) Ensuring that plans are carried out in line with standards.

(*iii*) Is making something happen the way it was planned to happen.

(*iv*) The evaluation of work after it is performed in terms of predetermined standards. Control involves the establishment of performance standards, the measurement of work by recording and reporting, the evaluation of actual performance against the standard, and the institution of corrective action in terms of exceptions of variance.

(*v*) The process by which managers ensure that planned activities are completely and properly executed.

(*vi*) The action that implements the planning decision and evaluates overall performance.

(*vii*) The process by which managers ensure that planned activities are completely and properly executed.

CONTROL ACCOUNT

A master account that shows how the total balance tallies with various individual ledger accounts; central accounting.

CONTROL CHART

The graphic record of how closely samples of a good or service conform to standards overtime.

CONTROL DEPARTMENTS

Control departments include personnel, credit, budgeting, accounting and auditing and such departments typically have full authority to see that their particular functions are properly carried out everywhere in the organisation.

CONTROL FUNCTION

(*i*) Is computer activities that dictate the order in which other computer functions are performed.

(*ii*) Control function includes those activities designed to compel events to conform to plans or to recognise deviations therefore. It is thus the measurement and corrective function. It involves the establishment of control standards and the gathering of information required for evaluating performance, and provides the inputs for subsequent planning.

CONTROL GROUP

Identical sample to one which is exposed to experimental stimuli but to which no such stimuli is given. Thus, its reactions, or lack of them, can be compared with those of the experimental group giving a base point from which to make measurements.

CONTROL OF PUBLIC UNDERTAKINGS

Centralised administration within the enterprises leave less initiative to technical hands. Most of the public sector corporations, particularly the big ones, have an imbalanced organisational structure. Sometimes even small decisions are taken at the top level. Under such conditions, due participation of the employees, even technical and professional hands at various levels, is not fully availed of. However, in recent years, top managements in public enterprises have developed a progressive outlook and show no inhibitions in adopting new work methods and techniques. It is due this new trend that the capacity of public sector enterprises to provide accelerated growth in output is visible.

CONTROL SYSTEM

(*i*) A set of mechanisms, established as part of the control process, that are designed to increase the probability of meeting organisational standards and goals.

(*ii*) A subsystem, of an open system, in which activity is directed towards maintaining, or affecting in a prescribed way, the value of some parameter of the output of the system. The parameter so effected is called the 'Controlled Condition'.

CONTROL TOLERANCES

Specifications of how much deviation will be permitted before corrective action is taken.

CONTROL TOOL

Is a specific procedure or technique that presents pertinent organisational information in a way that helps managers to develop and implement an appropriate control strategy.

CONTROL UNIT

A subsystem of CPU that directs and controls the working of the other parts of computer.

CONTROL, SPAN OF

The number of subordinates who report directly to a manager.

CONTROLLABLE COST

Costs chargeable to a job or cost centre that can be affected by the actions of the person vested with the responsibility of controlling such a centre.

CONTROLLABLE ELEMENTS

Internal factors in the marketing environment that marketers can modify, such as their product mix, pricing, distribution, and promotion.

CONTROLLABLE OR MANAGEMENT ACCOUNTANT

A staff-functionary who uses accounting information for management planning and control.

CONTROLLER

(*i*) Is the staff person whose basic responsibility is to assist line managers with the controlling function by gathering appropriate information and generating necessary reports that reflect this information.

(*ii*) The senior manager responsible for the finances of an organisation.

CONTROLLING

(*i*) Is the process managers go through to control. It is a systematic effort to compare performance to predetermined standards, plans, or objectives to determine whether performance is in line with those standards or needs to be corrected.

(*ii*) The process of comparing actual performance with standards and taking any necessary corrective action.

(*iii*) The management function that is aimed at regulating organisational activities so that actual performance conforms to expected organisational standards and goals.

CONVENIENCE PRODUCT

A relatively inexpensive, regularly purchased consumer product bought without much thought and with a minimum of shopping effort.

CONVENIENCE SAMPLE

(*i*) A non-probability sample made up of the subjects most conveniently available.

(*ii*) As the name implies, a research sampling technique using the most practical or convenient selection method to provide the necessary respondents.

CONVENTIONAL CHANNEL OF DISTRIBUTION

A channel of distribution characterised by loosely aligned, relatively autonomous marketing organisations that carry out a trade relationship.

CONVERGENT THINKING

A way of thinking related to creativity in which an individual attempts to solve problems by beginning with a problem and attempting to move logically to a solution.

CONVERSION COST

The cost of converting inputs into finished products.

CONVERTIBILITY

The degree to which something is convertible especially the extent to which the holder of a specified currency is permitted to convert it into other currencies.

CONVERTIBLE AND NON-CONVERTIBLE DEBENTURES

Convertible debentures are those which have the option of getting a part of full value of their investments converted into equity shares on a fixed date or after sometime. They are issued to allow the debentureholders to participate in the future prosperity of the company. Non-convertible debentures do not enjoy any such right to get themselves converted into equity shares.

CONVERTIBLE BOND

A bond which can be converted at the holder's option into shares in the issuing company, usually within a specified time period.

CONVERTIBLE SECURITIES

(*i*) Those preference shares and debentures which can be redeemed by converting them into new class of shares or debentures.

(*ii*) A security which can be converted into other securities under certain agreed conditions on which the holder has an option.

CONVEYANCE

The transfer of title to land from one person to another: the instrument that effects and records the transfer.

COOK-BOOK

A receipt book which shows the way to achieve a particular objective. It is used in hotels, hostels, guest-houses, etc.

COOLING-OFF PERIOD

A period during which a trade union is forbidden to call a strike or an employer is forbidden to enforce a lockout.

CO-OPERATION

Productivity of a business cannot be increased without close and personnel cooperation between management and workmen. Specialisation, delegation of authority, encouragement to personal initiative, freedom to act within their powers, are essential for better efficiency workers.

CO-OPERATIVE ADVERTISING

Advertising paid for jointly by a supplier and a customer—for example, by the manufacturer of a product and a retailer.

CO-OPERATIVE BANKS

Co-operative banks are organised on co-operative lines. They encourage thrift, accept money on deposits and extend loans to the members at a relatively reasonable rate of interest. Co-operative banks are primarily intended to help agriculturists by providing loans at low rates of interest and on easy terms. They are organised both at State as well as District levels. Their idea is not to earn big profits but to render service. They use most of their profits for the welfare of the farmers or artisans.

CO-OPERATIVE ORGANISATION

(*i*) A group of independent retailers that combine resources and expertise to control their wholesaling needs, as through a centralised wholesale buying centre.

(*ii*) Co-operation is a form of organisation wherein persons associate together voluntarily for the furtherance of their common economic interests. Co-operatives may undertake production not for earning profits, but for the benefit of their members. Similarly, consumers may join hands to establish direct contacts with the manufacturers and to eliminate middlemen's profits and thereby to provide consumer goods cheaply to the members of the co-operative society.

CO-OPERATIVE

A group of producers or purchasers who set up a trading organisation, the profit from which is shared out among the members of the group.

CO-OPTING

(*i*) An approach to influencing the environment that involves absorbing key members of important environmental elements into the leadership or policy-making structure of an organisation.

(*ii*) The method of increasing power and creating alliances in which individuals or groups whose support is needed are absorbed into another group.

(*iii*) Inviting someone to join an already established group because of some particular quality or skill, the need for which may not have been foreseen when the group was set up.

CO-ORDINATE

To time, unify, and integrate work as it takes place. Co-ordination refers to the activities the manager undertakes to ensure that different kinds of work, or work performed by different people, proceed harmoniously and in balance toward the desired end result.

CO-ORDINATION

(*i*) Ensuring that all efforts are bent forward a common objective and that there is no duplication of work that results in wasted effort. Includes resolution of differences of opinion.

(*ii*) Is the orderly arrangement of group effort to provide unity of action in the pursuit of a common purpose. It involves encouraging the completion of individual portions of a task in an appropriate, synchronised order.

(*iii*) The process of ensuring that persons who perform interdependent activities work together in a way that contributes to overall objective attainment.

(*iv*) The process of integrating all the parts and function of an organisation.

CO-OWNERSHIP

Shared ownership and usually control of an enterprise by employees.

COPY

(*i*) The process of duplicating the text, graphics or any other type of matter on the screen into a buffer for placing that elsewhere in the same or other file and leaving the original text or matter intact without any disturbance.

(*ii*) In the context of advertising, any words contained in an advertisement.

(*iii*) In advertising this refers to the text of an advertisements.

(*iv*) The written or broadcast words used in an advertisement.

COPY TEST

Test of advertising copy, either before or after publication aiming to discover reader's comprehension, interest, brand preference, company image, etc.

COPYRIGHT

(*i*) A law offering protection to prevent the copy of one's work without the permission of that person or organisation. Some applies to computer software also.

(*ii*) The right of an author (or other originator) to control the copying and distributing of books, articles, movies, or other creative works.

COPYWRITER

(*i*) Person who writes copy for advertisements or other promotional material. Usually employed by an advertising agency, but in technical areas, will more frequently be employed by the firm manufacturing and/or distributing the producers concerned.

(*ii*) Someone who writes copy for advertisements.

CORE MEMORY

A magnetic main memory composed of the doughnuts made out of ferrite (toroids) which can be magnetised in on direction to represent a binary digit 0 and in the other direction to represent a binary digit 1.

CORE TIME

Particular periods in Flexible Working Hours during which all employees must be in attendance. Outside this core time employees are free to choose their working hours.

CORPORATE CHAIN

A chain with 11 or more stores.

CORPORATE CULTURE

(i) The system of shared values, beliefs, and habits within an organisation that interacts with the formal structure to produce behavioural norms.

(*ii*) Is a set of shared values and beliefs that organisation members have regarding the functioning and existence of their organisation.

CORPORATE ENTERPRISES

The business entities which are independent of their owners are known as *Corporate Enterprises.* These are recognised by virtue of the legislation, administrative regulations or registration.

CORPORATE IMAGE

The impression of itself that an organisation presents to the outside world.

CORPORATE MANAGEMENT

The overall management of an organisation, as opposed to departmental or sectional management.

CORPORATE PHILANTHROPY

Corporate contributions for charitable and social responsibility purposes.

CORPORATE PLANNING

A planning process which takes into account the whole organisation as a set of resources and considers future development in the context of markets, competitive environment, legislative environment, new technologies, etc.

CORPORATE SOCIAL RESPONSIBILITY

(*i*) A term often used in reference to the concept of

organisational social responsibility as applied to business organisations.

(*ii*) Is the managerial obligation to take action that protects and improves both the welfare of society as a whole and the interests of the organisation.

CORPORATE SOCIAL RESPONSIVENESS

A term used in reference to the concept of organisational social responsiveness as applied to business organisations.

CORPORATE STRATEGIC PLANNING

Long-term planning for the organisation as a whole, carried out by top management.

CORPORATE-LEVEL STRATEGIC PLANNING

The process of defining the overall character and purpose of the organisation, the businesses it will enter and leave, and how resources will be distributed among those businesses.

CORPORATE-LEVEL STRATEGY

A type of strategy that addresses what businesses the organisation will operate, how the strategies of those businesses will be co-ordinated to strengthen the organisation's competitive position, and how resources will be allocated among the businesses.

CORPORATION

A collection of individuals acting as a single entity which has a legal status and autonomy in business dealings.

CORRECTIVE ACTION

Is managerial activity aimed at bringing organisational performance up to the level of performance standards.

CORRECTIVE READING

Instruction in reading a new reading in which an attempt is made to correct bad habits and deficiencies in this skill.

CORRELATION COEFFICIENT

In statistics this is a measure (denoted by the letter r) of the extent to which two variables are correlated. It can range from zero correlation to perfect positive correlation (1.00), where the variables are always associated in the same way, or perfect negative correlation (-1.00), where the variables are always associated but in different ways.

CORRELATION

A statistical technique for analysing the co-variation or closeness of relationship between two or more variables.

CORRIDOR PRINCIPLE

A principle which states that the process of beginning a new venture helps entrepreneurs visualise other opportunities that they could not envision or take advantage of until they started the initial venture.

COSMOS

A communication package developed by *Norsk Data Norway* for resource sharing providing the perfect solution for distributed data processing overwide or logical area networks.

COST

The amount of expenditure (actual or notional) incurred on or attributable to a given thing.

COST ACCOUNTANT

(*i*) An accountant or accounts officer whose job concerns the fixing of monies due for work done in manufacturing a product (*i.e.*, reckoning the cost of material and labour consumed) but who is increasingly called upon the estimate to probable unit cost of a manufacturing process so that the price to the buyer can cost of a manufacturing process so that the price to the buyer can be determined by the company for the purpose of making a tender.

(*ii*) An accountant specialising in recording and analysing cost data in order to advise on future cost control within business.

COST ACCOUNTING

(i) A branch of accounting which analyses the cost component of an activity. It has evolved and developed as a result of defects and limitations of financial accounting.

(*ii*) Planning, decision-making and control are the basic managerial functions. The cost accounting system provides the necessary tools such as standard costing, budgetary control, inventory control, marginal costing, and differential costing etc., for carrying out such functions efficiently. Hence, cost accounting is considered as a necessary adjunct of management accounting.

COST ANALYSIS

The assignment of costs to strategic business units, departments, products, sales territories, customer, or other meaningful categories to determine and evaluate the use of resources.

COST AUDITOR

A qualified accountant, who examines cost accounting records, cost statements and other books and papers of a company.

COST EFFECTIVENESS

A measure of the extent to which money has been effectively spent on something. It is found by seeing whether the benefits that have resulted could have been obtained with a lower expenditure.

COST LEADERSHIP

Is a strategy that focuses on making an organisation more competitive by producing products more cheaply than can.

COST LEADERSHIP STRATEGY

A generic business-level strategy outlined by *Michael E. Porter* that involves emphasising organisational efficiency so that the overall costs of providing products and services are lower than those of competitors.

COST LEDGER

A subsidiary ledger for the accumulation of accounts used in computing of summarising the cost of goods manufactured or of services produced.

COST OF GOODS SOLD

(*i*) The purchase process of goods sold during a specified period, including transportation costs.

(*ii*) One of the two components of financial accounting to arrive at the gross results of a business concern during a particular trading period.

COST PER THOUSAND (CPT)

Used in advertising as a measure of cost per thousand people viewing or reading the advertisement.

COST PLUS PRICING

A pricing approach where an agreed percentage is added to the costs of a product.

COST REDUCTION STRATEGY

(*i*) A product line extension strategy that involves lowering cost, used especially during a product's maturity or decline product marketing strategy that involves redesigning a product to lower production costs.

(*ii*) A product marketing strategy that involves redesigning a product to lower production costs.

COST, UNIT

Wages and fringe benefits.

COST, VARIABLE

Costs that a change with the level of company activity.

COST-BENEFIT ANALYSIS

Is the process of comparing the cost of some activity with the benefit or revenue that results from the activity to determine the activity's total worth to the organisation.

COST-EFFECTIVENESS

A technique adopted by management in the public sector for analysing specific expenditures to determine whether the same expenditure could be used more effectively in another direction, or to ascertain whether the expenditure can be reduced without negatively affecting the expected benefit.

COSTING

A branch of financial accounting; a technique and process of ascertaining costs.

COSTS, STANDARD

Unit costs set in advance of production by determination of the labour and material needed, plus a standard amount of overhead costs.

COUNT AND RE-COUNT OFFERS

Salesman count stocks of their product held by wholesale retail customers, then recount on next call and pay bonus on stocks sold in meantime.

COUNTER CONFORMITY

A form of non-conformity in which a person's judgment and action are impelled by group pressure to deviate even more widely from the group norm than if the pressure had been omitted or relaxed. The counter conformist tends to actively oppose the group and compulsively dissent from it.

COUNTER POWER

Leaders exert power on subordinates, and subordinates exert power on leaders. Power is a two-way flow.

COUNTER TRADE

Large-scale international barter.

COUNSELLING DEFINED

Counselling is a professional form of interpersonal communication whose purpose is to assist the employee with which eventually to question the knowledge store. It is a planned systematic intervention in the life on an individual who is capable of choosing the goal and the direction of his own development.

COVER

Outer faces of a magazine usually available for advertising purpose, *i.e.* front, back, inside front and inside back cover.

COVER NOTE

A provisional document issued by an insurance company to bid over the time between the acceptance of a risk and the issuing of a policy.

COVERAGE

The percentage of a selected target audience that have an opportunity to see a particular advertisement.

COVERED TIME

Time spent on work for which a bonus or piece work scheme exists but where it is not used. Instead of payment by result, payment is one a daywork or other time related payment scheme.

COW

Expression used to describe products whose performance past their best but which remain profitable. They are 'milked' *i.e.* provide a source of funds for new product development. Co-worker: Someone that a person works with who is neither his superior nor a subordinate.

CPI

Characters Per Inch.

CPU

Central Processing Unit.

CPU CYCLE

The amount of time required to access and execute an instruction.

CPU TIME

Amount of time actually devoted by central processing unit in execution of a program.

CRAFT TRAINING

Training which, in conjuction with appropriate further education, and usually under terms of an apprenticeship, leads to status of craftman, or, a little more archaically, journeyman.

CRAFT UNION

A labour union whose membership is limited to people who work at the same craft.

CRASH

Term used when the computer stops due to the malfunctioning of hardware.

CREATIVE GROUP

Collection of individuals specialising in the development of creative ideas, particularly for the origination of advertising campaigns.

CREATIVE PROCESS

In the context of advertising. The generation of ideas and the development of the advertising message or concept for the advertising strategy.

CREATIVE SELLING PROCESS

The six step process by which creative selling is carried out: (1) locating and qualifying prospects, (2) approaching the prospect, (3) making the sales presentation, (4) handling objection, (5) closing the sale, and (6) following up.

CREATIVITY

(*i*) The ability to generate ideas that are both innovative and functional.

(*ii*) The cognitive process of developing an idea, concept, commodity, or discovery that is viewed as novel by its creator or a target audience.

CREDIT CARD

A card issued to an individual which identifies him and permits him to obtain goods or services on credit. Credit cards are either two-party or three-party. A two-party card is issued by a retailer and may be used only to purchase goods from that retailer.

CREDIT FUNCTION

Provision of credit service to another member of a distribution channel.

CREDIT NOTE

A document issued by a vendor giving credit to the debtor for, say, goods returned, or overcharges acknowledged on an invoice.

CREDIT POLICY

It consists of the norms and guidelines for determining whether and to what extent credit can be granted to customers in general and various categories of customers in particular.

CREDIT RATING

An indication of the creditworthiness of an individual or company, based on an assessment of their ability to repay the amount of credit advanced.

CREDIT REPORTING AGENCY

An organisation that will supply information about the financial standing of individuals or firms. (Also known as a 'credit agency' or 'credit bureau').

CREDIT SQUEEZE

(*i*) A popular term for the state's interference with normal market forces (through Reserve Bank) in an attempt to regulate the level of economic activity by reducing the money supply. It is effected by making credit more expensive in the following ways: through direct instructions to banks; by raising the minimum lending rate quickly enough to force other organisations linked to the money market to increase their rates accordingly: by making changes in the hire-purchase regulations so as to deter prospective purchasers.

(*ii*) The government control of credit, aimed at making credit more difficult and expensive to obtain, by imposing high interest rates, restrictions on hire-purchase and back lending, and similar measures. The goal is to damp down demand in order to reduce the risk of inflation.

CREDIT TERMS

The terms extended by a firm to its debtors for payment.

CREDIT

Although generally used as an adjective (credit card, credit note, etc.) the word credit has a more precise meaning in the business world where it is considered as the opposite of cash. Transactions are made on a 'credit' basis where no cash changes hands. The introduction and acceptance of credit in business transaction has been the principal cause of great expansion in trade and industry over the past hundred years.

CREDITORS

A party in a transaction which gives goods or services or money on credit; a person to whom a sum of money is due.

CRISIS PROBLEM

A type of problem in managerial decision-making involving a serious difficulty that requires immediate action.

CRITERION

In performance evaluation, the dependent or predicted measure for appraising the effectiveness of an individual employee.

CRITERION BEHAVIOUR

Term used particularly in programmed learning, but also in some other areas of training, for a detailed specification of what is expected of a trainee/student after training or a defined part of it.

CRITICAL INCIDENTS

An observable human activity that permits inferences and predictions to be made about the person performing the work.

CRITICAL PATH

(*i*) Is the sequence of events and activities within a program evaluation and review technique (PERT) network that requires the longest period of time to complete.

(*ii*) The path in a PERT network that will take the longest to complete.

(*iii*) The planning and control technique that involves the display of a complex project as a network, with one time estimate used for each step in the project.

CRITICAL PATH SCHEDULING

A method of scheduling work by means of diagrams that show which jobs must be completed before other jobs can be started. Jobs are indicated by arrows; hence the technique is sometimes called *Arrow Diagramming*.

CRITICAL QUESTION ANALYSIS

Is a strategy development tool that consists of answering basic questions about the present purposes and objectives of the organisation, its present direction and environment, and actions that can be taken to achieve organisational objectives in the future.

CRITICAL READING

The interpreting and thoughtful evaluation of reading materials.

CROP INSURANCE

Insurance of crops against risks and losses from natural calamities like drought, floods, bad weather, cold waves, and plant diseases.

CROSS DOMINANCE

Control that is right-handed and left-eyed or left-handed and right-eyed.

CROSS-CLASSIFICATION MATRIX

A grid that helps isolate variables of interest in the market. For example, a geographic variable might be cross-classified with some other variable of interest, such as income.

CROSS-CULTURAL MANAGEMENT

The study of the behaviour of individuals in organisations around the world.

CROSSED CHEQUE

A cheque may be either an open cheque or a crossed cheque. Crossing is an indication appearing on the faces of the cheque that it should be paid only through a banker; it is usually done by drawing two parallel lines on the face of the cheque. Crossing has been evolved to avoid wrongful persons from obtaining payment on it.

CROSS-ELASTICITY

Elasticity in the demand for one product in relation to the process of substitutable or complementary products.

CROSS-FRONTIER COMPANY

Company which operates outside national boundaries, as distinct from multinational company which has separate companies registered in each country.

CROSS-FUNCTIONAL TEAM

Is an organisational team composed of people from different functional areas of the organisation who are all focused on a specified objective.

CROSS-REFERENCING

Cross-referencing means that a card or sheet describing a particular paper is placed in other positions in the files when someone might look for that paper. Usually cross-reference sheets are of some colour that will make them distinctive from other field materials. All commercial filling systems provide a cross-referencing form.

CROSSWALK

A diagram showing the relationship between items in programme budgets and those in budgets that have been prepared for departments or other budget centres of an organisation.

CRYSTALLISATION

Bringing into public consciousness something about which people are either vague or which exists in their subconscious mind.

CULTURAL ENVIRONMENT

That part of the environment, domestic or foreign or both, that is shaped by humankind.

CULTURAL LEVEL

Stage of enlightenment and refinement of taste acquired by intellectual and aesthetic training.

CULTURE

(*i*) Explicit and implicit patterns of and for behaviour acquired and transmitted by symbols, constituting the distinctive achievement of human groups, including their embodiment.

(*ii*) The institutions, values, beliefs, and behaviours of a society; everything we learn, as opposed to that with which we were born in artifacts.

CULTURE SHOCK CYCLE

A three-phase cycle (fascination and interest, frustration and confusion, and adaptation) which most individuals sent to another culture experience.

CUM-BONUS

Bonus shares issued by a company, the price of which includes the bonus.

CUMULATIVE PREFERENCE SHARES

A form of preference shares on which dividends may be accumulated if profits are poor in one year and then paid at the end of the next year when they improve.

CUMULATIVE QUANTITY DISCOUNT

A price discount determined by the amount purchased over some specified time period.

CUMULATIVE REACH

Number of people in a target audience reached without duplication by a given promotional schedule over a particular period of time.

CUMULATIVE TIMING

A method of timing a job using a stopwatch in time study in which the hands of the stopwatch are allowed to continue to move without returning them to zero at the end of each element of the job. The time for each element is obtained subsequently by subtraction.

CURRENCY DEPRECIATION

The extent to which the value of a currency has fallen in terms of its exchangeable value for other currencies. If the currency of one country is tied to another, the extent of its depreciation is reflected in the increase in the cost of the other. If, on the other hand, country's currency is said to be floating freely in the foreign exchanges then the extent of its depreciation will vary according to the value of the currency with which it may be linked.

CURRENT ACCOUNT

An account with a bank where the customer makes demand deposits and asks for repayment of the deposits by drawing cheques.

CURRENT ASSETS

(*i*) All assets held by a firm with the objective of converting them into cash within the operating cycle or one year, whichever is longer. Current assets include items such as cash, receivables, inventory and prepayments.

(*ii*) Assets which can be converted into cash within an accounting year; also called circulating assets.

(*iii*) The broad categories of current assets include such items as cash (including fixed deposits with banks) sundry debtors, bills receivable, marketable securities, inventories, advances recoverable and prepaid expenses. Generally, the term 'current assets' may be used to designate any asset which is reasonably expected to be realised in cash, or consumed during the normal operating cycle of the business.

CURRENT DEPOSITS

They are deposits engaged in some form of business where usual frequency of operations in the account is expected. There are no restrictions placed on the number of withdrawals of deposits in the account The deposits are withdrawable without any prior notice and banker has always to be ready to meet huge withdrawals on such accounts.

CURRENT INCOME

Income relating to a current accounting period.

CURRENT LIABILITIES

All claims against the assets of the firm which are to be met out of cash or other current assets within one year or within the operating cycle, whichever is longer. Usually, these include items such as accounts payable, tax or other claims payable and accrued expenses.

CURRENT MATURITY

The portion of a long-term obligation that is to be retired during the next twelve months; usually classified as a current liability.

CURRENT RATIO

The ratio between current assets and current liabilities.

CURRICULUM VITAE(C.V.)

A document which sets out a record of an individual's experience, qualifications and achievements. When given to a prospective employer, it offers a brief background to the individual on which an assessment of his suitability for a post can be partially based.

CUSTOM DUTY

A tax payable on goods exported or imported from a country.

CUSTOM MARKETING

A marketing effort in which the marketer seeks to satisfy each customer's unique set of needs. In effects each customer is an individual market segment.

CUSTOMER

(*i*) Person or organisation actually making the purchasing decision not necessarily the 'consumer' or 'user'. Legally, a party to a contract for the sale of goods.

(*ii*) In marketing it is generally anyone buying a product or service.

CUSTOMERS

The element of the task environ ment that includes those individuals and organisations that purchase an organisation's products and/or services.

CUSTOMER DIVISIONS

A form of divisional structure involving divisions set up to service particular types of clients or customers.

CUSTOMER GROUP

Classification income form, *e.g.* demographic, of members of the population likely to be customers.

CUSTOMER PROFILE

Total list or estimate of all customers divided into pertinent categories, *e.g.* age-groups, with each group expressed in percentages of the total.

CUSTOMER SATISFACTION

"Customer's satisfaction is our motto", this is one of the slogans mostly found in the offices of business houses and various stores. Customer satisfaction means providing the material and services to the customer without any inconvenience to him and meeting his requirements. In these days of tough competition, customer satisfaction in one of the important factors responsible for the success of a business.

CUSTOMER-BASED ORGANISATION

An organisational structure based on the specific needs of customer groups.

CUSTOMER S ACCOUNT

Personal account of a client, buyer, seller, lender, etc.

CUSTOMISATION STRATEGY

A product line extension strategy by which a product is made in relatively small lots for specific channels of distribution or specific customers.

CUSTOMISATION STRATEGY

A plan by which a marketer adapts its marketing strategy to each country in which the product is marketed.

CUSTOMS QUOTAS

The practice of allowing a certain amount of commodity (being imported) at a favourable duty and after that point charging normal duty.

CUT-RATE

Reduced rate at which goods are sold. Goods sold at cut prices or rates are called "Cut-price goods" and stores offering them are known as "Cut-price stores".

CYBER

Family of supercomputers and mainframe manufactured by *Control Data Corporation*.

CYBERNETIC CONTROL SYSTEM

A self-regulating control system that, once it is put into operation, can automatically monitor the situation and take corrective action when necessary.

CYBERNETIC

(*i*) From a Greek term meaning something like 'steersman' introduced in 1984 by *Norbert Wiener*, an American computer engineer. It is usually defined briefly as the study of regulatory mechanisms (like thermostats). Out of this field come the analogy of the brain as a computer and the model of psychological processes, as systems of messages with their own built-in feedback.

(*ii*) The science of communication and control. The word is derived from the Greek word for *Steersman* (*kubernetes*), and the study itself is important in the development of management information systems. Especially those that utilise computers.

CYCLE OF ADVERTISING DEVELOPMENT

Four stages; moving strategy definition (what to say and to whom); creative development (how to say it); communication assessment (have we said it); and campaign evaluation (what was the effect of what we said?).

D

DAMAGES

A sum of money claimed or awarded as compensation for loss or harm suffered by a person or by his property or reputation.

DANGLE

An arrow in an activity—in arrow network that has no preceding or succeeding event or activity at one end.

DATA

(*i*) Facts and recorded measures of phenomena.

(*ii*) Data are the facts and figures that are reduced and filed in the memory of a computer. This information is not intended to be retrieved immediately for decision-making *e.g.* various day books being made on the computer.

DATA (PLURAL OF DATUM)

(*i*) Something given or admitted, as a fact on which an inference is based;

(*ii*) Something, actual or assumed, used as a basis of reckoning.

DATABASE

A set of interrelated records stored in a manner that multiple applications can have access to same file without modification and easy to grow in future thus reducing the redundancy.

DATABASE MANAGEMENT SYSTEM

An integrated system that has DDL to create and modify the structures of database files, a centralised data pool, DML to manipulate, access and edit the database files and database administrator to manage all these components.

DATA BUS

A set of parallel wires that transforms information in the form of electronic signals in the computer from one location to another say from register to memory or from memory to secondary storage devices.

DATA COLLECTION SYSTEM

An organisation's manner of systematically collecting data. It includes internal records and reports systems, a marketing research system, and a marketing intelligence system. The data collection system is part of the marketing information system.

DATA COMMUNICATION EQUIPMENT

All electro-mechanical and electronic equipment for transmission of data from one place to another *e.g.*, concentrators, modem.

DATA DICTIONARY

The document that contains clear and precise definitions of the data that will be used in setting the database management system. It includes the list of all the files, fields and system with storage structure and accessing method.

DATA ENTRY

The conversion of human readable data into the form so that computer system can interpret by putting it into the system with the help of input device like keyboard. Also called Data Capture or input preparation or data preparation.

DATA LOGGING

The collection of data about various performance characteristics in a production system or item of equipment for example production rate at machine utilisation time lost for breakdown etc. It is used as an input to production management.

DATA PROCESSING

The use of computer and its peripheral devices to process, sort, classify, summarise and to perform a series of operations then on data to convert it from the raw form to useful meaningful information.

DATA REDUCTION

Refers to the selection and editing of operands to derive facts from large volumes of raw data.

DATA SECURITY

The protection of data from accidental or malevolent modification, deletion, destruction or disclosure.

DATA STORAGE DEVICE

The device that stores millions of characters by means of pulses, magnetic, laser or any other technology, typically a card, magnetic disk.

DATA TERMINAL

The device or point in a computer system or a data communications network from which data can be entered or retrieved.

DATA DREDGING

In statistical analysis the process of examining data that have been collected for specific purposes but that contain much more information than has been used for the original investigation.

DAY BOOK

Day book is a book wherein all the transactions of business for a particular day are recorded. Day book is prepared on a daily basis. It may also be called Waste Book. This is prepared in the order to avoid dependence on memory of the businessman.

DAY RELEASE

Arrangement under which employers given their employees a period off from work or duty (typically one day a week) without loss of pay in order that they can attend a course of further edition.

DAY SHIFT

1. A shift that is worked mainly during the hours of daylight.
2. The morning shift in a three shift system.

DAYS OF GRACE

In insurance it is the period of time given even when the premium is due and is paid without any loss of the insurance cover or any penalty.

DEED

(*i*) A person's statement made in writing on paper, parchment, or vellum bearing the person's seal and his signature, which the person has 'delivered' meaning that he has indicated that the statement is to take effect so that he will have to abide by it.

(*ii*) A legal document under seal containing an agreement, signed by two or more parties.

DEED OF TRUST

A document that creates a trust; also, a document by which an organisation or person transfers ownership of land to an independent trustee for holding until a debt on the land (a mortgage) is paid off.

DEALER

A trader who carries on the business of buying and selling and has other business dealings; also known as a Commission Agent.

DEATH DUTY

Tax on the property of a deceased payable by his heirs; also called Estate Duty.

DEBENTURE

(*i*) A bond issued against the general credit of the company does not carry a lien against physical assets,

(*ii*) A type of Security on which interest is paid as percentage of its nominal value.

DEBENTURE LOAN

Funds raised by the issue of debenture bonds.

DEBIT

Entry in an account recording a sum of money owed to a person; the left-hand side of an account on which such entries are made.

DEBIT AND CREDIT

Conventionally, the left side of an account is called the debit side (abbreviated Dr.) and the right side thereof is called the credit side (abbreviated Cr.). Amounts entered on the left (debit) side are termed debits and the account is said to be debited; and the amounts recorded on the right (credit) side are termed credits and the account is said to be credited. The difference between the total debits and the total credits is the account balance. But when the sums of debits and credits equalise, the account is said to be in balance.

DEBIT NOTE

Note sent to correct or reconcile errors in an invoice.

DEBT

(*i*) A debt is money owed by one person or firm to another. It may carry interest covering the period during which it is due but not paid, although common business usage allows an agreement. It also applies for obligation of goods and services.

(*ii*) A pecuniary liability arising out of an obligation to pay a person's dues.

DEBT CAPITAL

Money lent to a company on a long term basis (at least one year) which must be repaid first if the company is liquidated.

DEBT-FINANCED INCOME

Income generated from debt-financed real or personal property that is owned for the purpose of generating income. The debt must have been incurred in order to acquire or improve the income-generating property, but need not have been incurred prior to acquiring or improving it. Debt-financed income is important in determining a non-profit organisation's unrelated business income.

DEBT FINANCING

Raising capital by borrowing.

DEBT RATIO

A comparison of total debts to total assets; an accounting ratio used to evaluate the risk of increased debt to or opportunity for expansion or development of an organisation.

DEBT REDEMPTION

Repayment of debt.

DEBT, NON-GUARANTEED

A long-term debt payable solely from pledged specified sources, such as from earnings of revenue-producing activities. Non-guaranteed debt included only debt that does not constitute an obligation against any other resources if the sources pledged are insufficient.

DEBTOR

The person or organisation that owed goods, services or money. The person or organisation to whom it is due is known as the creditor.

DEBTOR'S LEDGER

An important register in which various accounts of nominal, real and personal accounts are opened.

DEBUG

(*i*)The process of removing the errors or bugs from any computer program.

(*ii*)To trace and eliminate faults; especially errors in a program for a computer.

DEBUGGING

The process of detecting, locating and removal of mistakes or errors or bugs of a computer program.

DECASUALISATION

Process by which the workers in an industry are switched from a casuals labour system to regular employment.

DECENTRALISATION

A system of management in which the responsibility of making decisions is passed down to lower levels in the hierarchy. The systematic and consistent delegation of authority to levels at which work is performed.

DECENTRALISATION OF AUTHORITY

Decentralisation means dispersal of authority and the power of decision-making to lower levels of the organisation. According to Louis Allen, "It refers to the systematic effort to delegate to the lowest level all authority except that which can only be exercised at central points."

DECENTRING

The process of continuing to perceive a situation in a way that changing circumstances have rendered ineffective. A psychological version of culture lag.

DECEPTION

To provoke spontaneous and revealing responses under motivational depth interviewing research respondents may be deliberately deceived by given information challenge's them to refute statements and so expose attitudes.

DECIDER

(*i*) Used in studying industrial buying as the person who makes the purchase decision, usually in a formal capacity.

(*ii*) The buying-centre role played by the organisation member who makes the actual purchasing decision.

DECISION

(*i*) A means to achieve some result or to solve some problem. The outcome of a process that is influenced by many forces.

(*ii*) A kind of flow chart used to summarise a possible sequence of decisions in which alternative choices are open at each stage and where each alternative is dependent on choices already made.

DECISION ACCEPTANCE

An important criterion in the Vroom-Yetton Model that refers to the degree of subordinate commitment to the decision.

DECISION PACKAGE

A mechanism used in zero-base budgeting to examine the effects of programmatic resource requirements, products, and levels of performance at alternative levels of funding.

DECISION QUALITY

An important criterion in the Vroom- Yetton Model that refers to the objective aspects of a decision that influence subordinate's performance, aside from any direct impact on motivation.

DECISION RULE

Any rule set-up to help make decisions in the face of uncertainty.

DECISION SUPPORT SYSTEM

A computer system that stores data and transforms the data into accessible information. It includes a user interaction system, software that manages the interface between the user and the computer system; a database, the collection of stored data on which the computer system and the user operate; and an analytical models system, which contains various software that operates on the data. The decision support system is part of the marketing information system.

DECISION TREE

A technique of evaluating the risks and uncertainties of capital budgeting decisions; one of the alternatives to assuming risky investment projects.

DECISION-MAKER

Anyone charged with the formal responsibility for making decision in an organisation. Usually applied to senior management people.

DECISION-MAKING

(*i*) Choosing among alternatives in cases where there is some uncertainty about the final result of each possible course of action.

(*ii*) A process aimed at the making of a evaluative judgment. It includes the cognitive activities of memory, thinking, and information processing.

DECISION-MAKING SKILLS

(*i*) Adequate conceptual understanding is required for taking sound decisions. With the development of intellectual, communication and organisational understanding skills, the manager reaches that stage of awareness when he can take effective decisions. The decisions so made will have to be carried out at working level and hence the most difficult task is to see that such decisions are carried out at the proper time by the right people.

(*ii*) It is the making of a choice from among alternative courses of action. More broadly constructed decision-making also involves all the actions that must take place before a final choice is made. The process or activity of selecting, from among possible alternatives from future course of acting.

DECISIVE THINKING

Thinking that is concerned with successfully arriving at decisions.

DECLARATORY JUDGMENT

A judicial decision defining the rights and duties of parties to a dispute, but excluding payment of damages or an order compelling one of the parties to take a specific action.

DECLINE STAGE

The stage in the product life cycle when the product loses market acceptance because of such factors as popularity obsolescence, and market saturation. (See Fig. 1)

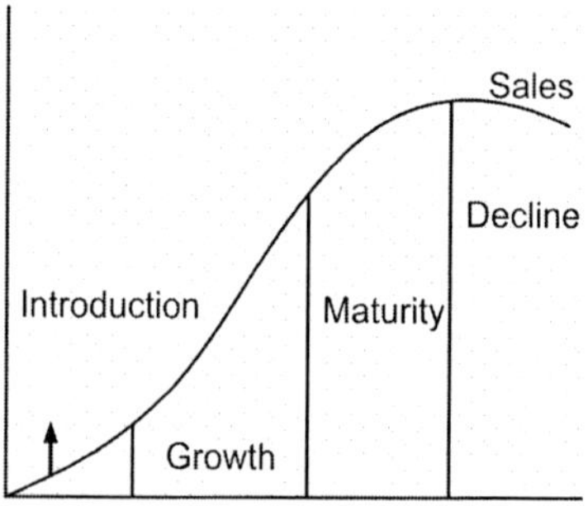

Fig. 1: Product Life Cycle

DECLINING BALANCE

A method of calculating depreciation of a fixed asset in

which the amount of depreciation is a fixed percentage to the previous year's depreciated value (Also known as Diminishing Balance).

DECODING

(*i*) The mental process that the receiver of a message goes through to decipher the message.

(*ii*) In communication theory, the process by which the receiver of a message interprets the message's meaning.

DECREE

An order of the Court.

DEDUCTION

Mode of reasoning which starts with premises or propositions.

DEDUCTIVE REASONING

A form of thinking which proceeds from the whole to parts or minor premises.

DEED WARRANTY

A deed containing a covenant of guarantee in which the grantor assures that the title is free from defects that the property is free of encumbrances other than those listed and that the grantor agrees to protect the grantee against any loss by reason of the existence of many other title or interest in the property at the time the deed is executed.

DEFECATION

The failure of a person to account for money entrusted to his or her care. There is the assumption that the money was misused.

DEFECTIVE

A unit of production which is some way does not conform with specified requirements.

DEFENCE BONDS

Securities issued by a government to raise funds from the public generally during periods of war.

DEFENSIVE BEHAVIOUR

Defense mechanisms evoked when an employee is blocked in attempts to satisfy needs to achieve goals. They include withdrawal, aggression, substitution, compensation, repression, and rationalisation.

DEFERRAL OF BUDGET AUTHORITY

In the federal budget, any action or inaction by the executive branch, including the establishment of reserves under the Anti-deficiency Act, that temporarily withholds, delays or effectively precludes the obligation or use of budget authority.

DEFERRED ANNUITY

An annuity that does not start until after a specified period or until the annuitant reaches a specified age.

DEFERRED ASSET

The incurrence of expenditure on an asset in advance before the benefits from such an expenditure are realised.

DEFERRED REBATE

A rebate or discount on a purchase which is accumulated

for a specified period to encourage customers to remain with a particular supplier. Also it is called *Aggregated Rebate.*

DEFERRED WAGE INCREASE

A negotiated pay increase that does not become effective until a specified future date.

DEFICIENCY

(*i*) It is the excess of liabilities over assets of an enterprise on a given date. It is equal to the debit balance in the profit and loss statement.

(*ii*) State or quality of being deficient or lacking in some quality.

(*iii*) A statement of the changes in the assets and liabilities of a bankrupt over the twelve months, preceding the date on which a receiving order was made against him. It forms part of the bankrupt's statement of affairs.

DEFICIT

(*i*) The result of an expenditure in excess of income, a lack or inadequate amount of something.

(*ii*) Excess of expenditure over income; debit balance in the profit-and-loss account.

DEFICIT FINANCING

The financing of projects which cost more than the organisation has available as cash or current assets and for which it therefore needs to borrow.

DEFLATIONARY GAP

The amount by which the theoretical volume of spending necessary to maintain full employment or to absorb all available goods and service at prevailing price exceeds actual private spending and government's expenses.

DEFLATOR

Present price level divided by price level at some past date is termed as deflator.

DEFRAUD

To cheat another or to withhold wrongful that which belongs to another to deprive one of some right by deceitful means.

DEFUNCT COMPANY

A company that has been struck off the official register of companies because it has ceased to function. This may arise after a winding up or where, after proper formalities have been completed.

DEGREE OF CONTROL

It means how close a control needs to be maintained. It is necessary to record production every hour, day or week. Must an accurate inventory count be made of all parts at all stages in their processing. It is obvious that there is a point of diminishing returns where the value of such controls no longer justifies the cost of their accumulation.

DEL CREDRE AGENT

He is an agent employed by a principal to buy or sell goods on credit. He ensures the recovery of payments. In the case of the default of the purchaser in paying the price, he shall indemnify the seller of the goods for any loss arising on account of bad debts. He gets extra commission for bearing this extra risk. Such commission is called *Del Credre Commission*.

DELEGATE

To entrust to another the performance of responsibility of the exercise of authority.

DELEGATED STRATEGIES

Organisational change strategies that allow active participation by subordinates.

DELEGATED STRATEGIES

Organisational change strategies that allow active participation by subordinates.

DELEGATION

(*i*) Delegation means devolution of authority on subordinates with a view to make them perform the assigned tasks or duties. It is that part of the process or organisation by which an executive, manager or administrator makes it possible for others to share in the work of carrying out the organisational objectives.

(*ii*) Passing authority and responsibility to lower levels.

DELEGATION OF AUTHORITY

The process by which authority is distributed downward in an organisation.

DELEGATION OF RESPONSIBILITY

Job enrichment's basis is delegation of more responsibility to the worker. The worker is allowed to take various decisions many of which were previously taken at higher level. Thus more autonomy is enjoyed by the worker as a result of job enrichment.

DELIVERED PRICING

Pricing that includes delivery within a specified area. Also called *Freight-Allowed Pricing.*

DELIVERY ORDER

An order requesting a warehouse keeper or dock to deliver goods.

DELIVERY PERIOD

The interval between sending an order for goods and receiving them. The interval between receiving an order for goods and dispatching them.

DELPHI METHOD

(*i*) A method of obtaining forecasts of future developments in which a number of experts are asked to give their individual forecasts: these are collected, and summarised; a summary of all forecasts is sent to each expert and each is asked whether he would reconsider his views in the light of what others have said; the process is repeated until the predictions are satisfactorily uniform.

(*ii*) A forecasting technique using the opinions of a panel of experts to develop qualitative forecasts.

DELPHI PROCESS

A technique used to improve group decision-making that involves the solicitations and comparison of anonymous judgments on the topic of interest through a set of sequential questionnaires interspersed with summarised information and feedback of opinions from earlier response.

DEMAND CURVE

A graphic representation of the relationship between various prices and the amount of product that will be demanded at those prices. Also called a *Demand Schedule.*

DEMAND DEPOSIT

A sum of money deposited by someone in a bank on condition that he can withdraw it on demand.

DEMAND DRAFT

(*i*) It is drawn by a bank or its another branch or it may be drawn on another bank.

(*ii*) An order for immediate payment of money by a bank.

DEMAND FUNCTION

Relationship between demand and the determinants of demand such as price substitute products income or credit facilities.

DEMAND INFORMATION

Reversal of traditional supply of information such as news with individual demanding what he wants forms view data of passive participants.

DEMAND MANAGEMENT STRATEGY

A strategy used by service marketers that requires accurate forecasting of the need for services. Examples include selling a service in advance and requiring reservations. Also called *Capacity Management Strategy.*

DEMARCATION DISPUTE

In industrial relations this is a disagreement between trade unions about the way in which work should be divided between different groups of workers, where each union claims the right to do certain types of work exclusively for its own members.

DEMARKETING

Activities that intentionally discourage all or some customers from buying or consuming a product, on a temporary or a permanent basis, generally because of a shortage of the product.

DEMOGRAPHIC

Information relating to broad population statistics, such as age, sex, income, education level or martial status.

DEMOGRAPHIC CATEGORY

A grouping based on age, sex, educational background, income, or some other demographic variable.

DEMOGRAPHY

(*i*) The sociological and statistical study of pollution and places defined by geography, class, and time intervals.

(*ii*) The study of the size, composition, and distribution of the human population in relation to social factors such as geographic boundaries.

DEMONETISE

To declare something to be no longer legal tender.

DEMONSTRATION FORMAT

An advertising format in which a clear-cut example of product superiority is presented.

DEMOTION

(*i*) Demotion is just the opposite of promotion. It is a downward movement of an employee in the organisational hierarchy with lower status and lower salary. It is a downgrading process and is insulting to an employee. Demotion is a punishment for incompetence or mistakes of serious nature on the part of an employee. It is a serious type of penalty or punishment and should be given rarely and only under exceptional circumstances and also tactfully.

(*ii*) Shifting or changing to a lower position or rank. It is accompanied by decreased pay and privileges, status or responsibilities.

DEMURRAGE

These are liquidated damages included in a contract, say a building or shipping contract. Normally it provides for a specified sum for each day the completion is delayed or ships are kept waiting. The fact that the loss is less than the demurrage would make no difference in making the claim. There are also charges incurred for late collection of goods from a carrier or a warehouse.

DENIGRATION

Advertisement should not unfairly attack or discredit other products advertisers or advertisements directly or by implication.

DEPARTMENT

(*i*) A functional or administrative division of an organisation.

(*ii*) Generally, a group of executives and employees engaged in performing a single function or a group of closely related functions.

DEPARTMENT MANAGEMENT

A departmentally managed undertaking is the oldest and the most traditional type of public enterprise in all the countries of the world. It has been mainly used for railway, communications, power, posts, etc. Under Departmental Management, the enterprise is managed by the officials of the government in one of its departments, under the charge of the Secretary of the Ministry concerned. They are managed by civil servants who are government employees and who work under the control of a Minister.

DEPARTMENTAL STORE

A departmentalised retail outlet, often large, offering a wide variety of products and generally providing a full range of customer services.

DEPARTMENTALISATION

The process in which an organisation is structurally divided. Some of the more publicised divisions are by function, territory, product, customer, and project.

DEPARTMENTALISING MANAGERIAL PLANNING

A number of enterprises have a department of managerial planning in their organisation structure. Commonly this department is established because top managers feel that the importance of planning warrants such a department or there is general belief that the amount and calibre of planning should be done unless a planning department exists.

DEPERSONALISATION

The loss of ones identity or self-image. In a work organisation this occurs when people are treated like machines. It is often associated with the Assembly line but is more a matter of management philosophy than production technique as such.

DEPLETION

It is a measure of exhaustion of a washing asset represented by period write off the cost or other substituted value.

DEPOSIT ACCOUNT

An account with a bank from which deposits are repayable only to the depositor, who is required to give notice in advance if he requires repayment.

DEPOSIT RECEIPT

An acknowledgment by a banker that a sum of money or a cheque had been deposited for collection.

DEPOSITION

Testimony in a law case given under oath a particularly as a written statement by a witness for use in Court.

DEPRECIATION

Money set aside each year to amortise investment in capital assets whose value declines over time.

DEPTH

The degree of influence or discretion that an individual possesses to choose how a job will be performed.

DEPTH INTERVIEWS

A research technique involving detailed discussions with individual respondents to explore in detail issues such as motivation, beliefs, etc.

DEPTH OF INTENDED CHANGE

In the context of organisational development, the scope and magnitude of intended change effort. A key issue in managing change.

DEPTH OF PRODUCTION LINE

The number of different items in a product line.

DERIVATION

(*i*) That from which a thing is derived.

(*ii*) The development of a word from its more original or radical elements.

DERIVED DEMAND

(*i*) Demand for a product that depends on demand for another product.

(*ii*) The demand for a component or intermediate product dependent on the sale of the final good or service.

DESCRIPTIVE ESSAYS

A performance evaluation method wherein the rater provides a description in her own words of the ratee's strengths and weaknesses.

DESCRIPTIVE MATERIAL

Material which are used to picture or portray objects, places, or events.

DESCRIPTIVE STATISTICS

Statistics that summarise or describe a set of measurement, *e.g.*, measures of central tendency. Compare with inferential statistics.

DESIGN

In marketing used as a generic term embracing all types of visual work *e.g.* rough typography graphics finished art for all kind of application-advertising exhibitions print work house styling.

DESIGNED DECAY

Manufacture and marketing of disposable *e.g.*, nappies, handkerchiefs and bottles.

DESK RESEARCH

A term used in market research to describe the gathering collation and analysis of available data opposed to fieldwork which generates fresh data. It is often used as the preliminary stage of a new project. It is the opposite of field research.

DESK TOP PUBLISHING

A computerised system of preparing the camera-ready documents for publishers to use for printing.

DE-SKILLING

Modifying method of performing a job to reduce the level of skill or skills demanded.

DEVALUATION

(*i*) A government action decreasing the value of the domestic currency in relation to that of a foreign country.

(*ii*) An instrument of national fiscal policy whereby a government chooses to reduce the value of its currency against orders.

DEVELOP

To build by successive additions. Development refers to the process followed in creating plans and ideas by pooling the suggestions of many people, or in building by increments from simple beginning.

DEVELOPED COUNTRY

An economically advanced country characterised by a high level of specialisation, full-scale marketing structures and activities, large markets, and extensive possibilities for importing and exporting.

DEVELOPER

In organisation behaviours a manager who uses a high relationship orientation and a low task orientation in a situation where such behaviour is appropriate he is perceived as having implicit faith and trust in people and as being primarily concerned with developing them as individuals.

DEVELOPING COUNTRY

A country characterised by social change and increased economic activity. Features include some specialisation of resources, growth of certain industries, an emerging business-based middle class and some export and import activity.

DEVELOPMENT

(*i*) A criterion of effectiveness that refers to the organisation's ability to increase its responsiveness to current and future environmental demands. Equivalent or similar terms include institutionalisation, stability, and integration.

(*ii*) Changes in an organism from its origin to its death, but more particularly the progressive changes from origin to maturity.

DEVELOPMENT AGE

Combination of all indices of development to indicate the person's relative status.

DEVELOPMENT ALLOWANCE RESERVE

It is a reserve created by a enterprise in accordance with the conditions for claiming development allowance under Income Tax Act.

DEVELOPMENT DIRECTOR

A person who manages a development programme in larger organisations.

DEVELOPMENT OF MORE RESOURCES

Marketing promotes the development of economic resources of a country and puts it on the road to faster economic development. The revenues generated by business houses are invested in exploiting more and more economic resources of the country.

DEVELOPMENT READING

Reading instruction given to children in accordance with their individual maturity levels.

DEVELOPMENT STAGE

The stage in new product development when a new product concept is transformed into a prototype. The basic marketing strategy also develops at this time.

DEVIATION

Generally speaking a departure from the norm whether social, psychological or statistical. In statistics it refers to the difference of a given score from the mean.

DEWEY DECIMAL SYSTEM

A way of classifying books in the library which makes use of numbers and decimal fractions.

DEXTERITY

Manipulative ability achieved through good coordination of motor and perceptual skills.

DEXTERITY TESTS

Tests designed to determine an individual's capacity to coordinate the use of different parts of the body.

DEXTRAL

Right-handed and right-eyed.

DIADIC

Paired comparison test involving informants reporting on two products or advertisements one against the other.

DIAGNOSIS

In reading, this means the discovery of reading deficiencies and their causes through the use of standardised and informal tests, instruments, observations, and interviews.

DIAGONAL COMBINATION

(*i*) This type of combination takes place where ancillary services such as repair works, distribution services such as transport or packing are run along with the main activity of production. Dependence on other for such services is done away with to ensure speed and continuity of production.

(*ii*) Communication that cuts across functions and levels in an organisation; important when members cannot communicate through other channels.

DIAL TIME RECORDER

A machine having a dial around the clock normally installed at the gate office of a factory that automatically records the arrival and departure time of a worker on a roll of paper when he presses the radial arm against his number.

DIALECTIC THEORY

In the contest of marketing, the theory that an existing institution (the thesis) is challenged by another institution (the antithesis); the interaction of the two yields a new institution (the synthesis), which has some characteristics of both.

DIARY METHOD

Research technique in which respondents keep a regular written record of events such as reading a publication viewing television or purchasing certain goods.

DIAZO OR OZALID

It is also known as blue-printing. It is used for copying plans, charts etc. The matter is drawn on a semi-transparent sheet of paper placed in a printing frame in direct contact with a sensitised paper and exposed to sunlight or artificial light. The positive copy is then developed and washed like a photograph.

DICTION

(*i*) Choice of words to express ideas.

(*ii*) Manner of speaking or singing, especially in public; enunciation.

DIFFERENTIAL

A difference between wage rates to total remuneration of different individual or group of employees which is part of a planned or negotiated pay structure.

DIFFERENTIAL APTITUDE TEST

Actually a battery involving eight difference tests of aptitudes like verbal reasoning and spatial relations. The test is used to assess educational and vocational performance.

DIFFERENTIAL COST

The different between the total cost incurred on alternative operations or processes.

DIFFERENTIAL PRICING STRATEGY

A strategy whereby different prices are charged to different buyers for the same product. Also called *Variable Pricing Strategy.*

DIFFERENTIATED

A separation of a total product from competitors. Can be a marketing mix unique to one supplier.

DIFFERENTIATED MARKETING

(*i*) A marketing effort in which the marketer selects more than one target market and then develops a separate marketing mix for each. Also called Multiple Market Segmentation.

(*ii*) A marketing strategy which is making different offerings to each segment of a market.

DIFFERENTIATED

A separation of a total product from competitors. Can be a marketing mix unique to one supplier.

DIFFERENTIATION

An important concept in the *Lawrence* and *Lorsch* research that refers to the process by which subunits in an organisation develop particular attributes in response to the requirements imposed by their particular sub-environments. The greater the differences among the subunits' attributes, the greater is the differentiation.

DIFFERENTIATION STRATEGY

Strategy in which the marketer offers a product that is unique in the industry, provides a distinct advantage, or is otherwise set apart from competitors' brands in some way other than price.

DIFFUSION

The rate at which new products move through various adoption categories.

DIFFUSION PROCESS

The spread of a new product through society.

DIGITAL COMPUTER

The type of computer most frequently used in business, including health care management. In contrast, analog computers tend to be used most frequently in scientific mathematical, and aerospace applications.

DILUTEE

Term often pejorative for a worker who has undergone shortened training and often experiences difficulty in gaining trade union acceptance as a semiskilled worker on the grounds that this would dilute the level of skill in the work on the grounds that this would dilute the level of skill in the work place.

DIMENSIONS OF MANAGEMENT

Management touches and influences the core of nearly every human being. Management makes us aware of our potential, shows the way towards better accomplishment, reduces obstacles, and causes us to achieve goals that we probably would not otherwise attain.

DIMINISHING BALANCE METHOD

It is the method in which the depreciation of an asset is calculated by applying a fixed percentage to its original cost or substituted amount less accumulated depreciation.

DIPLOMACY IN MANAGEMENT

Some managers adopt diplomacy in dealing with others and collect information from various sources within the organisation and utilise the same for their own development for getting favour and authority. These managers are so clever that no one suspects any foul play till it is too late in the day. They borrow ideas from others in the enterprise and present them as their own to earn credit.

DIPTHONG

The sounds of two vowels so closely blended together that they give the impression of one sound, such as OI and OW.

DIRECT ADVERTISING

Advertisements that are distributed to their audience as individual items and not as part of a publication containing other material. The most common examples are leaflets, brochures and catalogues distributed by retailers, by post or by door-to-door distribution.

DIRECT COST

(*i*) A cost that is clearly identified with a particular segment of and cooperation and directly allocated to that segment.

(*ii*) The cost which can be conveniently identified and allocated to a particular cost centre or cost unit.

DIRECT EXPENSES

All costs directly attributable to a project or an accounting centre.

DIRECT EXPORTING

A practice by which domestic producers sell products directly to foreign buyers.

DIRECT FINANCE

Finance provided by the Government, mainly for agricultural operations.

DIRECT FOREIGN INVESTMENT

Investment of capital in production and marketing operations located in a host foreign country.

DIRECT LABOUR

Work done on a product or to deliver a service, and which is a specific contribution to its completion. Indirect labour consists of all overhead and support work that do not contribute directly to the completion of a product or delivery of a service.

DIRECT LABOUR COSTS

The costs associated with those members of the work force direcdy involved in the production of goods and services. Compare with indirect labour costs.

DIRECT MAIL

A form of below-the-line advertising where personalised letters are sent directly from the advertiser to potential customers.

DIRECT MARKETING

(*i*) Also known as direct response marketing selling direct to customer using media such as direct mail, catalogues shopping, magazine, off the page press advertisement, telephone phone, view data or telex.

(*ii*) An approach offering products without intermediaries where the supplier sells directly to customers.

DIRECT TAX

A tax levied directly or income or profits—as distinct from indirect taxes such as *Value Added Tax.*

DIRECT WORKER

An employee whose work is directly concerned with the production of his employer's product (Also known as a *Direct*).

DIRECT

To command, direction implies giving orders that will require another person to do something. Direction implies authority, and, hence the power to invoke sanctions in case of disobedience. A manager directs that action be taken. This direction may be by letter, telephone, at first hand, or farther removed. Supervision denotes one kind of direction, that is, personal direction.

DIRECT-ACTION ADVERTISEMENT

An advertisement designed to stimulate immediate purchase or encourage another direct response.

DIRECTED READING ACTIVITY

A reading activity carried on under the direction of a teacher for the purpose of instruction.

DIRECTING

Directing in management involves guiding and leading subordinates, whether they be managers or non-managers. Although this concept is very simple, the methods of directing may be of extraordinary complexity. The superior manager should calculate in his subordinated a keen appreciation of enterprise traditions, history, objectives and policies.

DIRECTION

Seeing that subordinates do their work and do it as well as possible. Includes issuing orders, providing instruction, enforcing discipline, and developing *esprit de corps.*

DIRECTOR TREE

The hierarchical representation of the directories and subdirectories of a disk.

DIRECTOR'S REPORT

The annual report on the affairs of a company's business presented to its shareholders.

DIRECTORS, BOARD OF

A group elected by stockholders to provide general guidance for a corporation and to appoint and dismiss the chief executive.

DIRECTORS, OUTSIDE

Directors who are not executives of the company.

DIRECTORY

Every disk is divided into logical areas for fast accessing purpose. The name given to each of that area is the director where a set of files can be stored.

DIRECT-RESPONSE RETAILER

A non-store retail operation that sells goods by television or telephone and fills orders by mail.

DISAGGREGATED MARKET

A market containing no unidentifiable groups, or aggregates. The result is that products must be made to order for each buyer.

DISBURSEMENT LIST

A printed list containing the identity and quantity of parts and assemblies to be withdrawn from stock and dispatched the starting point of manufacture or assembly on a given day.

DISC

Same as disk. In fact this is the original spelling of disk.

DISCIPLINARY FINE

A fine that a union or professional association may levy against a member for violating provision of its bylaws.

DISCIPLINE

(*i*) According to *Michael Jucius,* "Discipline used a noun and preceded by the adjective 'good' means that the worker willingly abides by company rules and executive orders..." Disciplinary action or "to discipline" means that steps are taken to correct disobedience and if possible its cause.

(*ii*) The use of some form of sanction of punishment when employees deviate from the rules.

DISCONTINUOUS INNOVATION

A product so new that no previous product performed an equivalent function. Such a product requires the development of new consumption or usage patterns.

DISCOUNT

(*i*) A retailer who specialises in selling goods (especially consumer durables) at low prices.

(*ii*) A reduction from list price or a reimbursement for performance of a specific task—for example, a promotional discount offered by a manufacturer to a retailer in return for the retailer's advertising a specific product.

(*iii*) A percentage reduction from listed price allowed to business purchases for buying in bulk, paying in advance of due date, or performing functions or services that stimulate the sellers' sales or reduce their costs of distribution.

DISCOUNT CASH FLOW

A method used for evaluating capital project returns; also known as the present value return on investment.

DISCOUNT RATE

(*i*) The interest rate that a commercial bank pays when it borrows from Reserve Bank. The discount rate is one of the tools of monetary policy used. Or we can say that a discount is the percentage reduction from listed price allowed to business purchases for buying in bulk, paying in advance of due dale, (TTperforming functions or services that stimulate the sellers' sales or reduce their costs of distribution.

(*ii*) The interest rate that a commercial bank pays when it borrows from Reserve Bank. The discount rate is one of the tools of monetary policy used.

DISCOUNTED CASH FLOW (D.C.F.)

Any profitable investment, whether it can be the purchase of shares or an i income-earning asset, investor with a; cash return over a period, the return I being monies earned by the asset after; deduction of the costs of making the asset productive.

DISCOUNTED HOUSE

Large store or branch of chain offering mainly durable consumable at heavily discounted prices but providing little or no handing delivery or credit services to customers.

DISCOUNTING OF BILLS

The bank purchases them at their present worth. The bill is purchased (by the bank at the face value less the | interest at the current rate till the time when the bill falls due. This is known 1 as Discounting the Bills. This is a form of lending to the business community. Discounting of bills facilitates modem business transactions in a big way.

DISCOVERY METHOD

Method of teaching in which work is arranged and topics chosen so that rainee/pupil learns for himself rather han learning directly from the instructor/teacher sometimes known as Heuristic Method.

DISCRETION

Competence of a person to make a specified decision according to his own judgment alone.

DISCRIMINATING PROTECTION

The police of protecting the goods produced by a few select domestic infant industries from the invasion of foreign goods through either banning of such importations or levying prohibitive protective tariffs.

DISCUSSION CONSIDERATION

Describe aspirational reference groups with regard to career positions. What behaviours have students observed that they are now using to guide their own purchases of clothing or other behaviours?

DISECONOMIES OF SCALE

The disadvantages resulting from a large as opposed to a small-scale of operations in an organisation. They include difficulties of co-ordination, communication and adaptability to changing circumstances. Compare with economies of scale.

DISKETTE

The flat magnetic media used for storing data, records and programs in mini and microcomputer system, e.g., winchester disk and floppy disk.

DISMISS

To carry out the dismissal of an employee.

DISPAUPER

A person who is allowed to sue in form a pauper is but losses his right 'i to do so before the suit ends.

DISPERSION MEASURE

A statistic which indicates the degree to 5 which a frequency distribution or a probability distribution spreads out around its mean. The most frequentiy ! used dispersion measure is the I standard deviation.

DISPLAY ADVERTISEMENT

A printed advertisement which forms: part of a newspaper, magazine, book or similar publication which has been especially designed with the :intention of attracting the attention of readers.

DISPOSITIONAL ATTRIBUTIONS

Emphasise some aspect of the j individual such as ability or skill to explain behaviour.

DISPUTE

Traditionally industrial relations idisputes in general have been known as trade disputes with the term industrial dispute becoming more common in modern times disputes involving interjunion rivalry may be demarcation j . disputes jurisdiction disputes or I recognition disputes.

DISSOCIATION

A condition in which mental processes lose their usual modifying influence upon one another.

DISSOCIATIVE GROUP

Type of reference group brought together for the purpose of examining consumer buying motivate.

DISSOLUTION

Act of closing a business entity, which could be a partnership or a company.

DISTRESS MERCHANDISE

Merchandise that has been reduced in price to increase the probability of sale.

DISTRIBUTED PRACTICE

A technique of learning in which the lessons or periods of practice are spread out as widely as the available time permits. This is a much more effective method of learning in most cases than massed practice with which it is usually contrasted.

DISTRIBUTED REPETITION

An act repeated at intermittent intervals, short periods of study distributed over a period of time. This term is opposed to Concentrated Repetition.

DISTRIBUTION CHECK

Survey taken at retail oudets to measure levels of distribution being achieved.

DISTRIBUTION (PLACE)

An element of the marketing mix involving all aspects of getting products to the consumer at the right location at the right time. In economics, it is the study of how wealth is spread through a population.

DISTRIBUTION

(*i*) A marketing term for a retailer who deals in the wares of certain specified manufacturers, having perhaps the sole agency for an area. He buys and sells on his own account and is not therefore an agent for a single manufacturer.

(*ii*) In statistics, this is the term for the arrangement of data in categories and their display in the form of a graph or table; in economics it is the study of how wealth is spread through a population.

(*iii*) In statistics, this means an arrangement of tally marks or numbers, which shows the frequency of occurrence of each successive value or range of values. This can be expressed in a table or graph.

DISTRIBUTION CHANNELS

Routes through which products go from the supplier to consumer.

DISTRIBUTION CHECK

Survey taken at retail outlets to measure levels of distribution being achieved.

DISTRIBUTION NETWORK

The wholesalers, retailers and other firms in an economy that do not manufacture or produce goods but participate in the process of changing the ownership of goods from producer to consumer.

DISTRIBUTOR

(*i*) A marketing term for a retailer who deals in the wares of certain specified manufacturers, having perhaps the sole agency for an area. He buys and sells on his own account and is not therefore an agent for a single manufacture. Firm which buy and sells on its own account but which deals in the goods of certain specified manufacturers common in trades where special representation stocking and service facilities are required *e.g.*, motor transport,

(*ii*) A person or organisation who distributes goods. Distributors take ownership from suppliers and are responsible for collecting payments.

DISTRIBUTOR BRAND (PRIVATE BRAND)

A brand owned by a retailer, wholesaler, or other distributor rather than by manufacturer of the product, also called a *Private Brand.*

DIVERSIFICATION

(*i*) Branching out into new fields.

(*ii*) A process of introducing new products into new markets unrelated to an organisation's current customers.

(*iii*) The strategy of marketing new products to a new market.

DIVERSION IN TRANSIT

Direction of a rail shipment to a destination not specified at the start of the trip.

DIVERSITY

Used to describe human qualities such as race, gender, and ethnicity that are different from our own and outside the groups to which we belong.

DIVESTMENT

Action or process undertaking by a firm of transferring ownership and control of part of its activities to another firm.

DIVIDEND

A payment made to holders of shares or other securities, usually expressed as a percentage of the nominal value of the security held.

DIVIDEND COUPON

An instrument attached to each share warrant.

DIVIDEND

(*i*) A payment made to holders of shares or other securities, usually expressed as a percentage of the nominal value of the security held.

(*ii*) Amount of money received by a shareholder on the face value of shares out of the distributed profits of the company.

DIVISIBILITY

The quality of a product that provides the opportunity for consumers to sample small amounts.

DIVISION

A segment of a corporation whose head is in charge of all functions necessary to make and market a product in a given geographical area.

DIVISION OF LABOUR

(*i*) Most of the organisations are based on the classical theory of division of labour with division of specialisation as rigid hierarchical positions, rigid and close control and supervision and distinct hierarchy of authority.

(*ii*) The process of dividing work into relatively specialised jobs to achieve advantages of specialisation.

(*iii*) Most of the organisations are based on the classical theory of division of labour with division of specialisation as rigid hierarchical positions, rigid and close control and supervision and distinct hierarchy of authority.

DOC FILE

In MS-word package the files are created with extension DOC and also they are known as doc (document) files.

DOCK WARRANT

A document of title to the goods issued to the owner of goods stored at a dock warehouse.

DOCUMENT FILE

A file created with a word processing package with some formatting like font setting, type setting, margins, indents, alignment, headers and footers.

DOGS

Products liked by managements but probably uneconomic and should be dropped.

DOMESTIC ENVIRONMENT

The environment in an organisation's home country.

DOMESTIC EXPORT

Exports of goods or commodities produced within the country of origin.

DOMINANCE

Control of the actions of another. Ocular Dominance; preferential use of one eye so that objects are usually fixated by that eye only, the other eye remaining a little off from exact fixation. Manual Dominance: preferential use of one hand.

DOMINANT COMPETITIVE STRATEGY

A concept defined in the *Lawrence* and *Lorsch* research to refer to the subenvironment that is crucial to the organisation's success. The dominant strategy may be production, marketing, or product development, depending on the industry.

DONOR

Any person who makes a gift, donation to another.

DOS

Disk Operating System or OS for micro-computers.

DOS KEY

A command of DOS. When installed, the OS maintains the history of last few commands entered at the DOS prompt. Any user if wants to execute any of these commands can to that command using the cursor control keys.

DOS PROMPT

A string of characters displayed on the screen which prompts the user to enter some DOS command there. In case it does not appear on screen it means some problem in the execution of the last command has occurred.

DOT PROMPT

A prompt which appears in the Dbase for Foxbase environment as a period "o". This is the prompt against which the database commands are typed and executed.

DOTTING TEST

Sometime used in psychological testing of fatigue and concentration the person being tested has to mark with a dot the centres of circles passed in front of him or her at a regular rate but in irregular positions.

DOUBLE BUFFERING

This is a device or technique of first storing the information to be transferred between the computer and peripheral device and the transferring it.

DOUBLE DECKER

Two outdoor advertising panels sited one above the other.

DOUBLE INSURANCE

Insuring the same risk or subject matter twice or more with different insurers.

DOUBLE PAGE SPREAD

Two facing pages in a magazines or newspaper used in advertising as if they were one single sheet *i.e.* the design carries right across the gutter in the centre.

DOUBLE PLACEMENT

Product testing technique (used by Home Testing Panels subsidiary of Willian Schlackman Ltd.) in which product A is tested against new product B. Combination of panel and interview methods used 200 interview being conducted by field work 200 panel members completing a postal questionnaire.

DOUBLE TAXATION

A situation where a firm or individual becomes liable for tax on the same income in two or more countries or states simultaneously.

DOUBLE-DABBLE

Another method for converting the binary number into decimal equivalents.

DOWN PAYMENT

A partial payment of the total purchased price rendered by a buyer to a seller at the time of purchase with the understanding that the rest will be paid late according to the terms of their agreement.

DOWNER

Short strike or stoppage intended to draw attention to a particular grievance it usually involves workers in doing tools but not leaving the factory premises downer is a form of demonstration strike.

DOWNTURN

A contraction of economics activity leading to the period of depression or slump.

DOWNWARD COMMUNICATION

Communication that flows from individuals in higher levels of the organisation's hierarchy to those in lower levels.

DRAPER

A trader in textiles.

DRIVE

(1) A device (unit) which reads or writes data of any external storage device by placing the read/write hear on the surface of the device, *e.g.* hard disk drive or floppy disk drive. (2) When a person is aroused because he is deprived or stimulated. (3) In psychology this mean a persistent or recurrent urge.

DROP SHIPPER

A limited-service wholesaler, often dealing in bulky products, that takes customer orders and arranges for shipment of merchandise form the producer directly to the customer. Also called a *Desk Jobber.*

DRUM

Large cylindrical metal container mainly used for bulk packing of liquids.

DRY RUN

The execution of the program by the programmer or any person manually to test the validity of program. This is done by manually giving the values for variables and following each step as a computer executes.

DUAL DATE

In purchasing the expected date or receipt for a part in manufacturing the expected completion date of a part.

DUAL PRICES

A system in which goods are simultaneously sold at two different prices within a given area.

DUE DATE

Date to give effect to transactions for payment; a fixed day on which a transaction falls due.

DUMMY

An arrow in an activity-on-arrow network that is inserted only to show that two events must take place simultaneously also known as Zero- Time Activity.

DUMP

This is an action that causes the pattern of binary bits in a computer displayed on the output device or stored on secondary storage device.

DUMPING

(1) Sale of the same product in different markets at different price.
(2) Selling large quantities of a product in a foreign market at prices below their fair market value in the domestic market.

DUOPOLY

(*i*) A market situation in which two sellers control the market it may be either a perfect duopoly or an imperfect one depending on whether or not there is product differentiation.
(*ii*) A situation where there are only two firms producing similar goods.

DUOPSONY

The condition that exists when two buyer control the demand for goods and services offered by many producers.

DUPLICATING MACHINES

Duplication is a substitute for printing. Duplicating machines are used when the number of copies required is more than the capacity of typewriters, and yet not large enough to justify printing. Various duplicating machines are available for use in those offices where some letters have to be reproduced promptly, efficiently and with secrecy.

DUPLICATION ANALYSIS

The degree of inter purchasing between brand sizes or varieties the analysis can be used to evaluate the structure of a market brand loyalty size, loyalty range, loyalty or segmentation.

DURABLE GOOD

A physical, tangible item that functions over an extended period, such as an automobile or a refrigerator.

DUTY

(1) A duty is a number of tasks. Counselling students is a duty of a college instructor. A general accounting clerk's duties might include preparing the monthly income statement and distributing the weekly payroll checks.

(2) A tax levied by a national government on imports.

DYNAMICALLY CONTINUOUS INNOVATION

A product that is different from previously available products but that does not strikingly change buying or usage patterns.

DYSFUNCTIONAL CONFLICT

Any confrontation or interaction between groups that hinders the achievement of organisational goals.

DYSPITUITARISM

A faulty functioning of the pituitary body.

E

E.A.M.

Abbreviation of *Electrical According Machines.*

E AND OE (ERRORS AND OMISSION EXPECTED)

An abbreviation often found on bills or statements which attempts to cover errors and omissions in the document which are the fault of the issuer. The legality of the phrase is doubtful.

EAR SPACE OR TITLE CORNER

Advertisement at the top of the front page of a newspaper on either side of the title or masthead.

EARLIEST FINISH TIME OF AN ACTIVITY

(Or earlier finish date of an activity or earliest finish.) The earliest possible time at which an activity in an activity-on-node network can be completed.

EARLY ADOPTER

A member of the group of consumers who purchase a product soon after it has been introduced, but after the innovators.

EARLY MAJORITY

A group of consumers in the diffusion process; usually solid, middle-class people who purchase more deliberately and cautiously than early adopters.

EARNED PREMIUM

A portion of a premium payment for which the protection specified in an insurance policy has already been given. For example, 75 per cent of an insurance company's premium is earned after a period of nine months of the 12-month contract term of the insurance policy has elapsed.

EARNING DRAFTS

Extent to which wage or earnings rise above national rates through the influence of such factors as local rates overtime workplace bargaining payment by-results schemes, bargaining creep etc. Also known as *Wage Drift:*

EARNING OF UNDERTAKING OR MANAGEMENT

What remains of a businessman's profit after deducting interest on his capital at the current rate (allowing where necessary for insurance) is generally called his *Earning of Undertaking or Management.*

EARNING RELATIONSHIP

Relationship between the levels of earnings of the different work or groups occupation in a factory or plant.

EARNING REPORT

A statement issued by a company showing its earnings or losses over a given period usually one fiscal year.

EARNINGS

Any payment received for work done or services rendered, such as wages, salaries, profit, interest, etc.

EASEMENT

A formal grant or privilege to use a parcel of land adjacent to an owned parcel. The use is typically for a special purpose such as a road, highway entrance, irrigation ditch, or other need that is not in conflict with the manner in which the landowner uses his or her major property.

EASY MONEY

When loanable funds are available in the market at a low rate of interest, it is called *Easy or Cheap Money*.

ECHO

A command of DOS which creates a copy of message as it is on the screen.

E-COMMERCE

A contraction of Electronic commerce.

ECONOMETRICS

(*i*) A technique of making economic predictions by use of mathematics.

(*ii*) The branch of economics that deals with the mathematical or statistical relationships between economic variables.

ECONOMIC ACTIVITY

The production and distribution of goods and services also the contribution of persons to the production and distribution of useful goods and services.

ECONOMIC BATCH QUANTITY (EBQ)

The quantity of a manufactured item made in batches that should be produced in one batch in order to meet a particular regular demand with minimum production and stockholding costs.

ECONOMIC DETERMINISM

The concept that one's place in the economy, or even what one does for a living, determines one's views of society and politics. This concept is usually traced back to *Karl Marx*.

ECONOMIC DYNAMICS

Analysis of economic systems through time and particularly in relation to behaviour of market firms and the national economy in general.

ECONOMIC ENVIRONMENT

The conditions under which man conducts struggle to satisfy his wants.

ECONOMIC GROWTH MODELS

Growth pattern based on certain theories of economic growth. Economists around the world have developed several economic group models: The *Harrod-Doner* growth model, Mrs. *John Robinson's* growth model etc.

ECONOMIC INDICATOR

(*i*) A figure which provides some idea of how an economy is performing for example, the rate of inflation, the exchange rate or the rate of growth.

(*ii*) Treasury figure and charts published monthly and quarterly covering national output and investment income consumption and price external position money and credit unemployment. These form important appraisal aids as also the basis for management decisions and hence serve to reduce entrepreneurial. These include market research series price indices production indices income and expenditure series import and export statistics.

ECONOMIC MAN

(1) An invention of economists to support the belief that the motivation of workers depends solely on rational financial, reward and punishment. The beauty of the invention is that it saves them from thinking about complicated things like group norms or unconscious motivation. (2) In economic theory, an ideal human being who behaves in a totally rational fashion who is perfectly informed and whose economic motivation, when making decisions is towards maximising utility.

ECONOMIC MAN THEORY

The theory that money is the principal factor in human motivation.

ECONOMIC MODEL

An abstract framework representing the relationships between the elements of an economics system seeks to explain the behaviour of persons and institutions in the economy.

ECONOMIC OF WASTE

An economic analysis in which there can be many unemployed resources man and machines which could be usefully employed.

ECONOMIC ORDER QUANTITY (E.O.Q.)

A mathematically determined purchase order size that yields the lowest total cost of order processing and inventory holding. The calculating formula of *Economic Order Quantity* is as follows:

$$\text{E.O.Q.} = \sqrt{\frac{2 \times R \times C_p}{C_h}}$$

Where;

R = Annual requirement.

C_p = Cost of placing an order.

C_h = Ordering cost or carrying cost.

ECONOMIC PLANNING

A totality of arrangement decided upon in order to carry out a project concerned with economic activity.

ECONOMIC PROFITS

Profits arrived at by deducting imputed cost from accounting profits. The former relate to self-owned factors used in business and ignored in accounting profits.

ECONOMIC SYSTEM

The system through which a society allocates its scarce resources.

ECONOMIC UTILITY

(*i*) The ability of an organisation marketing a product to satisfy a consumer's wants or needs. Economic utility includes *Form Utility* (created by conversion of raw materials into finished goods that meet consumer needs), *Place Utility* (created by making goods available where consumers want them), *Time Utility* (created by making goods available when consumers want them) and *Possession Utility* (created by transfer of physical possession and ownership of the product to the consumer).

(*ii*) The ability of an organisation marketing a product to satisfy a consumer's wants or needs. Economic utility includes *form utility, place utility, time utility,* and *possession utility.*

ECONOMICS

A social science that deals with the production, distribution and consumption of wealth; of goods and services, and the human activities involved in these processes. It is, therefore, concerned with issues like business confidence, economic growth, inflation and unemployment.

ECONOMICS AND MONETARY UNION

One of the basic element necessary in setting up a common market.

ECONOMICS OR PRODUCTIVE EMPLOYMENT

Employment which bring about a net addition to total product by the count.

EDEOLOGY

Causative factors of disabilities.

EDITING

(*i*) In market research checking that questionnaires are complete and ready for coding and analysis also checking returns from respondents or panel member for inconsistencies and referring queries to interviewers before report are processed computer edit runs card made to check data against standard criteria.

(*ii*) Checking surveys or other data collection forms for omissions, incomplete or otherwise unusable responses, illegibility, and obvious inconsistencies 80/20 principle. In marketing, a principle describing the situation in which a relatively small percentage of customers accounts for a disproportionately large share of the sales of a particular product.

EDITORIAL ADVERTISEMENT

Advertisement designed in the form of a piece of editorial matter such advertisement must however be clearly labelled 'advertisement'.

EDITORIAL PUBLICITY

Space in journal or newspaper in which a product service or company is discussed or publicized at the discretion of the editor.

EDP

Electronic Data Processing (*EDP*); the term used to designed the processing of the data using computers.

EDRIDGE-GREEN LANTERN TESTS

Form of colour vision test in which the subject is presented with a member of lights of different colours and different degrees of brightness.

EDSAC

Acronym for *Electronic Delay Storage Automatic Calculator.*

EDUCATION TECHNOLOGY

Organised design and implementation of learning system taking advantage of modern visual aid is and communication and teaching methods. A system's approach to the teacher learning process.

EDUCATIONAL AGE (E.A.)

A pupil's average accomplishment in school subjects stated in terms of the average accomplishment of those of similar chronological age.

EDUCATIONAL FACULTIES

Some companies maintain special educational facilities and employ specialists, others rely upon regular personnel and facilities and still others make use of both approaches for different types of training. A few companies operate their own educational plants with faculties in many fields of knowledge.

EDUCATIONAL GUIDANCE

Assisting pupils to select the best programme of studies in the light of their capacities, interests, plans, and general circumstances. Remedial instruction is occasionally included.

EDUCATIONAL MEASUREMENT

Methods of determining school attainments by means of standardised tests or other types of examinations and the use of this method to determine the effectiveness of various educational procedures.

EFFECTIVE SUBSTITUTION

The policy of promoting managers only when they have subordinates able to take their place. To accomplish this end, managers are forced to delegate authority. Moreover this policy removes a major cause of hoarding authority the desire of a manager to gain indispensability by making sure that his duties cannot be handled by any of his subordinates.

EFFECTIVENESS

In the context of organisational behaviour, effectiveness refers to the optimal relationship among five components: *Production, Efficiency, Satisfaction, Adaptiveness,* and *Development.*

EFFICIENCY

A short-run criterion of effectiveness that refers to the organisation's ability to produce outputs with minimum use of inputs. The measures of efficiency are always in ratio terms, such as benefit-cost, cost-output, and costtime.

EFFICIENT MARKET HYPOTHESIS

The theory that in a market with numerous investors who prefer the highest possible yields with the lowest possible risk for their investment a market like the stock market for example no amount of information will influence the outcome for the investor can achieve no more (and no less) than a fair return relative to risk.

EG ADAPTER

Enhanced Graphics Adapter a mode of the monitors.

EGOCENTRIC DRIVE

Concern with ones self; urge to satisfy self.

EGOISTIC NEEDS

Industrial psychologist's term for the personal source of job satisfaction order than remuneration these including self-respect, the respect of sense of achievement, status, prestige, etc.

EJECT

A dbase command and causes the paper to move so that the printer's head is positioned at the top of next page.

ELASTICITY

(*i*) Sensitivity of customer demand to changes in price.

(*ii*) The ratio of proportionate change in one variable to a given change in another variable.

ELASTICITY OF DEMAND

A measure of the sensitivity of demand for a product or service to change in either its price (price elasticity) or in the income of the people demanding the product or service (income elasticity. Price elasticity is the ratio of the percentage change in demand to a percentage change in price.

ELECTRIC TYPEWRITER

Electric typewriter operated electrically by typist. It has the advantage of speed with little exertion of the typist. The slightest touch of fingers sets the keys in motion and the impressions are uniformly perfect even with erratic touch of fingers. It can produce as many as 30 copies with carbon paper as against six produced by the standard typewriters. Moreover, typists can type faster on such machines.

ELECTRODE

The conductor that collects, emits and controls the motion of electric charge.

ELECTRONIC CALCULATOR

Electronic calculator which is operated electronically, *i.e.,* by the use of values or transistors just like radio or television. The machines can perform calculations in a thousandth part of a second. These may be of full-bank or ten-key type. The machine operates silently and much faster than any other kind of machine.

ELECTRONIC CATALOGUE

An interactive videotext system in which consumers see products on their home TV screens but use touch-tone phones to control the order in which the products are shown and to place orders.

ELECTRONIC COMMERCE

Electronic commerce is a technique of selling the products over the web. It not only helps in marketing but also in competing the sale. Customers using the web specify what do they want, where do they want and their mode of payment for the purchase and business delivers accordingly.

ELECTRONIC DATA PROCESSING

Any kind of collection, manipulation or analysis of data that makes use of a computer.

ELECTRONIC MAIL

(1) Process of sending, receiving, storing and forwarding the textual messages as well as graphic patterns in digital form through telecommunication channels, or the transmission and distributor of text and picture material in electronic form over communication network.

(2) The system of transmitting communications electronically between individual computer terminals or within networks of such terminals. It includes the facsimile transmission of hard copy.

(3) Communication based on computer networks which allows users to send and receive store and foreword massages sent between terminals and to obtain hard copy for their records if necessary.

ELECTRONIC OFFICE

A term used to describe an (ideal) office which has taken maximum advantage of computerisation and the latest developments in office automation and information technology. Such an office would exhibit the following features among others; desktop publishing, electronic mail, facsimile transmission, micro-computers, teleconferencing, tele-working and word processors.

ELEMENT (OF WORK)

Originated with work study practice of braking work down into very small elements for method study and work measurement large element are appropriate in training except for example in skills analysis training of operative.

E-MAIL

A contraction of *Electronic Mail*.

EMBARGO

(1) Any prohibition imposed by government on commerce or trade. When it is forbidden to export goods to certain countries, then goods are said to be subject to embargo. The embargo may be imposed by either side; it prevents the unloading and loading of certain goods. It may also take the form of preventing ships entering or leaving certain ports.

(2) A government prohibition of trade, especially in a particular product.

EMBEZZLE

The act of stealing money or property entrusted to him or her by that employee.

EMBEZZLEMENT

(*i*) The fraudulent appropriation of property (personal or real) that has been entrusted to another person's care. For example, the taking of money from a bank by an employee or trustee with concealment of this act by the falsification of accounting records.

(*ii*) The practice of fraudulently using goods or money placed in one's care for one's own personal benefit

EMBLEMS

Gestures much like sign language that quickly convey an understood word or phrase.

EMERGENCY

A situation or condition that has a high probability of having consequences that are disabling or immediately life threatening; situation that requires immediate intervention to assist a person with potentially disabling or life-threatening conditions.

EMERSON SYSTEM

The system which lays down a certain task but the task is usually not so severe being designed for the average worker and the bonus is equivalently smaller and is graduated according to the nearness which the work gets to the task.

EMOLUMENT

The return from personal labour received or accrued in the form of compensation such as a salary wage fee commission award price concession or other personnel benefit.

EMOTION

State involving subjectively experienced feelings of attraction or repulsion.

EMOTIONAL BIAS

Prejudice resulting from feeling.

EMOTIONAL BLOCKING

Inhibition of thinking or of other forms of adjustive response due to excessive emotions, usually of the fear group.

EMOTIONAL CONFLICT

An unpleasant emotion resulting from a discrepancy between two opposing goals or between a goal and actual attainment.

EMOTIONAL MATURITY

Extent to which an individual is able to control impulses and emotions consistent with his stage of development.

EMOTIONAL STABILITY

Consistent and dependable emotional reactions.

EMPLOYEE RELATIONS

Relations between an employer and his employees regarded as individuals rather than as members of unions.

EMPLOYEE RELATIONS INDEX

Assessment of the quality of employee and personnel relations by noting trends in such factors as labour turnover, absenteeism, safety, medical needs, use made of suggestion schemes, grievances.

EMPLOYEE STOCK OWNERSHIP PLAN (ESOP)

Employee share in the ownership of the company under employee stock ownership plans.

EMPLOYEE'S CONTRIBUTORY NEGLIGENCE

If in a case for industrial injury compensation, it can be shown that the employee in question acted in a negligent fashion which contributed to his accident or to the seriousness of his injuries—for example, by failing to wear a safety helmet—the damages may be reduced.

EMPLOYEE-CENTRED LEADER

A person who only generally supervise the work of others, permitting them a sense of autonomy.

EMPLOYEES

Employees are concerned about the major social problems of poverty-crime, drug and liquor abuse, social inequity and environmental pollution because these problems directly affect the quality and security of their lives. Employees are at the same time concerned with the survival of the business entity or necessarily because they love it so well, but because they fear the insecurity of seeking their economic incomes and perhaps their psychic income elsewhere.

EMPLOYEES' PROVIDENT FUND

Retirement benefits in the form of provident fund, family, pension and deposit linked insurance are available to the employees under the *Employees Provident Fund.*

EMPLOYER

(1) Person or organisation that enters into a contract with someone who thereby becomes an employee.

(2) Person or organisation that has employees.

EMPLOYER REFERENCE

Where an employer seeks to use a disputes procedure or a grievance procedure. Such a step by the trade union side is known as a *Union Reference.*

EMPLOYERS' ASSOCIATION

A body whose members are employers and whose principal activities include regulating relations between employers and employees.

EMPLOYERS' FEDERATION

An association of employers within a sector or country. Typical activities include negotiations with trade unions, lobbying government, providing advice and assistance to members and generally representing their interests.

EMPLOYMENT

(*i*) Level of employment in a community ranging from mass

unemployment, when slump conditions are experienced, to full employment, when the dangers of inflation are present particularly in a laissez-faire economy.

(*ii*) Working for someone else in a job, usually paid, and part of an organisation.

EMPLOYMENT AGENCY

A firm which finds people toward for other firms. An employment agency usually receives fees from the firms to which it supplies workers. (Also called a *Personnel Agency.*)

EMPLOYMENT COSTS

Wages or salary paid to an employee plus the related payments for insurance, pensions, etc. that have to be met by the employer. Overheads related to the employee may also be included.

EMPLOYMENT EXCHANGE

An office at which work people seeking employment and employers requiring work people may notify their respective needs. It is a market place for labour, intended to replace the unguided individual reach for work or for employees.

EMPLOYMENT INTERVIEW

It is a dialogue between the employer and the prospective employee for determining the ability of the candidate or suitability of the candidate for the job. *Strauss* and *Sayles* observes, "the objective of the interview is to measure the applicant against the specific requirements of the job and to decide whether these will be a good fit".

EMPLOYMENT MEDICAL ADVISOR

A doctor appointed to carry out medical examinations of particular groups of workers—such as those in dangerous jobs or young people—whose health may be affected by their job.

EMPLOYMENT MULTIPLIER

The ratio of increase in total employment (N) to the increase in primary employment (N2) in the same way in which the investment multiplier is the ratio of increase in income to the increase in (primary) investment.

EMPLOYMENT RATE

Usually expressed as a percentage of total population, and sometimes as a percentage of labour force.

EMPLOYMENT TEST

(1) Set of questions or exercises or other means of measuring a person's suitability for a particular job, or for working in a particular occupation or a particular organisation.

(2) In case of jobs which require technical skill, trade test is generally necessary to find out their capabilities for the type of job for which they are being considered. They are taken as additional methods for the assessment of the suitability of the candidates nature, skill and abilities for the job.

EMPORIUM

A big shop in a market place; a retail business shop generally located in a central market place.

ENCODE

To convert the information in one form into another form which is using different set of symbols not understandable to every person.

ENCODER

The program or device that encodes the data.

ENCODING

(1) The conversion of an idea into an understandable message by a communicator.

(2) In communication theory, the process by which the sender translates the idea to be communicated into a symbolic message, consisting of words, pictures, numbers, gestures, or the like, so that it can be transmitted to the receiver.

ENCUMBRANCE

A claim, charge, or liability on property, such as a lien or mortgage, that lowers the property's value.

ENDOCRINE DYSFUNCTION

Faulty functioning of the endocrine glands.

ENDORSEE

(1) In finance, to execute a legal signature on a document authorising a financial agreement or financial exchange.

(2) To make an endorsement on a negotiable instrument. To give one's endorsement to a product. To write an endorsement to a product. To write an endorsement on a licence.

(3) The person designated in an endorsement as the one to whom the endorser is the transferring the right to receive money.

ENDORSEMENT

(1) A term used with particular reference to bills of exchange. When a bill is negotiated, the person negotiating will write his name on the reverse of the bill. A valid endorsement must be written on the bill itself or on an allied bill. It must be done for the entire bill and by all parties to whom the bill is made out unless one has authority to act for the others.

(2) A note or signature appended on the back of a document or on a slip of paper attached to it.

ENDOWMENT

It is a term used with reference to assurance policies. An endowment assurance is one where the holder of the policy, by paying a certain annual premium, is entitled to a fixed sum at the end of a stated period.

ENGINEERING CHANGE NOTE

(Concession request form: Engineering query note.) A document which lists any changes or queries to the original design and accompanying drawings in a development project. This provides an up-to-date record of how the design has been altered during its development.

ENHANCED MODEL

A model that extends the product line because of its distinctive features, which consumers perceive as better.

ENIAC

Contraction for *Electronic Numerical Integrator and Calculator.*

ENTER KEY

A large size key found on usually all the keyboards that is used to trans the cursor to next line.

ENTERPRISE

(*i*) A business undertaking. Unless otherwise qualified the entirely of an organisation rather than a unit or subdivision.

(*ii*) Organised endeavour.

ENTITY

Any object of concern in some particular application. Like in a banking system clients, their accounts are the entities.

ENTREPOT TRADE

Business consisting of re-exporting of imported goods, with or without any additional processing.

ENTREPRENEUR

(1) A person who is skilled at identifying products or sometimes new methods of production, setting up operations to provide new products, marketing the products and arranging the financing of the operations. Also a person who risks his or her judgment—and often capital—in a search for profit from new business opportunities. Such a person is considered to have a high need for achievement.

(2) Originally meant an owner-manager, often the founder of a business the man who combined land, labour, and capital for productive use. Now sometimes used (*e.g.*, by the Economist *Joseph A. Schumpeter*) for the innovating manager, who may or may not be owner, or for the manager who makes the crucial decisions in a company (*e.g.*, by *Lord Keynes*).

ENTRY

(1) The act of making or entering a formal record by writing it down; for example, to make an entry in an accounting journal.

(2) The process of keying-in the data.

ENVIRONMENT

(*i*) Any or all physical, behavioural, or social characteristics, conditions, elements, or factors that comprise an organism's surroundings and influence its health, growth, development, status, survival, and behaviour.

(*ii*) Refers to surrounding conditions of an activity, particularly in marketing, the social, physical and psychological conditions.

ENVIRONMENTAL CERTAINTY

A concept in the *Lawrence* and *Lorsch* research that refers to three characteristics of a sub-environment that determine the subunits requisite differentiation. The three characteristics are *The Rate of Change, The Certainty of Information,* and *The Time Span of Feedback* or *Results.*

ENVIRONMENTAL DIVERSITY

A concept in the Lawrence and Lorsch research that refers to the differences among the three sub-environments in terms of certainty.

ENVIRONMENTAL FORCES

Forces for change beyond the control of the manager. These external forces include marketplace actions, technological advancements, and social and political changes.

ENVIRONMENTAL SENSOR DEPARTMENT

Department in a company which tests the market or provides intelligence helpful to marketing, *e.g.* market research, economic, customer relations, public relations, legal departments.

ENVIRONMENTALISTS

Activists who seek to protect nature from damage by industry and produce articulate pressure groups which present industries with serious PR Problems. Topics include pollution, food additives, unclear reactors, hairspray aerosols, disposable plastic containers, lead content of petrol and motorcar exhaust fumes, effluent in rivers and so on.

EPROM

Acronym for *Electrically Programable Read Only Memory.*

EPROM ERASER

A device which is used for erasing the programs already stored in ROM by loading the ROM chip in this device for a number of minutes.

EQUAL PAY

Pay is the same for men and women who perform the same or similar work.

EQUILIBRIUM QUANTITY

The quantity of a good that is bought and sold when a market is in equilibrium.

EQUITABLE

Fair, reasonable, and evenhanded.

EQUITABLE PAYMENT

The remuneration which would be generally considered fair (at a particular time and in a particular country) for employees with a particular time-span of discretion.

EQUITY

(*i*) Ownership, equity financing is financing by the sale of stock.

(*ii*) An ordinary share owned by an investor in the capital stock of a company.

EQUITY CAPITAL (EQUITY SHARE CAPITAL)

Capital raised by issuing shares or equity shares in a business.

EQUITY MULTIPLIER

This is used to derive the Return on Equity from the Return on Investment, computed by dividing equity by total assets.

EQUITY ORDINARY

Shares in a Company.

EQUITY SHARE

(*i*) A company share with no restriction either on the amount of dividend or the share of surplus on winding up that may be paid to the holder.

(*ii*)A type of share issued by a company; a unit of the equity capital of the company.

EQUITY THEORY OF MOTIVATION

A theory that examines discrepancies within a person after the person has compared his/her input/output ratio to that of a reference person.

ERG THEORY OF MOTIVATION

A theory developed and tested by *Alderfer* that categorises needs as existence, relatedness, and growth.

ERGONOMICS

(1) The aspect of technology that is concerned with the application of biological and engineering data to problems related to human beings and the machine. Also known as *Biotechnology*.

(2) The study of the interaction between people and the environment in which they work, and in particular their relationship to machines and equipment. It draws most heavily on psychology as well as on anatomy and physiology. The field owes a great deal to the early twentieth century pioneers like *Frank Gilberth* and *F.W. Taylor*.

EROM

Contraction for Erasable Read Only Memory.

ERROR DETECTING CODE

A code in which the taboo pulse combination produced due to gain or loss of a bit will indicate the wrong bit.

ERROR FILE

A file that is created during the execution of a program, which contains the errors as detected by the program. Usually the extension of this file is ERR.

ERRORS OF COMMISSIONS

These errors include wrong posting of wrong amounts, on the wrong side, in the accounts.

ERRORS OF OMISSION

These errors are very difficult to discover, because they do not affect the agreement of the trial balance. They arise when a transaction is wholly or partly omitted from being recorded in the books.

ERRORS OF OMISSIONS EXPECTED (E.&O.E.)

These initials are often included at the end of an invoice, retaining the person issuing the invoice from clerical errors.

ESCALATION

In purchase contracts, a provision for unforeseen changes in basic costs-labour or materials or both-that may make it necessary to increase the final price.

ESCALATOR CARDS

Advertisements placed alongside underground escalators.

ESCALATOR CLAUSE

A clause in a collective agreement which states that wages should increase at the same rate as a specified cost-of-living index.

ESCAPE KEY

A control key on keyboard on the upper-left most corner. This is used in most of the software applications to abnormally terminate the execution or to take the control of computer away from a program.

ESCHEAT

An old legal term giving right to the grant of land or interest in land granted to anyone by retaining the land if the tenant dies leaving no heir.

ESCROW

(1) An arrangement in which a bond, deed or other document is adopted by two parties and given to a third for safekeeping to be surrendered only when some condition emerges. Or we can say that money, property, or documents that belong to organisations that are held by organisation B until organisation. A takes care of an obligation to organisation C. For example a mortgage company may require a nursing home with a mortgage on a building to make monthly payments into an escrow account to take care of a future payment when it comes due.

(2) Property placed by one person in the hands of a second person, usually a trust company, for the delivery to a third persons upon the fulfilment by the latter of certain specific obligations.

ESCROW AGREEMENT

An agreement that may be made during arbitration of wages in an industrial action between a trade union and management under which an employer delivers to the arbitrator a specified sum of money to be used to pay a wage increase if the arbitrator rules the increase to be warranted.

ESTABLISHMENT

A place where people work together to accomplish predetermined goals.

ESTATE AGENT

A person whose job is to sell landed property such as houses and land; a broker dealing in sale, letting, valuation of estates and lease-hold property.

ESTIMATED WORK

Work for which standard times have been set without using work measurement (*e.g.* they have been based on practical experience or previous production records).

ESTIMATING

Strictly, producing an estimate of the cost/price of an activity particularly in one-off jobs and in contracting.

ETHICAL DILEMMA

A predicament in which a marketer must resolve whether an action, although it benefits the organisation, the individual decision-maker, or both, maybe considered unethical.

ETHICS

A system of behaviours, expectations and morals comprising standards of conduct for a population or profession.

ETHNOCENTRISM

Belief in the superiority of ones own culture.

EUROPEAN COMMUNITY (EC)

A 12-member community of European nations within which all barriers to trade between members have been eliminated; formerly called the *Common Market.*

EUROPEAN ECONOMIC COMMUNITY (EEC)

A common market for all products except those covered by the European Coal and Steel Community (ECSC). EEC was established by a treaty signed by seven countries in Rome on 25th March 1957. The membership has since risen to twelve.

EUROPEAN FREE TRADE ASSOCIATION (E.F.T.A.)

This was formed in 1959 by the Stockholm Treaty as an alternative to the Common Market but with more limited aims. The emphasis was on eliminating tariff between members but not, as with the Common Market, presenting a common tariff to the outside world. It has other aims, such as improvements in both productivity and standards of living; these are sought through the friendly exchange of ideas rather than by the enactment of laws.

EUSTRESS

A term made popular by *Dr. Hans Selye* to describe good or stimulating stress.

EVALUATED DATA

Evaluated data is highly useful for a specific problem and for a certain individual at a certain time to achieve a definite goal. As problems vary from person-to-person or change as time passes, the value of information differs. That is, the value of information is not detached and permanent in itself.

EVALUATED MAINTENANCE PROGRAMME

A form of planned maintenance which uses a historical analysis of previous performance and costs to develop future maintenance plans.

EVALUATION RESEARCH

The systematic study of the effects and effectiveness of a research of training or intervention programme.

EVENING SHIFT

A shift that is worked mainly in the evening—*e.g.*, from 1600 to 2400.

EVIDENCE

Verifiable information, physical objects, documents, and opinions about an alleged claim, often submitted as part of a claimant's application. Evidence is employed in proving a claim ranging from a claim for health insurance payment to a Court trial.

EX

A financial accounting software developed by Tata Consultancy Services (TCS). A machine register in microprocessors of Intel family such as 8088,8086,80286.

EX OFFICE

By virtue of holding a particular office.

EX-ANTE INVESTMENT

Business plans for expansion.

EXCEPTED PROVIDENT FUND (EPF)

Also called retirement benefit scheme or cloth cap pension scheme. A type of pension scheme in which the whole of the benefit may be taken as a lump sum at normal retirement age instead of a pension proper.

EXCEPTION PRINCIPLE, MANAGEMENT BY

A method of control under which only exceptional results, good or bad, are flagged for management attention.

EXCEPTION REPORT

A report on a deviating from a plan that is presented to someone practising management by exception.

EXCESS CAPACITY

Unused or idle capacity. When the productive factors are not fully utilised, the phenomenon of excess capacity arises. In simple language, the term excess capacity indicates that the output can still be increased with the given factors.

EXCHANGE

Transfer of property, money, services, currencies of other countries for a consideration.

EXCHANGE MANAGEMENT

The term in contra distinction with free exchange market, denotes all kinds of interference by the monetary authorities of a country in the foreign exchange transactions designed primarily to prevent the free fluctuations in the rate of exchange. Exchange management is one of the devices for correcting disequilibrium in the international balance of payments.

EXCHANGE PROCESS

The interchange of something of value between two or more parties.

EXCHANGE RATE

(1) The rate at which currencies of different countries are exchanged for each other.

(2) The value of one currency in relation to that of another.

EXCHEQUER TALLY

A notched piece of wood, 8 or 9 inches in length, which, at one time, was given in U.K. as a form of receipt to a person who deposited money with the Government. A similar notched stick was retained in the Exchequer Department, and when the depositor wanted his money he produced his portion of stick, and if the two sticks 'tallied', that is, the notches on the one agreed with the notches on the other, he was paid his money. It is said that a notch of 1½ inches represented 1,000, 1 inch 100, 3/8 inch 10 and 3/16 inch size half a notch of that size 1.3/16 inch is the smallest notch.

EXCISE DUTIES (EXCISE TAX)

A tax levied on goods sold within a country as distinct from customs duty which covers goods imported into a country.

EXCISE DUTY

A tax charged on goods produced or manufactured on licenses; on betting and gaming.

EXCLUSION CLAUSE

In a guarantee clause which protects giver from complaints over which he has no control, such as exaggerated claims by salesmen.

EXCLUSIVE DEALING

A situation in which distributor carries the products of one manufacturer and not those of competing manufacturers.

EXCLUSIVE DISTRIBUTION

A distribution strategy in which only one outlet in a given area is allowed to sell a product.

EXCLUSIVE TERRITORY

An area, defined by geographical boundaries or population, assigned to a retailer, wholesaler, or other dealer with the understanding that no other distributors will be assigned to operate in that area.

EXE FILE

A executable file under DOS environment.

EXECUTE

To run a program on a computer so that some output may be obtained.

EXECUTED TRUST

A type of trust to be executed without any other supporting document or instrument.

EXECUTION

(*i*) Seizure by a public official of a person's goods for the purpose of enforcing a judgment order of a Court.

(*ii*) Format in the context of advertising, the style in which the advertising message is delivered.

(*iii*) The carrying out of plans.

EXECUTION TIME

(*i*) The amount of time required to perform the execution cycle.

(*ii*) The portion of an instruction cyde during which the actual work is performed, or the operation is executed; for example, the time required to decode and perform an instruction.

EXECUTIVE

(*i*) In organisational behaviour, descriptive of a manager how uses a high task orientation and a high relationships orientation in a situation where such behaviour is appropriate and who is therefore more effective. Such a manager sets high standards, treats everyone somewhat differently, prefers team management, and is therefore often perceived as a good motivating force.

(*ii*) A manager in the higher levels of the organisation. The specific level is a matter for arbitrary determination. The term "manager" is to be preferred.

EXECUTIVE DIRECTOR

A director of a company who is also a full-time employee of the company (Also known as on *Inside Director*).

EXECUTIVE GIFT

Advertising gifts as presented at Christmas to clients. Typical gifts are desk diaries, quality pen sets, calculators, wines and spirits.

EXECUTIVE OFFICE

Term used where a number of executives are shown in the top box on an organisational chart. This may indicate a form of group management at the top in some cases; in others, the executive office consists of the chief executive and his principal subordinates and advisers.

EXECUTIVE ORDER

A rule of regulation issued by a chief administrative authority.

EX-GRATIA PAYMENT

Payment made as a gift or favour and not in fulfilment of a contract or legal obligation.

EXHIBITION

Putting on display a company's products or services for promotional purposes.

EXIM BANK

The abbreviated form stands for *Export and Import Bank of India.* It is the largest public sector statutory financial institution.

EXIT INTERVIEW

(*i*) An employee who is leaving a company generally fell free to express his view regarding his work. A senior officer may arrange to meet him for brief discussion regarding the various aspects of his work in the organisation knowing that the employee is likely to bring up a large number of complaints. Repeated exit interviews have revealed important weaknesses in the organisation thus providing the basic data for further investigation.

(*ii*) Interview of an employee who has given notice to end his employment in order to gain information about his reasons for leaving.

EXPANDED MEMORY

Additional installed memory in AT (Advance Technology) family of micro-computers which is not directly addressable by memory. It uses a fixed block of address space in the first megabyte of main memory.

EXPATRIATE MANAGER

A manager from the firm's home nation who's on a foreign assignment.

EXPECTANCY

The perceived likelihood that a particular act will be followed by a particular outcome.

EXPECTANCY THEORY OF MOTIVATION

A theory in which the employee is faced with a set of first-level outcomes and selects an outcome based on how this choice is related to second-level outcomes. The preferences of the individual are based on the strength (valence) of desire to achieve a second-level state and the perception of the relationship between first-and second-level outcomes.

EXPECTED SERVICE-PERCEIVED SERVICE GAP

The situation where consumers' expectations do not match the perceived level of service received. A gap can be negative or positive.

EXPEDITING

In business and industry, the job of seeing that materials are at the right place when needed.

EXPENDITURE

A relinquishment by a firm of money or some other asset or an incurrence of liability in exchange for a benefit received or to be received.

EXPENSE, ADMINISTRATIVE

Outlay for management, clerical, and staff expenses.

EXPENSES

Expenditures that must be covered by current revenues if the company is to make a profit, in contrast to capital investments, only a portion of which (annual depreciation) is chargeable against current revenues in a single year.

EXPERIMENT

(*i*) An investigation containing two elements: manipulation of some variable (independent variable) and observation of the results (dependent variable).

(*ii*) A research method in which the research we changes one or two variables and observes the effects of those changes on another variable.

(*iii*) A research approach which evaluates alternatives to identify the optimum mix.

EXPERT

A person trained in a particular field, such as a lawyer, solicitor, doctor, engineer, scientist, accountant, auditor, valuer, actuary, etc.; one who has acquired skills or knowledge in a subject.

EXPERT POWER

(*i*) Capacity to influence related to some expertise, special skill, or knowledge. Expert power is a function of the judgment of the less powerful person that the other person has more ability or knowledge.

(*ii*) Power issuing from expertise and knowledge.

EXPERT SYSTEM

A computer system developed to act as an expert of the particular domain showed knowledge-base is attached with.

EXPERT WITNESS

A technically skilled and experienced person in a particular field who may be called to give evidence in Courts of Law, public enquiries, in quests and other examination processes.

EXPIRATION DATE

The time established in a contract or by a collective bargaining agreement for the contract or agreement to terminate; for example, the date that an insurance policy terminates.

EXPLOITATION OF LABOUR

The payment to labour of less than its proper wage. It arises from the unequal bargaining strength of employers and employed.

EXPLORATORY RESEARCH

(1) A pilot marketing research used to review a problem in general forms before committing larger expenditure to the study.

(2) Research to clarify the nature of the marketing problem.

EXPORT

To transmit the data out from one application to a file in the format of other applications like text files or graph files or any other format.

EXPORT AGENT

Person or company acting on behalf of an exporter in another country. Two types of agents are the *Commission Agent* and the *Del Credere Agent.*

EXPORT DECLARATION

Details, to be submitted within six days, of the export of all goods from the country.

EXPORT DEPARTMENT

An organisational unit developed to deal directly or indirectly with foreign customers.

EXPORT DUTIES

Taxes levied by the Government on goods being exported from a country, considered as indirect expenses and evidently, as a charge to the profit & loss account.

EXPORT HOUSE

(*i*) An organisation specialising in selling other people's goods abroad. It sets itself as a market expert owing to language and local conditions abroad. It deals with packing, shipping, insurance, import regulations, tariffs, quotas, licenses, exchange, and payment terms. Export House sells goods of producers on commission or on behalf of foreign importers. They also help to finance exporters, *e.g.* by buying direct and guaranteeing payment. When acting for the overseas buyer they supervise the quality of goods packed and receive a commission from the buyer.

(*ii*) To transmit the data out from one application to a file in the format of other applications like text files or graph files or any other format.

EXPORT INCENTIVES

These are inducement subsidies given by the state to promote exports. They may be in the form of grants or cash subsidies to exporting industries, additional credit facilities, tax exemptions, duty drawbacks, import licences, etc.

EXPORT MANAGEMENT COMPANY

An intermediary that specialises in buying from sellers in one country and marketing the products in other countries.

EXPORTING

Selling domestically produced products in foreign markets.

EXPOSITION

Sometimes used as synonym of 'exhibition', but usually to imply a larger or more serious event, often accompanied by a conference or seminar.

EXTENDED MEMORY

Memory beyond 1 Mb and which is directly accessible by 24 and 32 bit microprocessors.

EXTENDED PARTITION

Dividing a single physical device into many logical partitions. Like dividing a single hard disk into many drives say C, D and E.

EXTENDED USE TESTS

Similar to placement tests but used, especially in industrial marketing, where it is necessary for findings to be derived from use of the product in a work situation over a long-term period.

EXTENSIVE PROBLEM-SOLVING

In-depth search for and evaluation of alternative solution to a problem.

EXTERNAL HOUSE JOURNALS

House journals producted for a specific external readership such as distributors, users of consumers.

EXTERNAL LABOUR MARKET

The labour market outside, but affecting, the individual employing organisation.

EXTERNAL REPORTING

The preparation of financial statements for use by external interest groups like shareholders and the government.

EXTERNAL SOURCE

All sources of data external to a firm.

EXTERNAL STORAGE

Storage accessible to the processor only via input-output channels. It is considered as a peripheral device, example hard disk drive.

EXTINCTION

In a learning situation, the decline in the response rate because of non-reinforcement.

EXTRACTIVE INDUSTRIES

Industries which obtain products by exploiting natural resources—mining, oil and gas etc.

EXTRA-CURRICULAR ACTIVITIES

Activities which form part of the life of students but are not part of the courses of study.

EXTRAMURAL SERVICES

Extramural services are those which are provided outside the factory (such as education, housing, transport, recreation, etc.).

EXTRAORDINARY GENERAL MEETING

A general meeting that is not an annual general meeting. The word 'extraordinary' is used because an annual general meeting used to be called an *Ordinary General Meeting.*

EXTRAORDINARY RESOLUTION

A resolution of the members of a registered company approved by three-quarters or more of the votes cast on it at a meeting of the members of which notice was given specifying that the resolution was to be proposed as an extraordinary resolution.

EXTRAPOLATION

Forecasting by projecting trends to date into the future.

EXTRINSIC REWARD

Rewards external to the job, such as pay, promotion, or fringe benefits.

EXTRINSIC REWARDS (EXTENSIVE FACTORS)

Various kinds of external rewards offered to an employee-salary, bonuses, fringe benefits, travel etc.—as distinct from the internal rewards of Motivation.

EYE MOVEMENT

Change in position of the eyeball.

EYE PAUSE

Brief moment during which the eyeball is at rest. Only during such a moment is it possible to make visual discrimination.

F

F.O.B,

'Freight on board' or 'Free on board'; together with further information, law term that identifies the point at which title passes from seller to buyer. For example, 'F.O.B. factory' means that the buyer takes title at the factory and is responsible for all shipping charges.

FACE AMOUNT

The amount stated on the front of an insurance policy which is payable upon the death of the insured or in accordance with a specified schedule (a unity) after certain conditions have been met (such as payment overtime of a specified amount of money in premiums, or the occurrence of partial or total disability).

FACE-TO-FACE SELLING

Personal selling usually on a one-one basis, *i.e.*, a personal meeting between buyer and seller in which each can state a case and/or hear the other's point of view. Vulgarly referred to as 'belly-to- belly selling.

FACE VALUE

Nominal value; Par value: The amount, excluding interest, due on maturity to a holder of a bond or security.

FACIA

In exhibitions, the headboard above a stand. Sometimes used for advertising purposes, *e.g.*, featuring a brand-name, but usually carries the identity of the exhibitor.

FACIA BOARD

Board or panel bearing shopkeeper's name which may be supplied by a firm whose name or product is incorporated in the design as a permanent and prominent advertisement.

FACSIMILE

An exact copy; for example, facsimile signatures are mechanically imprinted signatures on cheques, stock certificates, and bonds.

FACTOR

(*i*) A data element or variable that could be operated mathematically.

(*ii*) A financial intermediary or agent; one who transacts business for others on a commission. Factoring is a method by which book debts can be quickly realised by way of outright sale or accounts receivable to a factor.

FACTOR ANALYSIS CHART TECHNIQUE (FACT)

Job evaluation approach to determining the relative worth of management positions within a salary structure. Involves assigning points to the major elements of jobs.

FACTORING COMPANY

Firm that does not manufacture goods itself but acts either as a wholesaler or as an agent for a manufacturer.

FACTORS OF PRODUCTION

The resources required to produce a commodity. They are usually divided into three categories—*land, labour,* and *capital*—which however, are admittedly arbitrary, since often a given resource may belong to more than one category.

FACTORY

(*i*) A unit of production declared or registered under the Factories Act, 1948; a building where goods are manufactured.

(*ii*) Defined under Factories Act as any premises in which or in precincts of which persons are employed in manual labour in manufacturing or related processes by way of made or for purposes of gain.

FACTORY AGREEMENT

Product of collective bargaining on behalf of employees from the whole of a factory, as distinct from work place bargaining on behalf of a smaller group on large scale bargaining such as for company agreements, house agreements, or industry-wise agreements.

FAD

A passing fashion or craze that many people are interested in for only a short time.

FAIR

A public exposition or market, usually held at regular intervals, for the purpose of exhibiting, exchanging, and/or selling goods. The practice of holding fairs dates from ancient times and became an important feature of economic life in medieval Europe. Today fairs are used less for actual trading than for exhibiting merchandise, both to producers within a field or industry and to the public.

FAIR TRADE

Trade conducted in a manner that is fair and equitable to the trading partners as per the provisions of the state fair trade laws and federal acts.

FAMILY

According to the *U.S. Census Bureau,* a group of two or more persons related by birth, marriage, or adoption and residing together.

FAMILY BUDGET

The term adverts to a detailed statement of the income and expenditure of a family for a period of time, say, a month.

FAMILY COMPANY

Where one person holds practically the whole of the share capital of a company and takes a few more dummy members simply to meet the statutory requirements of the minimum number of persons (6 more persons in case of a public company and one other person in case of a private company). A family company is perfectly in order in the eyes of law and is regarded to have a separate entity, as distinct from the majority shareholders.

FAMILY LIFE-STYLE

Manner for style of living adopted by a family according to its background, income, or aspirations is becoming subject to closer scrutiny in the development of psychographics.

FAMINE

Famine is a situation in which there is acute shortage of food and water. It may be caused by natural calamities like floods, cyclones etc.

FANTASY

A daydream: In the contest of advertising, a type of association format in which the intention is to link the product with the target buyer's wildest dreams and hopes.

FASHION OBSOLESCENCE

The pattern of products becoming out to date because of changes in the preferences for particular styles.

FAST-MOVING CONSUMER GOODS (FMCG)

Regularly purchased products, usually of low value.

FATAL ERROR

The errors that prevents the execution of a program and cause processing to cease immediately.

FEASIBILITY STUDY

A study made to determine the way in which procedures would have to be modified if a computer were to be employed and whether or not the use of a computer would be worthwhile.

FEDERAL TRADE COMMISSION (FTC)

Federal agency established in 1914 by the Federal Trade Commission Act to investigate and put an end to run fair methods of competition.

FEEDBACK

(*i*) Part of the output of a system that is used to evaluate the performance of the system.

(*ii*) The ability of a machine to sense and correct its own mistakes, may also be used in connection with systems of communication among members of an organisation if the results of communications from the top may be easily ascertained by those who issued them.

FEUDALISM

It is a form of economic organisation in which the owners of productive assets like land and capital also own and make use of labour as their serfs.

FICTITIOUS ASSET

Items grouped in the balance sheet which has no real value. For example: the debit balance of the profit and loss statement, underwriting commission, discount on issue of share or debenture etc.

FIDELITY

A contract of guarantee insurance under which the insurer

indemnifies the assured against losses caused by dishonesty of one or more of the assured's employees.

FIDUCIARY

Involving or depending on confidence or trust.

FIELD

An individual element of information of some data type.

FIELD EXPERIMENT

An experiment in which the investigator attempts to manipulate and control variables in the natural setting rather than in a laboratory.

FIELD RESEARCH

Research conducted outside the laboratory or an establishment, which involves the collection of primary, rather than secondary (existing published material and records), data; necessitating the study of natural, rather than laboratory conditions.

FIELD SALES MANAGER

(*i*) Executive responsible for organisation, derivation, control motivation and training of the field selling force in whole or in part.

(*ii*) A district or regional sales manager so-called because his or her main concern is the salespeople in the field. Field selling non-retail selling that takes place outside the employer's place of business, usually in the prospective customer's place of business.

FIELD WORK

(*i*) The activity of gathering information in the marketplace.

(*ii*) That part of a market research survey which involves face-to-face interview with respondents by research investigators, compared with other means of obtaining data, such as postal or telephone empires and the searching of relevant published material.

FILLER

Pre-prepared advertisement by publisher used to fill the gap left in a page after make-up.

FILTER QUESTION

Strip Question: Market research term for a question which an interviewer only puts to an informant if it is made relevant by the answer given to the previous question.

FINAL AVERAGE PAY

An individual's earnings during the final period of employment or participation in a compensation plan, typically the last three, five, or ten years' average pay. It is used particularly in the calculation of pension benefits.

FINAL GOODS

The finished articles which are the end products of production.

FINANCE

(*i*) The management of public revenues; the conduct or transaction of money matters generally and particularly those affecting the public as in the field of banking and investment.

(*ii*) Finance is the life blood of every business. Modern money (iii) economy is totally based on finance. No business can commence its activities, survive or grow without adequate supply of funds. Finance is needed for the production of goods and services as well as their distribution. A business enterprises needs finance to commence its operations, to continue operations and for expansion and modernisation of business. Finance controls the policies, activities and the decisions of every business. Success of a business largely depends upon favourable procurement and economic utilisation of finances. Sound financial management is as important in business as the production and marketing of goods.

FINANCE MINISTRY

Ministry of Finance is charged with the responsibilities of raising the resources for the overall expenditure of the Government of India. Thus, it is an agency which exists more for other Ministries and Departments than for itself. It has to see to the desirability of the demands of other departments, taking into consideration interest of the taxpayers.

FINANCIAL ACCOUNTING

Activity process of systematically recording and analysing information in monetary terms, relating to the transactions of a firm, primarily in order to provide information to people other than the management of the firm, *e.g.*, the owners (stockholders, or shareholders) of the firm, creditors, government agencies, or members of the public who might be persuaded to buy the firm's securities. Also the body of knowledge concerning such work.

FINANCIAL BILL

A bill of exchanges; also called *Accommodation Bill*. It is drawn and accepted without consideration for raising short-term funds required by the parties to an instrument.

FINANCIAL CONDITION

The financial condition refers to the assets and liabilities of an accounting entity as per the balance sheet. It is said to be good if the total value of the assets is more than the total value of the liabilities.

FINANCIAL LEVERAGE

The ratio of a person's or organisation's total debts to total assets. Other measures of financial leverage (such as those comparing cash inflows to committed cash outflows) are used for particular purposes or because of individual preference.

FINANCIAL PLANNING

It refers to the plan that indicates the requirements of finance, the source from which it is raised and the application of funds. In this way, financial plan provides a vivid picture of inflow and outflow of money sources of funds and uses of funds. The main objectives of financial planning is to secure adequate funds at minimum costs for the planned project. A good financial plan should take care that the cost of fixing capital should be reasonable.

FINANCIAL REPORT

Fortnightly confidential newsletter containing comment and analysis on worldwide financial matters.

FINANCIAL RESOURCES

The organisation's capital and cash flow.

FINANCIAL STATEMENT

A statement which gives information about the financial performance of a firm or organisation. These can take many forms but the most common are *Balance sheet* or *Profit and Loss Account.*

FINANCIAL SYSTEM

It consists of those institutions which are mainly concerned with the creation, destruction and exchange of claims.

FINANCIAL YEAR

The twelve month chosen by an organisation as its accounting period.

FINANCIER

A person who undertakes financing, like a small trader with his earnings. He usually charges a high rate of interest.

FINDER

A person, acting as an individual or as an enterprise, who brings together a buyer and a seller and earns a fee for the service.

FINE CONTROL SENSITIVITY

Type of psychomotor skill: An individual's ability to make delicately controlled muscular adjustments, particularly where larger muscle groups are involved.

FINISHED GOODS

Final goods which are for the enjoyment of the ultimate consumer and instrumental goods which are for use. In process: Finished Goods = Final Goods + Investmental Goods = Fixed Capital + Hoards.

FINK

A derogatory word, used as either a noun or a verb, to describe a member of a labour who exhorts his employer on the activities of the union and of his fellow employees. It was the practice to expel from the union any person behaving in such a way as to be identified as a *Fink.*

FIRM

The name given to a partnership business though more often used for proprietary firms. Any organisation or individual person engaged in any form of activity of which an important aim is the production of goods or services for sale to others. Used as an all inclusive term for units of economic activity. An organisation formed to carry out the business of a partnership.

FIRM'S PROFILE

Used in establishing the payment system appropriate to the firm.

FIRST COME, FIRST SERVED

Decision-making rule for scheduling: This rule places orders in line as they arrive at a processing point. The next order to be processed is the one that is first in line.

FIRST-IN FIRST-OUT

It is the method of valuing stock or taking Inventory in which the prices of the oldest items purchased are applied to the entire stock. Items received first are then first to be sold; a method of choosing people for redundant.

FISCAL AGENT

Fiscal Intermediary or Third-Party Administrator, a person or organisation that serves as another's financial agent; and agent who processes claims, provides services, and issues payment on behalf of certain private, federal and state health benefit programmes, or other insurance organisations; a contracted insurance company, management firm, or other private contractor that processes and pays provider claims on behalf of a government group. Fiscal agents are rarely at risk themselves, but rather serve as administrative units for handling the payment of bills. The same fiscal agent or contractor maybe the fiscal agent for more than one programme, under separate contracts. Use of a fiscal agent is a major practice among large employer groups who self-insure the cost of health benefits.

FISCAL MANAGEMENT

Administration of the financial affairs of a care organisation or professional practice, including planning, conducting financial operations, exercising controls, and reporting. Activities within fiscal management include resources planning and development, budgeting, accounting, purchasing, billing investing, and collecting.

FISCAL MEASURES

Government action to counteract deflation or inflation by tax changes. A budgetary surplus, where the government collects more than it spends, should have a deflationary effect—and *vice versa.*

FISCAL YEAR

A financial year: A fiscal year consists of twelve consecutive months which may start and end at any time during the calendar year.

FIVE PUBLIC

Most affected by the activities of business enterprise are the employees, the owners, the customers, the residents of the business enterprise, local environments and the general public. All five of these public are concerned in different but related ways with both the inadequacy of current governmental social problem-solving and the survival of the business enterprise as a socio-economic entity.

FIXATION PAUSE

The length of time required for the eyes to fixate on a given part of a line in reading.

FIXATION

Holding the eyeballs in position for vision to function in reading a part of a line in print as the eyes travel across the page.

FIXED ASSET

(*i*) Any tangible long-term asset, usually having a life of more than one year. It includes items such as land, building, plant, machinery, motor vehicles, furniture and fixtures.

(*ii*) Those business assets which are purchased for continued use in manufacture (*e.g.*, land, machinery, etc.). They are written off against profits over their anticipated life by charging an annual amount calculated to eliminate the original cost over that period.

FIXED BUDGET

Budget which is based on a forecast of ideal or normal capacity. It does not take account of possible variations in the level of activity as would a flexible budget.

FIXED CAPITAL

Needs relate to the investments that the business is required to make in purchasing real estate or permanent and fixed assets, *i.e.*, land, buildings, stores, plants and machinery, interest during the period of construction of these assets. Fixed assets do not mean that they are immobile or their values will always remain fixed. They only indicate that they will not be resold for profit and will be used by the business for generating profit. They also include intangible asset as goodwill, patent rights, etc. Fixed capital is used in producing commodities continuously over a long period of time.

FIXED COST

The cost which remains constant or fixed irrespective of any increase or decrease in the volume of output.

FIXED-SHIFT SYSTEM

A shiftwork system where each team of workers always works the same shift.

FIXED WORKING CAPITAL

The amount that remains more or less permanently invested as working capital in business.

FIXTURE

(*i*) An article that has been installed in or attached to a building or land in a more or less permanent way, so that legally it is considered part of the real estate. Fixtures and Fittings items attached to the structure of a building but not forming part of it.

(*ii*) Anything fixed to a building or land that cannot be removed easily.

FLAG

A variable whose value indicates a particular state.

FLANKER BRAND

An item that extends the product line in order to deny shelf space to competitors.

FLAT RATE

An overall price for an entire job or group or jobs. For example, a painter may offer rate covering both item and materials, rather than working for an hourly fee plus the cost of the paint.

FLEA MARKET

A market, held either outdoors or indoors, where numerous merchants at separate stalls sell old or used household goods, antiques, and curios. Prices are usually subject to bargaining.

FLEXIBLE MANUFACTURING TECHNOLOGY (FMT)

Modern manufacturing methods that combine computer and robot to achieve high levels of production as well as high levels of flexibility.

FLEXIBLE SPENDING ACCOUNT (FSA)

An employee benefit in the form of an account with a maximum amount set aside by the employer for medical, legal and other services that the employee and (sometimes) his or her dependents may need.

FLEXIBLE TIME

Term use in an application of flexible working hours (who) for the periods during the day when each employee can choose his or her own working hours. The rest of the day is core time when all employees are expected to be present.

FLEXIBLE WORKING HOURS (FWH)

An arrangement under which each employee in an organisation may choose the times at which he starts and finishes work each day to suit himself. In most arrangements of this kind, an employee must be at work during one or more periods of 'core time' and must work for a minimum number of hours in each week or month.

FLEXI-TIME

A flexible work schedule in which workers can, within a prescribed band of time in the morning and afternoon, start and finish their workday at their own discretion as long as they complete the total number of hours required for a given work period, usually a month.

FLIP-FLOP

The electronic circuit element which can exhibit either of two stable states and can with between these states.

FLOAT

(*i*) A data-type in C programming language to represent the real numbers.

(*ii*) In critical path scheduling, extra time available for a job because work cannot proceed further until another job that will take longer is completed.

(*iii*) To launch a new company; a small amount of cash used for expenses or in making change; to allow a currency to find its own exchange rate in the market, as opposed to maintaining a particular rate by central bank intervention;

used in network analysis to denote the amount of time that can be added to a given activity without extending the total time of the whole project.

FLOATING COSTS

Floating costs are incurred in the process of raising funds. These costs include the cost of advertisements, commissions, brokerage etc., for the issue of collections of funds.

FLOATING CURRENCY

A currency is said to float when it is allowed to find its own level in relation to other world currencies.

FLOATING DEBT

A debt consisting of short-term obligation. The term is used in contradiction to long-term or funded debts.

FLOATING EXCHANGE RATE

Where a country ceases to have an official exchange rate for its currency with other currencies but allows its currency to float or find a natural exchange rate. This can in effect by a devaluation.

FLOATING LABOUR

(*i*) Part of the national or regional workforce (usually unskilled) which has no stable employment but which moves, around both in terms of job category and geographical location on a short-term basis.

(*ii*) Workers who change their jobs and/or job locations from time to time.

FLOOR TRADER

(*i*) A person, usually a member of the stock exchange entitled to trade on the floor of that exchange.

(*ii*) Also, *competitive trader; registered trader,* A member of a stock exchange who trades for his or her own account rather than for customers.

FLOW LINE PRODUCTION

Method of organising work used mostly in mass production but also sometimes in batch production. Successive operations on a product are carried out in such a way that work flows in a single direction through the factory or workshop, the product being passed from operator to operator or from section to section for further work on it.

FLUCTUATING WORKING CAPITAL

The amount of working capital over and above the fixed minimum amount of such capital. It may fluctuate from period to period depending upon various factors.

FLYBACK TIMING

A method of timing a job using a stopwatch in time study in which the hands of the stopwatch are returned to get at the end of each element of the job. (Also called *Snapback Timing.*)

FLYING PICKETS

Groups of individuals which can at short notice be sent to any location to picket a place of work. Normally used to reinforce local pickets so as to bring more pressure to bear on the management.

FOCAL POINT INTERVIEWING

Focusing interviews upon certain point or theme in whatever is being researched, *e.g.*, TV commercial, so that respondent becomes more closely involved in a situation in which his responses can be recorded.

FOCUS GROUP

A research technique where groups of consumers are brought together to discuss their views and attitudes to a specific topic.

FOLDER TECHNIQUE

Field research technique, used in copytesting or pretesting press features, in which respondents are shown alternative advertisements, usually presented in folder containing plastic sleeves.

FOLDING MACHINES

Folding machines are used where a large number of letters and other documents have to be folded each day. These machines, operated electrically, can automatically fold the letters in the desired way at the rate of 10,000 to 20,000 fold per hour.

FOLK MEDIA

Traditional media as found in rural areas of developing countries, or used for PR purposes. It is either traditional or is a means of communicating with people whatever their tribal languages or dialects. It includes folk or village theatre, mimicry and puppet shows.

FOLLOW-UP

(*i*) Sales contact, telephone call or letter sometimes but not always as a result of an expression of interest by a prospect and usually after his/her receipt of an initial promotional piece, *e.g.*, *A Direct MailShot*.

(*ii*) The final step in the creative selling process, wherein the salesperson, after the sale has been made, contacts the buyer to make sure everything connected with the sale was handled properly.

FORCE CLOSURE

Collection of a debt (usually a mortgage) by seizing and selling the debtor's property or security.

FORCED SAVING

The prevention of spending by individuals, which compels them to save more than they ordinarily would. It may occur through a shortage of consumer goods (as in wartime), or as the by-product of a fiscal policy to curb inflating through levying higher taxes, thus limiting consumption.

FORECASTING

Predicting future business conditions and the state of the economy on the basis of various statistics describing past and current conditions, particularly those selected as indicators.

FOREIGN COMPANY

A company that is incorporated in a country outside India under its own laws having an established place of business in India.

FOREIGN CORPORATION

A corporation organised and chartered in a state or a country different from that in which its status or performance is being considered.

FOREIGN DEBT

Debts incurred outside India from persons not residing in the country.

FOREIGN TRADE LEAKAGE

It means that employment at home increases less than it would if all spending were for products produced within the domestic economy.

FOREMAN

(*i*) Generally, the first-line supervisor, one level above the hourly employee.

(*ii*) In manufacturing, construction, and similar industries, a person in direct change of production workers, generally considered a member of middle management.

FORESHIFT

The morning shift in a three-shift system.

FORFEITURES

Funds relinquished by a terminating employee in a qualified profit-sharing or thrift plan.

FORGERY

The alteration or false writing of an instrument with the intent of deceiving and injuring another person; for example, signing someone's name to a cheque without his or her consent. It means signature by a person other than the true person. Thus, if A signs as B it is forgery. Forgery may also mean, under certain circumstances, signing without proper authority to do so.

FORM LETTER

A word processing term for a letter sent to deferent people with only the name and address and some other particulars changed to give it the appearance of being personally written. The computer automatically inserts a new name and address etc., each time the letter is printed. It is often used in conjunction with a *Mail Merge Facility.*

FORMAL AGREEMENT

Express undertakings between the various business units concerning trade conditions or prices. In so far as they do not mean any collective control of the quantity of output to be marketed.

FORMAL COMMITTEES

Formal committees are constituted as a part of the organisation structure and their jurisdiction is also formal.

FORMAL ORGANISATION

Formal organisation refers to the structure of well defined jobs, each bearing a definite measure of authority, responsibility and accountability. The structure is consciously designed to enable the people of the organisation to work together in accomplishing the common objectives. Thus, formal organisation is more or less an arbitrary structure to which the individual must adjust. It tells him to do certain things in a specified manner, to obey orders from designated individuals and to work co-operatively with others. Co-ordination also proceeds according to a prescribed pattern in the formal organisation structure. The formal organisation facilitates the determination of objectives and policies. But the degree of success of these objectives will be determined by the capacities and attitudes of the people within the organisation.

FORMALISATION

A dimension of organisation structure that refers to the extent to which rules, procedures, and other guides to action are written and enforced.

FORMULA PENSION

The category of pension covering most salaried employees, under which a rate formula is applied to individual earnings to calculate the employee's pension.

FORWARD BUYING

A buying practice whereby a future contract to buy or sell is made on the basis of spot rates.

FORWARD CONTRACT

A contract for the delivery of goods at a specified future date (an 'outright' forward contract) or at a date to be chosen by either the buyer or the seller within specified limits (an 'option' forward contract).

FORWARD INTEGRATION

Where the manufacturer or main supplier of a product or service acquires or takes over certain customer or retail outlets in an endeavour to secure a further part of the market for the product or service.

FORWARDING AGENT

A shipping agent who specialises in moving goods from a factory or port of entry to their proper destination.

FOUNDATION

A non-profit organisation set up for charitable or other benevolent purposes, such as supporting scientific research, artistic endeavour, educational institutions, etc.

FOUR-DAY WEEK

An arrangement under which employees in an organisation work for only four days each week but work the same number of hours that were previously spread over five days. Also known as 'four-day, forty-hour week' because the number of hours worked is commonly 40 a week.

FOUR P'S OF MARKETING

(*i*) Shorthand way of indicating the principal factors to be included in the marketing mix, *i.e.*, *Product, Price, Place* and *Promotion.*

(*ii*) The basic elements of the marketing mix: *product, place* (*distribution*), *price,* and *promotional.* Also called the controllable variables of marketing, because they can be controlled and manipulated by the marketer.

FRACTIONAL (OR FRAGMENT) BARGAINING

Form of collective bargaining on behalf of a minority of employees or to deal with a particular grievance.

FRAGMENTATION

(*i*) More sophisticated market segmentation when segments are sub-segmented in a highly competitive market and new sources of sales are sought.

(*ii*) Process of storing the file in the form of fragments when continuous memory of the file size is not available. This slows down the retrieval time because DOS has to read the file from several parts of the disk, one at a time.

FRANCHISE

(*i*) A right, usually an exclusive right, granted by a government to an individual or firm, to perform some service or activity of a public nature. Or we can say that licence given by manufacturers who wish to limit the distribution outlets of their products or who wish all their sales in one country to be handled by specified persons.

(*ii*) A contractual agreement between a franchiser and a franchisee by which the franchisee distributes the franchiser's product.

(*iii*) A business in which exclusive rights are purchased for selling goods or services under a specified trade name and within a specified geographical area. The franchise or supplies the product or reaches the service to the franchise who then sells it, paying in returns a fee and/or royalty on the sales.

FRANCHISE POLICY

A marine insurance policy which disallows claims below a stated minimum unless the ship is stranded or sunk. The policy has the double purpose of avoiding petty claims and restricting liability on very risky cargo.

FRANCHISING

(*i*) A contractual relationship between a seller and an outlet which uses the seller's format, product and name.

(*ii*) Manufacturer's products, or to operate a service in which the manufacturer has a monopoly of equipment or supplies, *e.g.,* washing machines and launderettes.

FRANCO DOMICILE

Price including free delivery to customer's address.

FRANCO

'Franco' price covers the price of

goods delivered free of any charge to a specified destination.

FRAUD AND FORGERY

(*i*) Fraud under Sec. 17 of the Indian Companies Act means acts committed by a party to a contract or with his connivance, or by his agent, with intent to deceive another party thereto or his agent, or to induce him to enter into the contract.

(*ii*) *Deceit:* The practice of trickery or deception with intent to gain some advantage at the cost of others.

FRAUDS AND ERRORS—DETECTION OF

The detection of frauds and errors is a subsidiary object of auditing. In the present computer era, detection or errors and frauds by the auditor may be little more difficult. Auditor may not be able to locate errors and frauds in the accounts unless he knows the details of computer programming, which itself is a very technical and complex job. A minor deviation in the program may change the whole course of the figures and specifically, where it is done deliberately. Fraud may be classified as:

(*a*) Misappropriation of cash;

(*b*) Misappropriation of goods;

(*c*) Manipulation of falsification of accounts without any misappropriation of cash or goods.

FREE FLOAT

The length of time for which an activity in a network may be delayed or extended without delaying the start of any succeeding activity.

FREE GOOD

A good which, at a given time and place is either in such abundance that anyone can obtain it without cost (*e.g.*, air) or is incapable of being sold (*e.g.*, sunshine).

FREE LANCE

A person who works on an independent basis, taking on assignments from one or more employers.

FREE MARKET

The kind of market that would exist under a free enterprise system. The term may be used in relation to the purchase and sale of any commodity where there is complete freedom to deal.

FREE PORT

(*i*) It is a port that accepts the landing of goods from abroad on the specific understanding that there would be no imposition of any import duty or taxation on the products that are imported.

(*ii*) A port which allows goods to be temporarily imported and held within the port area without paying duty.

FREE TRADE

Unrestricted international trade either with no customs duties or with customs duties that are used only to create revenue and not to exclude imports.

FREEHOLD PROPERTY

It is a property which is free of any lien or any other condition or cess for its holding by the owner.

FREIGHT

(*i*) The money paid by a charterer to a shipowner in consideration of the latter letting the space within the ship. The fee charged for carrying goods.

(*ii*) A fee charged for the transportation of goods from one place to another by water, land or air.

FREIGHT PREPAID

This expression means the seller will pay transportation charges to the carrier and the buyer will remit the full amount of the invoice without deduction for freight charges.

FREQUENCY

The number of times an advertisement is repeated in a given medium within a given time period, usually a month.

FRINGE BENEFIT

(*i*) A reward beyond the basic pay for the job. Example can range from subsidised meals and travel to pensions, holidays and sickness benefits.

(*ii*) Fringe benefits and employee welfare programmes have been in vogue in industry since long. Some of them like provident fund and gratuity have become statutory while others concerning housing, education, etc., are not statutory yet. The fringe benefits are non-wage benefits offered by the employer to the employees; they represents "a substantial cost-expense to the employee and a cost-saving to the employee".

FRINGE BENEFITS (EMPLOYEES' BENEFITS)

Rewards to employees beyond their basic remuneration package—such as free or subsidised food or travel, special low-interest mortgage rates, special price access to a company's products, etc.

FROZEN ASSETS

Assets tied up so that transactions in them are restricted. Where a company has floating debenture and they become repayable, the assets of the company are frozen from the point of view of the debenture-holders.

FRUSTRATION

(*i*) A sense of emotional or mental unease, the result of one's inability to satisfy a need or desire because of environmental or self-imposed obstacles.

(*ii*) In human behaviour, the blocking or thwarting of goal attainment, defined in terms of the condition of the individual rather than in terms of the external environment. Frustration may take different forms of expression, including aggression against unrelated persons or objects.

F-TEST

A statistical test used to decide whether two samples with different sample variance may be presumed to come from normal population with the same population variance. The F distribution is used for the test.

FULFILMENT HOUSE

Specialist firm which handles response to mailing, sales promotion offers, direct response marketing sales and other postal responses to advertising.

FULL COVERAGE

Insurance that pays for every rupee of a loss with no maximum and no deductible amount.

FULL EMPLOYMENT

A situation in which all those persons who are seeking work in a community are able to find suitable work fairly readily, with the consequence that a very high proportion of the working population is actually in work at any one time.

FULL SERVICE AGENCY

Advertising agency offering clients a wide range of activities and expertise over and above the normal creative and/or media facilities.

FULL-CAPACITY GROWTH

The 'required' rate of growth to avoid long-run disequilibrium and unemployment and to insure the full capacity use of a growing capital stock.

FULL-LINE STRATEGY

The product line strategy that involves offering a large number of variations of a product. Also called a *Broad Strategy.*

FULL-SERVICE MERCHANT WHOLESALER

Merchant wholesaler that provides a complete array of services, such as delivery, credit, marketing information and advice, and managerial assistance. Also called a *Full-Function Wholesaler.*

FUNCTION

A group of related activities that contribute to the performance of work by an organisation (such as the purchasing function, *i.e.* all activities related to purchasing materials for use by an organisation). Also the part of an organisation that performs such a group of activities.

FUNCTIONAL JOB ANALYSIS (FJA)

A method of job analysis that focuses on the worker's specific job activities, methods, machines, and output. Widely used to analyse and classify jobs.

FUNCTIONAL ORGANISATION

The object of functional organisation is to give a place to specialists at the supervisory level in the line organisation. Under this, the personnel and their work are organised on the basis of the type of activities. All activities of the same type are grouped together under one functional department which is managed by an executive who is expert in his field. There maybe separate departments on the basis of major functions like *Production Procurement, Marketing, Finance,* etc., every department performs its specialised function for the entire organisation.

FUND

(*i*) It is an account normally of the nature of a reserve or a provision which is represented by specifically earmarked assets.

(*ii*) To provide for a financial obligation by borrowing money for a specific period. To provide for a future financial obligation by setting aside money and lending it to earn interest; to create a sinking fund.

FUND FOR MULTINATIONAL MANAGEMENT EDUCATION

Aims to bring about greater understanding of role of private enterprise in economy development.

FUNDED DEBT

A debt that does not have to be repaid, especially one represented by an irredeemable security.

FUNDING

A term used in connection with a variety of operations concerning the replacement of short-term loans by longer-term ones.

FUNDS FLOW ANALYSIS

Analysis of the flow of purchasing power into and out of an organisation. Inward flows include sales revenue, sales of fixed assets and investments, and issues of debentures, loans and shares.

FUNNEL TECHNIQUE

Method of interviewing which directs open-ended questioning without topic of investigation. More disclipined depth interview.

FURNITURE

Office Staff need furniture to perform their duties. Clerical work is concentrated around chairs, desks, tables etc., but little attention is paid to their quality and design. Proper design of furniture can make a valuable contribution to increased productivity in the office. It is being realised that furniture is bought not only for its utility but also for its appearance. Artistic furniture makes the office look more attractive and appeals to the office workers who use it throughout their stay in the office.

FUSION PROCESS

The process by which the goals of an individual become identical, to some extent, with those of an organisation (term used by *E. Wright Bakke*).

FUTURE MOVEMENT

Somewhat fragmented futurist movement recognising that new intellectual approaches are necessary to face up to dramatic changes in future development.

FUTURES

Forward sales or forward purchases, often by speculators who have no intention of taking up or providing the goods personality.

FUTURES CONTRACT

A contract, arranged on an organised market, by which a seller promises to deliver a fixed standard quantity of a commodity of a standard quality to the buyer on a fixed future date.

G

GAINSHARING

(*i*) An innovative reward strategy wherein employees share in the financial rewards of achieving set objectives.

(*ii*) Operation of a premium bonus scheme in which the incentive payment per unit of time saved decreases as the time saved increases. It is argued that gains from producing at more than the standard rate of performance should be shared between the worker and his employer.

GALLOPING INFLATION

Slow price increases are one thing. But when each increase in prices becomes the signal for an increase in wages and costs, which again sends prices up still further, we may be in the midst of a malignant, galloping hyper inflation.

GANTT CHART

(*i*) A chart on which progress in the various parts of a project (*e.g.*, production of a total amount of product, construction of a buildings) is plotted against time.

(*ii*) A pictorial method for displaying and monitoring a process, project, or production schedule so as to evaluate performance against a time table. Gantt charts, if properly maintained, can serve as valuable tools for planning, scheduling, and controlling the various aspects of a production situation.

GAP ANALYSIS

(*i*) The type of analysis marketers use to identify the sources of the consumer's expected service- perceived service gap.

(*ii*) Methodical tabulation of all known 'consumer wants' of a particular product category, together with a crosslisting of the features of existing products which satisfy those wants. Such a chart shows up any gaps which exist and thus provides a pointer as to where new products might find an unfulfilled demand.

GARIBI HATAO

Hindi expression meaning "banish poverty". It is an objective of Indian planning. It was coined by (late) Mrs. Indira Gandhi, the former prime minister of India. The phrase having been internationalised with its adoption by the U.N.O. has freely entered into the English language.

GARNISHMENT

Any legal or equitable procedure through which earnings of any individual are required to be withheld for the payment of any debt. Most garnishments are made by Court order.

GATEKEEPER

A group member who controls the flow of information to the decisionmaker; the buying-centre role played by the organisational member who controls the flow of information related to the purchase.

GATT

(*i*) General Agreement on Tariff and Trade International agreement signed in 1947 by numerous countries to liberalise trade by the reduction and removal of tariff barriers and quota restrictions. The agreement has no legal force but has had considerable influence in postwar developments.

(*ii*) The General Agreement on Tariffs and Trade. It is an international agreement to reduce trade barriers and establish a code of conduct for international trade.

GAZETTEER

A geographical dictionary.

GAZUMPING

Backing out of a proposed sale of property because another buyer has offered more for it.

GEARING OF CAPITAL

After the ascertainment of the total needs of the industry, planning of capital structure involves the selection of the different modes of raising the total amount. Determination of some proper ratio between any two or more methods or raising capital is called *Gearing of Capital, i.e.,* the ratio of the fixed income securities to the total capitals.

GEARING

The gearing of a company is the relationships of its total debt, *i.e.,* loan stocks, debentures, bank borrowings, etc., to the total equity, *i.e.,* issued capital plus reserves.

GENERAL ADAPTATION SYNDROME (GAS)

A description of the three phases of the defence reaction that a person establishes when stressed. These phases are *cdled Alarm, Resistance,* and *Exhaustion*.

GENERAL APTITUDE TEST BATTERY (GATB)

Battery of 12 aptitude tests, presenting results in the form of a profile to be measured against standard profiles of 22 vocational groups. Used widely by occupational psychologists in vocational guidance.

GENERAL CLERICAL TEST

Three-part psychological test developed in the USA and measuring verbal, numerical and clerical skills. The test takes about 30 minutes.

GENERAL CREDITOR

An insolvent debtor who neither has any security for his debt nor is he entitled to any preference in its payment mode.

GENERAL EQUILIBRIUM ANALYSIS (THEORY)

When all prices are viewed as dependent upon one another, the theory of prices become general equilibrium theory.

GENERAL EXPENSE

An administrative expense, not identified with a specific process, product, or service generated by the operation of the facility. Also known as *Burden.*

GENERAL INFLATION

The inflation that accompanies full employment of all other resources.

GENERAL LEARNING ABILITY TEST

Term used particularly in the USA in psychological testing for a wide-ranging intelligence test (rather than achievement test). It may be a combination of tests forming a test battery.

GENERAL LEGACY

A general legacy should be distinguished from a specific legacy and a demonstrative legacy. A general legacy is a gift by will out of the personal estate of the testator but is not necessarily and particular part of the estate. General legacies are usually, but not necessarily, pecuniary legacies.

GENERAL LINE WHOLESALER

Full-service merchant wholesaler that sells a full selection of products in one product line.

GENERAL MANAGEMENT

(*i*) The work performed by general managers.

(*ii*) The general managers within an organisation.

GENERAL MANAGER

A manager who determines and influences the broad objectives of a whole organisation, determines the resources to be made available for attaining those objectives and has significant responsibilities in more than one major field of activity (usually working through managers who specialise in single fields of activity). A general manager is especially concerned with the formulation and interpretation of policy and with long-term planning.

GENERAL MEETING

A meeting which may be attended by all the members of an association and which gives them some opportunity to control the association's affairs.

GENERAL PARTNER

An active member of a partnership who has unlimited liability for the actions of the partners.

GENERAL PLANNING

May be general as well as detailed. General planning concerns itself with major issues only. It lays down only the broad outlines of future development.

GENERAL RESERVE

A reserve or fund created without making allocations for any particular purpose as opposed to a specific or special reserve.

GENERAL STORE

A type of retailing institution that usually sells a limited selection of a wide range of goods.

GENERAL STRIKE

A strike called by all or most of the workers in all or most industries simultaneously. It may involve a city or an entire country. Its purpose usually is not so much one of gaining specific concessions as it is to put political pressure on a government or to demonstrate the unity of the labour movement.

GENERAL UNION

Trade union whose membership is drawn from all kinds of workers as opposed to the more specialised membership of, for example, *A Craft Union.*

GENERAL VOCABULARY

Words used in everyday conversation and correspondence.

GENERALISATION

An inference or number of inferences based upon collection or observation of facts.

GENERIC COMPETITIVE STRATEGY

Broad company strategies identified by *Michael Porter* which affect the success of the business in term of overall cost leadership, focus and market differentiation. He identifies three generic strategies—differentiated, undifferentiated and concentrated.

GENERIC PRODUCT (GENERIC BRAND)

A product that carries neither a manufacturer nor a distributor brand. The goods are plainly packaged with stark lettering that simply lists the contents.

GENETIC INDUSTRY

An industry engaged directly in increasing the supply of some forms of plant or animal life. Farming and cattle raising are examples.

GEODEMOGRAPHIC SEGMENTATION

A type of market segmentation by which consumers are grouped according to demographic variables, such as income and age, as identified by a geographic variable, such as zip code.

GEOGRAPHIC MARKET CONCENTRATION

Some industries have classical geographic concentrations while other industries are dispersed according to resources, *e.g.*, paper-making and water. Certain other industries may be located in seaport or airport areas, or close to urban markets.

GEOGRAPHIC PRICING

Occurs when the price for the same product or service varies according to the class of store, retailer or shopping area, whether within one town, or from one part of the country to another, or indifferent countries, *e.g.* motor-cars.

GERONTOLOGY

Study of the social, psychological, biological, and health aspects of the aging and the aging process.

GESTALT PSYCHOLOGY

School of psychology particularly associated with *Max Wertheimer* is

1912, and based on premise that human beings perceive things in patterns or whole. A furnished room is seen, not individual bits of furniture. Similar or associated objects are mentally grouped.

GHOST WRITER

Journalist who writes speeches, articles or hooks which are credited to another who has commissioned them.

GHOSTING

(1) Providing an inner view of a package or product by cutting away part of the exterior.

(2) Shadow on television film.

GIFFEN GOODS

Giffen good is a special case of inferior good and is named after *Sir Robert Giffen* (1837-1910) who in the 19th century pointed out: "a rise in the price of bread makes so large a drain on the resources of the poor labouring families they consume more and less of it". "Giffen good is an inferior good, but every inferior good cannot be a Giffen good".

GIFT VOUCHER

Special incentive to purchase, usually involving money off against next purchase of qualifying brand or providing an opportunity for a special purchase.

GIFTS DEED

An instrument that transfers the title to real estate for which the consideration is love and affection, rather than material consideration.

GILES-ARCHER LANTERN TESTS

Form of colour vision test in which the subject is presented with a number of lights of different colours and different degrees of brightness.

GILT-EDGED STOCK

Government stocks which are considered as extremely safe investments because their interest and repayment is guaranteed by the government.

GIRI APPROACH

The plea of *V.V. Giri* that attempts are increasingly to be made to settle all industrial disputes by mutual negotiations between the employers and the employees failing which conciliation officers are to be approached instead of compulsory adjudication, is referred to as *Giri Approach.*

GLOBAL BRANDS

Goods which can have universal appeal and are marketed in many countries with little modification to product or image.

GLOBALISATION

The interdependency of transportation, distribution, communication, and economic networks across international borders.

GLOBALISATION STRATEGY

A plan by which a marketer standardises its marketing strategy around the world. Also called a *Standardisation Strategy*.

GO NO-GO GAGE OR GO NOT-GO GAGE

In manufacturing, a type of limit gage utilised to measure the dimensions of a mechanical part to determine whether or not the part is within allowable limits.

GOAL

A specific target that an individual is trying to achieve; a goal is the target (object) of an action.

GOAL APPROACH TO EFFECTIVENESS

A perspective on effectiveness that emphasises the central role of goal achievement as the criterion for assessing effectiveness.

GOAL DIFFICULTY

The degree of proficiency or the level of goal performance that is sought.

GOAL ORIENTATION

The focus of attention and decision-making among the members of a subunit.

GOAL PARTICIPATION

The amount of a person's involvement in setting task and personal development goals.

GOAL SETTING

The process of establishing goals. In many cases, goal setting involves a superior and subordinate working together to set the subordinate's goals for a specified period of time.

GOAL SPECIFICITY

The degree of quantitative precision (clarity) of the goal.

GOAL-ORIENTATED RESEARCH

Research of practical application as distinct from research for its own sake.

GOING-CONCERN CONCEPT

Assumption made when valuing an enterprises's assets and liabilities that the enterprise will continue to carry on its business through the foreseeable future.

GOLD HANDICUFFS

A term referring to the feeling of being bound to remain in a job because financial benefits would be forfeited upon resignation from it.

GOLDEN HANDSHAKE

Colloquial term for severance pay given to a senior executive on termination of his contract of employment or cutting short of his contract of service.

GOLDEN PARACHUTE

A bonus payment which directors of a firm agree to pay themselves in the event of losing a take-over battle. The payment is so-called because one likely consequence of such a battle would be that they would be made redundant.

GOLDEN RULE FALLACY

Fallacious view in some T-group training that there is a right way for all people to interact in all situations.

GOOD-FAITH BARGAINING

Criteria for good-faith bargaining in labour management disputes. They require that all parties in a collective bargaining situation genuinely try to achieve agreement and develop a system of communication that will prevent disputes or solve them where they already exist.

GOODS IN CONSIGNMENT

Goods Received Note: A document issued by a firm no receipt of a delivery which sets out what goods and how many items have been delivered.

GOODS RETURNED NOTE

A document issued by a firm on receipt of goods which is originally supplied and which have been returned because of faults, wrong type or quantity etc.

GOODWILL

(*i*) The intangible set of factors which develop in a business such as customer loyalty, reputation, special expertise etc. When the business is sold it is often the practice to put a value on such goodwill. In the words of *Lord Elden, 'Goodwill* is nothing more than a probability that old customer will resort to old place. *Lord Macnaughten* stated it as 'it is very easy to describe but very difficult to define'.

(*ii*) The likelihood that customers will return to the same supplier. Also an estimate of the value of goodwill of the supplier. The standing of an enterprise as a successful business house.

(*iii*) One of the intangible values of a business beyond its net worth. Goodwill may include such assets as general reputation, brand name recognition, technical know-how, location, and the historic ability of the company to retain its accounts on the basis, for example, of services.

GOVERNMENT BONDS

Certificates issued by a government acknowledging its debt. They may be issued at a discount, at par, or at a premium.

GOVERNMENT INSTRUMENT

A document that governs an organisation's actions.

GOVERNMENT SECURITIES

Securities issued by Central or State Governments to raise public funds; also known as *Gilt-Edged Securities.*

GRACE PERIOD

A specified period, after a premium payment is due on an insurance policy, during which a policyholder may make such a payment without penalty and still have the protection of the policy continue.

GRADE CREEP

Tendency to re-grade or reclassify employees as superstitious method of allowing increases in pay.

GRADE PLACEMENT

The grade in which the student is actually placed.

GRADE SCORE

Average achievement in terms of grade level. For example, a grade score of 3.2 means the performance level of an individual two months in the third grade.

GRADED HOURLY RATES

A form of payment system where employees are paid according to their merit ratings.

GRADING

Storing individual units or assigning lots, or a product according to predetermined quality standards.

GRANT CLOSEOUT PROCEDURES

The procedures specified by grant-making public agencies that define financial, reporting and asset-retention or—protecting steps that must be taken at the termination of a grant.

GRANT PROJECT

A grant that directs funding to specific project, in contrast to a general support grant.

GRAPEVINE

(*i*) Information based on rumour and hearsay, as 'heard on the grapevine', the information becoming more and more distorted as it is passed from one to another. Often the cause of industrial strife, provoked by lack of information from management.

(*ii*) An informal communication network that exists in organisations and short-circuits in the formal channels.

GRAPHIC RATING SCALES

The oldest and most widely used performance evaluation method, wherein the rater evaluates an employee's qualities and characteristics on a written form.

GRAPHICAL DISPLAY

SeeVDU.

GRATUITY

(*i*) A gift, especially of a small sum of money, made in response to service received or anticipated. A benefit given to the employees at the time of retirement or leaving a job after some fixed period.

(*ii*) Sometimes known as a lumpsum, it is an amount payable under some pension schemes at the time when the pension is due to commence. It is not liable to income tax.

GREEN MARKETING

Marketing activities beneficial to the physical environment.

GREEN PAPER

A publication of the government with a green cover usually a proposal to which the government is not committed but would like public comment on.

GRID TRAINING

A leadership development method proposed by *Blake* and *Mouton* that emphasises the balance between production orientation and person orientation.

GRIP

A Graphics Interactive Programming Language.

GROSS CURRENT ASSETS

The aggregate of all current assets including cash.

GROSS DOMESTIC PRODUCT (GDP)

The total value of goods and services that are produced within a specified country (including those produced by non-residents) over a period (usually one year) excluding all goods and services used during that period to produce further goods and services. Like gross national product, GDP may be measured at 'market prices' or at 'factor cost'.

GROSS INCOME

Revenues from service, investments, contributions, and all other sources, prior to any deductions such as expenses or the funding of reserves.

GROSS LOSS

The excess of cost of goods sold or services rendered over the amount of sales or revenues realised during a period.

GROSS MARGIN

It is equal to the difference of the proceeds of the goods sold and services rendered during a period and their cost, before taking into account the overheads like administrative, selling and other expenses. In case the cost is more than the sale proceeds, it is known as *Gross Loss*.

GROSS MARGIN PERCENTAGE

The percentage of revenues available to cover expenses and provide a profit: Gross Margin/Net Sales.

GROSS NATIONAL PRODUCT (GNP)

(*i*) The total value of all the goods and services that are produced by the residents of a specified country over a period (usually one year) excluding all goods and services used during that period to produce further goods and services. Unlike gross domestic products, GNP includes income that a country's own residents derive from assets owned abroad but exclusive the income of foreigners within the country. In economics, the total value of business activity—production, investments (both nationally and abroad), services, property—of a country.

(*ii*) The total value of all the goods and services produced by a nation's residents or corporations, regardless of location.

(*iii*) The monetary value of the goods and services produced in a country in a year, without subtraction of amounts chargeable to depreciation.

GROSS PROFIT

(*i*) A figure representing the revenue from sales of a product or service minus the cost of its production. No other costs of taxes are deducted at this stage in the accounts.

(*ii*) The excess of total revenue over expenditure without deduction of insurance, overhead charges, etc. It is equal to gross sales minus returns (net sales) plus cost of goods sold before accounting for general selling and distribution expenses.

GROSS PROFIT MARGIN

The difference between direct cost and selling price.

GROSS RATING POINTS (GRPS)

A measure combining reach and frequency. GRP equals reach (in percentage points) times frequency.

GROSS SALES

Total sales over a specified period, before deduction of returns and allowances.

GROSS WORKING CAPITAL

The total value of the current assets of a firm.

GROUP

Two or more employees who interact with one another in such a manner that the behaviour and/or performance of one member is influenced by the behaviour and/or performance of other members. According to *Homans*, a group is a "number of person who communicate with one another, often over a span of time, and who are few enough so that each person is able to communicate with all the others, not at second hand through other people, but face to face".

GROUP BANKING

A banking system in which two or more bans are directly or indirectly controlled by an association such as a corporation, syndicate or business trust.

GROUP COHESIVENESS

By group cohesiveness, we mean the degree of attachment of the members to their group. The greater the degree of attachment, the greater is likelihood that all members will conform strictly to the group standards and greater the likelihood that its leader will represent the feelings of all members.

GROUP DYNAMICS

(*i*) According to *Keith Davis*, 'The social process by which people interact face-to-face in small groups is called *Group Dynamics'* Group dynamics is concerned with the interaction of individuals in a face-to-face relationship.

(*ii*) The interactions among members of a group. Also the study of these interactions with a view to learning how groups can become more effective.

GROUP EXECUTIVE

A manager who coordinates the work of two or more divisions.

GROUP INSURANCE

Also group disability insurance, group health insurance, and group life insurance, any insurance plan that covers individuals (and usually their dependents) by means of a single group agreement, contract, or policy issued to an employer or association with which the insured individuals are affiliated.

GROUP TECHNOLOGY

A classification and coding system used in computer aided design for combining similar parts into families.

GROUPTHING

The deterioration of the mental efficiency, reality testing, and moral judgment of the individual members of a group in the interest of group solidarity.

GROWTH STAGE

The stage in the product life cycle when sales increase at an accelerating rate.

GUARANTEE

(*i*) A promise by one person (usually called the 'Guarantor') that he will make good any failure by a second person (called the 'principal debtor') to meet financial obligations owned to a third person.

(*ii*) A promise, given by a manufacturer will correct any defects in the goods found by a purchaser within a certain time. (In theory, it is the retailer's duty to correct defects and so the manufacturer is acting as guarantor of the retailer).

(*iii*) A promise; a written statement by the maker of a document undertaking to repay any debt if the person for whom he stands guarantor breaks his promise.

GUARANTEE INSURANCE

An arrangement by which an insurer promises to indemnify an assured if a specified person fails to carry out a specified obligation to the assured.

GUARANTOR

A person who promises that if a second person fails to fulfil some obligation then he will fulfil it instead or pay money up to a specified limit to compensate for any loss caused by the second person's failure.

GUI

Graphics User Interface, an environment with menus etc. provided by the software like Windows which presents pictures, graphics and commands in the form of small icons. Mouse is used to select and initiate the commands thus minimising the typing work.

GUI TOOLS

Tools which are used to design and develop the interfaces in the graphical form for the different purposes.

H

HACKING

The unauthorised breaking into the database of a computer.

HALF-DUPLEX

A transmission mode in which the data in transmitted in one direction at a time either from a terminal to the computer or from the computer to the terminal.

HALLUCINOGEN

Any drug that distorts perception, sensation, or emotion.

HALO EFFECT

The tendency of managers to assume that a subordinate who is good, bad, or average in one respect is equally good, bad, or average in all others.

HALO ERROR

A positive or negative area around a ratee that influences a rater's evaluation.

HAMMERING

Public announcement at the stock exchange that a member cannot pay his debts. In the past attention was drawn to announcements by an attendant striking a restrum three times with a mallet.

HANDLING OBJECTIONS

The step in the creative selling process wherein the salesperson responds to questions or reservations expressed by the prospect.

HANG

A state of computer where all the processing of computer stops immediately by itself because of some internal error and does not responds to any of the control signals.

HARD COPY

Copy of any file obtained in printed form on paper.

HARD CURRENCY

A national currency generally recognised as strong, stable and easily convertible, used in international trade because it has a stable or rising exchange rate *e.g., American Dollars* or *Swiss Francs.*

HARD DISK

Hard disks are on-line storage device. They are used as secondary memory for mass storage of information permanently. They store programs, data, operating system, compilers, application programs, etc. A hard disk is made of aluminium (or other metal or metal alloy) base with a thin coating of magnetic material (iron-oxide) over it. Standard hard disk sizes are: 5.25, 3.5 and 2.5 inch diameter. 3.5 inch disks are commonly used. 2.5 inch disks are used in portable computers. 5.25 inch disks were used earlier. Digital information is stored on the magnetic coating (film) by applying current pulses of suitable polarity to the magnetising coil of the read/write head. The logic 1 or 0 depends on the direction of management of the very small area of the magnetic film which comes under the read/write head.

HARD MONEY

Revenue from an assured, continuing source that is set aside for the operation of specific program, service, or facility. Examples include State and Local Government financing, endowments, and long-term contracts for health care delivery.

HARD SELL

A colloquial term for the aggressive advertising, marketing, promotion and selling of a product.

HARDINESS

A personality trait that appears to buffer an individual's response to stress. The hardy person assumes that he is in control, is highly committed to lively activities, and treats change as a challenge.

HARDWARE

(*i*) Formally, the mechanical, magnetic, electrical, and electronic components of a computer. Informally, any piece of computer or automatic data-processing equipment.

(*ii*) Physical equipment and peripheral of a computer system such as storage devices, printer, CPU or keyboard.

HAULAGE

The chart made for carrying goods, though not usually for loading or unloading them.

HAWTHORNE STUDIES

A series of studies undertaken at the Chicago Hawthorne Plant of Western Electric from 1924 to 1933. The studies made major contributions to the knowledge of the importance of the social system of an organisation. They provided the impetus for the human relations approach to organisations.

HAZARD

A situation or even that introduces or increases the probability or occurrence of (or extent of loss arising from) an accident; such as slippery floors, insanitary conditions, or congested traffic.

HEAD

The electronic component in disk drives which actually transfers the data to and from the surface from and to the memory or the disk drive.

HEAD MOVEMENT

Extraneous movement of the head while reading.

HEAD NOTE

A short text before the beginning of an article generally highlighting its salient features and giving some information about the author; a concise statement of the legal principles contained in a law report.

HEADER

Control bits which has the information about the message to be transmitted like source of destination.

HEADER FILE

Special library files in C which are included in the beginning of program so that whenever some function is used in program the program has a reference to the function in the file.

HEADING

Any device by which one can protect oneself against losses in a stock exchange.

HEAD-TO-HEAD COMPETITION

Positioning a product to occupy the same market position as a competitor.

HEALTH INSURANCE

A generic term for all forms of insurance and prepayment plans that reimburse (in whose or in part) an individual or organisation for the costs of hospital and medical care; insurance against loss from disease or accidental bodily injury. Health insurance takes various forms, under such names as accident and health insurance, accident insurance, sickness insurance, disability insurance, health insurance, service benefit plan, prepaid health plan, preferred provider plan, health maintenance plan, foundation medical plan, hospital insurance, and dental plan.

HELP

A command of DOS and dBase which is used to invoke the on-line help on how to use the program that is present on the hard disk in the form of a file.

HERTZ

The international standard unit of measuring the frequency. The speed of processor is measured in terms of hertz.

HERZBERG'S TWO-FACTOR THEORY OF MOTIVATION

Herzberg extended the work of Maslow and developed a specific content theory of work motivation. He conducted a widely reported motivational study on about 200 accountants and engineers employed by firms in and around Pittsburgh, Pennsylvania. He used the critical incident method of obtaining data for analysis. The professional subjects in the study were essentially asked two questions:

(*i*) When did you feel particularly good about your job—what turned you on? and

(*ii*) When did you feel exceptionally bad about your job—what turned you off?

Responses obtained from this critical incident method were interesting and fairly consistent. Reported good feelings were generally associated with job experiences and job content. An example was the accounting supervisor who felt good about being given the job of installing new computer equipment. He took pride in his work and was gratified to know that the new equipment made a big difference in the overall functioning of his department. Reported bad feelings, on the other hand, were generally associated with the surrounding or peripheral aspects of the job—the job context. An example of these feelings was related by an engineer whose first job was to keep tabulation sheets and manage the office when the boss was gone. It turned out that his boss was always too busy to train him and became annoyed when he tried to ask questions. The engineer said that he was frustrated in this job context and that he felt like a flunky in a dead-end job. Tabulating these reported good and bad feelings, Herzberg concluded that job satisfiers are related to job content and that job dissatisfiers are allied to job context. Herzberg labelled the satisfiers motivators, and he called the *Dissatisfiers Hygiene Factors*. The term "hygiene" refers (as it does in the health field) to factors that are preventive; in Herzbergs theory the hygiene factors are those that prevent dissatisfaction taken together, the motivators and the hygiene factors have become known as Herzbergs two- factor theory of motivation.

HEWLETT PACKARD

A California based manufacturing company engaged in manufacturing equipments, calculators, computers and printers.

HEXADECIMAL NUMBERS

A number of hexadecimal number system which is nothing but a combination of hexadecimal digits.

HIERARCHY

A way of arranging the hardware or software according to the rank, class, priority, etc. Or in other words, any organisational structure containing different levels of authority and often responsibilities. Any arrangement of things in succeeding levels, each one subsuming all preceding levels.

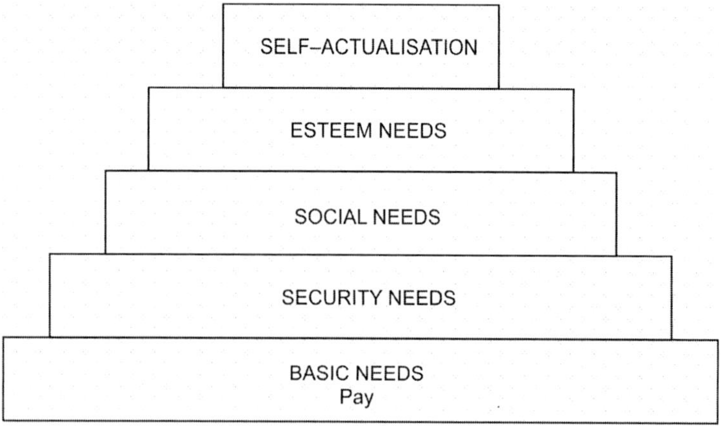

Fig. 2: A hierarchy of work motivation.

HIERARCHY OF NEEDS

Abraham Maslow, in a classic paper, outlined the elements of an overall theory of motivation. Drawing chiefly on his clinical experience, he thought that a persons motivational needs could be arranged in a hierarchical manner. In essence, he believed that once a given level of need is satisfied, it no longer serves to motivate. The next higher level of need has to be activated in order to motivate the individual. Maslow's identified five levels in this need hierarchy. They are, in brief, the following: (*i*) Physiological needs (*ii*) Safety needs (*iii*) Love needs (*iv*) Esteem needs (*v*) Needs for self-actualisation. Maslow did not intend that his need hierarchy be directly applied to work motivation. In fact, he did not delve into the motivating aspects of humans in organisations until about twenty years after he originally proposed his theory. Despite this lack of intent on Maslow's part, others, such as *Douglas McGregor*, in his widely read book: "The Human Side of Enterprise", popularised the Maslow theory in management literature. The need hierarchy has had a tremendous impact on the modern management approach to motivation. In a very rough manner, Maslow's need hierarchy theory can be converted into the content model of work motivation shown in Fig. 2. If Maslow's estimates are applied to an organisation example, the lower-level needs of personnel would be generally satisfied (85 per cent of the basic needs and 70 per cent of the security needs), but only 50 per cent of the social needs, 40 per cent of the esteem needs, and a mere 10 per cent of the self-actualisation needs would be met.

HIERARCHY

An arrangement in which personnel in an organisation are ranked or graded according to their position.

HIGH LEVEL LANGUAGES

A class of programming languages which has the statement in very simple languages. In these languages, control and data structures are problem oriented rather than hardware oriented.

HIRE

Payment of consideration for services rendered or using property belonging to another person; use of an asset in lease finance in exchange for money.

HIRE PURCHASE

An arrangement by which one person called the 'hirer' is lent goods (and pays rent for them) and has an option to purchase the goods outright, usually after paying a specified number of instalments of rent.

HIRE PURCHASE SYSTEM

A system of hiring anything such as a house, furniture, car, etc., against payment of hire charges in regular instalments on condition that the right of ownership of the goods hired rests with the owner.

HISTORY

A source of error in experimental results that consists of events other than the experimental treatment that occur between pre-and post-test measurement

HOBBY COMPUTER

A small, inexpensive computer for recreational and other home oriented uses.

HOLDING COMPANY

(*i*) A company which carries out listed or no business itself but which it has shares or other forms of security.

(*ii*) A company whose business consists wholly or mainly in holding the shares or securities of other companies. In particular one that holds shares or securities principally in companies that are 90 per cent subsidiaries or itself.

HOLDING GAIN

The difference in the worth of an asset from the time it was bought to a subsequent time (usually when it is sold, donated, or otherwise disposed of).

HOME ADDRESS

A field containing the cylinder on and the number of read/write heads used to access data on a track is stored on that track of a multiple disk memory.

HOME KEY

A key on keyboard marked 'Home' used to reach in the beginning of a file.

HOMONYM

A word having the same pronunciation as another but differing from it in origin, meaning, and often, in spelling, such as week, weak.

HORIZONTAL CHART

Horizontal charts which read from left to right and occasionally used. The pyramid lies horizontally instead of standing in the vertical position. The line of command proceeds horizontally, *i.e.*, from left to right showing top level at the left and each successive level extending to the right.

HORIZONTAL COMMUNICATION

Communication that flows across functions in an organisation; necessary for coordinating and integrating diverse organisational functions.

HORIZONTAL COOPERATIVE PROMOTION

An approach whereby channel members at the same level jointly sponsor particular promotions.

HORIZONTAL DIFFERENTIATION

The different units existing at the same level in an organisation. The greater the horizontal differentiation, the more complex is the organisation.

HOST COUNTRY NATIONALS

Workers from the local population.

HOT MONEY

Apart from its use in the world of crime to describe stolen or counterfeit money, hot money is a term sometimes used in the sphere of international payments. It refers to funds that move quickly from one country to another in search of the highest rate of interest.

HOUSEHOLD

A group of people who all live regularly at the same address and can be treated as a unit. There are two basic methods of identifying households: by defining 'housing units' and treating all the people living in one housing unit as household; by identifying groups of people who regularly live together as a family—usually defined as a group who are catered for by one person for at least one meal a day.

HOUSEHOLD SECTOR

It is a sector which sells or gives on hire the various factor services like land, labour etc. to the production sector. The household sector receives income in the form of wages, rent interest etc. and with the money thus earned the household sector purchases the goods produced by the production sector.

HOUSING SOCIETIES

The societies formed to provide residential accommodation to their members either on ownership basis or at some reasonable rent. These are generally formed by middle class people. These societies arrange loans from various sources which are payable in easy instalments.

HTML

This is a system of stages and codes which tell a Web browser how to display documents. HTML is used for the Web. Hyper text itself is text on a Web page, which has links. Clicking on these links gives access to another page of hyper text.

HUMAN CAPITAL

That part of an organisation's capital represented by the ability, experience and skill of its work-force.

HUMAN ENGINEERING

An American term for Ergonomics.

HUMAN FACTOR IN EFFICIENCY

The necessity for constantly increasing efficiency is a basic fact of business life. Yet increasing generates forces which in the long run decrease efficiency and the problem is still unsolved; it may be worse than ever. So perhaps more can be gained by concentrating on weakening those forces which tend to decrease efficiency rather than strengthening the forces which tend to increase efficiency. Basically the only output is to obtain the participation of the employees themselves is alleviating the factor that they have created to keep production down.

HUMAN PROCESS INTERVENTIONS

A class of interventions with the intended effects of changing individual and group behaviours found in the informal part of the organisation.

HUMAN RELATIONS

Human relations is the term commonly applied to the process of focusing the methodology and findings of a number of behavioural science disciplines on human problems. The human relations approach was greatly influenced by the Hawthorne studies and the other work of *Elton Mayo,* and later by *Kurt Lewin,* and *Douglas McGregor.* It emphasises the importance of morale in an organisation and the need for good working relationships between management and the people managed, in the quest for organisational effectiveness and high productivity. According to Elton Mayo, the main elements of human relations are as follows:

(*a*) Treat people as human rather than a bundle of skills .

(*b*) Understand people better and communicate effectively.

(*c*) Make them feel useful and important in the organisation.

(*d*) Create a sense of satisfaction among people.

For this, the motives and desires of people must be understood. Some of the natural interests of any human being are:

(*a*) An individual desires to be treated courteously.

(*b*) He likes to feel importance in his job.

(*c*) He wants recognition, desires security, aspires for trust and confidence.

(*d*) He welcomes direction from superiors.

(*e*) He wishes to have a superior who commands respect rather than demands.

HUMAN RELATIONS IN MANAGEMENT

Management's task in harnessing human energy to organisational requirement involves a process of directing their efforts, motivating them, controlling their actions and modifying their behaviour to fit the needs of the organisation. Without this active intervention by management people would be passive, even resistant to organisational needs. They must therefore be persuaded, rewarded, punished, controlled and their activities must be directed. This is management task. We often sum it up by saying that management consists of getting things done through others.

HUMAN RELATIONS PROGRAM

Human relations program represents an attempt to improve employee morale and motivation through improved communication and through employees' participation in decision-making processes. According to *W.G. Scot,* "Human relations is a process of effective motivation of individuals in a given situation in order to achieve a balance of objectives which will yield greater human satisfaction and help accomplish company goals."

HUMAN RELATIONS SKILL

Human relations skills make a leader out of a manager. Every manager works with, for and through people. Good human relations are the relationship of one person to a group of others. It means the ability to get along with people.

HUMAN RESOURCE ACCOUNTING (HRA)

A concept that views the employees of an organisation as capital assets, like plant and equipment. While the concept is intuitively attractive, calculating the value, replacement cost, and depreciation of human assets poses significant problems.

In other words, precisely, HRA is the systematic recording of the transactions relating to the value of the human resources. It records the cost of acquisition of the knowledge of the human resources, development of their skill and utilisation of their energy for the organisation. *Sidney Davidson, Clyde P. Stickney, James S. Schindler*, and *Roman L. Well* defined human resources accounting as: "A term used to describe a variety of proposals that seek to report and emphasise the importance of human resources—knowledgeable, trained, and loyal employees—in a company's earning process and total assets."

HUMAN RESOURCE MANAGEMENT

The responsibility for making the best use of an organisation employees. One of the major functions of personnel management.

HUMAN RESOURCES

A general term for all of the employees of an organisation or the workers in a society. In other words, the number and quality of an organisation's employees.

HUMANISM

An individualised philosophy and social doctrine of values that emphasises personal dedication to and constant concern for human welfare in every real of human experience.

HUMANIST

An individual with an intense concern for human dignity and well-being; also, a person who is involved and concerned with the humanities.

HUMANISTIC PERSONALITY THEORIES

Theories that place emphasis on the growth and self-actualisation of people.

HYBRID BASIS OF ACCOUNTING

This system of accounting is a combination of accrual basis and cash basis.

HYBRID COMPUTERS

The computers which are combination of both digital and analog circuits and features.

HYPER-INFLATION

A term applied to inflation when it is running at extremely high levels.

HYPERMARKET

A mass merchandise outlet featuring an especially large variety of products and an especially large size. Also called *A Superstore.*

HYPOPITUITARISM

Under-functioning of the pituitary gland.

HYPOTHECATION

(*i*) Hypothecation is a charge against property for the amount of the debt where neither ownership nor possession is passed to the creditor. In hypothecation, goods are in the possession of the borrower, but are charged equitable to the bank Usually the hypothecation deed empowers the bank to require possession of goods to be handed over to him.

(*ii*) A tentative theory or assumption, supposition, or generalisation adopted as a basis for reasoning, the validity of which is to be tested with proper statistical techniques.

HYPOTHESIS

(*i*) An unproved proposition that can be supported or refuted by marketing research. Research objectives are often stated as *Hypothesis*.

(*ii*) A testable assertion, statement or preposition about two variables which are in some way related to each other.

I

I/O INTERRUPT

An interrupt caused by a signal generated by some I/O controller to indicate that input or output operation is complete.

I/P PORT

The circuits attached with the circuitry of central processing unit so that input output peripheral devices could be attached to the computer system.

IBM

International Business Machine—a corporation which is the largest computer manufacturer.

IBMBIO.COM

Another hidden system DOS file that gets executed automatically at the start up.

IBM-CARD

A 80 column punched card used for input purpose.

IBMDOS.COM

A hidden system file of DOS that gets executed automatically at the start up.

IC

Integrated circuit.

IDEA GENERATION STAGE

The stage in new product development that involves a continuing search for product ideas consistent with target market needs and the organisation's objectives.

IDEA GENERATION USAGE

The stage in new product development that involves a continuing search for product ideas consistent with target market needs and the organisation's objectives.

IDENTIFIER

An alphanumeric label assigned to a device or program objects like variables, constants, arrays or functions that identifies it in a program or in memory.

IDENTIFYING CONSEQUENCES

We try to foresee impact on all the various company goals when consequences are likely to be both desirable and undesirable, both immediate and long-range, both tangible and intangible, both certain and only possible.

IDIOM

A form of expression peculiar to a people, a district, a community or a class.

IDLE TIME

(*i*) The difference between the late time and the actual time booked for labour. Workers are paid for this time without any corresponding production. It may be normal or abnormal in nature.

(*ii*) The time during which some job waits for the CPU or any other resource but it does not get that. This situation usually occurs in a time-sharing environment.

ILLUSTRATORS

Gestures that give a picture of what is being said (*e.g.*, extended hands to illustrate the size of an object).

IMAGE

A mental reconstruction of sensory experiences. Three levels: after images (A.I.), eidetic images (E.I.), and memory images (M.I.).

IMAGE BUILDING

A promotional approach intended to communicate an image and generate consumer preference for a brand or product on the basis of symbolic value.

IMAGE CONSULT

A public relations practitioner who specialises in teaching executives how to project a more impressive image (both inside and outside their organisation) by dressing, speaking, socialising, and otherwise behaving in a more "executive like" manner.

IMAGE PROCESSING

A computer aided graphic technique that provides the means to process the images captured by satellites circulating around the earth.

IMAGE, COMPANY

The general impression the public has of a company.

IMAGE

(*i*) A mental reconstruction of sensory experiences. Three levels: after images (A.I.), eidetic images (E.I.), and memory images (M.I.).

(*ii*) The perceptions of a product, brand, or company by customers and consumers.

IMAGERY

Collective mental images; visual, auditory, kinesthetic, gustatory, olfactory, pain, thermal or tactual.

IMMOVABLE PROPERTY

Fixed assets not liable to be removed without loss or damage having the character of permanency.

IMPERSONALITY

A form of management that is mechanical in its approach and lacks the personal involvement of a human relations emphasis.

IMPLEMENTATION

The putting into action of policies, goals, objectives, and task; and interactive process among planning and action groups in which policies, goals, and objectives are used to provide the direction for action, while actions are directed to completing tasks (to fulfil objectives), generating experiences (or learning) or causing modifications of tasks, objectives, policies, and goals.

IMPLIED CONTRACT

An agreement derived from uncontested assumptions about

or circumstances surrounding a transaction or relationship between two or more persons or entities.

IMPORT

The command or an option in one software package, to use a file in a another file, which was originally created by some other software application.

IMPORT DUTY

A duty charged on goods or services imported into a country.

IMPORT LICENCE

A license given by a government to a trader which permits him to import specified goods into his country.

IMPORT QUOTA

A limit set by a government on how much of a certain type of product can be imported into a country.

IMPORTS

Goods or services purchased from other countries, involving the use of foreign exchange. Imports, like exports, may be visible or invisible.

IMPORTS-RESTRICTIONS ON TRADE

Various restrictions apply to imports. Duty rates on some goods vary according to the type of product and the nature of any existing agreement with the supplying country. Tendencies to impose restrictions are countered both by fear of reprisals by the other country and by the general agreement on tariffs and trade. Other goods may be the subject of quotas, *i.e.*, only a certain quantity may be imported in any one year. All nations have a list of goods, the importing of which is prohibited. Such lists vary widely from country-to-country.

IMPREST

(*i*) The term denotes a particular system of accounting for petty cash within a business. Under the imprest system, the petty cashier receives a fixed float for sundry expenses over a certain period. At the end of that period, or when the float is exhausted, vouchers for all expenses will be presented and the expenditure reimbursed, theoretically returning the float to its original level. The person responsible for petty cash has little opportunity for misappropriation because the reimbursement depends on the production of the vouchers; this gives the employer a reasonable degree of control over sundry disbursements.

(*ii*) A cash advance or loan used in petty cash transactions, where a float is given to the person responsible and the end of a period he provides details of expenditure against that float which is then made up again to its original level and the process repeated.

IMPUTED COSTS

Costs of self-owned factors used in ones own business.

IN KIND

A kind of property, income, payment, receipt, etc., transactions, *i.e.*, receipts or payments made in goods rather than in cash.

INCENTIVE

Financial or other award provided to a subscriber, members enrolled, or beneficiary of a health service, prepaid, or insurance plan, usually in the form of cash or higher benefit levels.

INCENTIVE PLAN CRITERIA

To be effective in motivating employees, incentives should: (*i*) be related to specify behavioural patterns (*e.g.*, better performance), (*ii*) be received immediately after the behaviour is displayed, and (*iii*) reward the employee for consistently displaying the desired behaviour.

INCENTIVE PLANS

Stimulating worker for higher outputs has led to the introduction of incentive plans in industry. Greater productive efforts are rewarded by suitable incentive payments. Norms or standards are carefully laid down either on basis of past performance of the worker or through work measurements. Worker is paid incentive wages by reaching the standard or by exceeding the same.

INCENTIVE WAGES PLAN

Incentive wages relate earnings to productivity and may use premiums, bonuses or a variety of rates to compensate for superior performance.

INCENTIVE

(*i*) Something believed capable of satisfying a particular motive.

(*ii*) Financial or other award provided to a subscriber, members enrolled, or beneficiary of a health service, prepaid, or insurance plan, usually in the form of cash or higher benefit levels.

INCENTIVES, FINANCIAL

Extra payment for production above a predetermined standard.

INCIDENTAL TEACHING

Instruction which is concerned with by-products as well as the accomplishment of an immediate goal.

INCOME

The financial return from one's business, labour or invested capital. The term is complex, varying in meaning.

INCOME AND EXPENDITURE STATEMENT

A profit and loss account used by the organisations which are non-profit-making (such as charities) to indicate the financial state of their operations.

INCOME AVERAGING

The merging of lower income from prior years with present income, divided by the number of years, to achieve an averaged income as the basis for income tax payment. This reduces taxes in the current year.

INCOME BOND

A bond on which interest is paid only when the issuing company has earnings sufficient to pay it.

INCOME PROPERTY

A property that is purchased more for current income generation than for capital appreciation.

INCOME RETURN

Either the annual gain from an investment or the percentage figure found by dividing the annual gain by the initial price of the investment.

INCOME SCHEME

A scheme, usually found in industry but not unknown in commerce, whereby employees are offered benefits (usually monetary) as a reward for increasing efficiency by their own efforts. In the case of non-productive work-force whose efficiency cannot be directly related to output, the incentive may take the form of a special bonus determined by overall profit.

INCOME TAX

(*i*) From a business perspective, a tax on profits from business or work, but not on growth in the value of investments of property. For an individual, an income tax is a tax on personal income from work, less allowable deduction, credits, and other factors.

(*ii*) A tax imposed by the Central Government on one's annual income which exceeds the prescribed limit.

INCORPORATORS

The people who organise an organisation and file its initial articles of organisation with a state.

INCREMENT

In personal management this is a regular and usually automatic, increase in a scale of pay. In ergonomics, it may refer to an increase in a stimulus from the environment of a standard amount, *e.g.*, of illumination. If a person is employed in a grade of 5000-150-6500-200-8500, it means that he is entitled to an increment of ₹ 150 in his salary after serving for one year (for 10 years) and after that is annual increment will be ₹ 200.

INDEMNIFY

To promise to someone that if he should suffer loss as a result of some specified event that he will be reimbursed (but he cannot claim more than he loses).

INDEMNIFY POLICY

An insurance policy or contract that provides cash payments limited by a fixed schedule of payments for covered services, groups of services.

INDEMNITY

This means "security from damage, loss". An assurance to compensate a person (x) for any loss or damage caused by a third person (y).

INDEMNITY FUND

A form of protection against the costs of Industrial Disputes which is provided by employers paying into a special fund.

INDENTURE

A property deed between two more parties.

INDEPENDENT CONTRACTOR

An organisation or person retained by another organisation or person to perform a defined task or produce a specific product. An independent contractor works without control by the contracting organisation, other than the latter's evaluation for satisfactory performance. Independent contractors may be retained for such task as constructing parking lots, installing outside lighting doing landscaping.

INDEPENDENT READING

Reading done without assistance from an instructor.

INDEPENDENT RETAILER

A retail establishment that is not owned or controlled by any other organisation.

INDEX

(*i*) A table that contains the keys to the records of a file and the location where they are stored.

(*ii*) A table, list, or file, usually arranged alphabetically, for facilitating reference to topics, names and objects.

INDEX FILE

Files which are created when any database file is indexed. These are the files with .NDX extension or .CDX in some particular case. These files contains the information which allows the user to access the database file fast and to seek a particular record fast.

INDEX LINKING

A mechanism for offsetting changes in the value of money by making systematic adjustment to payments, such as pensions in the line with changing prices—usually as reflected in the retail price index.

INDEX OF MEMBERS

As index to the register of members in an organisation. Private and public companies must maintain such an index if their total number exceeds fifty.

INDEXATION

The practice, or an instance, of indexing.

INDEXED SEQUENTIAL FILES

A file sequentially arranged in terms of unique record keys. The records in this type of file are organised in sequence and an index table is used to speed up access to the records without requiring a search of the entire file. The records of the file can be stored in random sequence but the index table is in sorted sequence on the key value. This provides the user with a very powerful tool. Not only can the file be processed randomly, but it can also be processed sequentially. Since the index table is in a sorted sequence on the key value, the file management system simply accesses the data records in the order to the index values. Thus indexed sequential files provide the user sequential access, even though the file management system is accessing the data records in a physically random order. This technique of file management is commonly referred to as the Indexed Sequential Access Method (ISAM). Files of this type are called *ISAM files.*

INDIAN COIN

A metal stamped and issued by the Government of India for use as money, under Section 230 of the Indian Penal Code 1860.

INDIANISATION

The transfer of the shares of an industrial units (also ownership) from foreign shareholders to Indian shareholders.

INDIGENOUS CAPITAL

Indigenous capital means the capital resources which are at the disposal of the domestic entrepreneurs.

INDIRECT COST

A cost that is not directly traceable to a particular segment of operation. Also called a *Common Cost*

INDIRECT EXPORTING

Exporting through an intermediary.

INDIRECT LABOUR COSTS

The costs associated with those members of the work-force not directly involved in the production of goods and services, but whose labour is essential to the running of the organisation, *e.g.*, maintenance and secretariat staff. Compare with *Direct Labour Costs.*

INDIRECT TAX

(1) A tax levied in such a way that the person who pays it can recover the amount from sometime else (the payer is said to 'shift' the tax), the excise duties on numerous items like cigarettes, bear, whisky, television, air-conditioners and so many other consumer products are examples of indirect taxes.

(2) A tax levied not on income or profits but on goods or services purchased—for example, Value Added Tax, or Customs and Excise Duty.

INDIRECT-ACTION ADVERTISEMENT

An advertisement designed to stimulate sales over the longer run.

INDIVIDUAL BRAND

A brand assigned to a product within a product line that is not shared by other products in that line.

INDIVIDUAL DIFFERENCES

Individuals are similar, but they are also unique. The study of individual differences such as attitudes, perceptions, and abilities helps a manager explain differences in performance levels.

INDIVIDUAL FACTOR

With reference to perception, characteristic of a person that affects how the person perceives a stimulus.

INDIVIDUALISM-COLLECTIVISM

Individualism emphasises pursuit of individual goals, needs, and success. Collectivism emphasises group need, satisfaction, and performance.

INDORSEE

A person whose name is specified in the indorsement of any instrument, in whose favour a bill, etc., is endorsed.

INDUCTION

Induction refers to the introduction of a person to the job and the organisation. The purpose is to make the employee feel at home and develop a sense of pride in the organisation and commitment to the job. The induction process is also envisaged to the doctrinate, orient, acclimatise and acculturate the person to the job and the organisation.

INDUCTION TRAINING

Employee orientation or induction training is nothing but introduction of the organisation to the newly employed person. The purpose is to give a 'bird's eye view' of the organisation where he has to work.

INDUCTION

(*i*) A process of introducing or orienting new employees to the environment of the organisation. It is very much a socialisation or personalisation problem. A new employee must be made to feel at home after he has been placed on a particular job. He must get himself familiarised with the new environments, new colleagues and new challenges. This will generate in him a sense of belonging and self-confidence.

(*ii*) Act or process of reasoning from a part to a whole, from particulars to generals.

INDUCTIVE REASONING

A form of thinking which proceeds by induction.

INDUSTRIAL BANKS

These are the banks which provide long-term and medium-term loans to the industrial organisations. These banks also assist the industry by providing technical and management assistance to the industries.

INDUSTRIAL DEMOCRACY

A situation in which the management in an organisation or an industry share power with the workers or their representatives in making decisions about their work and about the organisation in general.

INDUSTRIAL DISCIPLINE

In simple words, the term 'discipline' connotes that members of a group conform to the rules and regulations framed by an organisation.

INDUSTRIAL DISEASE

A disease whose origin is directly attributable to conditions in the environment of the work being done *e.g.*, the lung diseases of *silicosis* in minors and *asbestosis* in building workers.

INDUSTRIAL ESPIONAGE

Specifying on an organisation to obtain information of economic (or sometimes in an industrial dispute, political) value that the organisation wishes to keep to itself. In the United Kingdom stealing a trade secret is not itself a criminal offence. Other countries have different laws on industrial espionage.

INDUSTRIAL GOODS

Products which are required by industrial organisations.

INDUSTRIAL MEDICINE

Medical research and practice carried out in an industrial working environment and specialising in industrial disease.

INDUSTRIAL PEACE

Industrial peace is an ideal situation for industrial growth. It is, therefore, desirable to establish cordial labour-management relations. The responsibility of creating industrial peace goes to employers, employees and the government. Industrial peace is possible only when all the three parties take suitable steps for maintaining cordial industrial relations.

INDUSTRIAL RELATIONS

"The term 'industrial relations' refers to the relationships between management and employees or among employees and their organisation that arise out of employment." Its usage is therefore much broader than its original industrial or manufacturing context and extends to issues and procedures concerning employment in any worker environment.

INDUSTRIAL REVOLUTION

The industrial revolution is the name given to the historical process, beginning in the late eighteenth century that led to the industrialisation of the United Kingdom, making it the first industrialised nation and the richest economy the world had ever seen.

INDUSTRIAL UNREST

Industrial unrest is the result of a absence of cordial industrial relations. Strikes, lockouts, demonstrations, picketing, disputes, "go slow", etc. are the usual consequences of industrial unrest. Industrial unrest is visible through strikes, lockouts, demonstrations and so on at the industry, state or national level.

INFANT INDUSTRY

A new industry which is still in the development process is known as *Infant Industry.*

INFANTILISM

Manifestation by an adult or adolescent of infantile traits, physical or mental. Many symptoms of mental disorder are held to be infantilism.

INFERENCE

Judgment; reasoning based on facts, opinions, or observations that are indicative but not conclusive with regard to some circumstances.

INFLATION

In economics this term describes a situation in which prices are rising relatively quickly, as measured by the retail price index, thus causing a fall in the real (as opposed to the nominal) value of money.

INFLUENCE

A transaction in which a person or a group acts in such a way as to change the behaviour of another person or group. Influence is the demonstrated use of power.

INFLUENCER

(*i*) A group member who attempts to persuade the decision-maker, the buying centre role played by organisational members (or outsiders) who affect the purchase decision by supplying advice or information.

(*ii*) The buying-centre role played by organisational members (or outsiders) who affect the purchase decision by supplying advice or information.

INFORMAL COMMITTEES

Informal committees are formed to advise on some problems requiring special skill; and these are not part of organisational structure.

INFORMAL GROUP

A group formed by individuals and developed around common interests and friendships rather than around a deliberate design.

INFORMAL ORGANISATION

Informal organisation refers to the relationships between the people in the organisation based on personal attitudes, emotions, prejudices, likes, dislikes, etc.

INFORMAL TEST

A test which is prepared and given informally, as contrasted to one which has been standardised by statistical procedures.

INFORMATION

(*i*) Data in a format useful to decision-makers.

(*ii*) Generally, knowledge provided by the specific arrangement of language or data elements (or both) in a medium of communication. This definition precludes the use of "data" and "information" as synonyms. Information is the content of a communication, and a communication system is the vehicle for its delivery. The interrelationship between content and communication assures that information is not conveyed without both being present.

(*iii*) The processed, well formatted, meaningful form of the raw data.

INFORMATION FLOW REQUIREMENTS

The amount of information that must be processed by an organisation, group, or individual to perform effectively.

INFORMATION MANAGEMENT

(*i*) The planning, development, organisation, structuring, and transmission or sets of language symbols which, when properly received and interpreted, provide knowledge and influence human endeavour through comprehension and understanding the value of the added knowledge. Information management includes the processes of analysing and resolving problems and administering or facilitating technical, semantic, and effective communication.

(*ii*) This is concerned with applying information technology to the flow of information in an organisation with the intention of ordering it in the best way to achieve organisation goals.

INFORMATION OVERLOAD

A situation in which the sheer amount of information in an information system is simply too great to be coped with by the information management available.

INFORMATION SEARCH

An internal or external search for information carried out by the consumer to reduce uncertainty and provide a basis for evaluating alternatives.

INFORMATION SYSTEM

(*i*) A system, formal or informal, for collecting, and processing data and communicating it at the most appropriate time to all levels of management. The data flowing from the system is helpful to managers for making decisions in the areas of planning and control, or is otherwise needed for financial reporting required under the law.

(*ii*) Any systematic way of organising the handling of information, from informations gathering to information retrieval and use.

INFORMATION TECHNOLOGY

A name given by the intellectuals to signify that the information is now a marketable product and there is certain technology related with information maintenance and marketing.

INFORMATION THEORY

They study of information and the way it is communicated. It originated with mathematicians and engineers and draws heavily on concepts from these fields, but with advances in brain research it has also been used in linguistics and psychology.

INFORMATION

(*i*) Data in a format useful to decision-makers.

(*ii*) Generally, knowledge provided by the specific arrangement of language or data elements (or both) in a medium of communication. This definition precludes the use of "data" and "information" as synonyms. Information is the content of a communication, and a communication system is the vehicle for its delivery. The interrelationship between content and communication assures that information is not conveyed without both being present.

INFRASTRUCTURE

(*i*) The detailed hierarchical structure and function of an organisation; also the physical assets of a nation that relate to its industrial productivity, such as roads, dams, bridges and other resources.

(*ii*) The network of supporting services which underpins an industry or industrial society, such as roads, communications or utilities (Water, Gas, Electricity etc.).

INFRINGEMENT

A breach or violation of a right; also, the unauthorised making, use, selling, or distributing of something protected by a patent, copyright or trademark.

INHIBITION

Mental condition in which a person finds it difficult to begin or continue a course of action; there is a peculiar hesitancy and a feeling as if restrained by an outside agency. Sometimes equals suppression or repression.

INITIATE

To begin something. Initiation refers to the first act that gets a series of sequence of events under way. For example, a manager initiates plans by putting a subordinate to work developing a program or budget.

INITIATING STRUCTURE

Leadership acts that imply the structuring of job tasks and responsibilities for followers.

INJUNCTION

An order issued by a Court that forbids a specified person from taking specified action.

INLAND BILL

A bill of exchange drawn and made-payable within a country or drawn upon a resident within the territory.

IN-LINE PROCESSING

Getting the information from remote distance terminal by telematic method using communication channel.

INNOVATION

Development and/or introduction of new ideas, new ways of doing things, new products.

INNOVATOR

A member of the first group of customer to reduce uncertainty and provide a basis for evaluating alternatives.

INSEPARABILITY

A characteristic of services that reflects the fact that production often is not distinct from the consumption of a service.

INSERTION ORDER

A formal order from an advertiser or an advertising agency to a publisher that the publisher should include a specified advertisement in a publication at a specified time.

IN-SERVICE TRAINING

Training carried out while in employment, with the aim of developing skills or enhancing experience which will be useful in that employment in the future.

INSIDE SELLING

Non-retail selling from the employer's place of business.

INSOLVENCY

A person or organisation is insolvent when he or it is unable to pay debts when they become due.

INSTITUTIONAL ADVERTISEMENT

An advertisement designed to promote an organisational image, stimulate generic demand for a product, or build goodwill for an industry.

INSTITUTIONAL FINANCE

Large number of financial institutions started after the independence of the country to provide medium- and long-term funds to the industries. They are providing secured funds at reasonable rates of interest both for fixed and working capital requirements.

INSTRUMENT

A document by which any right or liability is, or purports to be created, transferred, limited, extended, extinguished or recorded [Section 2 (14) of the Indian Stamp Act, 1899]. Any tool of a profession or job including, for example, such diverse items as a scalpel, legal document, check, resonance fork, or microscope; and also, written document; a formal or legal document such as contract or will. Also, a negotiable instrument (such as a cheque).

INSTRUMENTALITY

In the expectancy theory of motivation, the relationship between first- and second-level outcomes.

INSTRUMENTATION

A source of error in experimental results, caused by changes in the measurement instruments or the conditions under which the measuring of participants' performance is done (*e.g.*, wear on machinery, fatigue on the part of observers).

INSURABLE RISK

A risk that is one of a large, homogenous group of similar risks that would incur a definable and quantifiable loss, for which the loss in individual cases is accidental or fortuitous; for which the potential loss is large enough to cause hardship.

INSURANCE

It provides an opportunity to businessmen to develop sense of independence and security and freedom from anxiety. Insurance stands for the security against heavy risks. It makes business operations very secure by making provision against all probable losses and damages. The function of insurance is to protect the trader against all such possible losses. Insurance is a co-operative device of mutual help. The amount of risk borne by individual trader is reduced by distributing the burden of loss over all the members engaged in the work of distribution. Insurance is based on the principle of pooling of risks' whereby a large number of people are made to contribute to funds, out of which compensation is paid to those who may happen to suffer from a particular type of loss. Transference of risk to someone else, especially by means of a contract of insurance.

INSURANCE COMPANY

Any corporation engaged in the business of furnishing insurance protecting to consumers and corporate or group purchasers.

INSURED LOAN

In the context of federal credit programmes, a loan for which a private lender is assured of repayment of the federal government for part or all of the principal or interest due. For example, *Guaranteed Student Loan* (GSL).

INSURER

A person, company or an organisation that undertakes to make good the loss (indemnify) to another in the event of his death, or any personal loss or damage caused to his goods or property; also called 'assurer' or 'underwriter'

INTAKE

The administrative and assessment process for admitting a person to a health care programme or facility.

INTANGIBILITY

A characteristic of services referring to the customer's inability to see, hear, smell, feel, or taste the service product.

INTANGIBLE ASSETS

Long-term assets of a business entity without any physical characteristics. These include goodwill, patents, franchisees, formation expenses and copyrights.

INTANGIBLE PROPERTY

A right to ownership of a specified benefits that is not a right to possession of an item of tangible property, *e.g.*, a debt, a share in a company, patent rights. Also a collective of such property.

INTEGRATED INJECTION LOGIC

A circuit design that uses bipolar transistors to achieve medium level of performance and low power consumption.

INTEGRATED INJECTION LOGIC

A circuit design that uses bipolar transistors to achieve medium level of performance and low power consumption.

INTEGRATION

(*i*) A concept in the *Lawrence* and *Lorsch* research that refers to the process of achieving unity of effort among the organisation's various subsystems. The techniques for achieving integration range from rules and procedures to plans, to mutual adjustment.

(*ii*) The process of organising different parts into a whole of a higher order. It is used widely in science, from the organisation of nervous impulse necessary for any kind of behaviour up to the organisation of a whole society.

INTEGRATION, BACKWARD

Acquisition by a corporation of sources of supplies.

INTEGRATION, FORWARD

Acquisition by a corporation of marketing outlets or of manufacturing facilities to reduce the number of intermediaries between the company and the consumer.

INTEL

A short form of Integrated Electronics. It is a firm which was established by *Gordon More* and *Robert Noyce* in USA to manufacture microchips which is a leading company in world for fabricating the microprocessors.

INTELLECTUAL SKILL

Logical thinking is the fundamental requirement for the development of intellectual skill. If a tactical strategy is to be developed in an organisation, the managers must have the ability for logical analysis with a deep understanding and insight into the problems involved. No longer can he depend upon initiator or preconceived notions. He must use judgment to analyse the data and find the correct solution.

INTELLIGENCE

Ability to exercise the higher mental functions.

INTELLIGENCE QUOTIENT (IQ)

Mental age in years and fractions of years divided by chronological age; *i.e.*, by the number of years and fractions of years one has lived.

INTELLIGENCE SCALE

A series of tests so arranged that different degrees of intelligence may be indicated by more or less equal steps.

INTELLIGENCE TEST

A device for measuring the intelligence of individuals. These are tests to measure one's intellect or qualities of understanding. They are also referred to as tests of mental ability. The traits of intelligence measured include: reasoning, verbal and non-verbal fluency, comprehension, numerical, memory and spatial relation ability.

INTELLIGENCE

Ability to exercise the higher mental functions.

INTELLIGENT SOFTWARE DEVELOPMENT TOOLS

Special programs developed to help the programmers and increase their productivity in various stages of software development. Also known as *Software Development Tools.*

INTENSIVE DISTRIBUTION

(*i*) A distribution strategy aimed at obtaining maximum exposure for the product at the retail level.

(*ii*) A policy of organisations to maximise the availability of products.

INTERACTION

(*i*) Any interpersonal contact in which one individual acts and one or more other individuals respond to the action.

(*ii*) Effects the confounding of results that arises when any of the sources of errors in experimental results interact with the experimental treatment. For example, results may be confounded when the types of individuals withdrawing from any experiment (mortality) may differ for the experimental group and the control group.

(*iii*) Reciprocal reactions of people in a group to each other or of variables in a situation or machine.

INTERCOM

Large commercial houses have generally an interdepartmental telephone system of their own. Any department can ring up the other and the executives can get into touch with different departments through the internal telephone connections. This saves the time involved in sending messengers from room to room. Messenger service is also, costly, wasteful and liable to error. Interdepartmental communication is economical and aids in efficient working of the office.

INTERDEPARTMENTAL STRIFE

Some foremen seek release from pressure by continuously trying to blame others for the troubles that exist. In some plants much time is spent by certain factory supervisors is trying to lay the blame for errors and problems on their fellow supervisors.

INTEREST

The fee received for lending money; money paid for the use of money; also a broad term for any right in property. For example, both an owner who mortgages land the person who lends the owner money on the mortgage have an interest in the land.

INTEREST GROUP

A group that forms because of some special topic of interest. Generally, when the interest declines or a goal has been achieved, the group disbands.

INTEREST ON CAPITAL

Interest charged by a proprietor in business or by partners in a partnership business on the invested capital.

INTERFACE

An electronic circuit that is fitted with the equipments to allow one type of electronic unit to communicate with another electronic or mechanical unit.

INTERGROUP CONFLICT

Conflict between groups, which can be functional or dysfunctional.

INTERIM AUDIT

(*i*) Interim audit is conducted for a part of the accounting period with some clear objectives in view, such a declaration of dividend or take some mid-term important decision regarding price, profits or investments etc. It involves the complete checking of the accounts pertaining to a period under review. It is a kind of audit which is undertaken between the two balance sheets audits. The work of the final audit becomes much easier if this type of audit has been already undertaken.

(*ii*)Audit conducted for a part of the financial year with the objective of declaring interim financial results.

INTERIM FACILITIES

Temporary facilities planned and built to meet short-term requirements (ten years or less) while decisions are reached about the planning and construction of permanent facilities.

INTERIM RATE

A uniform monetary amount for payment of a defined amount and a specified composition of health care service (or a defined level of a specified composition of services over given time period) which is assigned by an insurer or other third party payer to provide interim payments to a health care facility until a more accurate rate can be determined. Final payment is then established by adjustments to the total of interim payments based on the determined rate.

INTER-LOCKING DIRECTORSHIP

A device of inter-locking directorship has also been used by the Government to ensure control and co-ordination between different enterprises working in the same field. For example, the Chairman of the Air India International and Indian Airlines Corporation is one and the same person.

INTERMEDIARY

(*i*) A public or private individual, agency, or organisation functioning as an administrative, evaluative, deliberative, consultative, or arbitrative agent between a programme and one or more constituent or interest groups.

(*ii*) A general name for a person who acts as a link in the flow of goods from a supplier to a final consumer.

INTERMITTENT REINFORCEMENT

A schedule that results in reinforcing behaviour only after some responses and not after each response.

INTERNAL AUDIT

(*i*) The process of reviewing on a regular basis some aspect of a company's operations or organisation. Most common is a financial audit but other types include manpower audit, technology audit, social audit, innovation audit and energy audit.

(*ii*) A system of audit in which the auditors of an organisation audit its books of accounts.

INTERNAL FORCES

Forces for change that occur within the organisation and that can usually be traced to process and behavioural causes.

INTERNAL MARKETING

Marketing efforts aimed at a company's (especially a service business's) own employees who have contact with the ultimate consumers or who directly affect consumers' satisfaction with the product.

INTERNAL STORAGE

The addressable storage area inside a digital computer which is directly accessible to the central processing unit.

INTERNATIONAL DEPARTMENT

An organisational unit that manages the firm's international marketing operations.

INTERNATIONAL FRANCHISING

A form of licensing in which a company establishes foreign franchises. Franchising involves a contractual agreement between a franchiser, often a manufacturer or wholesaler, and a franchisee, typically an independent retailer, by which the franchisee distributes the franchiser's product.

INTERNATIONAL MARKETER

Any organisation that sells its products beyond its home nation's boundaries.

INTERNATIONAL MARKETING

(*i*)Across national boundaries.

(*ii*)The evolution of international markets is one of the most significant trends in contemporary marketing. The marketing knowledge and ability possessed by multinational firms can aid immensely in the development of balanced economies in the both new and changing politico-economic systems. Marketing managers must recognise, analyse and adjust to the marketing systems of each international market.

INTERNET

A very huge network which is spread in almost all the countries of world connecting about 150 million people world wide through computers.

INTERNSHIP TRAINING

This method of training refers to a joint program of training in which the technical and business houses co-operate. The object of such cooperations is to provide such training as will bring about a balance between theory and practice. For this purpose, students may be sent from their schools to factories for practical training during vacations.

INTERPERSONAL COMMUNICATION

Communication that flows from individual to individual in face-to-face and group settings.

INTERPERSONAL CONFLICT

The conflict that a person faces internally, as when an individual experiences personal frustration, anxiety, and stress.

INTERPERSONAL ORIENTATION

A concept that refers to whether a person is more concerned with achieving good social relations than with achieving a task.

INTERPERSONAL REWARDS

Extrinsic rewards such as receiving recognition or being able to interact socially on the job.

INTERPERSONAL STYLE

The way in which an individual prefers to relate to others.

INTERPOLATION

The process of estimating intermediate values between two known values.

INTERPRET

To explain the meaning of interpretation involves telling people what something means in terms of their interest and needs. A policy is interpreted when its meaning is clarified and applied to the situation or the condition prevailing in a specific unit.

INTERPRETER

A kind of translator which converts the program of high level language into a program of machine language. It converts one statement at a time and executes that immediately.

INTER-ROLE CONFLICT

A type of conflict that occurs when different individuals define a role according to different sets of expectations, making it impossible for the person occupying the role to satisfy all of the expectations. This type of conflict is more likely to occur when a given role was a complex role set.

INTERRUPT

An electrical signal which is generated by a device to disturb the currently ongoing processing when it requires attention from the central processor.

INTESTATE

Dying without making a will; and intestate person is someone who dies without making a valid will.

INTERVENTION

The process by which either outsiders or insiders assume the role of a change agent in the OD program.

INTERVIEW

Interview is an oral examination of candidates for employment. No selection process is complete without one or more interviews.

Interview is the most common and core method of both obtaining information from jobseekers, and decision-making on their suitability or otherwise.

INTERVIEWING, INDIRECT

In viewing in which the interview err does not guide the discussion but says only enough to encourage the person interviewed to express himself freely.

INTRAMURAL SERVICES

Intramural services are those which are provided within the factory (such as safety, health and counselling services).

INTRINSIC REWARDS

Rewards that are part of the job itself. The responsibility, challenge, and feedback characteristics of the job are intrinsic rewards.

INTRODUCTION STAGE

The stage in the product life cycle when the new product is attempting to gain a foothold in the market.

INTUITION

Intuition is characterised by the use of hunches, inner feelings, or the "gutfeeling" of the person reaching a business decision. Suggestions, influences, preferences and the psychological make up of the deciding individual play an important part; the subject element is vital. It is believed by many that the intuitive decider has more "precognitive" ability and is better able to anticipate the future in instances where reliable data are lacking.

INVENTORY

(*i*) Stocks on hand. May be stocks of raw material of work in process, or of finished goods.

(*ii*) The various forms of material held by a company at any time raw materials, partly finished products (work-in-progress) and finished goods awaiting dispatch. In accounting, the term is used to describe the costs of such materials.

(*iii*) A detailed descriptive list of goods, including merchandise, stock of goods, raw-materials, consumable stores, work-inprogress and items like stationery, spare parts and tools.

INVENTORY TURNOVER

The number of times the average inventory has been sold during a period. Its ratio is obtained by dividing the cost of goods sold during a period with the average inventory for the period.

INVENTORY, MANAGEMENT

A listing of the managers within the company and their qualifications, often with notations on when each will be ready for promotion.

INVESTMENT INCOME

Income used for computing the share of investment of a non-resident Indian under the existing income-tax laws.

INVOICE DISCOUNTING

The practice of obtaining money on the security of books debts (*i.e.* money to be received). A company which finds that it has too much working capital tied up in book debts may sell these debts to a finance company. This is known as invoice discounting.

INVOICE

A detailed list of goods supplied or services performed with a statement of their value or the charge made for them.

I.O.SYS

A DOS file which is an alternative to IBMBIO.COM.

IRRELEVANT MATERIAL

Facts for information unrelated to the subject under the discussion.

IRREVOCABLE CREDIT

A credit that can be withdrawn or amended only by agreement between the applicant and the beneficiary.

ISOLATION EFFECT

An effect by which a product appears more attractive than in isolation.

ISSUE

A block of securities that are issued at the same time and all carry the same rights.

ISSUED CAPITAL

(*i*) The amount of capital actually issued by a company. Authorised capital is issued normally in the form of shares. Share capital may come from sale of ordinary shares, preference shares, etc. Issued capital is not the same thing as called-up capital or paid-up capital.

(*ii*) The value represented by the face value of all the shares or other securities issued by a firm.

(*iii*) The normal value of all the shares in a company that have been allotted.

ISSUING HOUSE

A financial institutional which acts an intermediary between those seeking capital (usually industries) and those able to provide it. This house handles issues on behalf of companies, either by full prospectus or by an introduction or placing. They also often work as underwriters of share issues or as merchant banks.

ITEM ANALYSIS

A technique to determine the effectiveness of different items on a rest in its discrimination among the people who take it.

J

JAVA

An internet language with the help of which applets are developed.

JOB

(*i*) A job is a type of position within the organisation. If a large insurance company employs sixty life insurance actuaries, then there are sixty positions, but just one life insurance actuary job.

(*ii*) A piece of work or an order for a piece of work to be done. The term is also used more widely to describe one's livelihood. A job is therefore a unit of work large enough to be the basis of an occupation. Systematic determination of the proper relationships among the wages and salaries paid for various jobs within a company.

JOB ANALYSIS

(*i*) The process of defining and studying a job in terms of behaviour and specifying education and training needed to perform the job.

(*ii*) A job analysis is a systematic exploration of the activities within a job. It is a basic technical procedure, one that is used to define the duties, responsibilities, and accountabilities of a job. It is a key role for practitioners of industrial psychology where the elements masking up a job are studied in an attempt to match the tasks and skills necessary for successful preformation with the ability of the worker to perform them. Job analysis is an essential prerequisite for the study of jobs and job-holders and is therefore an important tool of personnel management.

JOB CARD

This is the card which carries the first JCL statement in a job to identify the beginning of the job.

JOB CONTENT

The specific activities required in a job. The physical environment and other working conditions, along with other factors considered to be extrinsic to a job.

JOB DEFINITION

The determination of task requirements of each job in the organisation. The first sub-problem of the organising decision.

JOB DEPTH

The amount of control that an individual has to alter or influence the job and the surrounding environment.

JOB DESCRIPTION

(*i*) It is desirable to define the responsibilities of a job (job description) and to specify the qualifications necessary to fill the particular job (job specification). At one extreme top management might appoint a general sales manager and just leave it to him to sell the product. At the opposite extreme, before looking for a general sales manager, a careful job description maybe drawn up of what the job involves and from that a specification made of the kind of man needed to fill it. The broad outline of what tasks a job consists of delineating its duties and responsibility and the position of the job within the organisation.

(*ii*) A written description of the scope, responsibilities, expectations, etc., of an individual's job.

JOB DESIGN

(*i*) The process by which managers decide individual job tasks and authority.

(*ii*) One of the central concerns of industrial society. In addition to providing all of our goods and services, work provides our social identities and is the single most significant determinant of our physical and emotional health. Organising work in a manner consistent with societal goals has always been the basic task of management. The scientific management movement, has concerned itself solely with the physical considerations of work; it was human engineering. A modern job design purview seeks to address to totality of these concerns. The process of relating all the tasks to be performed within an organisation to specific jobs.

JOB ENLARGEMENT

(*i*) An administrative action that involves increasing the range of a job by increasing the number of tasks. Supposedly, this action results in better performance and a more satisfied work-force.

(*ii*) Increasing the responsibilities or variety of a job.

(*iii*) Expanding the content of a job to include new responsibilities that will usually require training and the acquisition of new skills.

(*iv*) Widening the content or increasing the responsibilities of a job.

JOB ENRICHMENT

(*i*) A term often confused or used interchangeably with job enlargement. Enlarging a job-adding additional but similar duties to the job—does not substantively change and by no means enriches it; it is nothing more than horizontal loading—laying similar tasks alongside one another.

(*ii*) An approach, developed by *Herzbergy* that involves increasing the individual's discretion to select activities and outcomes. It seeks to improve task efficiency and human satisfaction by means of building into people's jobs greater scope for personal achievement and recognition, more challenging and responsible work, and more opportunity for individual advancement and growth.

JOB EVALUATION

(*i*) The assignment of dollar values to a job.

(*ii*) A method of comparing jobs for their relative value to an organisation and then determining on the basis a hierarchy of pay appropriate to each job. The method uses such factors as complexity, experience, responsibility, skill, etc.

JOB GRADING

Job Grading is the classification and analysis of each type of job being performed in an organisation. As a matter of fact, it is one of the methods of job evaluation. Grading involves rating for each job indicating how its contribution compares in value to all other jobs in the organisation and then grouping them on some specified basis such as kind of work or pay.

JOB LONGEVITY

The concept that length of time spent in a job is an important factor in determining what contributes most to an individual's job satisfaction. For example, there is evidence that after five years in a job, factors in the organisational environment like pay, fringe benefits and relationships with colleagues and supervisors are more important than the performance of the job itself.

JOB MOBILITY

The extent to which workers are prepared to change job, especially if a change requires geographical relocation.

JOB ORDER TECHNOLOGY

A form of production in which products are tailor-made to customer specifications.

JOB POSTING

A system that allows and encourages employees to apply for other job in their organisation.

JOB RANGE

The number of operations that a job occupant performs to complete a task.

JOB REDESIGN

Redesigning the jobs of individuals, usually along the lines suggested by the job characteristics model of job design, in order to improve performance. May be used as an intervention in organisational development.

JOB RELATIONSHIPS

The interpersonal relationships required or made possible on a job.

JOB REQUIREMENTS

Factors such as education, experience, degrees, licences, and other personal characteristics required to perform a job.

JOB ROTATION

(*i*) A form of training that involves moving an employee from one workstation to another. In addition to achieving the training objective, this procedure is also designed to reduce boredom.

(*ii*) The systematic moving of people at the same level in an organisation from one job to another. On the shop floor it is done to relieve boredom and monotony; as part of management development it is done to give managers a broader experience of the organisation.

JOB SATISFACTION

(*i*) The attitude that workers have about their jobs. It results from their perception of the jobs.

(*ii*) The extent to which a worker is content with the rewards he/she gets out of his/her job, particularly in terms of intrinsic motivation.

JOB SHARING

The partition or sharing by two persons working part-time of the same job.

JOB SIMPLICATION

The process of using people like machines by reducing their job to consist of the smallest task possible with the least amount of discretion in it. It is particularly the work on an assembly line. Compare with *Work Simplication.*

JOB SPECIFICATION

The job specification states the minimum acceptable qualifications that the incumbent must possess to perform the job successfully. Based on the information acquired through job analysis, the job specification identifies the knowledge, skills, and abilities needed to do the job effectively.

JOB TICKET

A document used to instruct a worker to perform a particular operation on specified pieces of work. It is usually returned by the worker to signify that the operation is complete, often with a statement of time spent from wages or costs may be calculated. Also called a *Work Ticket*.

JOB TRAINING

Job training relates to specific job which the worker has to handle. It gives information about machines, process of production, instructions to be followed, methods to be used and so on.

JOB TRANSITION

The process of moving from one job to another, either within the same organisation or between organisations. A time of heightened psychological activity and stress.

JOB VENTURE

An enterprise jointly undertaken by two or more companies that are independent of each other.

JOB

A piece of work or an order for a piece of work to be done. The term is also used more widely to describe one's livelihood. A job is therefore a unit of work large enough to be the basis of an occupation.

JOBBER

A merchant middleman who buys from an importer or manufacturer or some large wholesaler and sells to retailers.

JOBBERY

Originally a term of abuse for sharp practice in stock exchange dealings only, but now used more generally.

JOB-CENTERED LEADER

A person who closely supervises and observes the work of others.

JOB-FRAGMENTATION

Splitting an existing job up and dividing it amongst other jobs, or creating a new series of smaller jobs.

JOINT CONSULTATIVE MACHINERY

Institution and procedures that enable regular joint consultations to take place.

JOINT DEBT

Debt due from one or two persons to a creditor. For instance, debts due from a firm and also from each of its partners constitutes a joint debt burden.

JOINT DECISION-MAKING

Decision-making shared by all or some members of a group. Often, one decision-maker dominates the process. Decisions truly made jointly are syncratic decisions.

JOINT LIABILITY

Responsibility accepted by two or more persons to repay a debt, making them jointly liable for the same.

JOINT OWNERSHIP VENTURE

In international marketing, a joint venture in which domestic and foreign partners invest capital and share ownership and control.

JOINT PRODUCTS

Two or more products ordinarily produced under a given process. Production of one product also gives by-products of some kind. It is possible, however, to have alternate processes which yield differing quantities of the two products. Products that a manufacturer produces from the same initial materials and where some operations are performed before the products are separately recognisable.

JOINT STOCK

Stock or shares held in common by a voluntary association or by a group of persons jointly formed for a common purpose by subscribing capital.

JOINT STOCK BANK

Historically, a bank is a joint-stock company rather than a partnership. Some of the larger banks have numerous branches and conduct a substantial proportion of their business with customers or current account.

JOINT STOCK COMPANY

A form of limited liability company where the liability is limited to the nominal value of shares issued.

JOINT VENTURE

(i) A project of company in which two or more individuals or organisations participate, agreeing to share the risks and benefits according to some agreed formula.

(*ii*) A business contract or management effort between two persons, companies, or organisations involving risk and benefit sharing.

JOINT VENTURING

In international marketing, an arrangement between a domestic company and a foreign host company to set up production and marketing facilities in a foreign market.

JOURNAL

(*i*) A chronological recording of accounting transactions. After the journals are balanced at the end of an accounting cycle (usually a month), they are posted to the general ledger and to the subsidiary ledger accounts.

(*ii*) A book of Daily Record, containing entries used to aid subsequent entries in a ledger. It is a book of original or prime entry.

JOURNEYMAN

The traditional term for skilled worker who has completed a craft or trade apprenticeship but is not yet a master craftsman in self-employment. In previous times such a worker would need to travel around offering his skills to a master until such time as he could set up in business for himself.

JOYSTICK

A manual device with a control lever set in a box which could be moved and titled in various directions. This is attached to the computer and is used to control the position of cursor on screen. As it moves the cursor also moves.

JUDGMENT SAMPLE

A non-probability sample chosen according to the judgment and experience of the selector.

JUNIOR LEVEL MANAGEMENT

The term applied to managers who are relatively low in the hierarchy of an organisation because they are junior in age and/or level of responsibility and authority.

JUSTIFICATION

Reasons why a project should be undertaken. Generally stated as return to be expected on the investment, although in some cases projects may be justified by pointing out that they are necessary for such things as employee safety, company prestige, or preservation of market share.

JUST-IN-TIME (JIT) INVENTORY SYSTEM

A materials management system in which inventory arrives just in time for use.

JUVENILE

It refers to persons of adolescence and near-adolescence; immature behaviour.

K

KAIZEN

The Japanese concept of continuous improvement. Many Japanese manufacturer use several small incremental improvements generated with their *kaizen* programs to continuously upgrade the quality of their products and processes. All these minor improvements cannot be easily copied by competitors, and collectively they can provide a significant advantage.

KANBAN OR ZERO INVENTORY

A Japanese term referring to purchasing raw materials by using a special ordering form.

KAO

The dominant Japanese company in the branded packaged goods industry, the benefits of scale economies have been more than offset by failure to customise products to the tastes and preferences of non-Japanese consumers.

KEIRETSUS

Are collections of major business organisations whose managers effectively motivate organisation members. Japanese leaders describe the *Keiretsu* not as a closed society but as a society of long-term relationships. *Fortune* describes it as a system that "pulls together government, industry, capital, and the best information on high technology worldwide to create a machine that grinds competitors into powder".

KEY JOB

Represent a cross section of the jobs in an organisation, usually, reflecting a mix of scores on the compensable factors, various levels in the organisation, and sizable proportion of the organisation's work force. At least 25 to 30 per cent of an organisation's jobs are typically designated as key jobs.

KEY SUCCESS FACTORS

In determining which aspects to include in a functional audit, managers might find it useful to compile a list of the internal characteristics that appear to be the *key success factors* in the industry.

KEY TECHNOLOGY

A technology that has proved its worth but has yet to come into widespread use. Such a technology provides a competitive advantage because its dissemination is limited.

KICKBACK

Part of a person's payment for doing a job that he gives to someone else for getting him the job.

KILO CYCLES PER SECOND

One thousand cycles per second.

KINESTHETIC IMAGERY

Muscle imagery.

KINESIC BEHAVIOUR

A category of non-verbal communication that includes body movements, such as gestures, facial expressions, eye movements, and posture.

KINETIC REVERSALS

Confusion of directional sequence, such as left for felt.

KITE

An accommodation bill. A cheque drawn by someone who knows there is no money in the bank account he is drawing on.

KNOWLEDGE-BASED SYSTEMS

(*i*) Is a system that uses knowledge about a narrowly defined, complex area to act as a consultant to a human. In some instances, an organisation may rely significantly on the knowledge of one or more individuals in particular areas that may be captured in an expert system.

(*ii*) Although managers often switch companies and work in different industries, they are apt to run into difficulties if they don't have a reasonably extensive knowledge base relevant to their particular managerial job. A *knowledge base* can include information about an industry and its technology, company policies and practices, company goals and plans, company culture, the personalities of key organisation members, and important suppliers and customers. For example, *Kotter* found that one reason why the general managers in his study were able to accomplish so much within short periods of time was that they could take action with only small bits of information at their disposal. Their extensive knowledge base enabled them to attach the appropriate meaning to the information fragments they obtained.

KNOWLEDGE POWER

The power that comes from a person's possessing special knowledge or skills. It is considered by some to be the most effective type of power.

KNOW-HOW

A term used to describe saleable knowledge of technique or special skill which have been developed within an industry for use on certain projects. This may be the result of many years of intensive research and development in the manufacture of a valuable product. Knowledge of the techniques or practical details that enable a process or operation to be carried out efficiently.

KNOWLEDGE OF RESULTS

The process of giving people feedback on their performance of a task. In the study of learning this has been found to increase someone's motivation to perform better.

KNOWLEDGE WORKER

A term sometimes used for a person working in the communication of information particularly in information management.

KONDRATIEFF CYCLE

The term given by Economist *Bloke Kondratieff* noticed by the nineteenth century Russian Economist *Nikolai Kondratieff.* This was the appearance of long, but regularly occurring cycles or waves in economic activity that oscillated between boom and recession every fifty years or so.

L

LA PROSPECTIVE

A method of technological, or qualitative, forecasting that addresses a variety of possible futures by evaluating major environmental variables, assessing the likely strategies of other significant actors, devising possible counter strategies, developing ranked hypotheses about the variables, and formulating alternative scenarios that do not gready inhibit freedom of choice.

LABEL

(*i*) The paper or plastic sticker at tacked to a product that carries product information.

(*ii*) This is the identifier string which is used to identify an instruction statement or message or record or item or file. One command of DOS.

LABEL RECORD

This is a magnetic record that contains the information about the file stored on magnetic tape.

LABORATORY EXPERIMENT

(*i*) Experiments for which the environment in which the subject works is created by the researcher. The laboratory setting permits the researcher to control closely the experimental conditions.

(*ii*) An experiment in a highly controlled environment.

LABORATORY TECHNICIAN

Person trained to carry on technical work.

LABOUR-DIVISION OF

By division of labour we mean the division of work into various parts and sub-parts and each part is done by a specialised worker.

LABOUR FORCE

The people in an economy who are available to perform work. The collection of people who perform the work of an organisation.

LABOUR MOBILITY

Movement of workers from job to job.

LABOUR SUPPLY

The element of the task environment that consists of those individuals who are potentially employable by an organisation.

LABOUR TURNOVER

(*i*) 'Labour turnover' may be defined as the rate of change in the number of employees of a concern during a definite period, commonly a month. In other words, it is a measure of the extent to which old employees leave and new employees enter the service of the concern.

(*ii*) The percentage of the total labour force of an organisation leaving its employment and being replaced over a given period of time, usually a year.

LABOUR WELFARE

(*i*) The Oxford dictionary defines *Labour Welfare* as "efforts to make life worth living for workmen". These efforts have their origin either in some statute formed by the State or in some local custom or in a collective agreement or in the employer's own initiative. Means of 'labour welfare', 'worker's welfare' are used interchangeable to denote various services provided by the employers to the employees in addition to wages. According to *Arthur James Todd*, "Labour welfare means anything done for the comfort and improvement, intellectual or social, of the employees over and above the wages paid which is not a necessity of the industry".

(*ii*) Labour welfare work is necessary not only for the workers' benefit but all the more so in the employer's own interest. Welfare work has beneficial effects on the work. The welfare measures influence the sentiments of the workers and contribute to the maintenance of industrial peace. When the worker feels that the employer and the government are interested in his day-to-day life he would like to take advantage of such facility and make his to happier. Thus his tendency to grouse and grumble are likely to be reduced to a minimum.

LABOUR-INTENSIVE INDUSTRY

(*i*) An industry requiring small amounts of capital per employee.

(*ii*) A firm or process which relies mainly on labour rather than on technology to produce its goods or services.

(*iii*) The term used for relying mainly on labour in the production of goods and services as opposed to the investment of capital in the process of automation, *e.g.*, as in teaching or tailoring. It is, therefore, the opposite of capital- intensive.

LABOUR-MANAGEMENT RELATIONS

The process through which employers and unions negotiate pay, hours of work, and other conditions of employment; sign a contract governing such conditions for a specific period of time; and share responsibilities for administering the resulting contract.

LAG TIME

The number of days between the date a service is rendered and the receipt of a claim by an insurer, service plan, prepaid plan, or other third party for processing and payment.

LAGGARD

A member of the group of final adaptors in the diffusion process.

LAISSEZ FAIRE

(*i*) The doctrine that governments need not interfere in economic affairs.

(*ii*) The behavioural style of leaders who generally give the group complete freedom, provide necessary materials, participate only to answer questions, and avoid giving feedback.

(*iii*) The theory or practice of noninterference by government in the economic or industrial affairs of a country.

LAN

(*i*) *Local Area Network* which is the collection of interconnected systems within a single room or a single building or within the buildings in a single geographical area.

(*ii*) Local area networks (LANs) connect computers and other information processing devices within a limited physical area, such as an office, a classroom, a building, manufacturing plant, or other work site. LANs have become common place in many organisations for providing telecommunications network capabilities that link end users in offices, departments, and other workgroups. LANs use a variety of telecommunications media, such as ordinary telephone wiring coaxial cable, or even wireless radio systems to interconnect microcomputer workstations and computer peripherals. To communicate over the network, each PC usually has a circuit board called a *Network Interface Card.* Most LANs use a more powerful microcomputer having a large hard disk capacity, called a file server or network server, that contains a network operating system program that controls telecommunications and the use and sharing of network resources. For example, it distributes copies of common data files and software packages to the other microcomputers in the network and controls access to shared laser printers and other network peripherals. Main LAN types are:

(*a*) Client Server Networks,

(*b*) Peer-to-Peer Networks.

LANGUAGE PROCESSOR

Ready-made program that translates source language programs into a form that can be executed on a computer.

LANGUAGE TRANSLATORS

Programs which translates program of one language into another language programs. Also known as *Emulator Programs.*

LANGUAGE-RHYTHM CLUE

A word which suggests a relationship or an opposite such as one, two, three; up, down, high, low.

LANHAM ACT

A U.S. law declaring that brand names cannot be confusingly similar to registered trademarks.

LAPSE

In insurance the termination of an insurance policy due to a policy, holder's failure to pay the premium within the prescribed time period.

LARGE SCALE INTEGRATION

Refers Integrated circuits.

LARGE-BATCH AND MASS PRODUCTION

A type of technology in which products are manufactured in large quantities, frequently on an assembly line.

LASER PRINTER

A printer of non-impact category which uses laser beam to form the dotmatrix characters on a drum of photo-conducting material which is then transferred to the paper one page at a time.

LAST IN, FIRST OUT

A method of valuing stock or taking inventory in which the prices of the newest items purchased are applied to the entire stock. Items received last are then first to be sold; a method of choosing people or redundancy in an organisation where the last to be hired are the first to be made redundant.

LATE MAJORITY

In the diffusion process, a group of consumers who purchase a product after the early majority, when it is no longer perceived as risky.

LATERAL IMBALANCE

A tendency of one or both eyes to deviate inward or outward from their normal position.

LATERAL RELATIONS

An approach to horizontal coordination that involves coordinating efforts through communicating and problem-solving with peers in other departments or units, rather than referring most is sues up the hierarchy for resolution.

LAW

Most of the management decisions have to be taken in a legal environment where the requirements of a number of statutory provisions or regulations are to be fulfilled. Some of the Acts which have their influence on management decisions are as follows: *The Companies Act, The Controller of Capital Issue Act, MRTP Act, FERA Act, FEMA Act* etc.

LAW OF EFFECT

A concept on which reinforcement theory relies heavily which states that behaviours having pleasant or positive consequences are more likely to be repeated and that behaviour having unpleasant or negative consequences are less likely to be repeated.

LAW OF THE SITUATION

The factors in a situation which appear to indicate that a certain course is obviously the sensible one.

LAYING OFF

A business which is in financial trouble may need to reduce its level of operations and in doing so it may be necessary to reduce its work-force. This could also be brought about by a continual dislocation of production due to disruptions at the supplier's factory.

LAYMAN ACT

A U.S. Law declaring that brand names cannot be confusingly similar to registered trademarks.

LEAD AND LAG METHOD

A method of forecasting based on the idea that certain sets of economic indicators (statistics) have risen or fallen in advance of changes in the economy as a whole, whereas others have changed as the economy moved from prosperity to recession or *vice versa*, and still others have lagged behind changes in the economy.

LEAD TIME

The time taken to complete a cycle of activity. The term is usually used in reference to the production process, from the initial idea to the finished product, although it can refer to the time-lag in supplying an order.

LEAD

A short summary serving as an introduction to a news story or article.

LEADER-MEMBER RELATIONS

A factor in the *Fiedler Contingency Model* that refers to the degree of confidence, trust, and respect that the leader obtains from followers.

LEADERSHIP

(*i*) An attempt to use noncoercive types of influence to motivate individuals to accomplish some goal.

(*ii*) The process of influencing others to achieve organisational goals.

LEADERSHIP CLIMATE

The nature of the work environment in an organisation that results from the leadership style and administrative practices of managers.

LEADING

The management function that involves influencing others to engage in the work behaviours necessary to reach organisational goals.

LEADING INDICATORS

Explanatory models based on variables that tend to be correlated with the phenomenon of major interest but also tend to occur in advance of that phenomenon.

LEAF

The terminal node in the data structure tree. This is the node which has no children.

LEARNED NEEDS THEORY

A theory that proposes that a person with a strong need will be motivated to use appropriate behaviours to satisfy the need. A person's needs are learned from the culture of a society.

LEARNING

(*i*) The process by which a relatively enduring change in behaviour occurs as a result of practice.

(*ii*) Any change in behaviour or cognition that results from experience or an interpretation of experience.

LEARNING TRANSFER

An important learning principle that emphasises the carryover of learning into the workplace.

LEASE

(*i*) A contract renting land, a building, space in a building, or equipment, typically for at least one year but often longer. Under a lease, title (or ownership) does not change. Leasing is an alternative to purchasing capital items (that is, an alternative to incurring capital costs).

(*ii*) An arrangement whereby the owner of something—land, transport, property, etc., permits its use to someone else for a specified period of time but retains ownership.

LEASED DEPARTMENT RETAILER

An independent retailer that owns the merchandise stocked but leases floor space from another earlier and usually operates under that retailer's name.

LEASE-PURCHASE

A lease that includes a provision whereby the leaseholder may purchase the leased asset during the term of the lease—usually at a favourable price, or that a portion of the lease payments that have been made up to the time of purchase may be applied against the purchase price.

LEASING

Renting plant or equipment as opposed to purchasing. A wide variety of leasing arrangements are in use.

LEAST-PREFERRED CO-WORKER SCALE

A questionnaire used by *Fieldler* to assess a person's task and relationship leadership tendencies.

LEDGER

(*i*) A complete record of all the transactions carried by an individual or a firm. This covers all debit and credit notes, together with payments and discounts, and any other information about the financial transactions of the firm.

(*ii*) A business account book, usually recording day-to-day transactions and usually showing debits and credits separately.

LEDGER CARD

A card that holds one subsidiary ledger account.

LEGAL ENVIRONMENT

Laws and regulations and their interpretation.

LEGAL MORTGAGE

A form of charge in which a debtor transfers property to his creditor on condition that property will be transferred back again when the debt is paid. Also called *Mortgage.*

LEGAL RESERVES

The percentage of total funds that an insurance company or bank must set aside to meet possible claims.

LEGAL TENDER

A lawful medium of exchange, such as money.

LEGAL TENDER

Money which is legally acceptable in payment of public and private debts.

LEGAL-POLITICAL ELEMENT

The part of the mega-environment that includes the legal and governmental systems within which an organisation must function.

LEGISLATION

The process of creating laws; legislative bills (proposed statutes or ordinances) proposed or in the process of being considered for enactment; also, inaccurately used to mean laws or statutes.

LEGITIMATE POWER

Capacity to influence derived from the position of a manager in the organisational hierarchy. Subordinates believe that they ought to comply.

LENDERS

Bankers and other financial institutions that lend money to a business enterprise with a view to earn interest on money, are called *Lenders*.

LEO

Abbreviation of *Lyon's Electronic Office*, the name of the computer made by a British Company, J. Lyons & Co. which initiated in 1947 a project to build a computer to mechanise the clerical functions of their own offices.

LESS DEVELOPED COUNTRIES (LDCs)

(*i*) A group of non-communist countries, often called the "third world", that consists primarily of relatively poor nations characterised by low per capita income, little industry, and high birth-rates.

(*ii*) A country in which small, low-technology companies may be developing but in which sophisticated marketing mechanisms typically do not exist.

LESSEE

One who is given possession of someone else's property by means of a lease.

LESSOR

(*i*) A party to whom a lease is granted for using or acquiring the property or a special right belonging to another person on a consideration.

(*ii*) One who gives possession of his property to someone else by means of a lease.

LETTER OF CREDIT

A document issued by a bank or financial institution which

guarantees credit up to a stated amount.

LETTER OF INTENT

A preliminary understanding that forms the basis of an intended contract.

LETTER OF LICENCE

An insolvent debtor may come to some agreement with his creditors whereby they agree to give him some time to pay and not to take any proceedings against him until that time has elapsed.

LETTER OF PLEDGE

A document in which a customer of a bank agrees to pledge to the bank the bills of lading of goods for which the bank lends the purchase price. A letter of pledge normally sets out standard terms to cover numerous transactions (Also known as a *Letter of Hypothecation* or *Letter of Lien*),

LETTER-OPENING MACHINES

Letter-opening machines are used for opening envelopes of different sizes. The machines can be operated manually or electrically and can be adjusted to open envelopes of any standard size, 75 to 500 envelopes per minute can be opened with the help of these machines.

LETTERPRESS OFFICE PRINTING MACHINES

The letterpress office printing machines are now used to produce as well as facsimile typewritten letters, a wide range of printed work, including letter-heading; invoice forms, postcards, and sales literature such as leaflets with illustrations, catalogues, price lists, etc. Either typewriter-face types or printing-face types can be used. Both manual and electrically operated letterpress machines are available with or without automatic paper feeds, these feeds having a capacity of 500 to 5,000 sheets.

LEVEL PREMIUM

An insurance premium that remains unchanged throughout the life of the policy for which it is paid.

LEVERAGE

The ability to operate with a significant liabilities to gross assets ratio.

LEVERAGE RATIO

(*i*) A measure of the long-term solvency of a firm, which also given an idea of the equity cushion for long-term indebtedness.

(*ii*) An organisation's total debt divided by its total assets; one of many accounting ratios used for assessing an organisation's financial health.

LIABILITIES

(*i*) The current and long-term debts owned by an enterprise or jurisdiction, current liabilities are due and payable within a year, and include such items as accounts payable, wages, and short-term debt. Long-term liabilities are payable after more than a year and include items such as bonds.

(*ii*) An amount owed by one person (the debtor) to another (the creditor). In a balance-sheet it refers to all such claims against the assets of an entity other than those of the owners.

LIAISON ROLE

A role to which a specific individual is appointed to facilitate communication and resolution of issues between two or more departments, thereby facilitating lateral relations.

LIBERALISATION

Liberalisation is a process in which the government loosen its control over the industry by reducing its interference.

LICENCE

(*i*) Permission granted to an individual or organisation, usually by a competent public authority, to engage in a practice, occupation, or activity which otherwise would be unlawful.

(*ii*) A contractual arrangement with another firm so that the second firm may use the company's trademark.

LICENCEE

A person who is entitled to do something under the term of a licence. A person who is entitled to use some one else's property under the terms of a licence.

LICENCING

(*i*) A method of international entry that involves an agreement in which one organisation gives limited rights to another to use certain of its assets, such as expertise, patents, copyrights, or equipment, for an agreed-upon fee or royalty.

(*ii*) Granting a licence to manufacture a trade-marked and/or patented product to another company in return for a royalty on each unit sold.

(*iii*) In international marketing, an agreement by which a company (the licencer) permits a foreign company (the licencee) to set up a business in the foreign market using the licencer s manufacturing processes, patents, trademarks, trade secrets, and so on in exchange for payment of a fee or royalty.

(*iv*) A formal process by which a government agency grants an individual the legal right to practise an occupation, grant an organisation the legal right to engage in an activity.

LICENCER

A person who grants a right to use his property to some one else by means of licence.

LIEN

Legal claim on a person's property till he has repaid a loan or debt connected with it. The various forms of lien include maritime lien, judgment lien, common law lien, etc.

LIEN OF SHARES

The articles of association of company usually provide that the company has first lien on the shares of a member for his debts or liabilities. The lien may also apply to dividends.

LIEN

A claim, charge, or liability against property that is allowed by law, rather than one that is part of a contract of agreement.

LIFE CHANGE EVENTS

Changes that create stress for an individual. The work of *Holmes* and *Rahe* indicates that an excessive number of life change events in one period of time can produce major health problems in a subsequent period.

LIFE CYCLES

Predictable stages of development that organisations typically follow.

LIFE INSURANCE

Insurance that provides for the payment of a specific amount to a designated beneficiary in the event of the death of the insured.

LIFESTYLE

(*i*) The behaviours, activities, values and beliefs that influences the physiological, psychosocial, environmental, economic and religious aspects of a persons daily life.

(*ii*) An individual s activities, interests, opinions, and values as they affect his or her mode of living.

LIFESTYLE ADVERTISEMENT

An advertisement that reflects a target market's lifestyle or hoped for lifestyle.

LIFO

A method of inventory and cost-of-sales valuation in which the individual items constituting the inventory are valued according to the cost of the earliest acquisitions and the cost of articles sold or used are valued at the cost of the most recent acquisition.

LIKERT SCALES

Market research scale which use statements for respondents to indicate agreement or disagreement.

LIMITED COMPANY

(*i*) A company whose members are required to contribute capital to the company but only up to a known limited amount agreed between member and company. No further contribution can be required even if the company is unable to pay its debts.

(*ii*) A limited company whose shares are bought and sold in public and quoted on the stock exchange. Such a company must use the letters 'Ltd.' after its name.

LIMITED PROBLEM IN SOLVING

A level of decision-making intermediate between routinised and extensive problem-solving in which the consumer has some purchasing experience but is unfamiliar with stores, brands, or process operations.

LIMITED-LINE STRATEGY

The product line strategy that entails offering a smaller number of variations than the full-line strategy.

LIMITED-SERVICE WHOLESALER

Merchant wholesaler that offers less than full service and charges lower process than a full service merchant wholesaler. Also called a *Limited- Function Wholesaler.*

LINE

Concerned with the basic objectives of a company; *e.g.*, in a manufacturing concern, line executives would be concerned with production and sales.

LINE AND STAFF ORGANISATION

This system is a compromise between pure line system, and pure functional system. This system implies the combined role of line (actual doers of the work) and the staff (the persons who only advise about during the job) in attaining the objectives of the enterprise.

LINE AUTHORITY

The authority that follows the chain of command established by the formal hierarchy.

LINE INDEX

It is a method of indexing that maintains information through lists. The data to be indexed are entered on the data insertion strips. These strips can be inserted or taken out of the data frame conveniently at any moment of time.

LINE MANAGEMENT

The term used to describe managers who are responsible for an organisation carrying out its basic functions, *e.g.*, marketing, production, etc. and who give and receive orders via the chain of command, within the organisational hierarchy.

LINE OF CREDIT

The maximum amount of credit a customer has with a bank or other lending institution.

LINE OR STAFF COMMITTEES

When a committee is vested with some decisive powers and whose decisions are carried out invariably, it is known as *Line Committee.*

LINE ORGANISATION

(*i*) Line organisation structure is one of the oldest and simplest of organisational structures. It is also known as *Military Organisation, Scalar Organisation, Vertical or Departmental Organisation.* This type of organisation is most common in small-scale units and here authority flows vertically downwards from top to bottom.

(*ii*) This is the oldest method which has been followed in its pure form in military till recently. Under this system authority flows from the top to bottom. Directions are issued by the highest authority and are conveyed to the persons responsible for executing them through the chain of command. The highest officer gives order to his immediate subordinate who to his next subordinate and so on.

LINE POSITION

A position that has authority and responsibility for achieving the major goals of the organisation.

LINEAR PROGRAMMING

A mathematical technique employed to pick the best choice from among several alternatives. The economic theorists approach to the analysis of business behaviour and business problems is based on the concept of optimisation. This, however, does not mean that in applied operation research work the analyst pretends to be able to find the best of all possible decisions.

LINEARITY

The assumption of linearity is close enough to reality also. The influence of each element must be directly proportional to the quantity to each element must be directly proportional to the quantity to each element involved in any problem. LP is relevant when the problem to be solved is a production process involving a straight-line relationship with a number of alternative methods for reaching the objective. A hierarchy of management problems ranging for those most suited to quantitative treatment (on the technical side) to those in which quantification is most difficult (on the human and value side) can be solved mathematically.

LINK

A relationship between the data used in an application and the file from which it originated. Like using the figure of *CorelDraw* in *PageMaker*.

LINKAGE

A strategy relating two or more issues in negotiations, which are then used as trade-offs or pressure points, much as in a"carrot and stick" technique.

LINKER

A system software tool which combines the separately compiled object modules and library file object modules to an executable program file.

LINKING PIN

An individual who provides a means of co-ordination between command groups at two different levels by fulfilling a supervisory role in the lower-level group and a subordinate role in the higher-level group.

LINKING-PIN FUNCTION

An element of System-4 organisation that views managers' major role to be to represent the groups they manage to higher-level groups in the organisation.

LINUX

An operating system which is the brainchild of *Linux Trovalds* and a team of programmers which was conceived 8 years ago in 1990s. It is written on the open source code of Unix and came into limelight in 1998. Its transparency and outstanding capabilities, have made it a cool and easy operating system which can be run on almost every computer with wide hardware support.

LIP MOVEMENT

Extraneous movement of lips in reading spelling, or listening.

LIQUID ASSETS

Assets that are in cash and immediately available or that are easily convertible into cash, like securities or bank deposits.

LIQUIDATED DAMAGE

(*i*) A provision incorporated in a contract between parties, according to which a certain amount of money has to be paid as liquidated damages upon default. (*ii*) The money amount established by the parties to a contract that must be paid in the event one or more of the parties fails to fulfil the terms of the contract.

LIQUIDATION

A defensive strategy that entails selling or dissolving an entire organisation.

LIQUIDATOR

An official who supervises the winding-up of a company. He takes over the company's property, though it does not vest in him unless a court says so. He acts as a receiver and manager. Generally speaking he does everything necessary to conduct the winding up and calls meetings where necessary. The liquidator's powers and duties vary according to whether the winding-up is compulsory or voluntary. If compulsory, he is subject to court control. The liquidator must give notice of winding-up to creditors and tell them when proofs must be lodged they are to receive a share of the dividend (*i.e.* distribution). An individual appointed to manage the winding-up of a company.

LIQUIDITY RATIO

(*i*) A measure of the short-term solvency of a firm.

(*ii*) Financial ratios that measure the degree to which an organisation's current assets are adequate to pay current liabilities (current debt obligations).

LIST PRICE

The basic price quite, before adjustment.

LISTENING VOCABULARY

Number of words understood when heard.

LOAD

The use that is to be made of a production facility (*e.g.*, machine, a work centre, a worker) over a period. To assign loads to particular production facilities (*e.g.*, a factory, a shop, a machine, a work centre).

LOAN FUNDS

Financial transactions in the context of Mutual Funds Organisation. Loan means sales expense.

LOAN

To lend or advance money or other property or pensions for temporary use; a sum of borrowed money. For accounting purposes, a loan is an account receivable by the lender and an account payable by the recipient.

LOCAL AREA NETWORKS (LANS)

Interconnections (usually by cable) through which end-user computing can be managed that allow communications among computers in a single building or within close proximity.

LOCATION CLUE

A suggestion as to geographical placement.

LOCK

A group of coded characters that allows the access to specified software system.

LOCK-IN

A loan that does not permit prepayment. The borrower is "locked- in" for the period of the loan.

LOCK-OUT

Action taken by employers in the course of an industrial dispute which involves denying the workers access to the workplace by locking them out; *i.e.*, it is opposite to a strike in its effect.

LOCUS OF CONTROL

A personality characteristic that describes people who see the control of their lives as coming from inside themselves as internalisers. People who believe that their lives are controlled by external factors are externalisers.

LOG

A journal or control ledger used to record events or milestones achieved in projects and activities.

LOGIC

The science related to reasoning.

LOGIC DIAGRAM

A pictorial representation by lines, triangles, circles etc. of the logic devices in a computer.

LOGIC GATE

An electronic device formed with the help of flip-flops to implement the elementary logic functions.

LOGIC PROGRAMMING LANGUAGE

A class of programming language. Usually fifth generation languages come under this class.

LOGIC SYMBOL

A symbol that is, used to represent the logical operation. For *e.g.* is used to represent logical OR operation in C and && is used to represent the AND operation.

LOGICAL OFFICE

The concept that portable microcomputers allow an individual's office to be anywhere the individual is, rather than being restricted to one specific location.

LOGISTICS

(*i*) The activities involved in moving raw materials and parts into the firm, in-process inventory through the firm, land finished goods out of the firm.

(*ii*) A term that was originally used in the military sphere to describe the organising and moving of troops and equipment. It is now often applied to any detailed planning process in an organisation which entails the distribution or redistribution of resources.

LOGO

An interactive graphical language especially beneficial for young children in the age group of four to five years. This is becoming popular in the field of education as it allows the young children to work and learn a variety of concepts like colour, direction, letters, words, sounds, etc. on computers very easily.

LOOP

In a graph, an edge that has the same vertex at each end. A sequence of instruction in a program that are to be obeyed repetitively by the computer.

LOSS LEADER

A product priced below cost to attract consumers, who may then make additional purchases.

LOYALTY (ALSO BRAND LOYALTY)

The extent to which customers repurchase a particular product or brand.

LPC (LEAST PREFERRED CO-WORKER) ORIENTATION

A personality trait in *Fiedler's Contingency Model* that indicates the extent to which an individual places a higher priority or value on task accomplishment than on personal relationships.

LUDDITE

The term used to describe workers who are obstinately opposed to the introduction of new technology into their workplace. It derives from the followers of *Ned Ludd,* an early nineteenth century British worker, who saw new machinery as threat to their traditional craft skills and working practices and opposed its introduction violently.

LUXURY GOODS

Luxury goods are non-essential items. They are consumed for the pleasure that they impart, such as costly cars, carpets, five star hotel living, perfumes, entertainment etc.

M

MACHIAVELLIANISM

A term used to describe political manoeuvres in an organisation. Used to designate a person as a manipulator and power abuser.

MACHINE CODE

The operation code of a particular machine.

MACHINE CYCLE

The time taken by the processor to perform any one of its internal operation like fetching.

MACHINE INSTRUCTION

The instruction of machine language that the computer can read, recognise and execute directly without the need of compilation.

MACINTOSH

The trademark of Apple Computer Corporation used for marketing of personal computers.

MACRO

A user-developed control routine created and run within an application. A macro consists of a sequence of actions record. When the macro is executed the actions are performed automatically.

MACRO-ENVIRONMENT

The general external business environment in which a firm functions.

MAGNETIC CORE

A non-volatile memory which consists of small ferrite or iron oxide doughnuts of magnetic material strung on wires that provide electrical current that magnetises the cores. Data is represented by the direction of the magnetic field of group of cores.

MAGNUSON-MOSS WARRANTY ACT

Federal law requiring that guarantees provided by sellers be made available to buyers before purchase and that they specify who the warrantor is, what products or parts of products are covered, what the warrantor must do if the product is defective, how long the warranty applies, and the obligations of the buyer.

MAIL ORDER

A form of trading conducted mainly through a postal or delivery system which connects buyers and sellers.

MAIL-ORDER WHOLESALER

A limited service wholesaler that uses catalogues, mail or telephone ordering, and mail delivery.

MAIN HEADING

Brief statement of chief topic or subject in a chapter or other composition.

MAIN MEMORY

Immediate access memory located in the computer for programs.

MAIN PROGRAM

A program may contain more than one module. Main program is that portion of the program which contains the code to control the achievement of program objectives by calling the other modules as required and which is initially executed at start up time. This is the program which is called by operating system for execution.

MAINFRAME COMPUTER

Initially the term mainframe was used to refer to the main framework of a central processing unit. It is a large system that has capability of supporting many powerful peripherals and has generally more than one nodes attached to it working in time-sharing environment.

MAINTAIN

To keep in effective condition. Maintenance refers to the work necessary to keep something in a satisfactory condition. An organisation is maintained by being kept in a sound operating condition.

MAJOR PREMISE

In a syllogism, the proposition which contains the general truth from which the particular inference is deduced.

MAJORITY FALLACY

The error embodied by a marketing effort that blindly pursues the largest, or most easily identified, or most accessible market segment. The error lies in the fact that other marketers will be pursuing these same segments.

MAKE OR BUY DECISIONS

Choice between manufacturing a component of a product in the company's own plants or purchasing it from an outside supplier or suppliers.

MALADJUSTMENT

State in which a person falls short of being able to do what is expected of him by others or by himself.

MALLOC

A function of C language which is used to allocate the main memory to a data dynamically which is released afterwards when not required.

MANAGE

The meaning of the word 'manage' is to 'guide' and have under command or control. It has been derived from the French word *Manege* which refers to the managing of a horse.

MANAGEMENT

(*i*) The process of getting work done through people.

(*ii*) "Management is a distinct process consisting of planning, organising, actuating and controlling, utilising in each both science and art, and followed in order to accomplish pre-determined objectives."

(*iii*) Making the most effective use of available resources, whether in form of machines, money or people. The people responsible for the management of an organisation, *i.e.*, for the directing, planning and running of its operations, for the implementation of its policies and the attainment of its objectives.

MANAGEMENT AUDIT

A review designed to evaluate management efficiency and identify areas in need of management improvement within an organisation. Management audits are used to ensure effectiveness in meeting organisational goals. It is an inspection and evaluation of meeting organisational performance, including one or more of the following: organisational structure and compensation, operational effectiveness, quality of services and products, market effectiveness, fiscal performance, and integrity, customer (client or patient) relations, professional relations.

MANAGEMENT BY CRISIS

A management style that tends to set up crash programmes to deal with problems as they arise in an organisation rather than focusing on long-term planning or the overall objectives of the organisation. It is a style that suits a manager inclined to authoritarian management and is a way of making short-term crisis management into a permanent arrangement.

MANAGEMENT BY OBJECTIVES

(*i*) Management by objectives is a process whereby performance goals and objectives are set by each subordinate in collaboration with his superior at the start of the appraisal period. Progress is then tracked and results are evaluated periodically.

(*ii*) A process in which superior and subordinate jointly set goals for a specified time period and then meet again to evaluate the subordinate's performance toward previously established goals.

MANAGEMENT CALENDAR

A working calendar that displays significant events, periods of heavy workload, and other data and which is used for planning by an organisation's staff or committee members and directors.

MANAGEMENT CONSULTANT

Someone who offers a consultancy service in any area of management of the running of an organisation.

MANAGEMENT CYCLE

A conception of the programme management processes or functions in which the centre thrusts of power are innovation/motivation and staff development.

MANAGEMENT DEVELOPMENT

(*i*) Training of managers currently employed to improve their performance in their present jobs and/or to fit them for promotion.

(*ii*) The process of identifying training and generally equipping relatively junior managers with the experience or skill necessary for senior management positions with an organisation in the future. It is a process that, ideally, should be an integral part of a coherent personnel policy going from initial recruitment to ultimate retirement.

MANAGEMENT EDUCATION

Any course of introduction in management and related field—which is often known as business administration. Success in such a course is usually rewarded with an academic qualification whether the setting is an institution of higher education or an in-house programme tailored to a particular organisation. The term is often used interchangeably with management training, though the emphasis of management education is generally more formal and academic.

MANAGEMENT INFORMATION SYSTEM

(*i*) An information system which provides information to various management level to help them in taking the decisions and formulating the policies to achieve the overall objectives of organisation. The output of MIS goes to *Decision Support Systems*. MIS may or may not be computerised.

(*ii*) A centralised and usually computerised information system for use by the managers of an organisation in decision-making.

MANAGEMENT PREROGATIVES

The prerogatives management believes it cannot share with a union if it is to have freedom to manage effectively.

MANAGEMENT PROCESS SCHOOL

Management theory perceives management as a process of getting things done through and with people operating in organised groups. It aims to analyse the process to establish a conceptual framework for it, to identify principles underlying it and to build up a theory of management from them.

MANAGEMENT SCIENCE

The application of scientific methods and particularly quantitative methodology to the practice of mangement. The application of a behavioural science or social science perspective to the study of management.

MANAGEMENT SERVICE

Any service intended to help management function more effectively, such as data processing or market research.

MANAGEMENT STRATEGY

Managements strategy of convincing divisional executives that the objectives we have jointly agreed to are both desirable and attainable. We are deadly serious about our responsibility to persuade—so serious, in fact, that, when our plans go way, we charge the failure to our lack of salesmanship, not the division's lack of implementation.

MANAGEMENT STYLE

The general approach a manager has in dealing with other people at work and in particular the exercising of his or her authority with subordinates. This style is often characterised as tending toward authority management or democratic management, depending on the personality of the individual manager, but people can also have somewhat different approaches when faced with different situations.

MANAGEMENT TEAM

A vague term generally referring to a group of managers who, addition to their distinct responsibilities, are held jointly accountable (by a senior manager or governing body) for an organisation's performance in meeting established goals or providing services that fulfil the mission of a program with budgetary and revenue constraints.

MANAGEMENT TRAINING

Any form of training in the practices and techniques of management. One important form of management training is to have managers' study case histories of real-life issues in organisation and work on solution to problem; another is to play business games designed to deal with particular aspects of management. The term is often used interchangeably with management education though the emphasis of management training is generally more focused and less formal or academic.

MANAGEMENT WORK PLAN

A record used in programme or organisational management, usually as part of a management-by-objectives process. A management work plan supports and provides greater detail than a management-by-objectives form. It emphasises task and resources management.

MANAGEMENT, GENERAL

Overall management as opposed to management of a speciality.

MANAGEMENT, MIDDLE

Managers above the first-line supervisors who do not participate in decisions on overall policy.

MANAGEMENT, SCIENTIFIC

A system of management developed by *Frederick W. Taylor* and others early in the twentieth century.

MANAGEMENT, TOP

The company policy-makers (sometimes just president).

MANAGER

Anyone involved in the administration of an organisation with the authority to used organisation resources, whether money, labour or equipment in furtherance of the organisation's objectives.

MANAGER BUOYANT

(*i*) A situation in which the management of an enterprise make a bid to own it, whole or in part, by buying out the original shareholders, then operating as a separate concern on their own behalf.

(*ii*) One who plans, organises, motivates, coordinates, and controls the work of other people.

MANAGERIAL ECONOMIC

The application of economics to the kind of practical business decision that a manager has to take. As well as economics field draws on operational research, management accounting and marketing.

MANAGERIAL EMPLOYEES

Middle-level managerial cadres in business and industrial establishments have a sense of job security since a bill was passed by the Indian Parliament. It covers managerial employees hitherto left out by the Industrial Disputes Act, 1974. The benefits of the new legislative measure do not extend to those occupying "top management positions" like managing directors, chairmen or board of directors, executives directors and chief executive officers or heads of branches of regional offices enjoying substantial managerial powers.

MANAGERIAL GRID

Theory of leadership based on a particular optimal style of leadership that includes balance of concern for production and for people. Basic leadership and group development activities are undertaken in managerial grid interventions to bring about desired leadership and individual group behaviours.

MANDATORY BARGAINING ITEMS

Those collective bargaining items over which each party must bargain if they are brought up by the other party.

MANAGEMENT SUPERVISION

We exercise management supervision through the device of planning meetings and irregular store visits where we learn to know the organisation and see what they are doing on their home grounds. Prior to the planning meetings the central office makes a detailed study of the division's performance, its forecast of sales for the year ahead and for as much as ten years ahead.

MANPOWER ANALYSIS

An analysis of the employees in an organisation that attempts to identify patterns and trends in their employment. It will examine, for instance, the distribution of employees by age, sex, skill, job title and length of service. It is the first stage of systematic manpower planning.

MANPOWER NEEDS

Different business enterprises may need different types of people at different times. To main continuous supply of the required kind of people for a business, the personnel department may undertake a study of the present and future requirements of the concern to determine its manpower needs. It is also required to ascertain the different sources of supply of labour and must keep in touch with general factors effecting the supply of labour.

MANPOWER PLANNING

The process by which management determines how the organisation should move from its current manpower position to its desired manpower position. Through planning, management strives to have the right number and the right kinds of people, at the right places, at the right time, doing things which result in both the organisation and the individual receiving maximum long-run benefit. According to *Gordon MacBeath,* manpower planning involves two stages. The first stage is concerned with the detailed "planning of manpower requirements for all types and levels of employees throughout the period of the plan," and the second stage is concerned with "planning of manpower supplies to provide the organisation with the right types of people from all sources to met the planned requirements."

MANUAL SKILL

A skill that requires physical rather than mental ability.

MANUFACTURER BRAND

A brand owned by the maker of the product.

MANUFACTURERS' AGENT

Independent agent intermediary that represents a limited number of non-competing suppliers in a limited geographical area.Also called *A Manufacturers' Representative.*

MARGINAL ANALYSIS

Analysis to determine the point at which the cost of extra input of one factor (*e.g.*, another employee or another machine) will pay for itself.

MARGINAL APPROACH

In setting the promotional budget, a method whereby the marketer attempts to spend resources until additional expenditures would not be justified by the additional sales and profits they would generate.

MARGINAL COST

(*i*) The extra cost of production of unit additional at those already produced or planned.

(*ii*) The net addition to a firm's total costs that results from the production of one additional unit of product.

MARGINAL MEN

Groups not fully accepted by the society in which they live.

MARGINAL REVENUE

The addition to total revenue contributed by the sale of each additional unit of a service or product.

MARKET/PRODUCT MATRIX

A matrix containing the four possible combinations of old and new products with old and new products with old and new markets. The purpose of the matrix is to broadly categorise alternative SBU opportunities in terms of basic strategies for growth.

MARKET

A group of potential customers that may want the product offered and that have the resources, the willingness, and the authority to purchase it. Or we can say that a situation where buyers and sellers are in communication with each other. They may take several forms, *e.g.*, in person (as in a cattle auction) or electronically (as in the stock exchange) or through the mass media as in newspaper advertising columns; the nature of the demand for a particular product.

MARKET DEVELOPMENT

The strategy by which an organisation attempts to draw new customers to an existing product, most common by introducing the product in a new geographical area.

MARKET FACTOR

A variable associated with sales that is analysed in forecasting sales.

MARKET FACTOR INDEX

(*i*) A sales forecasting tool used in analysing the association between sales and a number of other variables. Also called the *Market Factor Index.*

(*ii*) A sales forecasting tool used in analysing the association between sales and a number of other variables.

MARKET FORCES

The factors determining supply and demand in a given market.

MARKET LEADER

The organisation which has the greatest share of sales by offering more of their existing product in new markets.

MARKET MANAGER

An individual responsible for administering all marketing activities that relate to a particular market, including forecasting, product planning, and processing.

MARKET NICHE

A unique place of gap in the market for a given product.

MARKET OVERT

A market place where goods are arranged or displayed for sales only on certain days; also called *Open Market.*

MARKET PENETRATION

The strategy by which sales of an established product grow because of increased use of the product by existing customers in existing markets. An amount of demand in a given market that is supplied by a particular organisation.

MARKET PENETRATION

The strategy by which sales of an established product grow because of increased use of the product by existing customers in existing markets.

MARKET POSITION

The way consumers perceive a product relative to its competition. Also called *Competitive Position.*

MARKET POTENTIAL

The upper limit of industry demand. That is, the expected sales volume for all brands of a particular product during a given period.

MARKET RESEARCH

(*i*) General research of external factors relating to an organisations marketplace.

(*ii*) 'Marketing decisions can be no better than the facts upon which they are based.' Importance of market research has increased very much with the widening of markets and increasing competition. Now-a-days goods may be manufactured for stock rather than to order. It is necessary to manufacture goods by keeping in view the future trends of demand.

MARKET SEGMENT

A portion of a larger market, identified according to some shared characteristic or characteristics. Dividing a heterogeneous market into segments is *Market Segmentation.*

MARKET SHARE

The percentage of total industry sales accounted for by particular firm, or the percentage of sales of a given product accounted for by a particular brand.

MARKET SHARE

(*i*) The amount of total demand in a market which a particular organisation supplies over a given period of time.

(*ii*) The relative sales of product in relation to the overall market sales can be measured in either sales value or sales volume.

MARKET STRATEGY

The long-term direction of an organisation relating to marketing actions and the interaction of controllable variables.

MARKET VALUE

(*i*) The price that goods would ordinarily fetch if put on sale in the open market. The market value of shares is the value quoted in a recognised stock exchange.

(*ii*) The current price that a particular item would fetch in the market.

MARKETING

(*i*) All activities connected with sales and distribution.

(*ii*) The process of planning and executing the conception, pricing, promotion, and distribution of ideas, goods and services to create exchanges that will satisfy individual and organisational objectives.

MARKETING AUDIT

(*i*) A comprehensive review and appraisal of the total marketing operation; often performed by outside consultants or other unbiased personnel.

(*ii*) A systematic appraisal of the strengths and weaknesses of a company in relation to its marketplace, and the evaluation of the opportunities and threats in that market.

MARKETING CONCEPT

(*i*) The underlying philosophy that companies should be customer- oriented and that all an organisation's staff should work together to achieve this focus.

(*ii*) Organisational philosophy that stresses consumer orientation, long range profitability, and the integration of marketing and other organisational functions. The marketing concept, which focuses on satisfying consumer's wants and needs, is the foundation of a marketing orientation.

(*iii*) The underlying philosophy that companies should be customer- oriented and that all an organisation's staff should work together to achieve this focus.

MARKETING ENVIRONMENT

The set of external factors that affect the market in which an organisation operates, *i.e., Cultural, Economic, Legal, Political, Geographical* etc.

MARKETING ETHICS

The principles that guide an organisation's conduct and the values it expects to express in certain situations.

MARKETING INTELLIGENCE SYSTEM

A network of diverse sources that provide data about the marketing environment; part of an organisations data collection system.

MARKETING MANAGEMENT

(*i*) The process of planning, executing, and controlling marketing activities to attain marketing goals and objectives effectively and efficiently.

(*ii*) Marketing management is primarily concerned with the stimulation of sales and promotion of consumers satisfaction. It includes analysis of markets, determination of marketing goals, sales forecasting and formulation of marketing plans, policies and procedures. An important function of marketing management is to evolve an appropriate marketing mix, *i.e.,* planning and development of a satisfactory product for a particular market demand and fixation of its prices.

(*iii*) The process of planning executing, and controlling marketing activities to attain marketing goals and objectives effectively and efficiently.

MARKETING MIX

(*i*) The specific combination of interrelated and interdependent marketing activities in which an organisation engages to meet its objectives.

(*ii*) The controllable elements of the marketing function, originally containing 12 factors but sometimes reduced to the 4P's of management *i.e., product, price, place* and *promotion.*

MARKETING MYOPIA

Failure to define organisational purpose from a broad consumer orientation.

MARKETING OBJECTIVE

A statement about the level of performance the organisation, SBU, or operating unit intends to achieve. Objectives define results in measurable terms.

MARKETING OPPORTUNITY ANALYSIS

The interpretation of environmental attributes and change in light of the organisations's ability to capitalise on potential opportunities.

MARKETING ORGANISATION

(*i*) The part of an organisation to which marketing responsibilities are assigned.

(*ii*) Organisational philosophy that focuses on consumers' wants and needs.

MARKETING PLAN

A written statement of the marketing objectives and strategies to be followed and the specific courses of action to be taken when (or if) certain events occur.

MARKETING PLANNING

The systematic process of analysing the environment and a company's resources. Then developing objectives and suitable strategies and action plans to meet those objectives. Also the feedback and control of such actions.

MARKETING PROGRAM

All of the activities associated with marketing research and the implementation and control of the individual elements of the marketing mix.

MARKETING RESEARCH

(*i*) Studies to determine the potential market for a company's products or services and/or how products can be made more saleable.

(*ii*) The systematic and objective process of generating information for use in marketing decisionmaking.

(*iii*) The collection of marketing information which may influence marketing decisions. It is an aid to decision-making but not a substitute for it.

MARKETING RESEARCH SYSTEM

System for gathering new data to solve specific problems; part of an organisation's data collection system.

MARK-UP

A cost plus pricing technique.

MARK-UP ON COST

A mark-up expressed as a percentage of the cost of an item.

MARK-UP ON SELLING PRICE

A mark-up expressed as a percentage of the selling price of an item.

MASCULINITY-FEMININITY

High masculinity in a culture designates assertiveness, dominance, and independence. High femininity in a culture designates interdependence, compassion, and emotional opinions.

MASS MEDIA

Forms of communication that large-usually nation wide audience, *i.e., Radio, Television* and *Newspaper.*

MASS MERCHANDISE RETAILER

A retailer that sells a wide variety of products at discount prices. Also called a *Mass Merchandise Discount Store.*

MASS PRODUCTION

The production of identical items on a very large scale.

MASSED PRACTICE

A technique of learning in which the lessons or periods of practice follow each other without a break. Generally speaking, and for most purposes, this is considered a less effective method of learning than distributed practice, which it is usually contrasted.

MASTER

A device that controls the functioning of other devices.

MASTER OF BUSINESS ADMINISTRATION (MBA)

A post-graduate degree in the field of business and management awarded by many UK universities and a growing number of polytechnics. Some courses aim to cover a broad spread of management subjects, while allow students to specialise heavily in particular subject areas; in addition, students are normally required to work on an individual, personally researched, project. Most full-time courses last one year, a few require two year. There are also a growing number of part-time MBA courses, based on day-release or evening teaching, and generally spreading over some three years. There is a substantial degree of variation in the respect generally felt for MBAs from different institutions.

MATCHING

An accounting concept which holds that expenses should be recognised in the same accounting period that is used to recognise the income they produced.

MATERIALS HANDLING

The use of muscle power, machinery, and other methods to

identify, check, load, and unload goods in inventory.

MATERIALS MANAGEMENT

The activities involved in bringing raw materials and supplies to the point of production and moving in-process inventory through the firm.

MATH CO-PROCESSOR

An additional processing chip that was used to extended the instruction set of 386 and earlier chips to include the instructions that improve the systems numerical and computational performance.

MATRIX ORGANISATION

(*i*) An organisational design that superimposes a product— or project-based design on an existing function-based design.

(*ii*) Matrix organisation is created by merging the two complementary organisations—the project and the functional. It represents a combination of vertical functional departmental organisation with project organisation. In it, projects cut across the functional lines.

MATURATION

(*i*) In experimental studies, a source of error that results from changes in the subject group with the passage of time that are not associated with the experimental treatment.

(*ii*) Development consistent with mental or chronological age.

MATURITY STAGE

The stage in the product life cycle when sales increase at a decreasing rate.

MATURITY

The time at which a debt or other obligation becomes due or a right becomes enforceable. It is usually the date on which the borrower of a loan note, or bond must pay the full amount of the debt for the instrument.

MEAL

(*Media Expenditure Analysis Limited*); A firm that collects and publishes information on major UK media use and cost by companies.

MEAN PRICE

Average market price of two or more items.

MEAN

(*i*) The most commonly used measure of central tendency. It is the arithmetic average, found by summing the value of a series of number of dividing this by the total number in the series.

(*ii*) The simple average of a set of measurements, obtained by dividing the sum of the measurements by the number of them. For example: if the ages of four members of a family are 48, 44, 25 and 23 years, then the average age of the family is (48+44+25+23)/4 = 35 years.

MEASURE, DIRECT

A variable that is measured directly rather than through some other, intervening variable or indicator.

MECHANICS OF READING

Habits developed in connection with reading but apart from the reading process itself, such as following lines of print from left to right across the page, from top to bottom of a page, and from one to another.

MECHANISTIC MODEL OF ORGANISATIONAL DESIGN

The type of organisational design that emphasises the importance of production and efficiency. It is highly formalised, centralised and complex.

MEDIA OWNERS

The controllers of media who try to encourage the use of their channel and often provide comprehensive data about readers and viewers.

MEDIA SCHEDULE

A schedule identifying the exact media to be used and the dates on which advertisements are to appear. Also called a *Media Plan*.

MEDIA SELECTION STRATEGY

Strategy involving the determination of which media are most appropriate for an advertising campaign.

MEDIA

Channels of communication such as television, radio, newspapers, etc.

MEDIATION

A mediator is a neutral party called in to assist in resolving a conflict. Unlike an arbitrator, a mediator is not given any authority to pass judgement. The role of the mediator is to make suggestions and recommendations to the parties in dispute in order to help them reach an agreement. See also *Arbitration*.

MEDIATOR

An individual who acts as an impartial third in order to help resolve disputes. A mediator's role is to help the parties to a dispute to reach an agreement.

MEETINGS

Meetings are well-known to be a standard part of the work of most managers, though there are some patterned variations. On the whole, the larger the company and the higher the individuals rank, the larger the proportion of time spent in formal meetings. Or to put it a little differently, there appears to be a line running from chief executive through general management and down the production management hierarchy, and all the positions on this line involve a significant amount of time spent in meetings, whereas there is more variation in the functional specialisms away from this line. Meetings vary in content in a common-sensical way so that, for example, production managers discuss manning, hold-ups, schedules, production plans and scrap rates, while purchasing officers talk to design engineers about specifications and see suppliers' representatives. On the other hand, it is possible to classify meetings more analytically by function and purpose, distinguishing those that serve primarily the ends of: 'information exchange and coordination'; 'information exchange for control purposes'; 'problem-solving'; planning/devising future initiatives though there may be some overlay between these types in practice. Probably most managers in most countries complain (to anyone who is willing to listen) about the time they spend in meetings (though the loudest complainers are often the most avid prolongers of meetings). Indeed there usually is a case for a periodic review of the panoply of meetings in a company with a view to discarding any series which became institutionalised by accident or have outlived their usefulness. More important is to see that existing meetings give 'value for money' within the normal constraints of time and human abilities, a responsibility especially for those initiating and chairing them. Apart form simple precepts such as: 'having the right people there'; 'providing relevant information in advance'; 'foreseeing obvious questions'; not to obverse them but to offer satisfactory replies; letting everyone have their say, while keeping the ball in play. Probably the most important thing for the initiator is to define the purpose and ground rules, saying in effect what those taking part are there to do or decide according to what criteria, and then or chest-rating individual contributions to that end.

MEETING-THE-COMPETITION STRATEGY

A pricing strategy whereby an organisation sets prices at levels equal lot those of competitors.

MEGABYTE (MB)

A unit of measure of the storage or memory in computer hardware, meaning one million bytes.

MEMBERSHIP GROUP

In reference to an individual, a group to which the individual belongs. If the individual has chosen to belong to the group, it is a voluntary membership group.

MEMORY

(*i*) A function of cognition which refers to the storage of information with reference to a computer, an electronic form of storing information.

(*ii*) The information-processing function involving the storage and retrieval of information.

MEMORY CYCLE

The minimum time required by memory to complete a read or write cycle.

MEMORY DUMP

Transferring the contents of main memory to backing storage device or sending to the printer.

MENTAL ABILITY

An untechnical term meaning intelligence or mental maturity.

MENTAL AGE

Level of development in intelligence expressed in terms of the age at which the average child attains that level.

MENTAL DEFICIENCY

Term for all degrees of lack in intelligence.

MENTAL MEASUREMENT

Quantitative determination of a person's abilities and tendencies.

MENTAL SET

An attitude.

MENTAL TEST

Measurement in which interest centres on the differences between different individuals' responses.

MERCANTILISM

Rules which appear to increase the wealth of a country, largely through governmental action, *e.g.*, imposition of tariffs.

MERCHANT INTERMEDIARY

A channel intermediary, such as a wholesaler or a retailer, that takes title to the product.

MERCHANT WHOLESALER

An independently owned wholesaling concern that takes title to the goods it distributes.

MERGER

(*i*) Combination of two companies, generally through an exchange of stock.

(*ii*) A combination of generally two companies through an exchange of stock; a process of combining an independent corporate entity with another for furtherance of certain common objectives. The term is also used in a Contract

(*iii*) An amalgamation of two or more organisations into a single new organisation by mutual agreement as opposed to a takeover. The formal combining of two or more separate entities (*e.g.*, firms) into a single organisation.

MERGERS, CONGLOMERATE

Mergers of companies in entirely different fields.

MERGERS, HORIZONTAL

Mergers of companies with their suppliers or their marketing outlets.

MERGERS, VERTICAL

Mergers of companies with their suppliers or their marketing outlets.

MERIT RATING

(*i*) A formal rating system that is applied to hourly paid employees.

(*ii*) Formal periodic reporting in writing on how well individual employees are doing their jobs. Similar to appraisal except that appraisal is generally used for rating of managers, merit rating for rating of the rank and file.

MERITORARY

A social system in which advancement is based on ability rather than birth or background.

MESSAGE

Collection of data to be transmitted.

METAPHOR

A figure of speech in which a word or phrase literally denoting one kind of object or idea is used in place of another in order to suggest a likeness or analogy between them.

METHODS

In studies of management and business organisations there is a contrast, even a conflict, between the doing of indepth studies of limited generality which are nevertheless rich in detail, and survey-style studies of large groups/numbers which are cheap and convenient but relatively shallow. Studies of the first kind are typically by interview or use observational methods, or are simply studies in-depth of particular cases; the work of *Carlson Mintzberg* and *Stewart* in management research are examples. An example of the second type of research is the *Aston Group* studies and surveys of the background and qualifications of managers are also of this type. In an ideal world researchers would be able to cross the two methods, but it is easier said than done.

MICROFILMING

It means the phototgraphing of papers documents, etc. in miniature on a thin (16mm) strip of film. The machine commonly used is called *Recordak*. Microphotography is used widely for copying papers and documents and for preserving records. Paper fed into a chute is automatically photographed at high speed on a single roll or film. Up to 6,000 photographs can be taken per hour. The roll is then developed, numbered and indexed suitably for easy location and preserved in a central place. If necessary for reference, the film is placed on a special projector and flashed on a groundglass screen. If required, any number of clear and full size paper prints can be obtained from the negative. Complete units, consisting of microfilming, projecting, developing and printing machines and equipment are available in suitable size for office use.

MICRO-MARKETING

The marketing activities in a single firm, as opposed to *Macro-Marketing*.

MIDDLEMAN

An individual or an organisation acting as a link between others, especially between producers and consumers or retailers, *e.g.*, a furniture wholesaler to a literary agent.

MINNESOTA MULTIPHASIC PERSONALITY INVENTORY (MMPI)

A widely used inventory for assessing personality.

MINOR PREMISE

In a syllogism, the proposition which introduces the minor term. It is the second proposition.

MINTZBERG, HENRY

Contemporary Canadian management writer best known for a study of the work of top managers (The Nature of Management Work, Harper & Row, New York, 1973). Mintzberg picks up the account of management work where *Carlson* leaves off. That is to say, Mintzberg, like carlson before him, documents the crowded, pressurised, hectic and non-contemplative nature of the work of senior managers, and indeed apostrophises such work as marked by brevity, variety and fragmentation but unlike carlson, mintzberg sees this as a natural state of affairs, not the product of disorganisation or lack of policy. Even senior managers will have to fight fires (who else will?); it is right that they should deal with the unexpected and problematic, the obscure and unprogrammable; if the work were routine it would not need managers to doit.

MINUTES

Written record of a meeting or discussion, and generally useful as a reminder of what was decided (or was not) and who is going to do what. There are two things to watch: first, processing minutes can become a ritual: don't do it, if it is not necessary; secondly, minute writing is an opportunity for political manipulation—if you cannot win the meeting, write the minutes.

MIRROR WRITING

Writing words or numbers backward. The term was derived from the fact that such writing can be read when held before a mirror, which reverses the order of the letters or numbers.

MIS

Acronym for Management Information System.

MISLEADING ADVERTISING

Advertising that, although not strictly untrue, leads consumers to less-than accurate conclusions. Also called *Deceptive Advertising.* Intentionally misleading consumers is an extreme form of this type of advertising.

MISSION

The ultimate, primary purposes of an organisation. An organisation's mission is what society expects from the organisation in exchange for its continuing survival.

MISSIONARY SALES PERSONNEL

Salespersons who visit prospective customers, distribute information to them, and handle questions and complaints but do not routinely take orders. Missionaries really serve as customer relations representatives.

MIXED DEXTRAL

Right-handed and left-eyed.

MIXED ECONOMY

In economics, this refers to the kind of economy in which the ownership of the means of production is partly in the private sector and partly in the public sector.

MIXED SINISTRAL

Left-handed and right-eyed.

MNP5

This protocol filters out interference in the telephone line and eliminates errors that can occur during the transmission and reception of data via modem. In addition, it encodes data at the sending end and decodes it at the receiving end. This is also called *Compression* and *Compression of Data.*

MODE

Method of display on the monitors like textual display, interactive or graphical mode.

MODEL

Any representation of an object, situation or organisation. It may be physical, verbal mathematical or produced by computer simulation.

MODEL, MATHEMATICAL

A description of a system (a machine or a situation) in which the factors are expressed in mathematical terms in such a way that effects of various changes in the real system can be simulated by changing the values given to the mathematical terms.

MODELING

A method of administering rewards that relies on observational learning. An employee learns the behaviours that are desirable by observing how others are rewarded. Proponents assume that behaviours will be imitated if the observer views a distinct link between performance and rewards.

MODEM

(*i*) Short for Modulator and Demodulator.

(*ii*) From the term 'Modulator-Demodulator'. It is an electronic device that converts information from a computer into a form suitable for transmission by telephone, thus enabling communication with other computers.

MODIFIED REBUY

An organisational buying situation in which a buyer is not completely satisfied with current suppliers or products and is "shopping around" rather than rebuying automatically.

MODULAR FURNITURE

To provide greater desk area (*i.e.,* table top area) and to save floor space many types of interlocking, L-shaped desks have come in the market, these are called *Modular Furniture.* Modular furniture is complete with bookcase, file and dwarfed portions. It can serve the purpose of an unscreened cabin also. Modular furniture is designed upon motion and time studies of clerks. It not only saves space but adds to work efficiency.

MONETARY POLICY

In economics this refers to a government's position on the regulation of the amount of spending power available in an economy and the cost of borrowing money, *e.g.*, deciding whether or not to impose a credit squeeze.

MONEY CHANGERS

Persons authorised by the Reserve Bank of India under the Foreign Exchange Regulations Act, 1973, to deal in foreign currencies. They purchase and/or sell such foreign currencies in the form of notes, coins or travellers' cheques.

MONEY SUPPLY

In economics this refers to the total amount of money circulating within an economy at any given time, whether in the form of notes, coins, bank deposits etc.

MONOPOLIES AND MERGERS COMMISSION

An agency set up by the UK government to identify abuses of monopoly power and to decide whether proposed mergers are likely to lead to a monopoly or a serious reduction in competition. The commission has the legal right to block mergers. In the USA the Federal Trade commission has a similar role, while the US 'antitrust' laws are considerably more powerful than the equivalent UK legislation. This is an area where the European Community is likely to develop an increasing interest.

MONOPOLISTIC COMPETITION

(*i*) A market structure characterised by a large number of sellers offering slightly differentiated products and exerting some control over their own prices.

(*ii*) A market structure characterised by a single seller in a market in which there are no suitable substitute products.

MONOPOLY

(*i*) A market structure characterised by a single seller in a market in which there are no suitable substitute products.

(*ii*) Control of the sale of a product by one supplier.

MONTAGE FORMAT

An advertising format that blends a number of situations, demonstrations, and other visual effects into one commercial to emphasise the array of possibilities associated with product usage.

MONTE CARLO TECHNIQUES

Techniques used in operations research that make use of the laws of probability.

MORAL BEHAVIOUR

In regard to marketers, how well an individual's or organisation's marketing activity exhibits the ethical values to which the individual or organisation subscribes.

MORTALITY

A source of error in experimental studies that occurs when participants drop out of the experiment before it is completed, resulting in the experimental and control groups not being comparable.

MORTGAGE

A loan made on the security of something—typically a property—where the ownership does not pass to the person taking out the loan until it is repaid but where he may have the use of it, provided he continues to repay the loan in agreed instalments.

MOTHERBOARD

The main component of any computer system. Different type of motherboards are available. Some motherboard includes the processor and related support chips, math coprocessor, memory and system bust sockets for peripheral boards. Some motherboards do not have processor on it to facilitate the upgrading of the processor chip. Some motherboards corporate even video subsystem or serial and parallel ports.

MOTILE

Motor-minded.

MOTION STUDY

The process of analysing a task to determine the preferred motions to be used in its completion.

MOTIVATE

To inspire, impel and encourage action. Motivation encompasses all the actions undertaken by a leader to encourage highest productivity. They includes selection, placement, compensation, communication, participation and development.

MOTIVATION

(*i*) A concept that describes the forces acting on or within an employee that initiate and direct behaviour.

(*ii*) An activated state that causes a person to initiate goal-directed behaviour.

(*iii*) The act of arousing or stimulating an inward urge to action in order to achieve a goal.

MOTIVATION RESEARCH

A type of marketing research that seeks to determine unconscious reasons why consumers buy given products, or at least the reasons that they are unwilling or unable to express clearly.

MOTIVATOR-HYGIENE THEORY

The *Herzberg* approach that identifies conditions of the job that operate primarily to dissatisfy employees when they are not present (hygiene factors—salary, job security, work conditions, and so on). Other job conditions lead to high levels of motivation and job satisfaction. However, the absence of these conditions does not prove highly dissatisfying. The conditions include achievement, growth, and advancement opportunities.

MOTIVE

An aroused need that energises behaviour and directs it towards a goal.

MOTOR CARRIER

In relation to physical distribution, a mode of transportation of products. The term usually refers to the trucking industry but may also include other carriers, such as *Greyhound's* package service.

MULTIFACETED INTERVENTIONS

Combinations of technostructural and human process interventions, required for most significant organisational change efforts.

MULTINATIONAL COMPANY

(*i*) A company whose interests cut across national boundaries, one which allocates its resources and its marketing efforts on a worldwide basis (Also called *Transactional Company* and *International Company*).

(*ii*) A company which operates in a number of countries and which uses an international strategy based on moving resources and operations around the world to secure local advantages such as labour costs, tax relief or access to local markets. It differs from an international company, which simply sells its products in different countries.

MULTINATIONAL MARKETER

An organisation that has substantial marketing activity in many countries.

MULTINATIONAL MARKETING GROUP

A group of countries aligned to form a unified market with minimal trade and tariff barriers among participating member countries; the *European Community* is an example.

MULTINATIONAL MARKETING

Marketing across national boundaries. Also called *International Marketing.*

MULTINATIONALS

A firm engaged in business in two or more countries may be referred to as a *Multinational Company* (MNC). Some authorities argue that the term multinational should be more narrowly defined, involving operations in a number of countries, a substantial proportion of assets abroad and a global management orientation. This type of enterprise offers a special challenge to managers. The MNC has to cope not only with the economic, political, legal and social environment of the domestic country but also of each country in which it operates. Managers exchanged between countries have to adapt their approach to a new environment. For example, a manager from the USA might find himself confronted with a workforce in another country where the law does not allow any employee to be dismissed. More subtle cultural differences also arise.

MULTIPLE CHANNEL STRATEGY

A plan for distributing products through various channels.

MULTIPLE DEBTORS

A tie-up of two or more debtors to a creditor, though the magnitude of the debt may be the same in each case.

MULTIPLE-UNIT PRICING

Selling more than one unit of a product at a price lower than the sum of the individual units' prices. *Two-For-One* offers are an example.

MULTI-STAGE SAMPLING

A market research technique often used in political sampling where several random samples are used to give a convenient sample, say, one street in one political ward in one constituency.

MUTUAL ACCOUNT

An account operated on terms agreeable to both parties (the debtor and creditor) so that there is reciprocity of transactions or dealings between them.

N

NARRATIVE MATERIAL

Reading matter which tells a story.

NATIONAL CULTURE

A set of values, attitudes, beliefs, and norms shared by a majority of the inhabitants of a country.

NATIONAL GROWTH AND MANAGEMENT

The objectives for national growth as set forth by our planners are: (1) A sizable increase in national income so as to raise the level of living of the people in the country; (2) Rapid industrialisation and utilisation of nation's economic and natural resources; (3) A large expansion of employment opportunities; and (4) Reduction of inequalities in income and wealth and a more even distribution of economic power.

NATIONAL RESPONSIVENESS STRATEGY

A strategy of allowing subsidiaries to have substantial latitude in adapting products and services to suit the particular needs and political realities of the countries in which they operate.

NATIONALISATION

The process by which a state takes over the ownership of a private company or industry and brings it within the control of the public sector. This may be due to practising the ideology of socialism or to the attempt to save a strategic part of the economy from collapse or foreign ownership.

NATURAL LANGUAGE SPECIFICATION

Automatic programming method that uses a specification written in ordinary language specification with queries from the computer.

NEED FOR ACHIEVEMENT (NACH)

The desire to accomplish challenging tasks and achieve a standard of excellence in one's work

NEED FOR AFFILIATION (NAFF)

The desire to maintain warm, friendly relationships with others.

NEED FOR POWER (NPOW)

The desire to influence others and control one's environment.

NEED HIERARCHY MODEL

Maslow assumed that the needs of a person depend on what he already has. This in a sense means that a satisfied need is not a motivator. Human needs organised in a hierarchy of importance are classified as physiological, safety, belongingness, esteem, and self-actualisation.

NEED

The perceived gap between actual and desired states.

NEEDS ANALYSIS

An assessment of an organisation's training needs that is developed by considering overall organisational requirements, tasks associated with jobs for which training is needed, and the degree to which individuals are able to perform those tasks effectively.

NEEDS

Deficiencies that an individual experiences at a particular point in time.

NEGATIVE AFFECTIVITY

A mode state in which an individual is very likely to express and experience negative stress such as anger, fear and depression.

NEGATIVE ENTROPY

The ability of open systems to bring in new energy, in the form of inputs and feedback from the environment, in order to delay or arrest entropy.

NEGATIVE REINFORCEMENT

(*i*) A type of reinforcement in behaviour modification, aimed at increasing a desired behaviour, that involves providing a noxious stimuli so that an individual will engage in the desired behaviour in order to stop the noxious stimuli.

(*ii*) Reinforcement that strengthens a response because the response removes some painful or unpleasant stimulus or enables the organism to avoid it.

NEGATIVE SYNERGY

The force that results when group process losses are greater than any gains achieved from combining the forces of group members.

NEGATIVISM

Marked resistance, the tendency to do the opposite of what one is requested to do.

NEGOTIABLE INSTRUMENT

A financial proof document which entitles the owner to payment another person (*e.g.*, a cheque or currency note).

NEGOTIATE

The process or act of attempting to achieve agreement between two or more parties by clarifying and discussing issues, establishing the areas of controversy, clarifying positions taken, proposing options for agreement, discovering and confirming areas of agreement, creating and clarifying the language and terms of an agreement, including the intent and duties of the respective parties.

NEGOTIATION

The essence of the collective bargaining process. It refers to the discussion of terms and conditions of employment by employers and employees, or their representatives, with a view to reaching a mutually acceptable outcome.

NET BENEFIT

A decision criterion based on the same information and used for the same basic purpose as a cost/

benefit analysis. A net benefit is calculated by subtracting costs from benefits (a cost/benefit analysis divides benefits by costs).

NET CURRENT ASSETS

The aggregate of all current assets (including cash) less current liabilities. It is also known as *Working Capital*

NET INCOME

Revenue and gains minus expenses and losses.

NET LEASE

A lease in which the tenant pays the rent plus all costs of ownership, such as taxes and maintenance. Sometimes a distinction is made between a net lease (rent plus some costs) and a net lease (rent plus all costs, such as taxes).

NET PRODUCT

A product new to a company. This relative term is influenced by the perceptions of marketers and consumers; in general, it refers to any recently introduced product that offers some benefit that other products do not.

NET PROFIT (OR NET INCOME)

It is the excess of 'revenue and gains' over 'expenses and deprival'. It results in an increase in the proprietor's equity. 'Net loss is the deficiency of revenue and gains' as compared to 'expenses and deprival', and leads to decrease in the owner's equity.

NET PROFIT (TRADING PROFIT)

The actual financial gain from activities, calculated by deducting all operating expenses from the total sales revenue for a specified activity. It may be calculated with or without allowance for tax and interest payments.

NET PROFIT PERCENTAGE

Percentage of net profit from each sales rupee. Also called Net Income Ratio. The calculating formula is as follows:

$$\frac{\text{Net Profit}}{\text{Sales}} \times 100$$

NET SALES

Gross sales minus returns and allowances over a specified period.

NET SUM

A sum arrived at after making all the deductions and including the permitted allowances.

NET TOTAL ASSETS

Total assets less current liabilities.

NET

The balance of items or amount remaining after some items or amounts have been removed; also, the amount or number of items free from encumbrances or obligations; also, the considerations that remain after discounting or removing those that have little or no bearing on the issue or problem at hand.

NETWORK

(*i*) A management process element consisting of a set of

cooperative relationships with individuals whose help is needed in order for a manager to function effectively.

(*ii*) System of interconnected computers.

NETWORK DIAGRAM

A diagram constructed as a step in setting up PERT that constitutes a graphic depiction of the interrelationships among the activities in a project.

NETWORKING

The interconnection of two or more networks, (*i*) Wide Area Networks (WANs): Telecommunications networks covering a large geographic area are called wide area networks (WANs). Networks that cover a large city or metropolitan area (metropolitan area networks) can also be included in this category. Such large networks have become a necessity for carrying out the day-to-day activities of many business and government organisations and their end users. For example, WANs are used by many multinational companies to transmit and receive information among their employees, customers, suppliers, and other organisations across cities, regions, countries, and the world. Fig. 3 illustrates an example of a global wide area network for a major multinational corporation, (*ii*) Local Area Networks (LANs), connect computers and other information processing devices within a limited physical area, such as an office, a classroom, a building, manufacturing plant, or other work site. LANs have become commonplace in many organisations for providing telecommunications network capabilities that link end users in offices, departments, and other work-groups. LANs use a variety of telecommunications media,

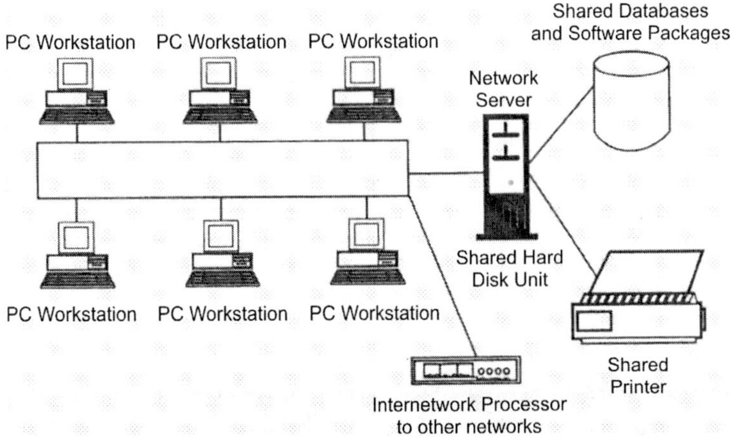

Fig. 3: A Local Area Network (LAN) Note how the LAN allows users to share hardware, software and data resources

such as ordinary telephone wiring coaxial cable, or even wireless radio systems to interconnect microcomputer workstations and computer peripherals. To communicate over the network, each PC usually has a circuit board called a *Network Interface Card*. Most LANs use a more powerful microcomputer having a large hard disk capacity, called a file server or network server, that contains a network operating system program that controls telecommunications and the use and sharing of network resources. For example, it distributes copies of common data files and software packages to the other microcomputers in the network and controls access to shared laser printers and other network peripherals.

NEUROLOGY

Science dealing with the nervous system.

NEUROSIS

Mental disorder generally of a milder character than a psychosis. "Nervousness" and "Nervous Breakdown" usually mean neurosis.

NEUTRAL

A term referring to any third party who is actively engaged in negotiations in order to facilitate an agreement.

NEUTRALISERS

Situational factors that make it impossible for a give leader behaviour to have an impact on subordinate performance and/or satisfaction.

NEW PRODUCT DEVELOPMENT

The process of identifying, developing and evaluating new offerings.

NEW PRODUCT

A product new to a company. This relative term is influenced by the perceptions of marketers and consumers; in general, it refers to any recently introduced product that offers some benefit that other products do not.

NEW PRODUCTS COMMITTEE

A group within an organisation assigned to such taste as creating and reviewing new product policies, evaluating options, and deciding whether to commercialise new products. Committee membership usually includes the heads of the organisation's functional departments and the new products director.

NEW TASK BUYING

An organisational buying situation in which a buyer is seeking to fill a need never before addressed. Uncertainty and back of information about products and suppliers characterise this situation.

NEW TECHNOLOGY

The term often used to describe the applied micro electronic devices to be found in the electronic office.

NEW VENTURE

An enterprise that is in the process of being created by an entrepreneur.

NEW VENTURE TEAMS

Temporary task forces or teams made up of individuals who have been relieved of their normal duties in order to develop a new process, product, or program.

NEW VENTURE UNITS

Either separate divisions or specially incorporated companies created for the specific purpose of developing new products or business ideas and initiatives.

NEWLY INDUSTRIALISED COUNTRIES (NICS)

Countries within the LDCs that are emerging as major exporters of manufactured goods, including such nations as Hong Kong, Taiwan and South Korea.

NEWS RELEASE

A brief written statement sent to the press or others describing a new product, a product improvement, a price change or some other development of interest. The release is intended to be newsworthy.

NICHE MARKETING

The systematic search for a market niche usually by a small specialist organisation. Its basic principal is the attempt to create a new market rather than increase market share of an existing market.

NICHE

A small discrete segment of a market which can be targeted with a distinct marketing strategy.

NODE

An indication of the beginning and/or ending of activities in a PERT network; also called an *Event.*

NOISE

(*i*) Any factor in the communication process that interferes with exchanging messages and achieving common meaning.

(*ii*) In communication theory, any interference or distraction that disrupts the communication process.

NOMINAL GROUP TECHNIQUE (NGT)

A technique for enhancing group creativity that integrates both individual work and group interaction within certain ground rules.

NON-ADOPTER

A member of the group of consumers who never buy a particular new product or adopt a certain new style.

NON-CRISIS PROBLEM

A type of problem in managerial decision-making involving an issue that requires resolution but does not simultaneously have the importance and immediacy characteristics of a crisis.

NON-CUMULATIVE QUANTITY DISCOUNT

A price discount determined by the size of an individual purchase order. The larger the order, the larger the discount.

NON-CYBERNETIC CONTROL SYSTEM

A control system that relies on human discretion as a basic part of its process.

NON-DURABLE GOOD

A physical, tangible item that is quickly consumed, worn out, or outdated.

NON-GOVERNMENT ORGANISATION

This term is usually applied to an organisation that operates internationally but is not supported, in the main, by direct government funding *e.g., Amnesty International* or *The Red Cross.*

NON-LINEAR PROGRAMMING

An operations research technique that may be used when some of the variables in the mathematical models are raised to a higher power (*e.g.*, X).

NON-OCCUPATIONAL POLICY

An insurance policy providing protection against off-the-job injury and illness. Injury or sickness covered by workers compensation insurance is excluded. Group accident and sickness policies are often non-occupational.

NON-PRICE COMPETITION

Competition emphasising marketing variables other than price—for example, *Product Differentiation.*

NON-PROBABILITY SAMPLE

A sample chosen on the basis of convenience or personal judgment.

NON-PROFIT ORGANISATION

(*i*) Any organisation whose ownership resides entirely with its members and whose financial operations are not intended to yield a profit for shareholders, *e.g.*, clubs or neighbourhood associations or charities.

(*ii*) An organisation whose main purposes centre on issues other than making profits.

NON-PROGRAMMED DECISIONS

Managerial decisions for which predetermined decision rules are impractical because the situations are novel and/or ill-structured.

NON-RATIONAL ESCALATION

(*i*) The tendency to increase commitment to a previously selected course of action beyond the level that would be expected if the manager followed an effective decision-making process; also called Escalation Phenomenon.

(*ii*) Models of managerial decision-making which suggest that information gathering and processing limitations make it difficult for managers to make optimal decisions.

NON-VERBAL COMMUNICATION

(*i*) Communication by means of elements and behaviours that are not coded into words.

(*ii*) Messages sent with body posture, facial expressions, and head and eye movements.

NORM

A social principle identifying what action is right or wrong in a given situation.

NORMS

A major group process factor involving expected behaviours sanctioned by the group that regulate and foster uniformity in member behaviours.

NORMAL DISTRIBUTION

The distribution of data from a random sample of the population. When these data are plotted on a graph they show up as a symmetrical bellshaped curve with scores clustered around the average and declining towards either extreme.

NORMATIVE DECISION-MAKING MODELS

Models of decision-making that attempt to prescribe how managers should make decisions.

NORMATIVE LEADERSHIP MODEL

A situational leadership theory model (designed by *Vroom* and *Yetton*) that helps leaders assess critical situational factors that affect the extent to which they should involve subordinates in particular decisions.

NORMING

A stage of group development in which group members begin to build group cohesion, as well as develop a consensus about norms for performing a task and relating to one another.

NORTON EDITOR

A word processor or a complete editor developed by *Peter Norton* for micro-computers.

NOTEBOOK COMPUTER

Small computer of briefcase size having a flat panel liquid crystal display.

NOT-FOR-PROFIT MARKETING

Organised marketing efforts used by not-for-profit organisations, including those involved in education, health care, philanthropy, social causes, ideas, land religious doctrines; used interchangeably with social marketing by some.

NOTICE BOARDS

These are found in every organisation, probably the commonness of the media has resulted in its receiving proper care. The location, style of display and the matter displayed over offer considerable scope for improvement.

NULL CYCLE

Time taken to execute a program without including data or new data.

NUMBER REPRESENTATION

Representating the numbers in an agreed format according to agreed rules.

NUMBER SYSTEM

A set of symbols and rules to providing meaning to them alongwith a set of operators and associated operations with those operators for number representation.

NUMERICAL CONTROL

Direction of machines by magnetic tape or punched cards.

NUTRITION

The science of food, nutrients, and other substances found in food. Nutrition is concerned with the actions, interactions, and balances of food and its component substances in relation to health and disease. The processes by which an organism ingests, digests, absorbs, transports, utilises and excretes food substances is also a part of this science. In addition, nutrition examines the social, economic, cultural, and psychological implications of food and eating.

O

OBJECT CODE

The code or output produced by an assembler or compiler in form of machine code to operate microprocessor or computer after translation of source code.

OBJECT LANGUAGE

A programming language in which the programs to the microprocessor or computer are written directly in binary code.

OBJECT LINKING AND EMBEDDING (OLE)

Integrating or incorporating the object of one window's application into other application.

OBJECT ORIENTED PROGRAMMING

A class of programming languages or a type of programming where the whole data items are treated as entities or objects and the programs are written following a different approach breaking the whole program into subprograms written oriented to those entities or objects.

OBJECTIVE AND TASK METHOD

A method of setting a promotional budget whereby the marketer decides the objective to be accomplished, determines the tasks necessary to achieve the objective, and budgets amounts sufficient to accomplish the tasks. Also called the *Task Method.*

OBJECTIVE

(1) In planning, a target to be achieved.

(2) More specific and concrete than goals, objectives enable managers to gauge the short-run progress of the organisation towards its goals.

(3) According to *Louis Allen*, "Objectives are goals established to guide the efforts of the company and each of its components." Objectives are key to effective planning.

(4) More specific and concrete than goals, objectives enable managers to gauge the short-run progress of the organisation towards its goals.

OBSERVABILITY

The quality of possessing advantages over existing products that are easily seen or understood by consumers.

OBSERVATION RESEARCH

(*i*) A research approach which involves studying customers' reactions and behaviour without any artificial stimulates.

(*ii*) The systematic recording of behaviour, objects, or events as they are witnessed.

OCCUPATIONAL BASED VALUATION

The first place to look for values within the objectives. If a firm wants to enter a new market its objectives indicate where to put the heavier weight.

OFFER MIX

The mix of product, price and availability offered to a customer. Not including communication of that offer.

OFFICE

(*i*) The dictionary meaning of office is "a place where business is carried on". From the point of view of a common man an "office" is a place where some clerks and a few officers sit on chairs with bundles of files on their table doing nothing but paper work. An office is defined as a central place where all sorts of clerical work is done to co-ordinate and control the affairs of the whole organisation.

(*ii*) A place from where a business or service organisation operates; a position or appointment which involves certain special duties.

OFFICE COMMITTEES

Office committees are those committees which are entrusted with the functions of office management. The responsibility of a committee is collective as the decisions are made by the committee as a body.

OFFICE MANAGER

The effective performance of the office functions is possible only if the office is managed properly. Generally, management of the office is entrusted to an executive known as *Office Manager*. It is the office manager who is responsible for planning, organisation and control of office operations and direction of office personnel for the achievement of the purpose of the office.

OFFICE MECHANISATION

Office mechanisation means introduction of machines and equipment with a view to increase the efficiency and quality of office operations. Mechanisation of office operations is preferred as it improves performance, achieves saving in time and clerical cost, ensures accuracy and provides a safeguard against fraud. Work done by the machines is neat and clean and the results are obtained more quickly than by manual operations. Therefore, mechanisation should be considered not as a fashion but to remove specific deficiencies in manual operations and to secure identifiable improvement in office work.

OFFICE SERVICES

This includes maintenance of proper data processing and other office management services, communication on best use of latest mechanical devices.

OFF-LINE

(*i*) Performing a job by a device which is not under control of a central processing unit.

(*ii*) The part of computer system which is not under the immediate control of the central processing unit and cannot therefore be accessed directly; *e.g. Long Intervals,* like a yearly bank statement or a quarterly electricity bill.

OFF-PRICE RETAILER

A specially discounter offering a limited line of nationally known brand names.

OFF-THE-JOB TRAINING

Off-the-job training covers a number of techniques-classroom lectures, films, demonstrations, case studies and other restimulation exercises, and programmed instruction.

OHIO-STATE PSYCHOLOGICAL EXAMINATION

A test used to predict ability to do academic work at the secondary, college and university levels. The test measures vocabulary, language usage, and achievement in reading.

OLIGOPOLY

A market structure characterised by a small number of sellers, who control the market.

OMNIBUS SURVEY

(*i*) A regular questionnaire-based field research survey with a large sample. Organisations can commission one or more questions to be asked; the survey includes questions from a number of different companies.

(*ii*) In market research this is a wide-ranging form of survey that seeks to obtain data on many topics for a number of clients.

ON COST

The share of indirect expenses allocated for a job or a commodity.

ONCE-OVER

A final, quick, and comprehensive check of a previous assessment or examination; a brief examination; or, a rapid, complete appraisal.

ONE-PLAN OFFICE

A single large room divided into various workplaces but with no fixed walls or barriers between them. It has been associated with a reduction in satisfaction.

ONE-PROCESS STRATEGY

A strategy whereby a single process is charged for a product regardless of the circumstances surrounding the sale, the quantity bought, or any other unique aspect of the exchange.

ON-LINE

(*i*) Term used when computer input or output is directly connected to the computer.

(*ii*) That apart of a computer system which is under the immediate control of the central processing unit and can make information immediately accessible to the user by being linked directly to a mainframe and operating in real time. Most common example is that of an airline seat reservation system.

ON-THE-JOB TRAINING

On-the-job training places the employees in an actual work situation and makes them appear to be immediately productive. It is learning by doing. For jobs that either are difficult to simulate or can be learned quickly by watching and doing on-the-job training makes sense.

OPEN DOOR

A term used to describe unscheduled and unlimited access or admission to, or availability of a person, service, or facility, policy adopted by a manager to assure open feedback and the participation of all employees in issues relating to management actions, policies, organisational performance and employees beliefs and attitudes.

OPEN FILE

The file in a database management system which is available currently for any kind of processing like reading, modification, writing or possibly both.

OPEN MARKET

A marketing method by which the trading activities of buying and selling are kept open to the general public.

OPEN-END AGREEMENT

A bargaining agreement providing for a contract that will remain in effect until one of the parties wants to re-open negotiations.

OPEN-END LEASE

A lease that may involve a balloon payment, based on the value of the item leased, when it is returned to the lessor.

OPERAND CONDITIONING

The process by which reinforcement of a behaviour results in repetition of that behaviour.

OPERANDS

Behaviours amenable to control by altering the consequences (rewards and punishments) that follow them.

OPERATING CYCLE

The time gap between the purchase of raw materials and sale of finished products in a manufacturing firm.

OPERATING EXPENSE RATIO

Percentage of operating expenses needed for each sales dollar: Total Operating Expenses/Net Sales.

OPERATING EXPENSE

An expense for salaries, rent, and other costs associated with operating a business.

OPERATIONAL AUDIT

A functional audit which appraises the various operations of an undertaking, such as production, sales, administration, marketing, etc.

OPERATIONAL DEFINITION

A definition of something which is based on the operation of the factors which produced it, *e.g.*, inflation is defined by the movement of prices and the real value of money. The term is also used more loosely to mean a 'working definition' or a 'rule of thumb'.

OPERATIONAL PLANNING

Planning that focuses on day-to-day functional activities, such as supervision of the sales force.

OPERATIONS RESEARCH

Application of quantitative methods to the solution of management problems. It includes a "systems approach" in which a larger number, rather than a few factors, are considered positively by a group of scientists from different fields.

OPERATIONS RESEARCH FOR PROBLEM-SOLVING

Current research on the machine simulation of higher mental processes suggests that we will be able to program much of the top job before too many decades have passed. There is good authority for the prediction that a decade or two a digital computer will be the world chess champion and that another will discover and prove an important new mathematical theorem, and that in the somewhat more distant future "the way is open to deal scientifically with ill-structured problems to make the computer coextensive with human mind".

OPERATIONS RESEARCH

Application of quantitative methods to the solution of management problems. It includes a "systems approach" in which a larger number, rather than a few factors, are considered positively by a group of scientists from different fields.

OPERATOR

The symbol denoting some kind of operation to be performed on the operands.

OPINION DEALINGS

A stock exchange term which refers to the right to buy or sell securities.

OPINION LEADER

A group member who, because of some quality or characteristic, is likely to lead other group members in particular matters.

OPINION POLLING

A form of survey research in which respondents are asked their opinions regarding goods, services or political candidates.

OPPORTUNITY COST

(*i*) In economics, this refers to the lost income, profit or time involved in foregoing an alternative course of action, *i.e.*, this is an economic cost and would not be included as an accounting cost.

(*ii*) The value of the benefit scarified by choosing a particular alternative or course of action.

OPTHALMOLOGIST

A physician specialising in hearing defects and diseases of the ear.

OPTICAL DISK

A storage device in which the digital data is recorded with the help of laser beam as microscopic marks in the form of concentric and spiral tracks.

OPTIMAL BALANCE

The most desirable relationship among the criteria of effectiveness. Optimal, rather than maximum, balance must be achieved in any case of more than one criterion.

OPTIMISATION

Any attempt to maximise or minimise a specific quantity, usually called an "objective", also, determination of the best mix of inputs to achieve an objective.

OPTIMUM

The course of action that minimises overall losses or maximises overall gains.

ORDER GETTING

An adaptive selling process that tailors sales efforts and product offerings to specific customer needs. An order getter is primarily responsible for developing business for the firm. Order getters seek out customers and creatively make sales. Also called *Creative Selling*.

ORDER PROCESSING

A systematic procedure for filling customer orders. Are received and ends when goods have been shipped and bills sent to customers.

ORDER TAKER

A salesperson who is primarily responsible for writing up orders, checking invoices, and assuring prompt order processing.

ORDINARY SHARES

Securities sold by a company which maybe traded within limitations (*e.g.*, if it is *Private Company*, etc.) and which constitute the equity share capital of that company. These shares usually carry voting rights and take third place, after debenture and preference shares, in entitlement to the distributed profits of the company.

ORGANIC MODEL OF ORGANISATION

The organisational design that emphasises the importance of adaptability and development. It is relatively informal, decentralised, and simple.

ORGANIC ORGANISATION

A term introduced by two British sociologists and management theorists, *Tom Burns* and *George Stalker*. It denotes a relatively open and informal type of organisation displaying flexibility in people's job descriptions, for example; an encouraging communication and the flow of new ideas out with the formal chain of command. This is in striking contrast to what happens in a mechanistic organisation.

ORGANISATION

(*i*) "Organisation is concerned with the arrangement of work, with the division of activities and with the allocation of duties, authority and responsibilities." In the words of *Leffingwell*, "A well organised office makes possible for the management to plan its operations intelligently, to put its plan into effect surely, to follow their progress currently, to determine their effectiveness promptly, to appraise the results without delay and to co-ordinate all the activities of the business".

(*ii*) A group of people brought together for the purpose of achieving certain objectives. As the basic unit of an organisation is the role rather than the person in it the organisation is maintained in existence, sometimes over a long period of time, despite many change of members.

(*iii*) The division of work into managerial positions in the corporate structure and the adaptation of the structure to the people in the organisation.

(*iv*) The process of identifying and grouping the work to be done, defining and delegating responsibility and authority, and establishing relationships to accomplish objectives.

ORGANISATION AND METHODS (O.M.)

These deal with organisations reducing cost and improving the efficiency of accounting, as also of office systems, procedures and operations, etc.

ORGANISATION AUDIT

An audit of all aspects of an organisation operations. In practice this is usually the same as a management audit.

ORGANISATION CHART

A diagram of positions and their relationship to one another.

ORGANISATION CHARTS

An organisation chart is a graphic portrayal of positions in the organisation and of formal lines of accountability among them. It provides a bird's eye-view of the relationships between members of the organisation.

ORGANISATION CONVENIENCE

A course of action that meets the (usually financial) interests of the organisation as a whole rather than the interests of members or customers, *e.g.*, moving to a cheaper, but less accessible, location.

ORGANISATION DEVELOPMENT

A process that affects the organisation as a whole as well as its individual members. It involves the application of behavioural science to process the functioning and the management of the organisation, especially in response to changes in the environment.

ORGANISATION FORMAL

The official relationships of the positions in a corporation, generally shown on an organisation chart and embodied in job descriptions.

ORGANISATION SIZE

The number of members an organisation has, can have a direct effect on its organisational structure. The larger the number, the greater the pressure to operate as a formal organisation with a high level of bureaucracy, relatively fixed chain of command and increased levels in a hierarchy of authority.

ORGANISATION STRUCTURE

(*i*) The formal pattern of how people and jobs are grouped in an organisation. The organisation structure is often illustrated by an organisation chart.

(*ii*) Organisation involves establishing an appropriate structure for the goal-seeking activities. The structure of an organisation is generally shown on an organisation chart or a job-task pyramid. It shows the authority and responsibility relationships between various positions in the organisation by depicting who reports to whom. It is significant to note that the organisation structure is directly related to the attainment of the organisational objectives.

(*iii*) The arrangement of the work of an organisation into the different functional roles and management roles.

ORGANISATION, INFORMAL

The unofficial (interpersonal) relationships in an organisation not shown on the organisation chart and even not consistent with it.

ORGANISATIONAL BEHAVIOUR

The study of human behaviour, attitudes, and performance within an organisational setting; drawing on theory, methods, and principles from such disciplines as psychology, sociology and cultural anthropology to learn about individual perceptions, values, learning capacities, and action while working in groups and within the total organisation; analysing the external environment's effect on the organisation and its human resources, missions, objectives, and strategies.

ORGANISATIONAL BEHAVIOUR MODIFICATION (OBM)

An operand approach to organisational behaviour. This term is used interchangeably with the term behaviour modification.

ORGANISATIONAL BUYING BEHAVIOUR

The decision-making activities of organisational buyers that lead to purchase of products.

ORGANISATIONAL CLIMATE

A set of properties of the work environment, perceived directly or indirectly by the employees that is assumed to be a major force in influencing employee behaviour.

ORGANISATIONAL CULTURE

The pervasive system of values, beliefs, and norms that exists in any organisation. The organisational culture can encourage or discourage effectiveness, depending on the nature of the values, beliefs, and norms.

ORGANISATIONAL DESIGN

A specific organisational structure that results from managers' decisions and actions. Also, the process by which managers choose among alternative frameworks of jobs and departments.

ORGANISATION DEVELOPMENT (OD)

A process that affects the organisation as a whole as well as its individual members. It involves the application of behavioural science to process the functioning and the management of the organisation, especially in response to changes in the environment.

ORGANISATIONAL MARKET

Market consisting of buyers that use the product to help operate a business or for resale. Also called *The Business Market.*

ORGANISATIONAL MISSION

A statement of company purpose. It explains why the organisation exists and what in hopes to accomplish?

ORGANISATIONAL OPPORTUNITIES

Marketing opportunities that fit the organisation's capabilities.

ORGANISATIONAL POLITICS

The activities related to acquiring, developing, and using power and other resources to obtain one's preferred outcome when there is uncertainty or disagreement about choices.

ORGANISATIONAL PROCESSES

The activities that breathes life into the organisation structure. Among the common organisational processes are *Communication, Decision-making, Socialisation,* and *Career Development.*

ORGANISATIONAL PRODUCT

A product or services that is used to produce other products and /or used to operate an organisation.

ORGANISATIONAL PROFILE

A diagram that shows the responses of the members of an organisation to the questionnaires that *Likert* devised to measure certain organisational characteristics.

ORGANISING

In a marketing contest, refers to the assignment of tasks, the grouping of tasks into organisational units, and the allocation of resources to organisational units.

ORGANISATION AUDIT

An audit of all aspects of an organisation operations. In

practice this is usually the same as a management audit.

ORGANISATION CONVENIENCE

A course of action that meets the (usually financial) interests of the organisation as a whole rather than the interests of members or customers, *e.g.*, moving to a cheaper, but less accessible, location.

OTS (OPPORTUNITY TO SEE)

The average number of viewing occasions for a particular advertisement.

OUTLAYS

Actual expenditure of funds, including cheques issued, the payment of interest accrued on debt and other payments (minus refunds and reimbursements).

OUTPLACEMENT

The process of helping people to find new jobs after notice of redundancy but while still employed.

OUTPUT

The result of a process; in a project-management or project-control sense, the results of the final process over which an organisation has control and which contributes directly to a desired outcome or impact.

OUTPUT CONTRACT

An agreement to purchase the entire production or output of a particular items.

OUTPUT DEVICE

The peripheral devices which are attached to a computer system which are used to obtain the output in the desired form, *e.g.*; *Printers, Plotters*.

OUTPUT MEASURE

An assessment of the result of an end process; when applied to the end product of a complex process output measures are assessments of productivity.

OUTPUT MEDIA

In data processing, paper print-outs and forms, tapes, diskettes, embossed plastic cards, and other matter and devices on which processed information appears.

OVER-COMPENSATION

(*i*) Producing a greater efforts than is needed to overcome a difficulty or resolve a defect. The term is often used in connection with attempts to overcome an inferiority complex.

(*ii*) An extreme form of compensation.

OVER-CONFORMING

This term is sometimes used to describe a person who is excessively slavish to the demands of authority or the convention of social norm.

OVERDRAFT

A method of taking a bank advance whereby the banker agrees to advance money to a client, which is over and above his balance but within a permitted ceiling limit.

OVERHEAD

(*i*) Any recurrent day-to-day expenditure incurred in running an organisation other than the costs of labour and material, *e.g., Rent Heading* and *Lighting*.

(*ii*) Costs that do not vary with output over a period of time.

OVERHEAD ABSORPTION

A process of charging or distributing overhead costs allotted to a particular department for its various units.

OVERSHOOT METHOD

A technique for forecasting economic activity based on the theory that whenever business activity rises beyond the normal trend level, a reaction is bound to set in.

OVERTIME

Any time worked outside normal working hours, for which people are paid at a higher rate than the basic level of pay, usually double or one and half-time.

OWNED FUNDS

These funds are those that have been contributed by the owners of the business, *i.e.*, proprietors, partners or shareholders as the case may be. Ownership funds are the real risk capital. Generally, it remains invested in the business as long as the business continues to exist. Owners of business can withdraw these funds from the business only at the risk of the closure of the business.

OWNER'S EQUITY

The owner's contribution towards the assets of a business entity. It could be expressed as the total assets of an entity less such claims of outsiders or liabilities and includes both contributed capital and retained earnings.

OWNERSHIP GROUP

An organisation made up of stores or small chains, each having a separate name, identity, and image but all operating under the control of a central owner.

P

PACKAGING

(*i*) An auxiliary dimension of the product that involves labels, inserts instructions, graphic design, shipping cartons, and sizes and types of containers. In other words, we can say that packaging is concerned with putting of the products in bags, boxes, bottles, cans, barrels or other categories of special containers, before they are despatched for sale. Packing of goods implies placing them in suitable packets to facilitate their easy and safe handling, to ensure their quantity and quality, to protect them from any kind of damage during transit or storage and to improve their attractiveness.

(*ii*) Packaging is concerned with putting of the products in bags, boxes, bottles, cans, barrels or other categories of special containers, before they are despatched for sale. Packing of goods implies placing them in suitable packets to facilitate their easy and safe handling, to ensure their quantity and quality, to protect them from any kind of damage during transit or storage and to improve their attractiveness.

PAGINATION

In desk top publishing software programs like word processors and spreadsheets, the process of dividing of a large file into hard copy pages.

PAGING

A process that automatically and continually transfers the pages between primary storage and direct access storage devices.

PAID-UP POLICIES

A person insured for life may sometimes find it difficult to pay premiums but may not like to terminate his interest. Provided the premiums have been paid for a stipulated minimum number of years, the policy-holder may exercise his option to treat the policy as paid-up'. The premiums then cease to be payable and the insured retains the claim till maturity of the policy.

PANELS (CONSUMER PANELS)

Groups of consumers who regularly monitor buying or usage information, often through keeping diary records.

PAR VALUE

Original or face value of stock, debenture or bond.

PARALLEL IMPORT

Importation of a branded product into a country by some firm other than a firm that has been granted exclusive rights to distribute the brand in that country.

PARAMETRIC STATISTICS

Statistics that deal with a normal distribution or other population of scores.

PARETO EFFECT

The 80/20 rule; The largest proportion of sale, value or profit will often come from a small proportion of customers.

PARITY

The perceived fairness of equal rates of pay between individuals of groups of people.

PARITY BIT

A check bit that is appended to an array of binary digits to make the sum of all bits including the check bit always either odd or even. If sum is to be made odd then it is known as *odd parity bit* If sum is to be made even then it is known as *even parity bit.*

PARKINSON, C. NORTHCOTE

English writer and academic best known for Parkinsons Law, which states that work will expand to fill the time available for its completion (Parkinson's Law and the Pursuit of progress, John Murray, London, 1958). More generally parkinson's name is associated with the critique of bureaucracy and especially the stern warning that unless checked bureaucracy will grow, with strangulating effect. The business implication is that it pays in both senses to keep a watch on the size and power of the headquarters staff and, indeed, of central for nations and staff units generally.

PART METHOD

A technique of learning in which the material is broken down into smaller parts to be learned separately and then recombined.

PARTICIPATION

(*i*) Payment by the insured person, under an insurance policy provision, of a certain percentage of any loss; also, a mortgage agreement in which the lender receives a share of the profits of a venture in addition to interest on the loan.

(*ii*) The term used to describe the involvement of people in the performance of the organisation they work for, *e.g.*, by employee ownership of profit sharing.

PARTICIPATIVE MANAGEMENT

A concept of managing of managing that encourages employee's participation in decision-making and matters that affect their jobs.

PARTNER

A person who is associated with another (or others) in an organisation, activity or endeavour. A full partner exercises authority and makes decisions, which commit and are binding on the resources of the organisation, activity, or endeavour. A silent partner is one who is not publicly known to be a partner. A limited partner is a partner with limited authority to participate in operating decisions or to commit the partnership's resources.

PARTNERSHIP

A business or professional unit based upon a formal legal agreement between two or more partners. It is not an incorporated company, which means that the individuals remain responsible for actions and decisions, and not the business unit itself.

PASSWORD

A code string that is used to identify a particular user and allow to access the data files if and only if the password is correct. This is a security feature to maintain the privacy.

PASTE

The feature of window based desk top packages which allows the user to copy a part of document and then paste it some other position in same or the other document.

PATENT

(*i*) An official record of specific rights awarded to an individual or group to prevent others (from copying a design for goods or manner of procedure (*e.g.*, a manufacturing process) invented by that individual or group for a specified time.

(*ii*) A monopoly right, awarded by law to an individual or group, granting sole right to make, use or sell an article or process they have invented. In the United Kingdom a patent normally lasts for twenty years during which time the patent holder is protected from any attempts by others to copy their invention.

PATH-GOAL LEADERSHIP MODEL

A theory that suggests that a leader needs to influence the followers' perception of work goals, self-development goals, and paths of goal attainment. The foundation for the model is the expectancy motivation theory.

PATH-GOAL THEORY

A type of contingency theory of leadership which is based on the expectancy theory of motivation. It concentrates on maximising the performance of subordinates in a given situation with the leader of manager having an enabling function of clearing a path for his or her subordinates towards their personal goals at work.

PATHOLOGICAL

Pertaining to disease.

PAY

An amount of money paid on a regular basis to people in regular employment. Payment may be of wages or salary, in cash or by cheque or by direct bank transfer.

PAY ORDER

A pay order is a cheque drawn by a branch of the bank on itself. To facilitate payments of local character due by the bank to third parties, this method is adopted. The payee can obtain payment at the office of its issue. The pay order may also be used for another purpose. For payments to local offices, for example, especially government offices involving huge amounts, cash may not be convenient. Cheques may not be accepted by them, but drafts or bank cheques are readily accepted. A branch cannot issue a draft on itself and the purpose is served by pay orders. Banks issue pay orders to their customers to facilitate payments.

PAY

An amount of money paid on a regular basis to people in regular employment. Payment may be of wages or salary, in cash or by cheque or by direct bank transfer.

PAY-AS-YOU-GO PLAN

A pension plan in which the employer pays pension benefits to retired employees out of its current income.

PAYBACK

The payback period is the length of time it is expected to take for the net cash inflows from a new project to cover the original capital investment. Many companies use the payback method to decide between projects for investment The method has the following advantages: (*a*) It is simple to use and understand, (*b*) It is based on the most easily predicted cash flows, *i.e.*, those in the near future, (*c*) Since payback involves choice of the project with the shortest payback period, it restricts the time cash is tied up in projects and so helps cash flow. On the other hand, critics argue that payback is a crude measure, ignoring the amounts of cash flows after the end of the payback period.

PAYEE

A person to whom a negotiable instrument (such as a check) is made out. For example, "pay to the order of John Smith".

PAYEE'S ACCOUNT CHEQUE

This type of crossing a cheque is a direction to the collecting bankers that the proceeds of the cheque are intended to reach the hands of the payee. Fie should therefore collect the cheque only by credit into the account of the payee. It is also a term used in double-entry book-keeping to indicate the records of the amounts charged to others for goods and services sold, and the amounts received. The cheque has a marking on the left hand top corner with two parallel line.

PAYROLL

The list prepared by a firm each week or month, giving details of wages and salaries. It states the name or number, or both, of the employee and amounts payable. It may also give information on how the net pay is calculated. For instance: basic pay, plus slips for inclusion in wage packets may be prepared at the same time—the one being a carbon copy of the other. A list of amounts to be paid by an employer to his employees. The total cost of wages and salaries to a firm over a period. Cash to be used to pay wages.

PBDIT

Profits before depreciation, interest and taxes, which amounts to gross cash flow.

PECKING ORDER

The hierarchy of status relationships formed among farmyard hens by their practice of pecking each other. The most pecked hen has the lowest status. The term is now routinely (and therefore dangerously) applied to status relationships in human groups. Similarly, the term hen-pecked has long been part of everyday speech though it is applied to males rather than females.

PEG

An exchange rate for a currency which is regarded as normal usually because Central banks will take action to prevent the rates at which the currency is actually bought and sold in the foreign-exchange market by deviating from the peg by more than a known amount. Also known as a 'Parity' or 'Par Value'.

PENSION

(*i*) Periodic payment made to public servants including members of the civil service who have either retired from service or resigned office; similar payment made by a company to its employees who have served in it for a certain number of years and retired.

(*ii*) A sum of money paid periodically to an individual who retires from employment (or simply from a particular organisation) because of age, disability, or the completion of a specified period of service. Such payments usually continue for the rest of the recipient's life, and sometimes extend to his or her legal survivors.

PERCEIVED JOB CONTENT

The characteristics of a job that define its general nature as perceived by the person who does the job.

PERCEIVED RISK

Consumers' uncertainty about the consequence of their actions. The perception on the part of a consumer that a product may not do what it is expected to do.

PERCENT OF SALES METHOD

A method of setting a promotional budget in which the amount budgeted is some set percentage of sales, often a standard percentage for a given industry.

PERCENTILE

A point in a distribution of scores so selected that a certain percentage of cases are above it and a certain percentage of cases are below it.

PERCEPTION

(*i*) The process by which an individual gives meaning to the environment. It involves organising and interpreting various stimuli into a psychological experience.

(*ii*) Mental awareness and integration of sensation.

(*iii*) The way a product or vent or stimulus is received and evaluated by a customer. The importance lies in the attempt to understand how people interpret messages

(*iv*) The processing of interpreting sensations and giving meaning to stimuli.

PERFORM

To carry out work; Performance refers to the process of accomplishing work to the point at which it is ready for measurement or evaluation. Performance implies continuing activity or observation until a designated end point is reached. A manager performs a function by working it constantly. Performance can be accomplished in part by delegation.

PERFORMANCE

The desired results of behaviour.

PERFORMANCE APPRAISAL

(*i*) Performance appraisal is the process of determining and communicating to an employee how he is performing the job. According to *W.D. Scott, R.C. Clothier*, and *W.R. Spreigel*, "Performance appraisal is the process of evaluating an employee's performance of a job in terms of its requirements."

(*ii*) It is the systematic periodical evaluation of the performance of an employee on his present job and also relation to future jobs that he may be required to take up. It measures and evaluates the results of the performance of the workers. It points out their potentialities and deficiencies.

PERFORMANCE RATING

Production is achieved in any organisation with the association of men, machines and raw materials and it is the responsibility of the management to provide for best possible interaction of the same so that productivity is maximised. Variables affecting ultimate output are numerous and all of them are not equally important.

PERIODIC DISCOUNTING

A pricing strategy whereby discounts are offered systematically and predictably.

PERMANENT COMMITTEES

Formal committees are more or less of permanent character. They are also known as *Standing Committees*.

PERPETUAL DEBENTURE

A type of debenture for which there is no period fixed for repayment of the principal of the debenture.

PERQUISITES

The special benefits, frequently tax-exempt, made available only to the top executives of an organisation. There are two basic kinds of executive perquisites: (1) Those with "take home" value (such as company cars, club memberships, etc.) and (2) Those that have no "take home" value, but service mainly to confer status (such as the proverbial executive washroom, office size and decor, etc.).

PERSONAL DEVELOPMENT PLAN

Establish a personnel development plan and integrating it into overall personal planning efforts are sometimes more difficult than obtaining a good manpower plan.

PERSONAL INTERVIEW

A research method where the researcher meets the respondents to carry out a survey.

PERSONAL SELLING

(*i*) An element of the promotional mix, where a supplier uses representatives to visit customers.

(*ii*) Person-to-person interaction between a buyer and a seller wherein the seller's purpose is to persuade the buyer to accept a point of view, to convince the buyer to take a course of action, or to develop a customer relationship.

PERSONAL SKILLS

The early management literature treated personal or social skills in a residual way (See Classical Management and Fayol), but more recent research and practitioner testimony have emphasised their importance. The relevance is to the ability to build and sustain relationships, motivate and communicate, and get some of it right by intuition rather than powers of analysis.

PERSONAL-BEHAVIOURAL LEADERSHIP THEORIES

Theories based primarily on the personal and behavioural characteristics of leaders. The focus is on what leaders do and/or how they behave in carrying out the leadership function.

PERSONALITY

(*i*) A stable set of characteristics and tendencies that determine commonalities and differences in the behaviour of people.

(*ii*) The sum total of all the factors that make an individual human being both individual and human; the inning, feeling and behaving that all human beings have in common, and the particular characteristics pattern of these elements that makes every human being unique.

(*iii*) The fundamental disposition of an individual; the distinctive patterns of thought, emotion, and behaviour that characterise an individual's response to the situations of his or her life.

PERSON-JOB FIT

The extent to which the personality of an individual fits harmoniously with the job he/she does. One the goodness of fit between the two will depend the crucial factors of work like job satisfaction, productivity and stress.

PERSONNEL

(*i*) The role of the personnel manager is to provide for the acquisition, maintenance and utilisation of an organisation's human resources. This role embraces a range of functions such as recruitment, selection, career planning, wage and salary administration, manpower planning and labour relations. Personnel managers may also be involved in developing the organisation structure. There is a growing trend for the personnel department to be involved with organising management development programmes, one result of which can be an enhanced status among other managers. The personnel manager can face a difficult conflict between two aspects of this role. On the other hand, in the pursuit of productivity the personnel department will be involved in monitoring the performance of workers. On the other hand, the personnel manager has a responsibility for each worker's long-term career development, and this may conflict with immediate productivity objectives. Put crudely, the personnel manager must represent the objectives of the organisation to the workforce and the objectives of the workers to the organisation.

(*ii*) The people employed in an organisation; the function of dealing with an organisation's employees as its human resources.

PERSONNEL AUDIT

(*i*) An audit of the personnel function can serve three basic purposes: (*a*) To ensure that sound personnel policies are being carried out. Thus any erosion of standards can be detected before a crisis arises, (*b*) To evaluate the costs and benefits of alternative personnel procedures. Most personnel objectives can be achieved in a variety of ways. For example, if the organisation needs more highly qualified staff then money can be spent either on recruitment from outside or on training existing staff. Thus it is desirable, to review periodically the cost effectiveness of the methods used. (*c*) To identify new challenges to the organisation calling for a revision of personnel policies.

(*ii*) The term "audit" is derived from the Latin word auditus meaning a "hearing". Thus an audit is a hearing of review resulting in a systematic evaluation. The meaning of audit in terms of accounting is well-known. Today in management it is also used in terms of *managerial audit, marketing audit* and *personnel audit.* Thus the personnel function can be audited resulting in a critical review and evaluation of the manpower management program including the employer-employee industrial relations situation.

PERSONNEL MANAGEMENT

"Personnel management is an extension of general management that of prompting and stimulating every employee to make his fullest contribution to the purpose of a business" According to *Flippo*, "Personnel management may be defined as the planning, organising, directing, and controlling of the procurement, development, compensation, integration and maintenance and separation of human resources to the end that individual, organisational and societal objectives are accomplished."

PERSONNEL MANAGER

Personnel manager occupies a pivotal position in a work organisation. The success of an organisation largely depends on the way in which the personnel manager discharges his functions. The personnel manager has been playing a variety of roles at different stages in the past, like that of a police agency, a legal defender of rights and a negotiator, a catering man meeting the welfare needs of the employees.

PERSONNEL POLICIES

The word 'policy' has assumed created significance in the sphere of human activities. When we talk of foreign policy, business policy or fiscal policy, what we attempt to comprehend is the course and direction of activities in these fields. "Policies are planned expressions of the company's official attitudes towards the range of behaviour within which it will permit or desire its employees to act."

PERSONNEL PRACTICES

Personnel practices refer to the manner in which personnel programmes are implemented in keeping with the procedures laid down for attaining the objectives as stated in personnel policies. Personnel practices are highly important as impact of policies of the employees is mostly felt at the level of implementation.

PERSONNEL PROCEDURES

Personnel procedures refers to the detailed manner of applying a policy to a particular administrative context. Policies are general instructions, procedures are specific applications.

PERSON-ROLE CONFLICT

A type of conflict that occurs when the requirements of a position violate the basic values, attitudes, and needs of the individual occupying the position.

PERT

Program Evaluation Review Technique; A type of flowchart of a graphical representation of the relationship between the different tasks/event of a project and the time required in accomplishment of each task/events.

PEST ANALYSIS (SOMETIMES STEP)

Elements of the macro, External environment, Political/Legal,

Economic, Social/Cultural and Technological.

PETER, LAWRENCE J.

Originator of the 'peter principle' that in a hierarchy every employee tends to rise to his level of incompetence. This is based on the observation that an employee who performs a job efficiently tends to be promoted to a new, more senior, job in the hierarchy. When the employee reaches a job which he cannot do well, then it is unlikely that further promotion will follow. The employee is unlikely to dismissed, because of legal and trade union restrictions on unfair dismissal, and also because those more senior in the hierarchy will not wish to admit that the promotion they have authorised has proved to be a mistake. Thus the employee is left stranded at the 'level of incompetence', to the discomfort of the employee and the detriment of the organisation. Dr. *Peter* based his principle, initially, on observation of the North American Educational System during his career as an academic. His satirical style of writing makes his works eminently readable, but may have resulted in his observation being taken less seriously than they deserve. Many organisations have noted the peter principle, responding in two ways: (*i*) Rigorous consideration of the qualities an employee will require in a new job, and assessment of whether the employee possesses the new qualities needed in addition to those already demonstrated, (*ii*) Structuring the hierarchy in such a way as to name it possible to transfer an employee who has been unsuccessful in a new post back to the field where achievement was displayed.

PETTY CASH

A fund administered by a clerical or supervisory person to make small amounts of money available immediately for sundry purposes, accountable on a general basis.

PHONETIC ALPHABET

The analysis of a word into its phonetic elements for pronunciation purposes; commonly used as a synonym for phonics.

PHONETICS

The science of the sounds of letters as used in speech.

PHONICS

The science of the sounds of letters as applied to the pronunciation of words in reading.

PHONOGRAM

A letter or group of letters forming a sound that can be articulated.

PHOTOSTATIC PROCESS

It involves the use of photocopying machine and the process, is used whenever an exact copy of any printed, written or drawn material is required. The photocopying machine takes a direct photograph of the document on a photographic paper without use of plates or films. The size of the copy can be made larger or smaller than the original and coloured copies can be obtained by using filters.

PICTOGRAPH (PICTOGRAM)

Pictograms, *i.e.*, pictures, are a very popular and fascinating medium of presenting data. They arouse an intense interest in the reader and are very useful for the presentation of data to non-technical persons. But their limitation is that they do not convey an exact idea of the variables, and are difficult to construct. In a pictogram, the relative values of items are represented by pictures. The number of pictures drawn or the sized of different pictures are in proportion to the values of the various items that are to be represented. The pictures may be human beings to represent populations, bags to represent money, and so on. It is necessary that the pictures should be self-explanatory.

PICTURE CLUE

An element in a picture which provides meaning.

PIE CHART

In a pie chart, circles are used instead of squares. A circular diagram is a hundred per cent graph. The circle is divided into parts, each part representing a percentage break-up of the relevant data. Since a circle has 360 degrees, one per cent works out to 3.6 degrees. An item representing 20 per cent of the total value of the data will be displayed by an angle of 72° (20 × 360/100) on a pie diagram. Each part of the circle or pie diagram is made distinct by using different colours, shades or designs. However, a pie diagram is not very effective in calculating values or making comparisons, for it is often difficult to grasp quickly the area covered by each part of the circle.

PIECEWORK

A form of payment by results where workers are paid for each piece of work they do rather than the number of hours they put in. It was based originally on the scientific management principles of *F.W. Taylor*.

PIGGYBACK SERVICE

Service by which loaded truck trailers or other sealed containers are carried by rail to destinations from which they can be moved by truck. Similar services are fishyback service, involving transport of containers by water, and birdyback service, involving transport of containers by air.

PILOT STUDY

A term used in market research or survey research, *e.g.*, when a proposed questionnaire may be tested on a few respondents before being used on a large-scale study, to see whether the questionnaire needs revising and whether the study itself is worth doing.

PIN MONEY

A specific amount of predetermined money payable to a married woman annually for her maintenance.

PIP TESTS

PIP tests are those which seek to measure one's personality, interests and preferences. These tests are designed to understand the relationship between any one of three and certain types of jobs.

PIPELINES

Systems of pipes through which products, such as oil and natural gas, are transported.

PITCH

Measurement of the size of a printer font. In some software applications this is referred to as point size also. The point side of majority of text of this book is 10.1 pitch size = 120/point size.

PLACE (DISTRIBUTION)

An element of the marketing mix involving all aspects of getting products to the consumer in the right location at the right time.

PLACE UTILITY

Economic utility created by making goods available where consumers want them.

PLACE

An element of the 4 Ps of the marketing mix.

PLACEMENT

It means putting the right man at the right job. Proper placement reduces labour turnover, eliminates wastes, increases productivity and improves morale. Determination of a suitable job for the worker and providing right type of worker for the job is called *Placement.*

PLANNED ECONOMY

An economy under the central direction and control of the state, *e.g.*, under the ideology of socialism, which would decide on matters like pay and production in the absence of market forces.

PLANNED OBSOLESCENCE

The practice of consciously attempting to make existing products out of date by frequently introducing new products at planned in travels.

PLANNING

(*i*) Setting the objectives to be accomplished by a corporation (or a segment of it) over different periods of time and deciding on the major methods of reaching them. In other words, the process of envisioning the future, establishing goals and objectives, and designing organisational and marketing goals to be implemented in the future.

(*ii*) The process of envisioning the future, establishing goals and objectives, and designing organisational and marketing goals to be implemented in the future.

(*iii*) Setting the objectives to be accomplished by a corporation (or a segment of it) over different periods of time and deciding on the major methods of reaching them.

(*iv*) Any attempt systematically to organise the future performance of people or money or goods and services within a given set of constraints and time horizon.

PLANNING STRATEGIC

A complete review of basic company objectives and methods of achieving them, which may result in major changes in either or both.

PLATEAU

A temporary halt in the progress of learning during which added units of practice bring no improvement.

PLURALISM

In general sociology the term pluralism is used to suggest that there are a variety of countervailing forces and disparate interests in society, and that they roughly balance each other out so that society is not actually torn apart. At a more specific level the term has also come be applied to the understanding of formal organisations in terms of the disparate interests within groups, functions and individuals. The pluralistic approach to the understanding of companies thus recognises: The difference of interest between capital and labour, and a shifting accommodation between them; different policy preferences within 'the ruling coalition' (=top management/people of influence in the company); the different interests and objectives of the various functions/departments; the fact that individuals may well be following 'war aims' which take priority over company objectives. Thus a pluralistic approach seeks to understand the variety of forces and interests, together with their resolution and outcome.

POINT OF SALE (OR POINT OF PURCHASE)

(*i*) A place where a product is shown to a customer and where the customer can purchase the product if he wishes. Usually applied by a manufacturer to a strategic position in a retail establishment where his products are offered for sale.

(*ii*) Usually in retail, the area where a retailer's customer buys a product supplied by that retailer.

POINTED-HOUR-RATIO

Shows the relationship between the total number of hour points earned and the number of semester or term hours for which the student is enrolled. An indication of scholarship.

POINT-OF-SALE ADVERTISING

A form of advertising material that is below the line and placed in retail outlets, *i.e.*, the point at which the sale is actually made.

POINT-SYSTEM

A method of job evaluation in which a number of job factors are defined; for each factor, a rating sale is defined with numerical values called 'points'; a rating according to the rating scale is given to each factor of each job and the total number of points for a particular job then represents its evaluation.

POLICY

(*i*) A general principle laid down for the guidance of executives in handling their jobs.

(*ii*) A standing decision to guide repetitive action. Policies are binding upon all parts of the organisation to which they apply.

(*iii*) A statement of an organisation's intention to act in certain ways when specified types of circumstances arise. It represents a general decision predetermined and expressed as a principle or rule establishing a normal pattern of conduct for dealing with given types of business events usually recurrent A statement of policy is useful in economising the time of managers and in assisting them to discharge their responsibility equitably and consistently.

POLITICAL APPROACH

A limitation of some theories of leadership and motivation is that they tend to overlook the existence within organisations of individuals and groups pursuing different interests. The political approach has grown up as a counter-poise to this element of blandness in the organisational behaviour literature: this approach take as its starting point individuals acting singly or in coalition to try to achieve the things they want; it sees the individuals proactive and wilful, and eschews semi-abstractions of the 'for the good of the company' and 'all pulling together' type. It deals in terms of power and influence, conflict and coalition.

POLITICAL ENVIRONMENT

The practices and policies of governments.

POPULATION

In marketing research, any complete group of entities sharing some common set of characteristics; the group from which a sample is taken.

PORTFOLIO

A collection of interdependent products, services, investments or securities upon which a business is based.

POSDCORB

Mnemonic propounded by *Luther Gulick,* management writer/consultant and one-time member of president *Roosevelt's* three-man Administrative Management Committee, to denote the function/responsibility of top management. The letters stand for: *Planning, Organising, Staffing, Directing, Coordination, Reporting, Budgeting.* Posdcorb is one in a series of semi-abstract formulations of the purpose/function of higher management starting with *Henri Fayol* in the First World War period Position: Work grouped for performance by one individual.

POSITIONING

(*i*) Planning the market position of the company wishes to

occupy. Positioning strategy is the basis for marketing mix decisions.

(*ii*) Product Positioning: The establishing of factors valued by consumers in purchase decisions. Then the matching of product features to those factors.

POSSESSION UTILITY

Economic utility created by transfer of physical possession and ownership of the product to the consumer.

POST TESTING

In the context of advertising, testing that takes place after an advertisement has been run to determine whether it has met the objectives set for it by management.

POSTAL SURVEY

A research method which communicates with a respondent using a postal questionnaire.

POST-DATED

To give a document especially a cheque of a date that is later than the actual date of writing the document.

POVERTY

The condition of having an inadequate supply of money, resources, goods, or means of subsistence. Poverty is a difficult concept to define in practice and there is no single national definition of poverty.

POVERTY AREA

A geographic area with a high proportion of low-income families. Normally, average income is used to define a poverty area, but other factors, such as housing conditions, illegitimate birth rates, and the incidence of juvenile delinquency are sometimes considered.

POWER

(*i*) The ability to get things done in the way that one wants them to be done.

(*ii*) A key variable in the analysis of companies/organisations. It is what makes things happen. Its strength and direction, together with the counter forces and obstacles in its way, determine the direction companies take and chart the course of events in the lives of individuals. A focal point for organisational behaviour literature on power is to make dear the different bases on which power may rest, which include: *Reward Power;* the ability to give people things they want, or at lest 'use your influence' to make this more likely. *Coercive power;* the converse of reward power, it is the stick rather than the carrot; coercive power is the ability to discipline, punish, burden or disadvantage people. *Legitimate Power;* the acceptance by those being influenced of the right of the power holder; subordinates may obey a supervisor because they believe he is the one who should tell them what to do irrespective of his ability to reward or coerce. Thus legitimate power is similar to the classical idea of authority, except that it does not come from the top down, but is given by the subordinates, and of course it is always possible that the subordinates give legitimate power to someone other than a formal superior. *Referrent Power;* based on people identifying with power holders, responding to their feeling that this is the way he should act and that they would act. In the same way if they were him. *Expert Power;* based on special abilities or knowledge, so that a manager may be obeyed because of respect for his technical know-how. It is the classic power base for managers in staff/specialist functions with regard to their colleagues in other departments or general management. It is important to understand that there are varieties of power base because: it means one is following different people for different reasons; the counter plays vary with the power base; there is seldom an exact overlap between the distribution of (various kinds of) power and the formal authority positions in a company.

POWER ILLUSION

The notion that a person with little power actually has significant power.

POWER OF ATTORNEY

A deed by which one person called the 'donor' appoints another person called the 'attorney' to act on behalf in specified matters. Also known as *Letter of Attorney.*

PRE-CONCEIVED IDEA

A predetermined point of view unmodified by the introduction of new and relevant concepts; a prejudice.

PREDATORY PRICING STRATEGY

An illegal pricing strategy whereby a product is priced low to eliminate competition and then raised to a high level after competition has been eliminated.

PRE-EMPTORY PLEAS

Pleas that go to the root of a case.

PREFACE

An introduction to a book, in which the writer declared his intentions.

PREFERENCE SHARES

A special class of equity in a company which may entitle the holder to payment of a fixed dividend irrespective of profits and first consideration for repayment of the face value of shares if the company is liquidated.

PREMISE

A proposition stated or assumed as leading to an conclusion; either of the first two propositions of a syllogism.

PREMIUM

(*i*) A sum of money paid by an insured person or policyholder (or on his or her behalf) to an insurer (or third party) for insurance coverage. The premium is typically paid periodically, in fixed sums. It is related to the actuarial value of the benefits to be provided but also includes a loading charge to cover administrative costs, profits and other expenses.

(*ii*) A product offered free or at reduced charge if another product is purchased.

PRESCRIBE

To direct specified action. This implies that action must be carried out in a specified fashion. A manager may prescribe on his own authority or through derived authority from a superior. When authority is derived, the source should be stated.

PRESS RELEASE

A formal statement made by an organisation to representatives of the media in the hope that it will be publicly disseminated (published or broadcast). Press releases are written descriptions of past or uncoming events or activities of significance, or statements about the organisations position.

PRESTIGE PRICE

A high price meant to convey an impression of high quality.

PRETESTING

Conducting limited trail of a questionnaire or other aspect of study to determine its suitability for the planned research project. In the context of advertising, research on the effectiveness of an advertisement that begins at the earliest stages of development and continues until the advertisement is ready for use.

PREVENTIVE MAINTENANCE

Servicing or refurnishing plant and equipment on a regular and scheduled basis, not reactively in response to breakdowns. The case for preventive maintenance is that it reduces uncertainty: you know when the 'down-time' is going to be because of the schedule, and breakdowns become less likely. Not generally a British strength.

PREVIEW

The act of asking a preliminary survey of chapter, book, or other written composition.

PRICE

Setting a price for the output of a business is one of the most important, and difficult, management decisions. Considerations to be taken into account include: Attitudes of customers: Generally one would expect that demand for output would increase as prices are reduced, but this is not always the case. For some goods a high price acts as a 'signal of quality to the buyer. This obviously applies to fashion goods, such as clothes and perfume. The same principle can sometimes apply in other cases. In one example; a commercial vehicle producer found that an increase in price led to increased demand, because the vehicles were perceived by buyers to be of higher quality. *Behaviour of competitors*: The amount that the business is able to charge is strongly influenced by the prices set by competitors. For many years one of the UK's largest motor manufacturers did not produce a car in the smallest range, because a major competitor was selling their small car so cheaply that a rival could not be produced at a comparable price. The price that can be charged for a product will also depend on the accompanying level of service provided. A business maybe subject to legal or trade restrictions on pricing policies. For example, in the U.K. lawyers are not allowed to charge for their services on a 'contingency basis', whereby the amount of their fee depends on the outcome of litigation; the reason for this restriction is to safeguard the integrity of the legal profession. Prices have to be set at a level where costs will be covered, so that the cost of the business will affect pricing policies. These example illustrate the variety of factors influencing the pricing decision.

PRICE ANALYSIS

This is a practice sometimes adopted by companies to assist them in their sourcing arrangements and negotiations with suppliers. Its essence is to calculate precisely and realistically the cost of an item the company doing the analysis wishes to buy from a supplier. This knowledge may then inform negotiations with potential suppliers. It is not just a case of powerful buyers intimidating defenceless suppliers (though it happens), but sometimes of helping potential suppliers to improve the efficiency of their costing and manufacturing methods.

PRICE COMPETITION

Competition based on price. It is especially important in the marketing of products that are not distinctive, such as raw materials.

PRICE LEADERSHIP

Strategy in which the marketer emphasises underpricing all competitors.

PRICE STABILISATION

A pricing objective aimed at avoiding widely fluctuating prices. The marketer with this objective sets prices to match competitors' prices or maintain existing price differentials.

PRICE

(*i*) The amount of money or other consideration given kin exchange for a product.

(*ii*) The fee charged or something. "Price" is contrasted with "payment" or "negotiated price".

PRICE-LINING STRATEGY

A strategy whereby a seller prices products in a product line in accordance with certain "price points" believed to be attractive to buyers.

PRICING

(*i*) Fixation of prices at which products are to be sold.

(*ii*) The decisions made by an organisation in setting price for the goods or services it provides, taking into account the cost of production and the nature of the market.

(*iii*) The decisions made by an organisation in setting price for the goods or services it provides, taking into account the cost of production and the nature of the market.

PRIMARY DEMAND

Advertising aimed at stimulating primary, or generic, demand.

PRIMARY RATIO

An overall measure of business efficiency, based on the widely criterion of the return on capital employed.

PRIVATE COMPANY

A company whose shareholders are restricted in sale of equity. The shares of a private company are not bought and sold in the open market.

PRIVATE SECTOR

The part of a mixed economy which is controlled by individuals or companies rather than the state.

PRIVATISATION

(*i*) The process of returning to the private sector property (such as public lands) or functions owned or performed by government.

(*ii*) The floatation of a previously state-owned organisations as a *Public Limited Company*, often with some remaining government interest, perhaps of a special nature.

PROBATE

The process of proving that a Will is genuine, and distributing the property of an estate as provided in a Will; also, some states, the name for a Court that handles the distribution of decedants' estates (dead persons' property) and other matters.

PROBLEM IDENTIFICATION

Problem identification is a major task case studies. Frequently, it requires deep and concentrated thought. A common criticism by the non-professional is that the case does not include all the facts. This is true; few case studies can include all the facts. But managers seldom have all the facts, a concept itself subject to wide interpretation by the researchers. So while not prefect case studies do have definite sense of reality. Attempting to determine a solution without full knowledge may be frustrating but actually it is part of the essence of managerial problem-solving.

PROCEDURE

(*i*) A discrete operation, frequently consisting of a set of closely related tasks producing a single desired result or discernible service.

(*ii*) A predetermined series of steps to be taken in doing a task.

PROCESS MOTIVATION THEORIES

Theories that describe and analyse how behaviour is energised, directed, sustained, and stopped.

PROCESS OF AUGMENTATION

A command that may be achieved by the man who can, through skill in persuading others, bring about acceptance of his decisions.

PROCESSES

Those activities that breathe life into the organisation structure. Common processes are *Communication, Performance evaluation, Decision-making, Socialisation,* and *Career Development.*

PRODUCT

A good, service, or idea that offers a bundle of tangible and intangible attributes to satisfy consumers.

PRODUCT BARGAINING

Collective bargaining that seeks increases in productivity in exchange for increases in wages and benefits. There are two basic approaches to productivity bargaining—*Integrative bargaining* and *Pressure bargaining.*

PRODUCT CATEGORY

A sub-set of a product class containing products of a certain type—for example, domestic automobiles for personal use.

PRODUCT CLASS

A broad group of products that differ somewhat but perform similar functions or provide similar benefits.

PRODUCT CONCEPT

The marketing strategist's selection and blending of a product's primary and auxiliary dimensions into a basic idea emphasising a particular set of consumer benefits.

PRODUCT DESIGN

A product's configuration, composition, and style; a characteristic that influences most product dimensions.

PRODUCT DIFFERENTIATION

A promotional approach in which the marketer calls buyers' attention to those aspects of a product or brand that set it apart from its competitors.

PRODUCT DIVERSIFICATION

The deletion of an item from an organisation's product mix.

PRODUCT ENHANCEMENT

The introduction of a new and improved version of an existing product to extend its life cycle by keeping it in the growth stage.

PRODUCT ITEM

A specific version of a specific good or service.

PRODUCT LIFE CYCLE

The different stages through which a product develops over time. It covers development, birth (or introduction), growth, maturity and decline. The stage a product has reached in its life cycle will affect the marketing mix decisions which should be taken.

PRODUCT LINE

(*i*) A number of related products offered by a supplier, which often cover the needs of several different segments.

(*ii*) A group of products that are fairly closely related.

PRODUCT MANAGEMENT

The function responsible for the tactical and strategic planning of a company's existing and new products.

PRODUCT MIX

The total range of products or services that an organisation offers.

PRODUCT MODIFICATION

The alterting or adjusting of the product mix, typically influenced by the competitive nature of the market or by changes in the external environment.

PRODUCT OBSOLESCENCE

A condition that occurs when an existing product becomes out of date because of the introduction of a new product.

PRODUCT ORIENTATION

Organisational philosophy that emphasises physical production and technology rather than sales or marketing.

PRODUCT PLANNING

Long-range planning includes product planning which provides good discussions material because products are familiar objects, they have wide interest, and they illustrate many excellent examples of planning techniques.

PRODUCT PORTFOLIO CONCEPT

A concept that focuses on the inter-relationships of different types of products within a product mix. The performance of the mix of products is emphasised rather than the performance of individual products.

PRODUCT STRATEGY

The planning and development of a mix of the primary and auxiliary dimensions of a products attributes.

PRODUCT WARRANTY

A written guarantee of a product's integrity and the manufacturer's responsibility for repairing or replacing defective parts.

Product

(*i*) A good, service, or idea that offers a bundle of tangible and intangible attributes to satisfy consumers.

(*ii*) The wide range of tangible and intangible benefits that a buyer might gain from a product after purchasing it.

PRODUCTION

A criterion of effectiveness that refers to the organisation's ability to provide the outputs that the environment demands of it.

PRODUCTION TRANSFERS

Such transfers are resorted to when there is a need of manpower in one department and surplus manpower in the other. Thus, production transfers are made from a department which is overstaffed to the other department where manpower needs have increased or vacancies have occurred through separations.

PRODUCTIVITY

It is defined as war against waste. Even if the technical and economic concept of productivity is taken into consideration, *i.e.*, productivity is ratio of output and input, this ratio could be favourable only when planned efforts are made to utilise the scarce resources as economically as possible to achieve the best results. Among several factors affecting productivity safety in industry is one of the most important factors to be kept in view for promoting productivity. The rate of output of a worker or a machine.

PROFESSIONAL MANAGER

The professional manager is an individual who manages an organisation by applying modern management techniques to develop and expand the business, to achieve and attain the ambitions, aspirations and expectations of the owners and society. Such a manager need not necessarily be an owner though divergent views are expressed as to the desirability or otherwise of his sharing the ownership of a business which he manages. The professional manager tackles all operating problems by applying scientific methods. Such methods include a well-planned, organised and systematic human approach to all organisational responsibilities.

PROFIT

The gain made by the sale of a good or service after deducting the value of the labour, materials, rents, interest on capital, and other expenses involved in the production of the goods or services. Economists define profit as return on capital investment.

PROFIT ANALYSIS

A study that organises profits by particular segments of the marketing operation in order to evaluate them.

PROFIT AND LOSS STATEMENT

A statement listing net sales, costs, expenses, and profit or loss for a specified period.

PROFIT SHARING

The distribution of part of a firm's profits to some or all of its employees, based on the profitability of the firm. A qualified profit sharing plan must provide specific criteria and formulas for which persons get what share of the profit.

PROFIT SHARING

The sharing of profits between an employer and his employees after payment of the wages of the latter.

PROFORMA

Proforma Profit and Loss Statement; preliminary profit and loss statement containing forecasts for sales, expenses, and so on for some future period.

PROGRAMME

(*i*) A major, mission oriented organisational endeavour that is defined in terms of the principal actions required to achieve a significant objectives. A program is an organised set of activities designed to produce a particular result or set of results that will have an impact on a specific problem or need.

(ii) A sequence of actions designed to accomplish a specific objective.

PROGRAMMER

A person who is responsible for planning, designing, writing and testing the computer programs.

PROGRAMMING

The process of planning, designing, writing and testing the computer programs.

PROGRESSIVE DISCIPLINE

Managerial use of a sequence of penalties for rule violations, each penalty being more severe than the previous one.

PROJECT GRANT

A grant of funds to a public or private organisation for a specified purpose, such as development of an emergency medical service system or conduct of a continuing education program. Project grants are usually discretionary. Applicants are typically chosen on the basis of merit, often competitively. The amount of a project grant is usually based on the estimated cost of achieving the goal of the project.

PROJECTING ALTERNATIVES

Some kind of forecast is crucial to the analysis of alternatives. We must predict what is likely to happen if we take action A or alternative B or likewise for each alternative on our list. For some decisions the tie between a proposed alternative and a result is almost mechanistic and we can predict outcomes with precision.

PROMOTION

A promotion may be defined as an upward (vertical) advancement of an employee in an organisation to another job commanding greater responsibilities, better pay, higher authority, better working environment, convenient working hours and facilities, and a higher rank. In the words of *Scott* and *Clotheir*, "A promotion is the transfer of an employee to a job which pays more money or one that carries some preferred status."

PROMOTION

(*i*) An element of the 4 Ps of the marketing mix, it covers the ways in which an organisation communicates with its markets.

(*ii*) In external relations, a very broad term meaning the presentation of a product (in the broadest sense of the work "product") for consumer or public acceptance, through a program of direct contact methods (such as direct mail) and/or a media-relations program.

(*iii*) The element of the marketing mix that includes all forms of marketing communications.

PROMOTIONAL MIX

The elements of promotion enabling an organisation to communicate with its market. These include advertising, personal selling, sales promotion and publicity.

PROOF

Inked impression of type, used for making corrections; the act of demonstrating or proving the truth of a fact, statement etc., record of evidence given in a Court.

PROOF OF LOSS

A sworn statement made to an insurance company of a loss suffered under an insurance policy.

PROPRIETARY

Owned, as in the case of property; private; profit-making; owned and operated for the purpose of making a profit, whether or not one is made.

PROSPECTING

(*i*) In sales, identifying likely customers. In prospecting, the salesperson may search lists of previous customers, trade association lists, government publications, and many other sources.

(*ii*) The selling technique involved with identifying new customers.

PROTESTANT ETHIC

Max Weber's term for the view that making money is a worthy occupation and that hard work and individual competitive effort are qualities to be admired for their own sake.

PROTOCOL

Standard, formal procedures for sending and receiving data while networking.

PROTOTYPE

A company version of a proposed version, which is designed to text the operations and suitability of the system.

PROVISION

An amount set aside to meet a known liability out of profits, which cannot be ascertained with much accuracy.

PROXEMICS

The use of space when interpersonally communicating with others.

PROXY

A person designated by a stockholder to represent him at the company's annual meeting and vote his shares. Also used for the card that the stockholder uses to appoint his proxy.

PSYCHIC INCOME

Satisfaction, other than monetary, from a job.

PSYCHODYNAMIC PERSONALITY THEORIES

Freudian approach which discusses the ID, superego, and ego. Special emphasis is placed on unconscious determinants of behaviour.

PSYCHOGRAPHICS

A base for segmentation derived from attitudes and behavioural variables.

PSYCHOLOGIST

One who studies human behaviour.

PUBLIC ADMINISTRATION

The study of or practice of organising and managing people and other resources to achieve the goals of government; also, a more gentle name for public relations; also, an expensive view of the academic field of public administration.

PUBLIC CORPORATION

Public corporations are legal bodies and may be defined as group of persons acting as a single legal personality. These enjoy governmental powers and yet possess initiative and flexibility so essential and imperative in a business enterprise.

PUBLIC DEPOSITS

Public deposits are funds deposited by the public in a financial institution, bank or a company authorised to accept public deposits both for short and long periods. Since no security is offered, they are attracted by the financial standing and reputation of the managerial personnel. The rate of interest also depends upon the credit and financial standing of the managerial personnel of the concern.

PUBLIC GOODS

Commodities typically provided by a government that cannot, or would not, be separately parcelled out to individual since no one can be excluded from their benefits. Public goods such as national defence, clean air, and public safety are neither divisible nor exclusive.

PUBLIC INTEREST GROUP

An organised pressure group seeking to develop positions and support causes relating to a broader definition of the public goods as opposed to any specific social or economic interest.

PUBLIC POLICY

Laws, rules, and administrative and Court decisions that lead to the establishment of social or communical objectives, and influence or control the behaviour of citizens and constituents of a government.

PUBLIC RELATIONS

(*i*) A management function that evaluates public opinion, identifies the policies and services of an organisation with the public interest, and develops and executes programs to earn public understanding and acceptance; the effort to promote a reservoir of community goodwill for an organisation and/or its programs in order to benefit specific development campaigns for funds, services, or other objectives. Public relations encompasses, for example, public information and education, media relations, and other fields.

(*ii*) The activities involved in actively seeking to manage the nature of the publicity an organisation receives.

(*iii*) A deliberate, planned and sustained effort to establish and maintain positive understanding between an organisation and its publics.

PUBLIC SECTOR

Industries or activities run by the government.

PUBLIC UTILITY

An organisation that provides an essential public service, like the supply of water or electricity, whether it is part of the private sector or the public sector.

PUBLIC WAREHOUSE

A storehouse appointed under the Customs Act for storage of goods on which custom duty is leviable as per the provision of the Customs Act, 1962.

PUBLICITY

(*i*) A message about a product, organisation, or event carried by a non-personal medium but not paid for by a sponsor, publicity involves a third party, such as a newspaper editor, who determines whether the message is newsworthy enough to transmit and what the nature of the transmitted message will be.

(*ii*) Publicity refers to a non-personal stimulation of demand for a product, service or an idea by placing significant news about it in trade journals, newspapers, radio, etc., that is not paid for by the sponsor.

PULL STRATEGY

A promotional strategy whereby a supplier promotes a product to the ultimate consumer with the aim of stimulating demand and thus pulling the product through the channel of distribution.

PUNISHMENT

An uncomfortable consequence for a particular behaviour response or the removal of a desirable reinforcer because of a particular behaviour response. Managers can punish by application or by removal.

PURCHASE JOURNAL

The journal used to record items ordered and purchased by an organisation. It contains information about the date of each item ordered and purchased, the nature of the item, the purchase-order number, the amount of the purchase, and which subsidiary or general ledger account is affected by the purchase.

PURCHASE RETURN

Also called 'Returns Outwards', it refers to the return of goods to the suppliers either because they do not (*i*) conform to the samples or (*ii*) correspond to the order placed. The return outwards book is used to record all such transactions.

PURCHASE SATISFACTION

The feeling on the part of the consumer that the decision to buy was appropriate.

PURE COMPETITION

A market structure characterised by free entry, a homogeneous product, and many sellers and buyers, neither of whom can control price.

PUSH STRATEGY

(*i*) A marketing strategy in which the manufacturer promotes directly to the final customers, and hopes that they will demand the product from intermediaries.

(*ii*) A promotional strategy whereby a supplier promotes a product to marketing intermediaries with the aim of pushing the product through the channel of distribution.

PYRAMID HIERARCHY

An organisational structure having different levels of authority with fewer people at each succeeding level, so that a chart of the hierarchy would like a pyramid in shape.

Q

QBASIC

A high level language which is an advanced version of BASIC.

QUALIFYING

In sales, evaluating a prospect's potential. Key questions are whether the prospect needs the product, can pay for it, and has the authority to make, or at least contribute to a decision to buy.

QUALITATIVE OVERLOAD

A situation in which a person feels that he lacks the ability or skill to do a job or that the performance standards have been set too high.

QUALITATIVE RESEARCH

Research which produces numerical data, often from large samples. This is sometimes called *Hard Data*.

QUALITY

(*i*) The nature, kind, or character of someone or something; the degree or grade of excellence possessed by a person, service or thing; the character of nature that belongs to or distinguishes a person or thing. The term is now used mainly as a way of measuring or describing how good or bad a product is at performing its function.

(*ii*) The totality of features and characteristics of a product or

(*iii*) service that bear on its ability to satisfy stated or implied needs,

(*iv*) Is the extent to which a product does what it is supposed to do —how closely and reliably it satisfies the specifications to which it is built.

QUALITY ASSURANCE

Is an operations process involving a broad group of activities that are aimed at achieving the organisation's quality objectives.

QUALITY CIRCLES

(*i*) A Japanese institution now widely adopted in the West. Its essence is that small groups of production workers meet during company time to discuss quality issues and recent quality performance, perhaps under the non-directive leadership of a first-line supervisor or inspector. The presumption is that this raises quality consciousness, and that the mutual exchange helps to generate solutions to practical quality problems 'at the coat face'.

(*ii*) Are small groups of workers that meet to discuss quality related problems on a particular project and communicate their solutions to these problems to management at a formal presentation session.

QUALITY CONTROL

Its objective is the maintenance of quality standards, and the savings attendant on the reduction of scrap. This objective often involves three distinct operations:

(*i*) good inward control, or the inspection of raw materials or bought-out parts when they arrive at the factory;

(*ii*) medial inspection, or checking the quality standard of partly manufactured goods, often in the form of checking major manufactured components or sub-assemblies;

(*iii*) final inspection of finished products before their dispatch to the customer or launch into the distribution system. In process industries, quality control is typically a laboratory based operation which takes the form of monitoring the process (rather than the product). The alternative responses to these inspectional exigencies are: (*a*) inspect everything; (*b*) inspect nothing (and hope for the best); (*c*) practice statistic quality control (SQC): this is sample inspection where applied mathematics define the likelihood of defects in the proportion not inspected thereby offering calculable levels of protection. The inclusion of (*b*) above, inspect nothing, is not frivolous: there is a survey evidence from Britain in the late 1970s suggesting that the number of firms practising the more sophisticated SQC is matched by the number doing nothing. A further ramification of quality control is that especially larged companies may inspect the quality control procedures of potential suppliers, perhaps even becoming involved in initial stages in the suppliers operations to raise standards. This is particularly likely where the rise relativities make the buyer dominant (see Quasi-Vertical Integration). Developments in quality control include: *Building quality* into the system, *i.e.*, using design, work organisation, and production engineering skills to inhibit faults and defects; *Quality circles; Placing* responsibility for as much as possible with production workers themselves, even if (some inspectors are employed as a 'second line of defence'. But perhaps the most dramatic change has been the emergence of the conviction that the customer has a right to quality. Not so long ago there was a widespread view that just because you paid for it that did not mean you could expect it to work.

QUALITY CONTROL, STATISTICAL

Control of product quality by sampling techniques.

QUALITY CONTROL

The operational function within a company responsible for carrying out quality policies through inspection and formal procedures.

QUALITY MARKET

A market in which the quality of a product is more important to the customer than the price.

QUALITY OF LIFE

The sense of well-being perceived by people in a society.

QUALITY OF WORK LIFE (QWL)

Management philosophy that enhances employee philosophy that enhances employee dignity, introduces cultural change, and provides opportunities for growth and development.

QUALITY IMPROVEMENT TEAMS

Small groups of employees who work on solving specific problems related to quality and productivity, often with stated targets for improvement.

QUALITY-ORIENTED POLICY

Is a standing plan that fiimishes broad, general guidelines for channelling management thinking toward taking action consistent with reaching quality objectives.

QUANTITATIVE FORECASTING

A type of forecasting that relies on numerical data and mathematical models to predict future conditions.

QUANTITATIVE METHODOLOGY

The use of research methods in behavioural science or social science which are concerned more with the precision and generalisability of the data being collected than their richness of content or complexity, *e.g.*, having a narrower but sharper focus than qualitative methodology. The experiment and the structured questionnaires are the most common methods used.

QUESTIONABLE PAYMENTS

An international social responsibility issue concerning business payments that raise significant ethical questions of right or wrong either in the host nation or in other nations.

QUARTILE

One of the three points on a frequency distribution which divide it into equal quarters.

QUASI CONTRACTS

These are contracts in which no proper contract exists. In such cases the Court may establish an obligation from one to another. The Court can review even illegal contracts and may allow one party to recover money from the other even through the contract was void.

QUASI-LOAN

An arrangement between two persons under which one agrees to meet some of the other's financial obligations on condition that the letter reimburses him.

QUESTIONNAIRE

Any set of written questions used in the collecting of information of purposes of comparison. It is widely used in market research and is the basis of all work in survey research.

QUEUING MODELS

Quantitative planning tools based on mathematical models that describe the operating characteristics of queuing situations, in which service is provided to persons or units waiting in line; also called Waiting-Line Models.

QUEUING PROBLEM

The problem of determining the facilities to be provided when the need for them varies at random, for example, the optimum number of ticket windows in cases where there may be long queues some times and no customers at all other times.

QUICK RATIO

The relationship between quick or liquid assets *i.e.*, Current assets - (stock + prepaid exp.) and current liabilities. While some scholars uses quick liabilities in place of current liabilities.

QUOTA

A limit set by a government on who much of a certain type of product can be imported into a country. These are quantitative limits fixed on the importation of specified commodities. The protection afforded by quotas is more certain than can be obtained by raising import tariffs as the effect of the latter will depend on the price elasticities of the imported commodities. Like tariff, quotas can also be used for preferred sources of supply.

QUOTA-BONUS PLAN

Compensation plan whereby a salesperson is paid a base salary related to achievement of a quota and a bonus for sales exceeding the quota.

QUOTA SAMPLE

A non-probability sample whose members' characteristics match a predetermined quota. A sampling method where those questioned have to match a defined proportion on a number of attributes, *e.g.*, sex, age, occupation.

QUOTA SAMPLING

The process of sampling data from each subgroup of a given population. This is a particular form of stratified sampling widely used in market research where an interviewer is given a set number of quota of interviews to carry out in a given stratum of the population and stops sampling when the quota has been achieved.

QWERTY

A key arrangement of keyboards which is most widely used. The term consists of the first six letters in the first row of alphabetic keys. The other type of keyboard arrangement is AZERTY.

R

RACK JOBBER

A limited-function wholesaler that contracts with a retailer to place display racks in a store and to stock those racks with merchandise.

RAIL ROAD

In relation to physical distribution, a mode of transportation by which products are shipped by train over railways.

RANDOM DISCOUNTING

A pricing strategy whereby discounts are offered occasionally and unpredictably.

RANDOM SAMPLE

A sampling method where everyone has an equal chance of being included.

RANDOM SAMPLING ERROR

Inaccuracy of results associated with random sampling and caused by chance variation.

RANK ORDER

Any series of numbers, items, or individuals arranged in order of magnitude, either increasing or decreasing.

RANKING METHOD

The ranking of ratees on the basis of relevant performance.

RAPPORT

Unconstrained, intimate, and friendly relationship between two persons.

RATE CARD

The published cost of advertising media.

RATE OF TURNOVER

An accounting term for the speed with which stock is turned over. In a retail business, for instance, if stock averaged Rs. 1,00,000 and annual sales were Rs. 7,50,000 the stock would be calculated as turned over seven and half times per annum.

RATE SETTING

An old fashioned term for the process of setting piecework rates of pay for a job. The process is more often included now under the term work measurement.

RATING

An estimation or assessment of something expressed in relative terms — especially when it is compared with a commonly used standard. Also a numerical value assigned to such an estimation in accordance with a rating scale.

RATIO

A mathematical relationship between two variables or a quantitative proportion of one thing to another; a proportional relationship between two items.

RATIO ANALYSIS

(*i*) A financial control technique that involves determining and evaluating financial ratios.

(*ii*) A method of judging company performance by examining the relationships between various figures, *e.g.*, the ratio of profits to investment.

RATIO NORM

Norm for different kinds of ratios either as an average overtime of the same firm, or an industry average or an average of a cross-section of firms, to evaluate and control performance.

RATIONAL MANAGEMENT

The opposite of participative mangement. The term is usually used to denote a management style that emphasises objective measures of input rather than human relations.

RATIONAL MODEL

A model of managerial decision-making which suggests that managers engage in completely rational decision processes, ultimately make optimal decisions, and possess and understand all information relevant to their decisions at the time they make them.

RATIONAL-ECONOMIC

A view of human nature which argues that people act only to maximise their self-interest. It is based on the philosophy of the thoughts of *Adam Smith*. A management style which acted on his view would be described as rational management.

RATIONALISATION

(*i*) In economics, the term is used to denote the application of the most efficient methods in the use of resources in an organisation. In organisational structure, which often implies one that is simpler and cheaper.

(*ii*) The strategy of assigning activities to those parts of the organisation, regardless of their location, that are best suited to produce the desired results and then selling the finished products where they are likely to yield the best profits.

RATIONING

A method of adapting to environmental fluctuations that involves providing limited access to a product or service that is in high demand.

RAW DATA

Information collected in a survey or experiment, before it has been processed for use in determining results.

RAW MATERIALS INVENTORY

The stock of parts, ingredients, and other basic inputs to a production or service process.

REACH

The number of people exposed to an advertisement carried by a given medium.

REACTIVE CHANGE

Change that occurs when one takes action in response to perceived problems, threats, or opportunities.

READ/WRITE HEAD

Digital information is stored on the magnetic coating (film) by applying current pulses of suitable polarity to the magnetising coil of the read/write head. The logic 1 or 0 depends on the direction of management of the very small area of the magnetic film which comes under the read/write head.

There are two types of recording technique: Longitudinal recording and Vertical recording. In longitudinal recording the magnetised regions are oriented parallel to the disk surface along the track. In the vertical recording the magnetised regions are vertical to the disk surface. The vertical recording stores many time more data as compared to longitudinal recording. During read operation a voltage is induced in the coil of the read/write head due to the change in the magnetic field in the vicinity of the head. The coil now serves as a sensing coil. Hard disks and read/write heads are placed in a sealed, air-filtered enclosure. This technique is called Winchester Technology. Example are Tape drive or Floppy drive or Hard disk drive.

READERS' GUIDE TO PERIODICAL LITERATURE

An index to magazine articles and periodical literature.

READINESS

A physical, mental, and emotional preparedness for a given learning activity.

READING

A process of securing meaning from symbols; a physical, mental, and emotional activity of identifying, interpreting, and evaluating messages conveyed through the medium of printed symbols.

READING DEFICIENCY

Lack of adequate skills in reading.

READING LABORATORY

A reading clinic or workroom in which corrective and remedial work in reading is carried on.

READING LEVEL

The stage of development which a person has reached in reading skill.

READING MALADJUSTMENT

Inability to adjust to the use of the reading process.

READING VOCABULARY

Words that can be identified and understood in context or in isolation from the printed page.

REAL TIME

A period of time during which an online computer is processing the data about a particular situation while that situation is actually in progress thus allowing for instant updating as in an airline or hotel reservation system.

REAL WAGES

Disposable income left after paying taxation, etc.; the buying power of a certain income as opposed to the actual money received.

REALISTIC JOB PREVIEW

A technique used during the recruiting process in which the job candidate is presented with a balanced view of both the positive and the negative aspects of the job and the organisation.

REAL-TIME OPERATION

Term used of a computer that is processing data fast enough for it to be used to control an operation.

REBATE

A rebate is similar to a discount in so far as it reduces an amount payable. Sometimes it is used as a synonym for discount in a trade. However, a discount is strictly a reduction allowed by the payee whereas a rebate is an amount returned to the payer often at a later date. The term rebate is associated with rent and rates as certain people who are considered to be of limited means are given back portions of rent paid to a local authority at specified rates. A deduction from a sum of money to be paid; a discount specifically a deduction from the sum to be paid according to a bill of exchange when the bill is presented for payment before the date specified on it.

RECALL TEST

In the contest of advertising, a research tool used to determine how much people remember about an advertisement. Unaided recall tests give those being tested no clues as to the specific material to be remembered. Aided recall tests provide such clues. Related recall tests measure recall of specific messages or images.

RECEIPT

A document issued by a creditor to acknowledge payment of a debt. At one time it was demanded as proof of payment. Now, if payment is by a Payee's Account only cheque, no receipt is legally necessary. A sum of money, or quantity of goods received. A written acknowledgment that one has received money or goods.

RECEIVER

Flow of information from one point to another. The point to which the information is transmitted from source is receiver.

RECEPTIONIST

He or she represents the company to callers of various types. Callers may include customers, prospective customers, sales representatives, solicitors and promoters, creditors, applicants for position and friends of the employer. It is the receptionist's job to handle each visitor in a manner that will build goodwill for the firm and conserve the time and energy of the person or persons for whom he or she works.

RECESSION

A lack of growth or a decline in trading or in the economy generally though not as seriously as in a depression.

RECIPROCAL INTERDEPENDENCE

A type of technological interdependence in which one unit's outputs become inputs to the other unit and *vice versa*.

RECIPROCITY

The principle that a response is produced by a combination of the duration and intensity of a stimulus.

RECOMMEND

To offer or suggest for use; Recommendation describes the presentation of plans, ideas or things to others for adoption.

RECOMMENDED RETAIL PRICE

The price for an item which a manufacturer suggests a retailer might results.

RECORD

A group or collection of data items or fields which are logically related to each other. This collection may be treated as single unit.

RECORDATIVE WORK

Routine recording and classified posting of financial transactions and events.

RECRUITMENT

(*i*) An activity in the staffing process that involves finding and attempting to attract job candidates whom are capable of effectively filling job vacancies.

(*ii*) Is the initial attraction and screening of the supply of prospective human resources available to fill a position.

(*iii*) Personnel management is required to select and recruit the right type of man for the right job and to maintain adequate records of their employment. He may invite applications, organise selection tests and conduct interview for this purpose in consultation with the departmental managers where the workers are actually expected to work. The higher the level of posts to be filled up, the process of selection becomes more elaborate and complex.

RECURRING DEPOSITS OR CUMULATIVE DEPOSITS

A fixed sum is payable monthly into the account and the full amount with cumulative interest thereon is repaid on maturity. Certain banks have formulated schemes combining the features of fixed deposit and recurring deposits.

RECYCLE BIN

A temporary storage on hard disk in which the deleted items are stored unless they are physically removed. A software feature available only Windows 95 onwards.

RED-TAPISM

Means delaying tactics used by the officials in disposing of management questions. Departmental management is usually taken to be a synonym for red-tapism. Rules, regulations and procedures are rigidly followed and the officers are discouraged from taking quick and independent decisions. They lack initiative and settle down as mere cogs in the huge machine.

REDEEM

To end an obligation to someone else by making a suitable payment. Specifically to buy back a security, to end a mortgage by paying off the relevant loan.

REDEEMABLE

Capable of being redeemed. Used to describe a security when the issuer may demand its surrender in return for a cash payment.

REDEMPTION

The process of paying back money that has been borrowed; repayment or return of a debt, as per the terms of borrowing. The term also relates to the return of the amount invested in a share issued by a company.

REDEPLOYMENT

The process of moving workers from one location to another often with the objective of finding them alternative employment.

REDUNDANCY

The dismissal of someone from his employment either because his job ceased to exit or skills are no longer required.

REFERENCE CHECKS

A selection method involving attempts to obtain job-related information about job applicants from individuals who are knowledgeable about the applicants5 qualifications.

REFERENCE GROUP

A primary or secondary group that influences an individual because that individual is a member of the group or aspires to be a member.

REFERENCE PRICING STRATEGY

A strategy whereby moderate price is set for a version of a product that will be displayed next to a higher-priced model of the same brand or next to a competitive brand.

REFERENT POWER

Power that results from being admired, personally identified with, or liked by others.

REFINDED DATA

With all this information at hand with a continuous feedback loop established for comparison and verification of the resulting refined data a truly valid and useful manpower plan can be developed. The prediction of a 95 per cent probability of securing an order that could not be filled without the addition of 10 or 20 experienced computer programmers within short time would have a compelling impact on any recruiting plan.

REFREEZING

Is the state in which an individual's experimentally performed behaviours become part of the person.

REFRESH

In the computers the images are formed on the screen by setting the pixels of screen. This image formed fades within a small faction of time. So to maintain the sharp and crisp image on the screen it become necessary to continuously refresh the image. The refreshing is nothing but redrawing of the image again and again which may happen upto 60-80 times per second.

REFUND

To return the money someone has paid for goods because he is dissatisfied with purchase. To repay a loan by means of a further borrowing.

REGENCY EFFECT

The finding that under certain conditions in the process of learning the last one of the series to be learned is remembered best.

REGISTER

A device in CPU capable of storing a specified amount of data such as one word. This is nothing but a collection of flip-flops connected together to load instructions and store data. Many common registers are accumulator, stack pointer, shift register and program counter.

REGISTERED COMPANY

A limited or unlimited company, usually with shareholders, which has been incorporated under the Companies Act, 1956, having complied with all required regulations.

REGISTERED TRADEMARK

A legally-defined Trademark owned by an individual or group in the Register of Trademarks.

REGISTRY

An organisation that conducts a registration program for health personnel and the list of individuals it has registered.

REGRESSION MODELS

Explanatory models based on equations that express the fluctuations in the variable being forecasted in terms of fluctuations in one or more other variables.

REGRESSIVE EYE MOVEMENT

Turning the eyes to the left to retrace a part of a line while reading from left to right across a line of print.

REGULATION

Regulatory programs can be classified by their purpose (*e.g.*, to control charges), the regulated (*e.g.* state government), or their method (such as prospective rate review). Most regulatory programs include certification, registration, licensing, or other similar components of control. Regulations may include programs or rules that seek to change behaviour through financial incentives. It does not include private accreditation programs, although they may be used by government regulatory programs.

REIMBURSEMENT, RETROACTIVE

Additional payment by a third party to an institution for services not identified at the time of initial reimbursement.

REINFORCEMENT

The process of strengthening the likelihood that a given behaviour will occur by providing it with some form of reward. This is the basis of all conditioning.

REINFORCEMENT THEORY

A theory of motivation that argues that our behaviour can be explained by consequences in the environment and, therefore, that it is not necessary to look for cognitive explanations.

REINFORCER

Any object or event that increases or sustains the response given by a person.

REINSTATE

To put back in place, or in a condition that was lost, taken away, or revoked.

RELATEDNESS NEEDS

The needs in ERG theory thqt address our relationships with significant others, such as families, friendship groups, work groups, and professional groups.

RELATIONAL DATABASE

The database in which the data is organised in the tabular form in rows and columns so that the relationship of any data item to any data field or data item can easily be determined. *E.g.*, ORACLE and SYBASE.

RELATIONAL OPERATORS

The operators which are used for comparison like <, >, =, >=, <=, and <>.

RELATIONSHIP MANAGEMENT

The sales function of managing the account relationship and ensuring that buyers receive appropriate services.

RELATIONSHIPS

Interpersonal relationships required or made possible on a job.

RELATIVE ADVANTAGE

The characteristic of offering clear-cut advantages over other existing, competing offerings.

RELEASE

To remove from an obligation or penalty; to give up for relinquish a claim on the person or organisation against whom the claim was made.

RELEVANT ALTERNATIVES

Are alternatives that are considered feasible for solving an existing problem and for implementation.

RELIABILITY

In search, the dependability of a measuring device, as reflected in the consistency of the results it provides when repeated measurements are made of the same parameter or group. A test is said to have a high degree of reliability when an individual tested today and tested again at a later time with the same test and under the same conditions gives approximately the same result. According to this meaning, reliability is the reproducibility of an experimented result. Reliability does not address whether or not a result is correct: that is a matter of "validity".

REMEDIAL READING

Clinical procedures in which particular effort is made to

discover the exact cause or causes of deficiency and means of removing or mitigating these casual factors, coupled with instruction designed to remove special reading deficiencies.

REMEDIAL TRANSFERS

These are transfers made to remedy some situation primarily concerned with employee on the job.

REMUNERATION OR COMPENSATION

Remuneration payable to an employee is one of the conditions in the contract of service which is generally in writing since it has legal importance. Remuneration paid to an employee is usually referred to his wave (or salary). It includes basic pay and certain other allowances like dearness allowance, house rent allowance, etc. The term wave or salary also includes any non-pecuniary benefit attached to money payment.

RENT

A payment made by one person usually at fixed intervals for the use of someone else s property. The difference between the amount actually paid for using a factor of production and a minimum payment which would bring it into use.

REORDER POINT (ROP)

The inventory level at which a new order should be placed.

REPATRIATION

Is the process of bringing individuals who have been working abroad back to their home country and reintegrating them into the organisation's home-country operations.

REPETITIVENESS DIMENSION

Of a plan is the extent to which the plan is to be used over and over again.

REPLACEMENT CHART

A partial organisation chart showing the major managerial positions in an organisation, current incumbents, potential replacements for each position, and the age of each person listed on the chart.

REPLACEMENT TRANSFERS

These are transfers of long-service employees to similar jobs in other departments where they replace or 'bump' employees with shorter service. The object of these transfers is also to retain the efficient and trained employees as long as possible but in this process some short-service employees may be thrown out of employment.

REPOSITIONING

Changing a product's design, formulation, brand image, or brand name to alter the product's market position.

REPRESENT

To speak or act under the authority of another, to attend or act on behalf of another.

REPRESENTATION

The procedure where someone acts on behalf of an individual

or a group of workers in an organisation. Usually this refers to the right of a trade union to represent its members in dealing with management on issues other than those dealing with pay and conditions of employment which are dealt with by collective bargaining.

REPRESENTATIVE

A person authorised to act or speak on behalf of others; a public official elected to the U.S. House of Representatives or a state or local legislative body.

REPRESENTATIVE ACTION

A class action; also, a lawsuit brought by one stockholder in a corporation to claim rights or to fix wrongs done to many or all stockholders in the company.

REPRESENTATIVENESS

A decision-making bias that involves the tendency to be overlay influenced by stereotypes in making judgments about the likelihood of occurrences.

REPRESSION

The rejection and shutting out of the awareness of reaction pattern (thought, feeling, impulse, memory) in order to avoid distress.

REPRIMAND

Formal censure for some job-related behaviour. A reprimand is less severe then an adverse action, more forceful than an admonition.

REQUISITION

A routine written request for supplies or services. Usually made by one person or department in an organisation to another.

RESALE PRICE

Attempts by the manufacturers or suppliers of goods to dictate the price at which, or the conditions on which, goods are to be sold by the retailer.

RESCIND

To take back; unmake; annual. For example, an organisation s board may rescind a previous action.

RESCISSION

In insurance, the cancellation of a policy with repayment of the premiums.

RESEARCH AND DEVELOPMENT (R&D)

The function within a company, responsible for discovering new ideas, or new applications of old ideas, which might be to the commercial advantage of the company at some point in the future.

RESEARCH BRIEF

A structured document given to a research agency including background to the organisation, objectives of the research, limitations and aiming.

RESEARCH DESIGN

A master plan that specifically identifies what tools and techniques will be used to collect and analyse data relevant to the research problem.

RESERVATIONS

Organisational units that devote full time to the generation of innovative ideas for future business.

RESERVE

An amount of money or other negotiable instrument set aside by an insurance company to assure the fulfilment of its commitments to pay future claims.

RESERVE MONEY

The sum of currency with the public, other deposits with the Reserve Bank of India, cash with banks and bankers deposits with RBI.

RESERVED RESPONSIBILITY

The work assigned to a person.

RESIDUAL VALUE

The difference between the original worth of an asset (for example, the purchase price or fair market value of a donated automobile) and that portion of it that has been amortized or written off (as a depreciation expense or loss).

RESIGNATION

An employee's formal notice that his or her relationship with the employing organisation is being terminated.

RESOLUTION

A term or measurement of clarity of sharpness of an image, based on the number of pixels user to form the image. More is the number of pixels better is the resolution and high is the cost of monitor. A measure of precision of hard copy also. In case of hard copy resolution is measured in terms of dpi (dots per inch).

RESOURCE DEPENDENCE

An approach to controls that argues that managers need to consider controls mainly in areas in which they depend on others for resources necessary to reach organisational goals.

RESOURCE DEPENDENCE MODEL

A view of the organisation-environment interface that highlights organisational dependence on the environment for resources and argues that organisations attempt to manipulate the environment to reduce that dependence.

RESPONDENT

A person interviewed or contacted in a market research survey.

RESPONSE

A person's behavioural activity that has resulted from a stimulus.

RESPONSE BIAS

A mental set to respond in a particular way to certain issue or questions, *e.g.*, on a questionnaire.

RESPONSIBILITY

Responsibility means the work or duty which the subordinate is expected to perform by virtue of his position in the organisation. Mental and physical efforts to be put in by a person to complete a given task is the responsibility of the person to whom the authority is granted. Responsibility or duty must be expressed either in terms of functions or in terms of objectives.

RESPONSIBILITY

The obligation to carry out duties and achieve goals related to a position.

RESPONSIBILITY CENTRE

A subunit headed by a manager who is responsible for achieving one or more goals.

RESPONSIBILITY GAP

It exists when certain organisational tasks are not included in the responsibility area of any individual organisation member.

RESTRAIN OF TRADE

Any activity which interferes with the operation of a freemarket process fixing or preventing a new competitor from entering the market.

RESTRAINING FORCES

Forces studied in force-field analysis that involve factors that pressure against a change.

RESTRICTIVE PRACTICE

This term usually refers to a work practice supported by a trade union in the interest of job security for its members which limits the scope of management especially in the allocation of particular kinds of work. The practice may not be officially agreed through collective bargaining.

RESTRICTIVE ENDORSEMENT

The signature of a negotiable instrument (such as a cheque) in a way that limits its negotiability; such as by endorsing a cheque with the words, "Pay to Arun Kumar Jain only".

RESTRUCTURING

A method of increasing organisational efficiency and effectiveness that involves making a major change in organisation structure and often includes reducing management levels and changing components of the organisation through divestiture and/or acquisition, as well as shrinking the size of the work force.

RESUMES

An experienced self-confident recruiter can scan and sort resumes at the rate of several hundreds an hour. An experienced self-confident preliminary interviewer can handle application at the door in a matter of minutes per person referring the most likely ones to recruiters almost as fast as they arrive.

RETAIL AUDIT

A market research technique which involves taking a representative sample of retail outlets and studying term to obtain data on distribution, sales, stock, etc.

RETAIL AUDIT

The research undertaken in retail outlets involving checking invoices, delivery notes and sales records to determine the precise volume of goods sold. Results are often syndicated to several suppliers.

RETAIL PRICE INDEX

A index designed to show the purchasing power of currency with regard to a basket of consumer item prices.

RETAIL SELLING

Selling to ultimate consumers.

RETAILER

A firm that buys consumer goods in order to resell them at a profit without altering them in any way to consumers.

RETAILING

The selling of goods and services in relatively small quantities directly to the consumer through a shop or other retail outlet.

RETAINER

An advance fee paid to a professional to assure the availability of his or her services in the future.

RETIREMENT

The process of finishing one's full-time work life at a designated or generally accepted age.

RETIREMENT ON THE JOB

A term sometime used on an employee who experiences such alienation from this job that he does the minimum possible in order to retain it while he waits for retirement.

RETIRING A BILL

Withdrawing a bill from currency, stating that it be payable later at a fixed time.

RETRENCHMENT

Is a strategy adopted by management to strengthen or protect the amount of business a strategic business unit is currently generating.

RETURN

Yield or profit; for example, the return on a public relations campaign.

RETURN ON INVESTMENT (ROI)

The ratio of profits to assets (or net worth) for an organisation, a subunit of an organisation, a product line, or a brand.

RETURNS

Goods sent back to the seller because of damage, late delivery, or some other reason.

RETURNS AND ALLOWANCES PERCENTAGE

Percentage of returns and allowances for each sales dollar: Returns and Allowances/Net Sales.

REVALUATION

Action by the government of one country to change a peg for its currency in terms of the currency of another country so that in future a unit of the first currency will be exchanged for more units of the second currency. A fresh valuation of assets.

REVALUATION ACCOUNTING

Revaluation or replacement value accounting is mainly concerned with ensuring that capital is maintained in real terms and profit is calculated on this basis.

REVENUE

Money received from all sources. Unless otherwise stated, gross receipts represent receipts prior to the deduction of expenses.

REVENUE BOND

A bond that is redeemed only with revenues generated from the completed, operations project for which the bond was sold. This is the typical bond issued for the financing of projects.

REVENUE CENTRE

A responsibility centre whose budgetary performance is measured primarily but its ability to generate a specified level of revenue.

REVENUE COST

Cost incurred to maintain the income earning capacity of a business, for example, the cost of maintaining an asset, or running a business.

REVERIE

A lower form of thinking* Dwelling upon a series of recollections without attempt to control their direction.

REVERSAL TENDENCY

The tendency of an individual to reverse letters or words while reading.

REVERSE DISCRIMINATION

Is the term used to describe inequities affecting members of the majority group as an outcome of programs designed to help underrepresented groups.

REVIEW

To examine critically; Review implies close scrutiny of something to determine its suitability or accuracy. For instance, a program is reviewed preparatory to approval or authorisation.

REVISED OPERATIONAL PROCEDURES

These outline what specific activities are to take place in the performance of specific work. In writing and using ROP the management must concentrate on the changes that are required. This is the information the employee really needs to know to carry out the change.

REVITALISATION

The renewal of the innovative vigour of organisations, sought in the elaboration-of-structure stage of the organisational life cycle.

REVOLVING FUND

A fund established to finance a cycle of operations through sums of money received by the fund.

REWARD

Any kind of return (usually positive) as a result of a given behaviour. It is most often used in employment to refer to monetary gains in return for an individual performance at work. These gains may be in the form of pay of fringe benefits of perks.

REWARD POWER

An influence over others based on their hope of reward; the opposite of coercive power. A subordinate perceives that compliance with the wishes of a superior leads to positive rewards, either monetary or psychological.

REWARD POWER

Power that is based on the capacity to control and provide valued rewards to others.

RIBBON

The thin tape made up of synthetic fabric type material which is used as inking medium in many impact and non-impact printers. The character heads strike on the ribbon and the impression is received on paper.

RIDER

A legal document that modifies the protection afforded by an insurance policy, either expanding or decreasing its benefits or adding or excluding certain conditions from its coverage. A rider differs from a waiver in that a waiver is a total removal of a specific coverage.

RIGHT TO BE INFORMED

The consumer s right to obtain the information that is require to make an intelligent choice from among the available products.

RIGHT TO SAFETY

The right consumers assume they are entitled to expect the products they purchase to be free from unneccesary dangers.

RIGHT-TO-WORK LAWS

State laws that make it illegal for collective bargaining agreements to contain maintenance of membership, preferential hiring, union shop, or any other clauses calling for compulsory union membership.

RISK

The likelihood, or the statistical probability, of failure in an enterprise, the essence of being an entrepreneur, and therefore of capitalism. The term is also used for the probability of damage or loss; the essence of insurance. In other words, the possibility, characteristic of decisions made under uncertainty, that a chosen action could lead to losses rather than the intended results.

RISK CAPITAL

Capital invested in an enterprise with a high degree of risk, though usually with the possibility of a large financial gain.

RISK CONDITION

Is the decision-making situation in which the decision-maker has only enough information to estimate how probable the outcome of implemented alternatives will be.

RISK MANAGEMENT

The function of planning, organising, directing, and evaluating a comprehensive programme of activities to identify, evaluate and take corrective action against risks that may lead to patient injury, employee injury, and property loss or damage with resulting financial loss or legal liability; all of an organisation's efforts to protect its assets, reputation, and human and physical resources against loss.

RISK-TAKING FUNCTION

Assumption of the responsibility for losses when the future is uncertain.

RISKY SHIFT

The finding that people will often make decisions of greater risk under the influence of a group than when they are alone.

RITE

A relatively elaborate, dramatic, planned set of activities intended to convey cultural values to participants and, usually, an audience.

RITUAL

Automatic activity or behaviour that has a cultural origin in an organisation, society, or sect.

ROBINSON-PITMAN

Act. U.S. federal law passed in 1936 and intended to halt discriminatory pricing policies by specifying certain limited conditions under which a seller may charge different process to different buyers.

ROBOT

A machine which can be programmed and controlled by computer to function like person for certain jobs.

ROBOTICS

The study of robots, their design, manufacture and applications.

ROLE

(*i*) A major work group input that involves a set of behaviours expected of an individual who occupies a particular position in a group; also used to denote a management process element consisting of an organised set of behaviours associated with a particular office or position.

(*ii*) A term widely used in social psychology to refer to the kind of behaviour expected of a given person in a given situation. The term has been applied generally to the organisation and the workplace.

ROLE AMBIGUITY

A person's lack of understanding about the rights, privileges, and obligations of a job.

ROLE AND RESPONSIBILITIES OF PERSONNEL MANAGER

Differing according to size and nature of the enterprise, taken as a specialised function:

(i) formulation of personnel policies, plans, programs, and procedures.

(*ii*) undertaking personnel research for better advice to management.

(*iii*) developing an effective system of recruitment, selection, training, placement, appraisal etc.

(*iv*) designing schemes of motivation and welfare.

(*v*) establishing effective communication system.

(vi) advising management in negotiating with employees.

(vii) facilitating the growth of cordial work relationships.

ROLE CONFLICT

A situation in which an individual is expected to play two or more roles which are in conflict or in competition with each other.

ROLE DIFFERENTIATION

The process of the division of labour and of specialisation within a group. The larger and more complex the group – from the family to the multinational company—the greater the degree of role differentiation.

ROLE EXPECTATION

The expectation other people have about the way a person will play his/her role in a given situation.

ROLE LEARNING

Learning attempted solely through repetition without any attempt to find order or meaning in the material.

ROLE MANAGEMENT STAGE OR SOCIALISATION

Socialisation activities undertaken or experienced during the stable career/ work stage.

ROLE MODEL

A person after whom an individual will model his/her own performance of a given role.

ROLE NEGOTIATION

This term is sometimes used to describe a process that may take during an interview with a candidate for a job where the exact role individual would play in the organisation is subject to negotiation.

ROLE OVERLOAD

An extreme form of role conflict where the number of different roles expected of an individual are simply too great for her to contain.

ROLE PLAYING

Acting the part of another person in a therapeutic or business game situation. Playing a certain role for the particular effect it will cause.

ROLE RELATIONSHIP

Any relationship between two people which is defined by the role they play, *e.g.*, boss and subordinate.

ROLE REVERSAL

A situation in which people agree to switch their usual role relationships, *e.g.* where army officers serve Christmas dinner to the troops.

ROLE SET

Individual's expectations for the behaviour of a person in a particular role. The more expectations, the more complex is the role set.

ROLE STRUCTURE

The extent to which a role is specified and defined or left open.

ROLE TRANSITION

The process of switching from one role to another a process in which socialisation is of great importance.

ROLE UNDERLOAD

The opposite of role overload. A situation in which an individual feels that his/her role is not big enough for him/her.

ROLLING PLAN

A strategy statement covering a standard future period (*e.g.*, give years ahead), which is updated annually to allow for changing circumstances.

ROOT DIRECTORY

The directory structure resembles the structure of a tree with up-side-down (*i.e.*, reverse tree). The main directory is the root directory from which the directories and if required subdirectories branch out.

ROUTINE

An ordered set of instructions which yield some output. The routine contains that set of instructions which is frequently required in that program.

ROUTING MODELS

Quantitative methods that can assist managers in planning the most effective and economical approaches to distribution problems also called distribution models.

ROUTINISED RESPONSE BEHAVIOUR

The least complex type of decisionmaking, in which the consumer bases choice on past behaviour and needs no other information.

ROWAN SYSTEM

In this plan if the worker completes his job in less than the standard time the wage payment time saved is calculated as a percentage of the time allowed and the worker is credited with a bonus for the time saved in the same percentage.

ROYALTY

A fee paid to an author or composer on each sale of published work for which he holds the copyright, or to an inventor for the use of an invention for which he holds the patent.

RPROM

Short for Reprogramming Read Only Memory.

RULE

(*i*) A standing plan that is a statement spelling out specific actions to be taken or not taken in a given situation.

(*ii*) A statement by a government agency of general or particular applicability and future effect, designed to implement, interpret, or prescribe law or policy; or a similar government agency statement describing the organisation, procedure, or practice requirements of an agency.

RUMOUR

An unverified belief that is in general circulation and that contains three components: the target, and the allegation, and the source.

RUNNING COSTS

Expenses incurred in the daily operation of a business or project.

RUN-TIME ERROR

The errors that occur at the time of execution of program. These are neither the result of logical error nor syntactical problem. In fact when user enters the wrong type data or ambiguous data such error occurs at that time as they hurdles the execution. Sometimes it may occur because of hardware failure.

S

SABOTAGE

Any of several illegal tactics used by workers during labour disputes, such as wilfully damaging machinery or other property of the employer, wasting or destroying materials, and obstructing or interfering with normal business operations.

SAFETY NEEDS

The needs in Maslow's hierarchy that pertain to the desire to feel safe, secure, and free from threats to our existence.

SAFETY NET

The capacity of social welfare programs to supply a subsistence standard of living to people lacking adequate essentials of daily living.

SAFETY OFFICER

Employee in an organisation who is responsible for recommending safe methods of working, educating employees in safe working methods and investigating accidents.

SALARIED STAFF

This term is usually applied to staff who are white-collar workers and whose pay is calculated on an annual basis and paid in equal monthly instalments. This is contrast to the blue-collar worker, for example who might be paid on an hourly basis or by the amount of work completed.

SALARY

A fixed regular payment to an employee for work done. Usually restricted to payments to non-manual workers and payments made at intervals of a month or longer. Also the amount a person receives as salary in a particular period.

SALARY ADMINISTRATION

Activities concerned with fixing and sometimes paying salaries in an organisation.

SALARY CLASSES

Salary brackets used in calculating entitlements and contributions under certain pension schemes.

SALARY INCREMENT

Regular increase in salary, usually annual, written into pay scales and individual contracts of employment. Particularly common in government and other public service.

SALARY PLUS COMMISSION

Compensation consisting of a regular salary plus a commission based on sales performance.

SALARY ROLL

The payroll for salaried employees.

SALARY STRUCTURE

The arrangement of pay within an organisation such that different grades of employees doing different jobs will receive different rates. These rates would be based (originally) on the process of job analysis and job evaluation increment of pay.

SALE

A change of ownership over goods in return for money. An agreement to sell specified goods to someone. *An auction:* An offer by a retail establishment or reduces in the prices of many goods for a restricted period. The total quantity of goods sold by an enterprise over a period. Synonym for Sales Revenue.

SALE AND LEASEBACK

A single business transaction in which a piece of equipment or machinery is sold to an individual or business, which then leases it back to the original owner.

SALE OF RETURN

Colloquial term for practice whereby only goods resold are charged to a dealer, any unsold goods being returnable for full credit.

SALES AGENT

A marketing term for the person employed by a company or manufacturer to control or supervise the distribution of his goods in a particular area. The sales agent strictly negotiates contracts between the manufacturer and a third party and may not himself be the contracting party.

SALES ANALYSIS

A detailed study of sales records of the aggregation and breaking down of sales information to reveal patterns that can be used to evaluate the effectiveness and efficiency of marketing efforts.

SALES BRANCH

Wholesaling establishment maintained by a manufacturer for its own product. It carries an inventory of the product.

SALES CALL

A visit made by a sales representative to a potential customer.

SALES CORRESPONDENT

A sales employee at company headquarters or at a branch office.

SALES FORECAST

The actual sales volume an organisation expects during a given period.

SALES FORECASTING

The process of estimating sales volume for a product, an organisational unit, or an entire organisation over a specific future time period. The breakdown method of forecasting starts with large-scale estimates (for example, an estimate of GDP) and works down to industrywise, company, and product estimates. The build-up method starts with smaller-scale estimates and works up to large-scale ones.

SALES MANAGEMENT

The marketing management activity that deals with planning, organising, directing, and controlling the personal selling effort.

SALES OBJECTIVES

The specific objectives that an organisation's sales effort will attempt to meet. Sales objectives should be precise and quantifiable, should include a time frame, and should be reasonable in terms of the organisation's resources.

SALES OFFICE

Wholesaling establishment maintained by a manufacturer for its own product. It does not carry an inventory of the product.

SALES ORIENTATION

Organisational philosophy that emphasises selling existing products, whether or not they meet consumer needs, often through aggressive sales techniques and advertising.

SALES POTENTIAL

The maximum share of the market an individual organisation can expect during a given period.

SALES PRESENTATION

The step in the creative selling process wherein the salesperson attempts to persuasively communicate the product's benefits and to explain appropriate courses of action.

SALES PROMOTION

Promotional activities other than personal selling, advertising, and public relations that are intended to stimulate buyer purchased or dealer effectiveness over a specific time period.

SALES PROMOTION — OBJECTIVES OF

The following are the main objectives of all sales promotion activities:

(*i*) Creation of demand

(*ii*) Educating consumers

(*iii*) Securing response in the desired manner

(*iv*) Establishing goodwill for the product.

SALES TAX

A tax levied on the sale of goods and services at one or more stages in the process of distribution.

SALES TEAM

The sales representative and those who support his or her efforts in making sales and servicing accounts. Support personnel may include technical specialists, missionary salespeople, sales correspondents, and others.

SALES TERRITORY

The specific and prospective accounts assigned to a salesperson. They may be based on geographical divisions, customer types, product lines, or selling tasks.

SALESFORCE COMPOSITE

A method of judgmental forecasting that is used mainly to predict future sales and typically involves obtaining the views of various salespeople, sales managers, and/or distributors regarding the sales outlook.

SALESFORCE ESTIMATION METHOD

Predicts future sales levels primarily by asking appropriate salespeople for their opinions of what will happen to sales in the future.

SALVAGE

The regard given to persons, who save, in part or whole, a ship or its cargo from shipwreck. The person rendering assistance must show that he did so voluntarily, that there was danger involved and that he showed enterprise, that the ship was in need of help and that some benefit did arise from what he did. Salvage reward is given by the owners of the ship and cargo to the saving persons.

SAMPLE

A portion or subset of a larger population.

SAMPLING

This is the process of analysing a sample drawn from a particular population when it is too difficult or expensive to deal with each member of that population. The most common ways to obtain a sample are by random sampling and stratified sampling including quota sampling.

SAMPLING ERROR

Errors arising in a sample survey due to inferences drawn about population, size, composition, etc., on the basis of observation of a few units.

SAMPLING FRAME

The background or catchment area of population from which a sample is to be taken.

SAMPLING ORDERS

Trial orders for a product by a prospective buyer who may place large orders if the samples meet his requirements for price, quality etc.

SAMPLING PROCEDURE

Practical rules for obtaining a sample from a population.

SANCTION

A penalty or disincentive designed to promote the use of preferred or contract providers of care. The term is most frequently used in alternative reimbursement and delivery systems.

SANDWICH LEASE

A transaction in which a person or organisation leases property and then sublets it for more money; this is often done in leasing an office building and renting out office space in it to others.

SATELLITE

An enterprise that sells its products to only one or two large firms and is, therefore, dependent on their success for its existence.

SATISFACTION

A criterion of effectiveness that refers to the organisation's ability to gratify the needs of its participants. Similar terms include morale and voluntarism.

SATISFACTION-PROGRESSION-PRINCIPLE

A principle incorporated into *ERG theory* which states that satisfaction of one level of need encourages concern with the next level.

SATISFICING MODEL

A non-rational model of managerial decision-making stating that managers seek alternatives only until they find one that looks satisfactory, rather than seeking the optimal decision.

SATISFYING

Adopting a course that is merely "good enough" from all viewpoints, rather than seeking the best possible course (term used by *Herbert A. Simon*).

SATURATION POINT

Level at which any further expansion of distribution in a market is unlikely to be achieved and where further sales are restricted to the potential arising from replacement needs or population growth.

SAVINGS-ACCOUNT LOAN

A loan secured by funds on deposit in the same financial institution.

SCALAR CHAIN

Chain of superiors from top to bottom is called the *Scalar Chain*. To facilitate quick communication between one link of the chain and the other, either the chain should not be very long or gang planks may be provided in-between to correspond directly.

SCALAR RELATIONSHIPS

Refers to the chain-of-command positioning of individuals on an organisation chart.

SCALPER

A speculator who buys and sells principally to make quick profits.

SCANNER

An input device which is used a scan a whole document both text or graphics type and store the scanned matter in the form. Text is stored as text file and graphic is stored as the .bmp or graphic file of desired format.

SCANNING

The act of examining point by point. Generally the term is used to describe paid reading for a specific purpose.

SCHEDULE

A series of items to be handled or events to occur at or during a particular period of time; a timetable.

SCHEDULE OF DEMAND

Demand schedule: It refers to a series of quantities of a good that will be taken by buyers at each of a corresponding series of prices.

SCHEDULE PLANNING

Concerns scheduling which is affixing time values to each needed activity and to the total project. Scheduling gives vitality and a practical meaning to a plan.

SCHEDULES OF REINFORCEMENT

Patterns of rewarding that specify the basis for and timing of positive reinforcement.

SCHEDULING

Is the process of formulating a detailed listing of activities that must be accomplished to attain an objective, allocating the resources necessary to attain the objective, and setting up and following timetables for completing the objective.

SCHEME ADVERTISING

Advertising normally of a below-the- line character.

SCIENCE

The accumulation of knowledge about humans and the environment.

SCIENTIFIC MANAGEMENT

(*i*) Scientific management is a thoughtful, organised, systematic approach to the job of management as contrasted with hit or miss, *rule of thumb*. It includes finding the most efficient methods of production, scientific selection and training of workers, proper allotment of work and achieving cooperation between workers and management. Scientific management refers to application of science to management practices.

(*ii*) An approach within classical management theory that emphasises the scientific study of work methods in order to improve worker efficiency.

(*iii*) Emphasises the "one best way" to perform a task.

SCIENTIFIC METHOD

The basic premise underlying the scientific method is a simple and abiding faith in the rationality of nature, leading to the belief that phenomena have a cause.

SCIENTIFIC NOTATION

A method of representing the large quantities or numbers using a two part notation-exponent and mantissa. This is an easy and convenient notation of writing the big numbers. This is used in calculators where there is limited space to represent the digits. Many high level languages also use this notation and thus supports a wide range of numbers.

SCOPE

The scale on which an organisational change is implemented (*e.g.*, throughout the entire organisation, level by level, or department by department).

SCOPE DIMENSION

Of a plan is the portion of the total management system at which the plan is aimed.

SCOPE OF THE DECISION

Is the proportion of the total management system that a particular decision will affect. The broader the scope of a decision, the higher the level of the manager responsible for making that decision.

SCORE

Credit or value given to a specific response to a test item. Sum of the credits obtained on all the items of a single test.

SCORE-KEEPING

The process of data accumulation or record-keeping which enables interested parties (internal and external) to ascertain how the organisation is performing.

SCRAMBLED MERCHANDISING

The offering of products of sale in a retail outlet knot traditionally associated with those products.

SCRAP

(1) Material which becomes unusable excess as a result of a production process.
(2) Faulty items resulting from poor work, which may or may not be recoverable by rectification.

SCREEN PROMPT

An instruction or symbol displayed on the screen whose appearance on screen assures the user that computer is ready to accept the instruction.

SCREENING STAGE

The stage in new product development that involves analysis of ideas to determine their appropriateness and reasonableness in relation to the organisation's goals and objectives.

SCREENING TASK FORCE

One technique for handling the deluge of candidates is to use a screening walk-in-candidates and resumes do not go directly to the recruiter. Instead they go to a small group of recruiters designated daily, weekly or monthly who are assigned to this task.

SCRIP

The abbreviation of subscription receipt, and a general term for any security.

SEAL

On a document, a symbol of a person's willingness to be bound by the statements and promises he makes in the document.

SEASONAL DISCOUNT

Discount offered by media owners to encourage business during what are considered to be slack periods in the year.

SEASONAL FLUCTUATIONS

Patterns of orders or sales that last for periods of less than one year.

SEASONAL INVENTORIES

Inventories whose levels are adjusted to absorb seasonal fluctuations in demand.

SEASONAL RATE

Rate in advertising which vary according to the time of year.

SEASONAL UNEMPLOYMENT

A form of unemployment that peaks at certain times of the year due to the nature of the industry in question, *e.g.*, construction or tourism.

SECONDARY ACTION

In an industrial dispute between an employer and his employees, secondary action is industrial action taken by the employees against persons who deal with the employer.

SECONDARY BOYCOTT

Attempts by a union through strikes, picketing, or other methods to stop one employer from doing business with another employer.

SECONDARY DATA

Data maintained by an organisation for use in its normal course of SEEK TIME operations, and which can be used for evaluative purposes; evaluation data which already exist prior to the initiation of an evaluation study.

SECONDARY GROUP

A group, generally larger than a primary group, whose influence or members is not as strong as the influence of primary groups.

SECONDARY MEDIA

Advertising media used to support the primary media in a campaign.

SECONDARY MEMORY

A general name given to any nonvolatile storage medium such as CDROM, tape, diskette. This means content of this memory will not loss even if the computer is switched off.

SECONDARY PICKETING

Picketing in furtherance of a trade dispute by individuals or groups not directly party to the main dispute.

SECONDARY READERSHIP

Indicates readership of a publication by location.

SECONDARY STORAGE

Storage supplement to the primary memory. *See* Secondary Memory.

SECOND-MARKET DISCOUNTING

A differential pricing strategy whereby a product is sold at one process in the core target market and at a reduced price in a secondary market.

SECONDMENT

Moving someone to another job or organisation for a temporary period.

SECRETARY

An individual who supports one or more executive in an organisation by typing, filling, arranging meetings, screening telephone calls, etc. An individual who is the executive responsible for arrangement of a group of organisations, *e.g.* the secretary of government department.

SECTOR

A section of one track only on diskettes that contains a specified number of bytes. A typical floppy disk has 9 sectors whereas hard disk has 17 sectors. One sector may hold either 128 characters or

256 characters or 512 characters depending on the operating system.

SECURITY

Prevention or protection of information against retrieval, alteration by authorised user.

SECURITY OF TENURE

The right of an individual to remain in a current position of employment or residence.

SECURITY, OR SAFETY NEEDS

Are maslow's second set of human needs-reflecting the human desire to keep free from physical harm.

SEED MONEY

The initial financing needed to start a project which is to be supplemented with larger, more permanent funding at a later date.

SEEK TIME

The time taken to locate a particular record in a disk and transfer that information to the CPU when found.

SEGMENT

A portion of a program or data file.

SEGMENT VALUE

A number which tells the position of segment in memory by considering the memory made up of 16-bits units.

SELECT

To make a choice between alternative courses of action as a result of a test.

SELECTION

(*i*) A source of error in experimental studies that occurs when participants are assigned to experimental and control groups on any basis other than random assignment. Any other selection method causes systematic biases the result in differences between groups unrelated to the effects of the experimental treatment.

(*ii*) An activity in the staffing process that involves determining which job candidates best suit organisational needs.

(*iii*) Is choosing an individual to hire from all those who have been recruited.

SELECTION BOARD

A committee that is given the task of selecting new employees from among application.

SELECTION INTERVIEW

(*i*) A relatively formal, in-depth conversation conducted for the purpose of assessing a candidate's knowledge, skills, and abilities, as well as providing information to the candidate about the organisation and potential jobs,

(*ii*) An interview that is intended to help the interviewer decide whether to select the interviewer for employment.

SELECTION OF PERSONNEL

Selection means making a choice by preference. This choice by preference is based on comparison between two factors: (i) What the job requires for successful execution?, and (ii) What the applicant has to offer? For the most part, the better the balance between these factors, the better the selection work and the more likely the attainment of a satisfactory working force.

SELECTIVE ATTENTION

A perceptual screening device whereby a person does not attend to a particular stimulus.

SELECTIVE DEMAND ADVERTISING

Advertising aimed at stimulating demand for a particular brand.

SELECTIVE DISTRIBUTION

A distribution strategy in which the product is sold in a limited number of outlets.

SELECTIVE EXPOSURE

The principle describing the fact that no individual is exposed to all stimuli.

SELECTIVE INTERPRETATION

A perceptual screening device whereby a person distorts a stimulus that is incompatible with his or her values or attitudes.

SELECTIVE PERCEPTION

(*i*) Is the tendency to collect information that not only supports one's own motives, beliefs, and attitudes but also minimises the emotional distress caused by unfamiliar or troublesome stimuli.

(*ii*) The screening out of certain stimuli and the interpretation of other stimuli according to personal experiences attitudes, or the like.

SELECTIVE RETENTION

The process by which a person remember information in which he or she is interested and forgets information that is of little interest.

SELF-CONTROL

A component of social learning theory involving our ability to exercise control over our own behaviour by setting standards and providing consequences for our own actions.

SELF COVER

Cover of brochure or other print item made of same paper as inside pages.

SELF-EVALUATION

In management, self-enrichment can be achieved through self-disclosure and group feedback, sensitivity analysis tests, management effectiveness seminars, self-analysis etc. If a manager adopts the following five steps to maturity, he could successfully operate in an organisation: (i) Self-examination; (ii) Self-expectation; (iii) Self-realisation power; (iv) Self (iv)deduction; (v) Broadened perception. The answer to the various questions we ask ourselves in the above areas will disclose the extent to which we differ from others.

SELF-ACTUALISATION NEEDS

(*i*) Are Maslow's fifth, and final, set of human needs-reflecting the human desire to maximise personal potential.

(*ii*) The needs in Maslow's hierarchy that pertain to the requirement of developing our capabilities and reaching our full potential.

SELF-ADMINISTERING TEST

Test in which instructions are so complete that a person can give the test to himself.

SELF-CONCEPT

The individual's perception and appraisal of himself or herself.

SELF-EFFICACY

(*i*) The belief in one's capabilities to perform a specific task.

(*ii*) The belief that one can perform adequately in a situation. Self- efficacy has three dimensions: magnitude, strength, and generality.

SELF-EMPLOYMENT PERSON

One working on his own, or in business on his own account.

SELF-ENRICHMENT

It is a virtue which can be achieved through self-disclosure and group feedback, sensitivity analysis tests, management effectiveness seminars, self-analysis etc.

SELF-INDEXING RECORDS

The index may either be kept apart from the records to which it refers or the records themselves may be so arranged as to be self-indexing. If the files are arranged alphabetically or chronologically or geographically in an alphabetical order, there is no need of having a separate index as the order of the files is self-indexing.

SELF-MANAGED TEAM

Is an organisational team established to plan, organise, influence, and control its own work situation with only minimal direction from management.

SELF-MANAGING TEAM

A work group given responsibility for a task area without day-to-day supervision and with authority to influence and control both group membership and behaviour; also called *An Autonomous Work Group*.

SELF-ORIENTED ROLES

Roles that are related to the personal needs of group members and often negatively influence the effectiveness of a group.

SELF-SERVING BIAS

Is the tendency to overestimate external causes of behaviour and underestimate internal ones when judging ones own behaviour.

SELF-SERVING BIAS

The tendency to perceive oneself as responsible for successes and others as responsible for failures.

SELLER'S MARKET

(*i*) A market situation in which sellers have more power to influence prices and conditions of sale than buyers, usually because demand exceeds supply. Always contrasted with buyer's market.

(*ii*) A situation where a few sellers dominate the market in terms of controlling the supply of goods, determining the price, etc.

SELL-IN

Process of selling goods to the retail trade prior to a consumer promotional campaign.

SELLING

Process of persuasion leading to a continuing trading arrangement, initiated and perpetuated at either a personal or impersonal level but commonly confined to oral representation supported by visual aids.

SELLING AGENT

Independent agent intermediary similar to a manufacturer's agent but representing a given product in every area in which it is sold, rather than in a limited geographical area.

SELLING FUNCTION

Activities associated with communicating ideas and making a sale and thus effecting the transfer of ownership of a product.

SEMANTIC BLOCKS

The blockages or communication difficulties that arise for word choices.

SEMANTIC NET

The network of words and word meanings that a given individual has available for recall.

SEMI-CONDUCTOR

A general name given to any Silicon, Selenium or Germanium based electronic component. These three materials are conductors in certain electrical conditions and nonconductors in other. That's why they have been named semi-conductors.

SEMI-SKILLED WORK

Work which is related between unskilled work and skilled work, usually on the basis of a requirement for dexterity but not decision-making or judgment.

SEMI-SKILLED WORKER

Generally taken to mean reasonably highly skilled operator-operative though not as highly skilled as a craftsman who has served as apprenticeship.

SEMI-SOULS

Advertisement which appears on a page containing another advertisement but which is not positioned adjacent to it.

SEMI-STRUCTURED

Research conducted by interviewer with guidelines but in which certain key questions may need to be answered.

SENDER

The initiator of the message in the communication process.

SENIOR MANAGEMENT

The term applied to managers who are relatively high in the hierarchy of an organisation because they are senior in level of responsibility and authority and often in age as well.

SENIORITY

Length of service; state of being old or older than others, official position or ranking of a person in an organisation.

SENSATION

Impression received by the sense organs.

SENSITIVITY TRAINING

A technique for trying to improve interpersonal communication and the quality of interpersonal relations in small groups. The orientation of this technique is based on the methods and experience of group therapy. Group leaders try to facilitate open and honest discussion of feelings within the group. The hope is that any new-found sensitivity to one dealing with other people will carry over to other areas of life, such as work groups.

SENTENCE COMPLETION TEST

Projective test, subject being asked to fill in blanks in sentences or phrases.

SEPARATION RATE

Ratio of number of employees who leave an employer for any reason during a period to average number of persons employed by that employer during that period.

SEQUENTIAL FILE

A file whose contents can be arranged in either ascending or descending order so that the records are accessed one after another in sequence.

SEQUENTIAL INTERDEPENDENCE

(i)Interdependence that requires one group to complete its task before another group can complete its task.

(ii)A type of technological interdependence in which one unit must complete its work before the next unit in the sequence can begin work.

SERIAL BONDS

Bonds of the same issue, put out at the same time, that have varying dates of maturity, so that the entire debt does not fall due at once. Usually, the groups of bonds carrying the longest term (in years) pays a higher rate of interest than bonds with shorter terms.

SERIAL TRANSMISSION

Involves the passing of information from one individual to another in a series.

SERVER

The centralised server which administrates the database at back-end in the client-server model.

SERVICE

Business have service functions to perform besides profit-making. *Timothy E. Shea,* Vice-President Incharge of Engineering of Western Electric Company has said: "Business is a vehicle through which man serves society." Such a view of service and profits requires a balancing of functions by managers. Customer service is one of the keys to survival and profit. The serving of customer needs profitably is the basic concern of marketing executives. Service to customers and to society concepts rest on the ethical view of business practice.

SERVICE ACTIVITIES

Staff may perform service activities by carrying out specified work for the line. For example the personnel department may recruit, select and employ people for the line and other staff departments. The purchasing department may buy materials and supplies for the line. Finance may install accounting, budgetary and reporting systems for the line organisation.

SERVICE DEPARTMENTS

Service departments are those assigned to carry out certain specific duties such as construction, purchasing, traffic, insurance, maintenance, engineering and research. These groups seldom advise and seldom have authority; they usually are referred to as "staff groups" since they do not actually work on the product.

SERVICE ENCOUNTER

A period during which a consumer interacts with the service provider.

SERVICE FUNCTION

Activities performed by chances members than increase the exchange process. Repair services and management services provided by intermediaries are examples.

SERVICE INCREMENTS

Increases in pay due after completion of an agreed length of employment.

SERVICE INDUSTRIES

Suppliers of services not directly involved with manufacturing, *e.g.*, travel, entertainment, health, insurance, professional and personal treatment.

SERVICE LEVEL

Extent of extra services provided to customer; often related to price.

SERVICE MARK

A symbol that identifies services. It distinguishes a service in the way a trademark identifies a product.

SERVICE QUALITY

A comparison of customers5 expectations with the performance of service providers.

SERVICE SECTOR

That sector of a mixed economy which is concerned not with the conversion of raw materials or the production of goods but with providing a service, such as advertising, education, health or transport.

SERVICES

Work carried out for others by an individual or organisation where no transfer of goods is involved, *e.g.*, banking, insurance, travelling.

SERVOMECHANISM

A system that has control over another system. Feedback from the system under control enables the servomechanism but homeostasis in the body can also be seen in this way.

SERVOMECHANISM CONTROL

Management information and control system which includes the feedback concept.

SERVOMECHANISM THEORY

A means for automatically filtering out spurious information on certain types of decision-making in management.

SET

A collection of objects of some sort is defined by a rule which unambiguously determines whether or not something is included in the collection. A state of psychological preparedness, of limited duration, which is characteristically taken up in anticipation of a particular type of stimulus or situation.

SET-OFF

A set-off is said to take place when two parties are indebted one to the other and one debt can be set off against another by mutual agreement.

SETTLEMENT

When a transaction or a business deal is fully completed inclusive of all the requisite legal formalities, it is called *Settlement.*

SET-UP DOMINANT SYSTEM

In this system if the original set-up is correct output will be standard.

SEVERANCE PAY

A payment made to an employee either because his contract of employment has ended or because he has to lose his job through no fault of his own, *e.g.*, redundancy.

SHAPING

A technique associated with positive reinforcement that involves the successive rewarding of behaviours that closely approximate the desired response until the actual desired response is made.

SHARE

One unit of stock in a profit-making corporation.

SHARE ACCOUNT

A type of account offered by a credit union that is similar to the time-and- savings accounts offered by commercial banks and thrift institutions.

SHARE INDEX

An economic indicator calculated for a basket of shares on a stock exchange. The prices of the shares are monitored on a continuous basis and the computed index is published as a measure of buoyancy in the market. Or in other words, we can say that share index number based on the prices of particular parcel of shares supposed to be representative and intended as a guide to overall market fluctuations. It may refer to share prices generally or to one particular group of shares.

SHARE WARRANT

A certificate, similar to share certificate, which states that the bearer is the legal owner of a number of shares in a company. No record of the bearer's name is kept by the company, however, and the warrant may be sold without the company's knowledge. The bearer must register with the company and exchange the warrant for a certificate to obtain voting rights and other privileges.

SHARED APPROACH

An OD strategy that involves managers and employees in the determination of the OD program.

SHELF LIFE

The amount of time a product has before it starts to deteriorate.

SHIFT TRANSFER

These are transfers of workers from one shift to another on the same type of work.

SHIFT WORK

The process of dividing the whole 24-hour day into work periods often of eight hours each, *e.g.*, midnight, 8.00 a.m. and 4.00 p.m. Shift work is used to obtain maximum use of plant in manufacturing or of the workforce in the service sector especially that part of it which includes the emergency services where continuous cover is required.

SHIPPER

A middleman who buys in one market or sells in another.

SHIPPING AGENT

A general agent specialising in the export or import of goods by sea. He deals with shipping documents, Insurance and customs and sees that cargo-space is available as needed. Some of the shipping agents are connected with particular steamship companies and these circulate information about available space to their agents.

SHIPPING BILL

A document used for claiming drawback or other facilities from the customs authorities or the Ministry of Commerce.

SHOP FLOOR

A term originally applied to the area of a factory in which production took place. It has been widened in its application to indicate the blue collar workers in an organisation as opposed to the white collar workers or even the workforce in general as opposed to the management.

SHOP STEWARD

A trade union official elected by fellow workers on the shop floor to represent them in their day-to-day dealings with the employers or their management representatives.

SHOP, CLOSED

An arrangement, embodied in a union agreement, under which the employer can hire only people who are already members of the union for jobs within the bargaining unit.

SHOP, OPEN

A shop in which it is not necessary for anyone to be a union member in order to get or keep employment.

SHOP, UNION

A union contract arrangement under which the employer may hire people who are not members of the union for jobs in the bargaining unit, but they must all joint union after a certain length of time, for example, after a sixty-day probationary period.

SHOPLIFTING

Stealing from retail stores with intention to evade payment for them for them leading to stock '*shrinkage*\

SHOPPING GOOD

Products which are considered purchases such as many consumer durables.

SHOPPING PRODUCT

A product for which consumers feel the need to make comparisons; seek out more information; examine merchandise; or otherwise reassure themselves about quality, style, or value before making a purchase.

SHORT TIME WORKING

(*i*) A situation in which a workplace is forced to work a reduced working week because of shortage of orders. This is seen as a temporary measure to cut labour costs while retaining the workforce intact.

(*ii*) State where shortage of work leads an employer to reduce hours of work to a part-time basis, hopefully temporarily.

SHORT-LIST

A list of the leading candidates for a particular job as the result of a recruitment process. People on the short-list will be asked to attend an interview and will perhaps be given some tests as well, before the final selection is made.

SHORT-TERM OBJECTIVES

Are targets to be achieved in one year or less.

SHOWCASE

Cabinet made of glass or clear plastic to display products protected against deterioration and pilferage.

SHUT DOWN

A command in Window 95 onwards to shut the computer so that the files from main memory are moved to their respective places on secondary storage and computer is ready for being switched off.

SHUT-OUT

As lock-out.

SIBILANT SOUND

A hissing speech sound. The sibilants in English are S,Z,SH,ZH and CH.

SICK PAY

Pay given to workers who are off work for reasons of illness or injury. As well as statuary provisions there are many occupational schemes and these are sometimes regarded as a fringe benefit of a job.

SICKNESS BENEFIT

Payment made to an individual to provide income to compensate for loss of earnings during absence during absence from work as a result of illness.

SIGHT APPROACH

The method of teaching children to read by recognising word wholes by sight, as contrasted to the phonetic method by which words are analysed into sound parts.

SIGHT WORD

A word that is memorised as a whole.

SIGNAL

Is a message that has been transmitted from one person to another.

SIGNATURE

(*i*) The formalised construction of a company's name as it appears on the stationery, advertisements, and other printed materials, often used interchangeably with logo type.

(*ii*) A printed sheet containing 4,8,12,16 or 32 pages, folded into a single unit, forming a part of a book or pamphlet.

SIGNATURE MACHINES

These machines are used for imprinting signatures on cheques and circulars or notices sent repeatedly and in large numbers.

SIGNATURE SLOGAN

Use of a slogan as a pay-offline at the end of an advertisement.

SILICON

Another semi-conductor element which is widely used in the manufacturing of electronic devices. It is retrieved from beach sands and occasionally from river gravels.

SILICOSIS

Progressive and potentially lethal disease of lungs resulting from breathing in silica in coal mining; quarrying, pottery, iron and still, refractory products and other industries.

SIMM

Acronym for *Single-In Line Memory Module,* These are the RAM chips which can be directly plugged into the motherboard without the requirement of an additional circuit board.

SIMPLE CONTRACT

A contract not continued in a deed.

SIMPLE RANDOM SAMPLE

A probability sample selected in such a way that all members of the sampled population had and equal chance of being selected.

SIMPLICITY OF USAGE

Ease of operation; a product benefit that offsets the complexity of the product itself.

SIMULATED TRAINING

Training in especially created conditions simulating real working conditions and giving opportunity for formal instruction.

SIMULATION

(*i*) A quantitative planning technique that uses mathematical models to imitate reality.

(*ii*) Use of a computer to simulate a process. If the mathematical model is correctly developed, changes in the values assigned to variables in the model may show exactly what will happen when changes are made in the variables of the process.

SINECURE

A job or office without regular duties but with regular pay.

SINGLE TAX

A tax which is the source of all revenue of the government of a country.

SINGLE-LIFE PENSION

Pension scheme providing for an employėe by his employer.

SINGLE-LINE STORE

A type of retail sales establishment that carrier a wide variety of one line of merchandise. The goods handled are related items.

SINGLE-PRODUCT STRATEGY

The product line strategy that involved offering one product item or one product version with very few options.

SINGLE-SOURCING

Purchasing a product on a regular basis from a single vendor.

SINGLE-USE PLANS

(*i*) Plans aimed at achieving a specific goal that, once reached, will most likely not recur in the future.

(*ii*) Are plans that are used only once — or, at most, several times — because they focus on unique or rare situations within the organisation.

SINISTRAL

Left handed and left-eyed.

SINKING FUND

Money or other assets put aside for a special purpose, such as to pay off bonds as they come due or to replace worn-out or outdated machinery or buildings.

SIPP

Acronym for *Single In-Line Pin Profile.* It is a RAM chip which has its electrical connections on one side only.

SITE SELECTION

Involves determining where a plant facility should be located. It may use a weighting process to compare site differences.

SITUATIONAL APPROACH TO LEADERSHIP

Is a relatively modem view of leadership that suggests that successful leadership requires a unique combination of leaders, followers, and leadership situations.

SITUATIONAL ATTRIBUTIONS

Attributions that emphasise the environment's effect on behaviour.

SITUATIONAL LEADERSHIP THEORY

A contingency theory (developed by *Paul Hearsey* and *Ken Blanchard*) based on the premise that leaders need to alter their behaviours depending on one major situational factor — the readiness of followers.

SITUATIONAL THEORIES

Theories of leadership that take into consideration important situational factors.

SITUATIONAL THEORIES OF LEADERSHIP

An approach to leadership that advocates that leaders understand their own behaviour, the behaviour of their subordinates, and the situation before utilising a particular leadership style. This approach requires the leader to have diagnostic skills in human behaviour.

SKILL

A learned response, often as the result of specific training which afford someone the ability to perform a particular task and achieve a particular goal.

SKILL TESTING

Testing for level of attainment in a particular skill, either to assess training required or to assess level attained after training.

SKILL VARIETY

A core job characteristic involving the extent to which the job entails number of activities that require different skills.

SKILL-BASED PAY

(*i*) A compensation system in which employees' rates of pay are based on the number of predetermined skills that the employees have mastered.

(*ii*) Wages paid at a rate calculated and based on the skills employees possess and display in performing their jobs.

SKILLED LABOUR

Work that requires considerable skill relatively long training and usually also considerable judgment on the worker's part. Also, workers engaged in such jobs.

SKILLS INVENTORY

(*i*) A data bank (usually computerised) containing basic information about each employee that can be used to assess the likely availability of individuals for meeting current and future human resource needs.

(*ii*) Summary of the skills possessed by employees of an organisation.

SKIMMING

A pricing strategy where an organisation sells at a high price initially to maximise short-term profit margins.

SKIMMING PRICE

A relatively high price, often charged at the beginning of

a product's life. The price is systematically lowered as time goes by.

SLACK

Latitude about when various activities on the noncritical paths in a PERT network can be started without endangering the completion date of the entire project.

SLACK RESOURCES

A means of facilitating horizontal coordination that involves a cushion of resources that aids adaptation to internal and external pressures, as well as initiation of changes.

SLICE-OF-LIFE FORMAT

An advertising format that dramatises a "typical" setting wherein people use the product.

SLIP EDITION

Localised edition to give newspaper special reader interest, as occurs at holiday times when slip editions are prepared for different resorts.

SLOGAN

Catchwords phrase or sentence associated with a product or company, encapsulating a particularly pertinent selling point in a succinct and sometimes entertaining fashion.

SLOWDOWN

A deliberate slowing of the normal work space in order to reduce output and force an employer to give in to some particular demand.

SMALL BUSINESS

A private venture that is limited in its number of employees or sales volume.

SMALL CLAIMS COURT

A special Court which handles small cases involving a legislatively amount of money.

SMART MONEY

Damages awarded as a punishment in addition to the actual damages sustained.

SMOOTHING

A method of adapting to environmental fluctuations that involves taking actions aimed at reducing the impact of fluctuations, given the market.

SMUGGLING

The practice of secretly importing goods, either to avoid paying customs duties or to obtain goods that may not legally be imported, such as narcotics.

SOCIAL/PSYCHOLOGICAL NEEDS

Needs stemming from people's interaction with the social environment.

SOCIAL ACCOUNTING

A particular concern with the social aspects of a cost benefit analysis.

SOCIAL ADAPTABILITY

The ability to live in a society, to have acceptable interpersonal relationships, and to conduct transactions within the restrictions and demands of society.

SOCIAL AUDIT

(*i*) A means for reviewing whether an organisation is accomplishing its mission in society; an investigation of the firm's place in the macromarketing environment.

(*ii*) A systematic study and evaluation of the social, rather than the economic, performance of an organisation.

SOCIAL CLASS

A group of people with similar levels of prestige, power, and wealth who also share a set of related beliefs, attitudes, and values in their thinking and behaviour.

SOCIAL CONTRACT THEORY OF BUSINESS

Melvin Anshen of Columbia University looks at this theory as an expression of an implicit movement of change the unwritten social contract that existed for almost over 200 years between private enterprise and the modern society.

SOCIAL CONTROL

The control that a group or culture or society exerts upon the individuals who comprise it. This control stems from the process of socialisation and is established as conformity pressures towards social norms.

SOCIAL DISTANCE

The degree of social intimacy someone will accept in relation to other individuals or groups.

SOCIAL ETHIC

Term used by *William H. Whyte. Jr.,* in "The Organisation Man" to mean the concept that man is primarily a group member and should subordinate his individuality to the group mores. Used in contradistinction to *Weber's* Protestant ethnic, which emphasises individualism.

SOCIAL FACILITATION

The stimulating effect on someone behaviour of other people, even the mere presence of other people. The *hawthome effect* is an example of social facilitation.

SOCIAL FORECASTING

The process of identifying social trends, evaluating the organisational importance of those trends, and integrating these assessments into the organisation's forecasting program.

SOCIAL INSTITUTION

A stable cluster of values, norms, roles, and other means that have developed overtime to fulfil a central purpose of a society.

SOCIAL INSURANCE

A mechanism for pooling risks by transferring them to an organisation (usually governmental) that is required by law to provide identity (cash) or service benefits to or on behalf of covered persons for certain losses.

SOCIAL LEARNING

The extension of Skinner's work initiated by noted psychologist

Albert Bandura. Bandura views behaviour as a function of a continuous interaction between cognitive (person), behavioural and environmental determinants. Contrary to Skinner, Bandura believes that cognitive functioning must not be ignored in explaining and modifying behaviour.

SOCIAL LEARNING THEORY

A theory of motivation having aspects of both cognitive and reinforcement theories which argues that learning occurs through the continuous reciprocal interaction of our behaviours, various personal factors, and environmental forces.

SOCIAL LOAFING

The tendency of individuals to expend less effort then working in groups than when working alone.

SOCIAL MARKETING

Activities aims at enhancing the acceptability of social causes, ideas, or desirable behaviours; sometimes used to refer to not-for-profit marketing.

SOCIAL NEEDS

Are maslow's third set of human needs-reflecting the human desire to belong, including longings for friendship, companionship, and love.

SOCIAL NORM

Behaviour that is expected of all the members of a society. The norm of social behaviour is therefore one way of defining social normality.

SOCIAL OBLIGATION APPROACH

Is an approach to meeting social obligations that considers business to have primarily economic purposes and confines social responsibility activity largely to conformance to existing legislation.

SOCIAL OVERHEADS

Municipal services, such as water supplies and public transportation.

SOCIAL PRODUCT

The total of all commodities produced and marketed in a community within an economic period.

SOCIAL RESPONSIBILITIES, MANAGEMENT

Management's responsibilities to those other than the owners, *e.g.,* to employees, the local community, or even the national or international economy.

SOCIAL RESPONSIBILITY

The ethical consequences of a person's or an organisation's acts and they might affect the interests of others.

SOCIAL RESPONSIBILITY APPROACH

Is an approach to meeting social obligations that considers business, as having both societal and economic goals.

SOCIAL RESPONSIBILITY OF BUSINESS

Awareness and acceptance throughout the free enterprise world, that companies, as well as public corporations, have irresponsibilities toward parties other than their owners. They owe a duty not merely to shareholders or to the state in case of public corporations — but to their employees, customers, suppliers and the community at large.

SOCIAL RESPONSIBILITY, SENSE OF

A management must have a keen sense of social justice. It must be fully appreciative of the rights and interest of men and women of work. It must have philosophy of social injustice based on this fundamental concept that industry is a partnership between men, money and management and whose objective is to earn profits through service.

SOCIAL RESPONSIVENESS

Is the degree of effectiveness and efficiency an organisation displays in pursuing its social responsibilities.

SOCIAL RESPONSIVENESS APPROACH

Is an approach to meeting social obligations that considers business to have societal and economic goals as well as the obligation to anticipate potential social problems and to work actively toward preventing them from occurring.

SOCIAL SCANNING

The general surveillance of various elements in the task environment to detect evidence of impending changes that will affect the organisation s social responsibilities.

SOCIAL SECURITY

By social security we mean the security as provided by the society to its members, against all contingencies or risks to which the members are exposed. An individual member cannot afford to meet the risks and contingencies by his meagre income and it is the duty of the state to promote social security and promote general well-being of people. Social security is a comprehensive term. It includes all the schemes of social insurance, social assistance, and commercial insurance. These insurance schemes protect individuals from falling prey to unforeseen contingencies and risks.

SOCIAL SUPPORT

The comfort, assistance, or information that an individual receives through formal or informal contacts with individuals or groups.

SOCIAL VALUES

(i) Are the relative degrees of worth society places on the manner in which it exists and functions.

(ii) In practice a manager often finds himself working with several means and chains. He is trying to choose a course of action that will contribute to several objectives and there will be mean end chain for each. Stable employment growth, short-term profit, low risk control are examples of internal objectives.

SOCIALISATION

Refers to the processes by which members learn the cultural values, norms, beliefs, and required behaviour that permit them to be effective contributors to the organisation.

SOCIALISATION PROCESS

(*i*) The process by which a society transmits its values, norms, and roles to its members.

(*ii*) The activities by which an individual comes to appreciate the values, abilities, expected behaviours, and social knowledge that are essential for assuming an organisational role and for participating as an organisation member.

SOCIALISM

An economic system characterised by state ownership of the means of production and distribution.

SOCIALIST ECONOMY

An economy in which the means of production are owned by the state and economic activity is co-ordinated by plan.

SOCIETAL MARKETING CONCEPT

Organisational philosophy that stresses the need for marketers to consider the collective needs of society as well as individual consumer's desires and organisational profits.

SOCIETY AND MANAGEMENT

No modem management can function for long in isolation and in disregard to the society in which it exists. Management holds itself accountable for the quality of life of the society. It has an obligation to be a real part of the society, not merely in its industrial life but in the other spheres of it also. Management must develop a deeper commitment to, involvement in, and engagement in the attack on pressing social problems beyond its normal economic activities.

SOCIO-CULTURAL ELEMENT

The element of the mega-environment that includes the attitudes, values, norms, beliefs, behaviours, and associated demographic trends that are characteristic of a given geographic area.

SOCIO-ECONOMIC GROUPS CLASSIFICATION

A grouping of the population according to the occupation of the head of the household: A, B, Cl, C2, D, E.

SOCIOGRAM

Is a sociometric diagram that summarises the personal feelings of organisation members about the people in the organisation with whom they would like to spend free time.

SOCIO-GROUP

Those who are associated for work, interest or pay.

SOCIOLOGY

The science that studies cultures, social institutions, groups and social interactions.

SOCIOMETRY

Is an analytical tool that can be used to determine what informal groups exist in an organisation and who the members of those groups are.

SOCIO-TECHNICAL INTERVENTIONS

In change efforts, an attempt to integrate social organisation and technological requirements. Many of these efforts can be seen in modern manufacturing. As industry after industry must adapt to innovative manufacturing methods that require different relationships among individuals performing these methods.

SOCIO-TECHNICAL SYSTEM

A system combining social and technical factor that underlie the interaction of people and machines in an organisation. It emerged from the approach to management of the Tavistock Institute of Human Relations in London, led by *Eric Trist* The objective of this approach was to jointly optimise tasks performance and job satisfaction.

SOFT AND HARD CRITERIA

Two types of criteria and used to measure the improvements: (1) Soft, and (2) Hard. Soft criteria includes leadership style, enthusiasm of manager, employee satisfaction, harmonious relationships and term spirit. To measure soft criteria a observations, personal interviews and prepared formats are used. The latter are printed forms which when filled out supply data to reveal the characteristics of the organisation.

SOFT CURRENCY

A currency which is not considered to be totally stable, perhaps reflecting a company's political position.

SOFTWARE

(*i*) Generally, media used to support instrumentation or hardware, such as the programmes, procedures, operating systems, programming languages, translators, and manuals used with a computer; and films *i.e.*, audio-tapes, training manuals, video-tapes, filmstrips and slides used in a training department.

(*ii*) The set of programs, documents, procedures, and routines associated with the operation of a computer system that makes the hardware capable of its various activities.

SOFTWARE APPLICATION

A general name given to any program.

SOFTWARE PACKAGE

Software programs supplied by the developers as their proprietary product.

SOLDIERING

A work practice whereby workers deliberately work at less than full capacity, the resolution of which led *Taylor* to develop his scientific management approach.

SOLE PROPRIETORSHIP

Single ownership or operation, such as in a solo professional practice. The primary advantage of sole proprietorship is simplicity in opening a business and in policy development, financial accounting, establishing personnel requirements for it, as well as the self-determination this permits. The disadvantages include sole legal and financial responsibility for the business, limited professional consultation resources, and limited opportunities for leisure time and professional development.

SOLE TRADER

One-man trading concern, representing the simplest and earliest form of business organisation.

SOLID-STATE

The technology concerned with solid materials that can change or mould the character of an electrical value without the use of moving parts or straight magnetic principles. Solid-state parts, *e.g.*, transistors produce effects through phenomena taking place within or at the junction of solid material.

SOLVENCY

Solvency means the capacity or ability of the business to meet its short-term and long-term obligations. The capacity to pay off the current debts of the company is represented by the liquidity ratio. The long-term solvency ratios enable shareholders, debenture-holders and other long-term creditors like financial institutions to analyse the capital structure of the company. They indicate the pattern of financing, whether long-term requirements have been met out of long-term funds or not.

SOMATIC

Having to do with the body. The "opposite" of psychogenetic.

SORTING FUNCTION

An activity performed by marketing intermediaries, in which accumulated products are classified as to grade and size, then grouped accordingly.

SOUL POSITION

The placing of an advertisement in the news or editorial section of a publication — away from other advertisements.

SOURCE

Flow of information from one point to another. The point from which the information is transmitted is source. In a file copy/achieve process, the source is the file which is to be copied or achieved.

SOURCE CODE

A program in its original form written in some high level language before it is compiled, assembled or interpreted.

SOURCE FILE

A program written in a high-level language that has been generated as an object file either by a translator or compiler.

SOURCE/ENCODER

Is the person in the interpersonal communication situation who originates and encodes information to be shared with another person or persons.

SOURCES OF FINANCIAL INFORMATION

Sources which provide information about economic, commercial and industrial matters, such as dailies, journals and periodicals which supply financial information, investors' guides, investors, encyclopaedias, directories, year books, etc.

SPACE

Term used to describe pages available for advertising purposes in a publication; constitutes the product available for sale after text matter has been accommodated.

SPAN OF ATTENTION

Number of letters, parts of words, or words that can be identified at one fixation.

SPAN OF CONTROL

The number of subordinates reporting to a specific superior. The span is a factor that affects the shape and height of an organisational structure.

SPAN OF MANAGEMENT

(*i*) A means of vertical co-ordination involving the number of subordinates who report directly to a specific manager; also called *Span of Control*

(*ii*) Is the number of individuals a manager supervises.

(*iii*) Synonym for *Span of Control*

SPAN OF SUPERVISION

It is a step in supervision which is designed to determine the number of subordinates who should report directly to each executive. Narrower the span, taller would be the structure with several levels of management.

SPEAKING VOCABULARY

Words that are used and understood in conversation.

SPECIAL INTEREST REPRESENTATION

Concern with social matters had led some business organisations to accept the idea of special interest representation on the board of directors representation of consumer of geographic regions, and, in case of the multinational companies of nationalities. Positive psychological values can be visualised in this structure.

SPECIAL POSITION

Insertion of an advertisement in what is regarded as a distinctive position in a publication.

SPECIAL TYPE OF PRODUCT

A consumer product that is not frequently bought, is likely to be expensive, and for which great care in purchase is likely.

SPECIALISATION

Part of the division of labour in which a given task is broken down as far as possible into subtasks, each of which then becomes the responsibility of a specialist worker. Specialisation is therefore an important basis for mass production.

SPECIALISATION OF LABOUR

The division of tasks into their component operations so that each worker becomes a specialist in one operation.

SPECIALISED STAFF

In contrast to personal staff the specialised staff advises and serves all line and other staff departments in a functional capacity. For instance the staff finance department reporting to the chief executive is available not only to advice and serve him but also to serve other departments that need help in financial matters. The specialised staff thus becomes a reservoir of special knowledge, skills and experience which the entire organisation can use.

SPECIALIST

An individual who is an expert in one particular field of study or in the use of certain ability or skill, or even in the performance of a particular task.

SPECIALIST WHOLESALER

Full-service merchant wholesaler that sells a very narrow selection of products.

SPECIALITY ADVERTISING

Advertising using advertising specialities.

SPECIALITY GOOD

Consumer goods for which customers are prepared or make an effort to acquire.

SPECIALITY SHOP

A retail establishment selling mainly or exclusively specially goods; usually offering a large and diverse selection of a very narrow range of goods.

SPECIALITY STORE

A retail institution that sells a limited line of products.

SPECIFIC UNEMPLOYMENT

Unemployment in particular industries.

SPECIFICATION

In marketing, this relates to the specified characteristics and performance required of a product, expressed in quantitative as well as qualitative terms.

SPEECH PROCESSING

The capacity of a computer to recognise and react to the spoken word.

SPEED OF COMPREHENSION

The speed at which one can read and still understand the import of text.

SPELL-CHECK

A feature of most of the wordprocessing software systems

which when activated automatically checks the spelling of each and every word in document from the dictionary attached to it. If any error is found it gives the suggestions also. Some word processors allow to create own dictionary as not all the words are present in the general dictionary.

SPIN-OFF

A method by which a company may divest itself of one of its divisions. An entirely new corporation is formed and the stock distributed to the shareholders of the first company.

SPLIT SHIFT

In shift work practice this term refers to a shift which has been divided into two more periods of times and/or groups of workers.

SPLIT-FUNCTION DEPARTMENT

In the split-function department, labour and personnel activities are completely separated. Executives heading labour relations activities and those Incharge of personnel administration report separately to a top line executive or to different line executives.

SPOKESPERSON

A person who, representing the advertiser, directly addresses the audience and urges them to buy the advertiser's product.

SPONSOR

A middle manager who recognises the organisational significance of an idea, helps obtain the necessary funding for development of the innovation, and facilitates its actual implementation.

SPONSORSHIP

An element usually considered part of the promotional mix where money is linked to an event or a participant in an event.

SPONTANEOUS RECOVERY

Reappearance of a conditioned response which had been extinguished, after a short rest period.

SPOOLING

An acronym for *Simultaneous Peripheral Operation On Line.* This is storing the input data from low-speed devices temporarily on high-speeds secondary storage units, which can be quickly accessed by the CPU.

SPOT ANNOUNCEMENT

A short, attention-getting, public service announcement broadcast on radio or television. Spot announcements are designed to stimulate a specific action, such as a donation, a call to volunteer one's assistance, and so forth.

SPOT PRICE

The price of goods or services as quoted for immediate delivery and payment.

SPREADSHEET

A technique, that originated in accounting, for displaying items in a wide series of columns (*i.e.,* on a spreadsheet of paper) so that calculation could be made by row or column as well as by items. The term has now largely been taken over by the computer world to refer to software packages that produce spread-sheets for visual display units from which rapid electronic calculations can be made.

SSAD

Structured System Analysis and Design.

STABILISED BOND

A bond that has its principal or interest adjusted to reflect changes in inflation or deflation as indicated by an index.

STABILITY

Is a strategy adopted by management to maintain or slightly improve the amount of business a strategic business unit is generating.

STABILITY STRATEGY

A grand strategy that involves maintaining the *status quo* or growing in a methodical, but slow, manner.

STAFF

A relationship which involves one position or element of the organisation providing advice and service to another position or element. "Staff" elements of the organisation have a predominantly advisory and service role.

STAFF APPRAISAL

The assessment of how well a member of staff is doing. It is usual to include a performance appraisal interview as part of this process.

STAFF AUTHORITY

Consists of the right to advise or assist those who possess line authority.

STAFF INSPECTION

A job analysis of all staff positions in an organisation as the first step in a process of rationalisation.

STAFF MANAGEMENT

The management of staff in an organisation; Managers who have a specialist service or advisory support function and are not in the chain of command of the organisation's hierarchy.

STAFF POSITION

A position whose primary purpose is providing specialised expertise and assistance to line positions.

STAFF SPECIALIST

Member of an organisation who provides specialised services or advice to line managers in the organisation.

STAFF VERSUS FACTORY STRIFE

When foremen try to diminish pressure by blaming the budget people, production control people and salesmen for their problems, staff and factory come into strife.

STAFF WORK, COMPLETED

Staff work whose end-product is a single recommendation which a line executive may either approve or disapprove without further investigation.

STAFF, GENERAL

Staff members who assist an executive with responsibilities he cannot delegate.

STAFF, PERSONAL

An *aide-de-camp* or private secretary who helps the manager by making his corporate life easier and more convenient.

STAFF, PERSONNEL

Positions or organisational elements created for the purpose of providing advice and service in one functional area, such as finance or personnel, to all appropriate management positions.

STAFF, SPECIALISED

Executives (and their subordinates) who handle specialised functions that contribute indirectly to the attainment of organisation goals. Also those who provide advice on and develop techniques for use in these specialised areas. In other words, we can say that staff specialised is such type of positions or organisational elements created for the purpose of providing advice and service in one functional area, such as finance or personnel, to all appropriate management positions.

STAFFING

(*i*) Selecting and hiring managers and employees.

(*ii*) The set of activities aimed at attracting and selecting individuals for positions in a way that will facilitate the achievement of organisational goals.

STAKEHOLDERS

Are all individuals and groups that are directly or indirectly affected by an organisation's decisions.

STAMP-DUTY

A Duty which must be paid for some documents (*e.g.*, title deeds to property) to record a transaction formally, with an official stamp.

STAMPING OR FRANKING MACHINES

Stamping or Franking machines are used in large offices for affixing postage stamps on envelopes. In large offices, where thousands of outgoing envelopes have to be stamped each day, these machines are very useful. They not only simplify postage accounting and save time, but also eliminate the possibility of errors in stamping or wastage and the misuse of stamps.

STANDARD

Is the level of activity established to serve as a model for evaluating organisational performance

STANDARD COST CENTRE

A responsibility centre whose budgetary performance depends on achieving its goals by operating within standard cost constraints.

STANDARD INDUSTRIAL CLASSIFICATION (SIC) SYSTEM

A numerical coding system developed by the U.S. Government and widely employed by organisational marketers to classify organisations in terms of the economical activities in which they are engaged.

STANDARD LABOUR RATE

An employee's base pay, plus any incentives and premiums in money, estimated to be attainable under efficient working conditions.

STANDARD LABOUR TIME

The time, in terms of man-hours of a specified quality, estimated to be required to produce a specific quantity of goods or services.

STANDARD OF LIVING THEORY

A wage theory which holds that employees should be paid more than a subsistence wage.

STANDARD-HOUR PAYMENT SYSTEM

Synonym for *Standard-Time Payment System.*

STANDARDISATION HOUR

Using one type of component, material, or machine for as many purposes as possible.

STANDARDISED POSSESSING TEST

A scientifically constructed measure both reliability and validity.

STANDING COMMITTEE

A permanent task group charged with handling recurring matters in a narrowly defined subject area over an indefinite, but generally lengthy, period of time.

STANDING ORDER

A continuing work order that directs the production of an item to meet specified sales objectives.

STANDING PLANS

Are plans that are used over and over because they focus on organisational situations that occur repeatedly.

STANDING PLANS

Plans that provide ongoing guidance for performing recurring activities.

START-UP

A new firm or venture started from scratch by an entrepreneur.

STATE LIST

List of subjects under the jurisdiction of the state governments as provided in the *Seventh Schedule of the Constitution of India,* which defines the powers of the Union and State Governments.

STATE TRADING

A system of conducting all or some international trade through a government agency.

STATEMENTS (OF ACCOUNT)

Documents sent to customers, listing all items of account outstanding. They are often treated as the official request for payment.

STATIC MARKET

Market which has a pattern over time substantially free from fluctuations, particularly of volume.

STATISTICAL PROCESS CONTROL

A statistical technique employed in quality control that uses periodic random samples taken during actual production to determine whether acceptable quality levels are being met or production should be stopped for remedial action.

STATISTICAL QUALITY CONTROL

Is the process used to determine how many products should be inspected to calculate a probability that the total number of products will meet organisational quality standards.

STATUS

In an organisational setting, status relates to positions in the formal or informal structure. Status is designated in the formal organisation; in informal groups, it is determined by the group.

STATUS AGREEMENT

Collective agreement granting staff to manual workers.

STATUS CONSENSUS

The agreement of group members about the relative status of members of the group.

STATUS GROUP

People who share common life-style, or common social, cultural, occupational or professional interest.

STATUTORY AUDIT

Audit of any business enterprise according to the statutory provisions of the law.

STEM

A word from which words have been developed by the addition of prefixes, suffixes, and inflectional endings.

STEREOTYPE

(*i*) A set of beliefs that one has about a group for other individuals.

(*ii*) Is a fixed, distorted generalisation about members of a group.

(*iii*) Is a positive or negative assessment of members of a group or their perceived attributes.

STEREOTYPING

The tendency to attribute characteristics to an individual on the basis of an assessment of the group to which the individual belongs.

STICKER

An individual who is content to remain in his current position rather than seek promotion.

STILL-LIFE ADVERTISEMENT

An advertisement that makes the product or package its focal point, emphasising a visually attractive presentation and the product's brand name.

STIMULUS

Some aspect of the environment that triggers a behavioural response.

STIMULUS FACTOR

A characteristic of a stimulus — for example, the size, colours, or novelty of a print advertisement — that affects perception.

STOCK

The shares owned by stockholders in a corporation. The capital stock of a company or corporation is divided into various classes or types of shares.

STOCK ACCOUNT

An account of stock in trade.

STOCK OPTIONS

Options granted to executives to purchase stock in the future at a given price approximating the current market price, regardless of its price at the time of purchase (Sometimes granted to employees as well).

STOCK TURNOVER RATIO

The number of times inventory, or stock, is turned over, or sold, over a specified period: Net sales/Average Inventory or Cost of Goods Sold/ Average Inventory. Also called *Inventory Turnover Ratio.* Turnover measures the speed with which inventory measures the speed with which inventory is sold.

STOCK, COMMON

Shares in ownership on which the return depends on what the company makes. That return may be nothing or it may be very high.

STOCK, PREFERRED

Shares in ownership on which dividends are fixed in advance. Preferred stock dividends must be paid in full before common stockholders receive anything.

STOCK-EXCHANGE

A nationally recognised, formally organised place of dealing in securities. Because of the importance of sales in securities, transactions may only take place between authorised people (jobbers and stockbrokers) acting on behalf of others. This business is restricted to stock exchanges, stock markets, which exist in major cities throughout the world. Membership of exchange is carefully controlled.

STOCKHOLDER

(1) An individual who owns Stock issued by a company. (2) A company which holds stocks of goods or materials to sell for use by other companies.

STOCKHOLDERS, INSTITUTIONAL

Insurance companies, pension funds, and similar institutions which hold company stock.

STOCKOUT COST

An inventory cost that involves the economic consequences of running out of stock (such as loss of customer goodwill and possibly sales).

STOP BIT

A bit which follows every word of data in serial communication system. They place the communications line in a marketing stage.

STORAGE

The holding and housing of goods in inventory for a certain period of time.

STORAGE FUNCTION

Is computer activities involved with retaining the material entered into the computer during the performance of the input function.

STORE IMAGE

Everything consumers see and feel about a store. Store image is affected by such things as personnel, merchandise, external and internal appearance, process, and services.

STORING

The keeping of goods or products over a period time, usually in a warehouse, a cold storage, plant or other special facility, depending upon the nature of the product.

STORMING

(*i*) A stage of group development in which group members frequently experience conflict with one another as they locate and attempt to resolve differences of opinion regarding key issues.

(*ii*) The second stage of the team development process, is characterised by conflict and disagreement as team members try to clarify their individual roles and challenge the way the team functions.

STORY

A narrative based on true events, which sometimes may be embellished to highlight the intended value.

STORYLINE FORMAT

An advertisement that gives a history or tells a story about the product.

STRAIGHT COMMISSION

Compensation based strictly on sales performance.

STRAIGHT LEASE

A lease for a fixed, agreed-upon price for a specific period, with regular payments of equal amounts. Also known as *Flat Lease.*

STRAIGHT REBUY

A type of organisational buying characterised by automatic and regular purchase of familiar products form regular suppliers.

STRAIGHT SALARY

Compensation at a regular rate, not immediately ties to sales performance.

STRATEGIC (BUSINESS) ALLIANCE

An informal partnership between a marketer and organisational buyer; all commitment between a wholesaler and a customer to establish a long-term relationship.

STRATEGIC BUSINESS UNIT (SBU)

(i) A distinct business, with its own set of competitors, that can be managed relatively independently of other businesses within the organisation.

(*ii*) A distinct unit, such as a company, division, department, or product line, of the overall parent organisation with a specific marketing focus and a manager who has the authority and responsibility for managing all unit functions.

(*iii*) Is a business portfolio analysis, a significant organisational segment that is analysed to develop organisational strategy aimed at generating future business or revenue. SBUs vary in form, but all are a single business (or collection of businesses), have their own competitors and a manager accountable for operations, and can be independently planned for.

STRATEGIC CONTROL

(*i*) A control type concerning mainly top managers that involves monitoring critical environmental factors that could affect the viability of strategic plans, assessing the effects of organisational strategic actions, and ensuring that strategic plans are implemented as intended.

(*ii*) The last step of the strategy management process, consists of monitoring and evaluating the strategy management process as a whole to ensure that it is operating properly.

STRATEGIC CONTROL POINTS

Performance areas chosen for control because they are particularly important in meeting organisational goals.

STRATEGIC CORPORATE GOALS

Broad or organisational goals related to the long-term future. The organisation's primary strategic corporate goal is identified in its organisational mission statement. Which explains why the organisation exists and what it hopes to accomplish.

STRATEGIC GAP

The difference between where the organisation wants to be and where it is.

STRATEGIC GOALS

Broadly defined targets or future end results set by top management.

STRATEGIC MANAGEMENT

A process through which managers formulate and implement strategies geared toward optimising strategic goal achievement, given available environmental and internal conditions.

STRATEGIC MARKETING PROCESS

The entire sequence of managerial and operational activities required to create and sustain effective and efficient marketing strategies.

STRATEGIC PLANNING

Is a long-range planning that focuses on the organisation as a whole.

STRATEGIC PLANS

Detailed action steps mapped out to reach strategic goals. Such plans are developed by top management in consultation with the board of directors and middle management.

STRATEGIC WINDOW OF OPPORTUNITY

A limited time during which an organisation's capabilities, resources, or competitive position provide it with certain advantages over the competition.

STRATEGIES

Large-scale action plans for interacting with the environment in order to achieve long-term goals.

STRATEGIES CONTINGENCY

An event or activity that is extremely important for accomplishing organisational goals. Among the strategic contingencies of subunits are the ability to cope with uncertainty, centrality, and substitutability.

STRATEGY

(*i*) An overall, long-term direction or approach which a company aims to follow, derived from the Greek word meaning to lead an army.

(*ii*) Is a broad and general plan developed to reach long-term organisational objectives; it is the end result of strategic planning.

STRATEGY FORMULATION

(i) Is the process of determining appropriate courses of action for achieving organisational objectives and thereby accomplishing organisational purpose. Strategy development tools include critical question analysis, *SWOT Analysis*, business portfolio analysis, and *Porter's Model* for Industry Analysis.

(*ii*) The part of the strategic management process that involves identifying the mission and strategic goals, conducting competitive analysis, and developing specific strategies.

STRATEGY IMPLEMENTATION

(*i*) The fourth step of the strategy management process, is putting formulated strategy into action.

(*ii*) The part of the strategic management process that focuses on carrying out strategic plans and maintaining control over how those plans are carried out.

STRATEGY MANAGEMENT

Is the process of ensuring that an organisation possesses and benefits from the use of an appropriate organisational strategy.

STRATIFIED SAMPLE

A probability sample resulting from a process by which the population is divided into subgroups based on characteristics of interest and then a simple random sample is taken from each subgroup.

STRESS

(*i*) An adaptive response, mediated by individual differences and/or psychological processes, resulting from any environmental action, situation, or event that places excessive psychological and/or physical demands on a person, (ii) Is the bodily strain that an individual experiences as a result of coping with some environmental factor.

STRESSOR

(*i*) An external event or situation that is potentially harmful to a person.

(*ii*) Is an environmental demand that causes people to feel stress.

STRICTNESS OR LENIENCY RATER ERRORS

Rater errors that occur when a harsh rater gives ratings that are lower than the average ratings usually given or a lenient rather gives ratings higher than the average ratings usually given.

STRIKE

In the words of *Patterson,* "Industrial strikes constitute militant and organised protests against existing industrial conditions. They are symptoms of industrial unrest in the same way that boils are a symptom of a disordered body" Strike as under: "Strike means a cessation of work by a body of persons employed in any industry acting in combination, or a concerned refusal under a common understanding of any number of persons who are or have been so employed to continue to work or to accept employment."

STRIKE PAY

Or *dispute benefit;* Paid by a trade union to its members to compensate for loss of income during a strike or other industrial action.

STRIKER

Person participating in a strike.

STRUCTURAL CHANGE

Is a type of organisational change that emphasises modifying an existing organisational structure.

STRUCTURAL FACTORS

Are organisational controls, such as policies and procedures.

STRUCTURAL UNEMPLOYMENT

Unemployment which is accepted by a government as part of the economic balance of the country.

STRUCTURE (IN GROUP CONTEXT)

The standards of conduct that are applied by the group, the communication system, and the reward and sanction mechanisms of the group.

STRUCTURE

Refers to the designated relationships among resources of the management system.

STRUCTURE BEHAVIOUR

Is leadership activity that (1) delineates the relationship between the leader and the leader's followers or (2) establishes well-defined procedures that the followers should adhere to in performing their jobs.

STRUCTURED INTERVIEW

One in which questions are determined in advance and set out in a questionnaire.

STRUCTURED PROGRAMMING

A method of program design, coding and testing designed to produce programs which are correct, well organised, easy to read and maintain. It uses the top down design methodology of programming.

STRUCTURED PROGRAMS

A program which uses modularising techniques so that the code could be managed easily. The whole code is in the form of logical sections.

STRUCTURED QUERY LANGUAGE (SQL)

A query language that is becoming a standard language to be used with relational database management systems.

STYLE

A distinctive execution, construction, or design of a product class.

SUBCULTURE

A group within a dominant culture that is distinct from the culture. A subculture will typically display some values or norms that differ from those of the overall culture.

SUBDIRECTORY

This is the directory which is subsection of another directory. Like WINDOWS is one directory. SYSTEM, CONTROL are the subdirectories.

SUB-EDITOR

Journalist who prepares copy for press, cutting, amending and marking up with typesetting instructions, *i.e.* subbing.

SUBOPTIMISATION

Is a condition wherein organisational sub-objectives are conflicting or not directly aimed at accomplishing the overall organisational objectives.

SUB-ROUTINE

The program module which is executed by either invoking it in the main program or by transferring the control to it unconditionally. Transfer is returned back to the original calling point after execution of sub-routine.

SUBSCRIPT

A numeric value that is used to identify each element of array. The text which is smaller than the routine sentence size and is hanged downwards. For example: *Text Subscript*

SUBSCRIPTION

An agreement to purchase a periodical, a series of theatre or concern tickets, or some other item to be used over a period of time.

SUBSIDIARY

A company controlled wholly or partially by another through ownership of its stock.

SUBSISTENCE

The minimum food, clothing, and shelter a person or family needs for survival.

SUBSTITUTABILITY

Extent to which other subunits can perform the job or task of a subunit.

SUBSTITUTES

Situational factors that make leadership impact not only impossible but also unnecessary.

SUBSTITUTES FOR LEADERSHIP

An approach that attempts to specify some of the main situational factors likely to make leader behaviours unnecessary or to negate their effectiveness.

SUBSTITUTES FOR LEADERSHIP

Task, organisational, and subordinate characteristics that can substitute for leader behaviours. A leader will have little or no effect if certain situations, skills, or tasks exist.

SUBSTITUTION

An attempt to replace one goal with another.

SUBSYSTEM

Is a system created as part of the process of the overall management system. A planning subsystem increases the effectiveness of the overall management system.

SUBTOPIC

A subheading in an outlined exposition.

SUCCESSFUL COMMUNICATION

Refers to an interpersonal communication situation in which the information the source intends to share with the destination and the meaning the destination derives from the transmitted message are the same.

SUFFIX

One or more syllables added at the end of a word to change the meaning.

SUGGESTIVE SELLING

Suggesting to a customer who is making a purchase that an additional item or service be purchased.

SUNK COSTS

Costs that, once incurred, are not recoverable and should not enter into considerations of future courses of action.

SUPER COMPUTER

A large size mainframe computer systems that are the most powerful systems available today. They are designed to handle massive computational problems. For example; *PARAM10000.*

SUPERLEADERSHIP

Is leadership that inspires organisational success by showing followers how to lead themselves.

SUPERMARKET

Any large, departmentalised retail establishment but especially one that primarily sells food items.

SUPERORDINATE GOALS

(*i*) Goals that cannot be achieved without the co-operation of the conflicting groups.

(*ii*) Major common goals that require the support and effort of all parties and on which the manager is sometimes able to refocus individuals or groups in conflict, thus reducing or resolving the conflict.

SUPERVISE

To direct personally; a supervisor exercises leadership by overseeing the activities of others in person. Supervision implies that the people supervised report directly to the person doing the supervision.

SUPERVISION, PLAN OF

The number of people supervised by a manager.

SUPERVISORY TRAINING

Courses and planned experience for supervisors/forcemen.

SUPPLEMENTS AND FEATURES

Special sections or extra pages in newspapers or magazines devised to attract advertisements.

SUPPLIER

(*i*) An organisation that provides raw materials, component parts, equipment, or other resources to a marketing organisation. Also called a *Vendor*.

(*ii*) Are individuals or agencies that provide organisations with the resources they need to produce goods and services.

(*iii*) The element of the task environment that includes those organisations and individuals that supply the resources an organisation needs to conduct its operations.

SUPPLY CURVE

A graphic representation of the relationship between various prices and the amount of product that will be supplied at those process. Also called a *Supply Schedule.*

SUPPLY OF LABOUR

The number of workers or the number of manhours of service or (where payment is made by results) the actual amount of work-performed.

SUPPORTIVE

A leader behaviour identified in path- goal theory that entails showing concern for the status, well-being, and needs of subordinates; doing small things to make the work more pleasant; and being friendly and approachable.

SUPPORTIVE LEADERSHIP

Management emphasis on the building up of good social relations within an organisation, a feature of the human relations school of thought.

SUPPRESSION

(1) Psychological blocking of vision in one eye. (2) Involuntary exclusion of anything from awareness.

SURETY

A guarantee provided by a third party in support of an application for a loan.

SURVEY

A survey usually attempts to measure one or more characteristics in many people, usually at one point in time. Basically, surveys are used to investigate current problems and events.

SUSPENSE ACCOUNT

A special account which is used to hold receipts and payments which are incomplete and required clarification.

SWAP FILE

An area of hear disk that is set aside for exclusive use by Windows in 386 enhanced mode. The information from memory is temporarily transferred to swap file by Windows so that memory is free for other information.

SWAPPING

The process of exchanging the modules of an application program or exchange the values of two variables.

SWEETHEART CONTRACT

A contract placed by a company with a supplier in preference to other potential sources, partly because of their special relationship.

SWOT ANALYSIS

(*i*) A method of analysing an organisation's competitive situation that involves assessing organisational strengths (S) and weaknesses (W), as well as environmental opportunities (O) and threats (T).

(*ii*) Is a strategy development tool that matches internal organisational strengths and weaknesses with external opportunities and threats.

(iii) SWOT is an acronym for *Strengths* and *Weaknesses*, *Opportunities* and *Threats*. The SW refer to internal resources of an organisation; the OT to the macroenvironment.

SYLLABICATION

Division of words into syllables, usually for purposes of pronunciation.

SYLLOGISM

A logical scheme or analysis of a format argument consisting of the major premise, the minor premise, and the conclusion.

SYMBOL

An object, act, event, or a quality that serves as a vehicle for conveying meaning.

SYMBOLIC PROCESSES

Components of social learning theory involving the various ways that we use verbal and imagined symbols to process and store experiences in representational forms that can serve as guides to future behaviour.

SYMPTOM

Is a sign that a problem exists.

SYNDICATED RESEARCH

Research conducted on behalf of more than one organisation. Such as: *Consumer panels*, *Retails audits* and *Omnibus studies*.

SYNDROME

Collection of symptoms which characterise a particular disorder or disease.

SYNERGY

A major characteristic of open systems that is the ability of the whole to equal more that the sum of its parts.

SYNONYM

One or two or more words of the same language having the same or nearly the same essential meaning. For example, *Little, Small*

SYNTAX

Rules of a language for forming the statements and expressions in that language. These are the rules similar to grammar rules in English which must be followed.

SYNTAX DIAGRAM OR FLOWCHART

A flowchart that displays the syntax of statements of a programming language or an application software with the help of pictorial representation.

SYNTAX ERROR

A computer programming error in syntax. This error occurs when a programmer violates the rules of grammar and expression of a computer language.

SYSTEM

(*i*) A set of interrelated parts that operate as a whole in pursuit of common goals.

(*ii*) Is a number of interdependent parts functioning as a whole for some purpose.

SYSTEM ANALYSIS

Analysing in detail the system, its components and requirements. This analysis requires the analysis of the needs of information of an organisation.

SYSTEM APPROACH

An approach of the problem-solving based on the scientific and synergy method which defines the problems and opportunities for a system not for the individual component. Many alternatives for solving the problem are identified and evaluated and best is then selected and implemented.

SYSTEM APPROACH TO MANAGEMENT

Is a management approach based on general system theory — the theory that to understand fully the operation of an entity, the entity must be viewed as a system. This requires understanding the interdependence of its parts.

SYSTEM CONTEXT

Recognising the systems, its subsystems and components in a particular situation.

SYSTEM DESIGN STANDARDS

Standards that are decided to promote the design of common features of system such as design of programming interfaces, user interfaces and telecommunication support.

SYSTEM DEVELOPMENT LIFE CYCLE

The process involved in the development and improvement of an computerised system. This cycle has six main phases. This is the cycle for developing an information system so it is known as information system development also.

SYSTEM DISK

A floppy disk that has systems startup information *i.e.,* boot information system files on it. This diskette can be used to bolt the system.

SYSTEM TERMINATION

A state of computer system when all the processing is stopped.

SYSTEM UTILITY PROGRAMS

A collection or set of programs that assist the system programmer to find the solutions to problem that may arise. These are also used to improve the overall efficiency of operation.

SYSTEMATIC BIAS

A research shortcoming or inaccuracy in the results because of flaws in the design or execution of a research study.

SYSTEMS CONCEPT

The idea that elements maybe strongly interrelated and may interact toward achieving a goal.

SYSTEMS DEVELOPMENT

Conceiving, designing and implementing a system. A series of operations which includes investigation, analysis, design, implementation and maintenance is performed.

SYSTEMS DEVELOPMENT LIFE CYCLE

A series of stages that are used in the development of most medium- and large-size information systems.

SYSTEMS TERMINATION

The state of the system when the complete processing of system is stopped.

SYSTEMS THEORY

(*i*) A view of management based on the notion that organisations can be visualised as systems.

(*ii*) An approach to the analysis of organisational behaviour that emphasises the necessity for maintaining the basic elements of input-output-process and for adapting to the larger environment that sustains the organisation.

T

TA

Transactional Analysis.

TAB

An indent from the left martin of some block of text. Most of the word processors provide the feature to create tabs of user defined steps.

TABLOID

Small page newspaper, opposite to broadsheet and printed lengthwise on the web.

TABULAR STANDARD

A monetary standard in which the standard is not the price of single commodity, but it is based upon the price of a representative list of commodities.

TACHISTOSCOPE

A device used in planning advertising technique such as *Subliminal Advertising*. An image is displayed for a brief controlled time and the viewer's response is used to judge the best exposure to be used in practice.

TACTIC

A method, technique, practice, or approach employed as part of a strategy.

TACTICAL CONTROL

A control type concerning mainly middle managers that focuses on assessing the implementation of tactical plans at department levels, monitoring associated periodic results, and taking corrective action as necessary.

TACTICAL GOALS

Targets or future end results usually set by middle management for specific departments or units.

TACTICAL PLANNING

Is short-range planning that emphasises the current operations of various parts of the organisation.

TACTICAL PLANS

Are used to support implementation of the strategic plans and achievement of tactical goals. Such plans are developed by middle management potentially in consultation with lower management.

TACTICAL PRICING

Short-term variations, usually reductions in price, to stimulate sales.

TACTICS

The specific operational activities undertaken in support of an organisation's strategy.

TACTILE, TACTUAL

Having to do with touch.

TACTUAL IMAGERY

The mental reconstruction of sensory experiences secured by touch.

TAILOR-MADE PANELS

Diary panels set up by market research company (*e.g., Mass Observation*) for individual clients to observe, measure, and check what is happening to clients5 brands.

TAINTED GOODS

Blacked Goods; Products or supplies that have been placed by a trade union.

TAKE-HOME PAY

Amount actually included in the pay check, that is, pay minus deductions for taxes and other purposes, such as contributions to a pension plan.

TAKEOVER

(*i*) A form of acquisition involving the purchase of a controlling share of voting stock in a publicly traded company and thus a potential reason for organisational termination.

(*ii*) The gaining of control by one organisation over another.

TAKEOVER PANEL

A voluntary organisation drawing its members from bodies concerned with investment and finance. The *Takeover Panel Administers* the city code on takeovers and mergers. The panel has no legal powers but transgressors who fail to comply are liable to encounter difficulties with the stock exchange which may suspend a share quotation or refuse listing for new securities.

TALL STRUCTURE

A structure that has many hierarchical levels and narrow spans of control.

TAPE DRIVE

An electro-mechanical device used to read from or write to magnetic tapes.

TAPE LEADER

This is the few meter tape in the beginning of magnetic tapes. These portion of take cannot be used for writing purpose.

TARE

The weight of the packaging, wrapping, containers, or other materials used in shipping goods. Tare weight plus net weight make up gross weight.

TARGET

Quantified aim or result to be achieved or bettered within a stated period of time.

TARGET AUDIENCE

The management of financial matters so as to lower taxes as much as is legally possible.

TARGET MARKET

A specific market segment toward which an organisation aims its marketing plan.

TARGET POPULATION

The population of interest in a marketing research study; the population from which samples are to be drawn.

TARGET RETURN PRICING

Setting prices to yield a particular, target legal of profit for the organisation.

TARIFF

(i) A type of trade barrier in the form of a customs duty, or tax, levied mainly on imports.

(ii) A tax imposed by a government on an imported product. A tariff is often intended to raise the price of imported goods and thereby give a price advantage to domestic goods.

TASK

The instruction or set of instructions give to the computer via some program or software or a batch file.

TASK ENVIRONMENT

The segment of the external environment made up of the specific outside elements with which an organisation interfaces in the course of conducting its business.

TASK FORCE

(*i*) A temporary task group usually formed to make recommendations on a specific issue; also called *An Ad hoc Committee.*

(*ii*) A group of managers and staff specialists, often drawn from a variety or organisational levels and functions, who collectively apply themselves to a particular assignment for the duration. The assignment is typically something both important and not quite routine—major organisational change, moving to a new site, bringing major facilities on stream or a takeover, merger or integration.

TASK GROUP

(i) A formal group that is created for a specific purpose that supplements or replaces work normally done by command groups.

(*ii*) A group of individuals who are working as a unit to complete a project or job task.

(*iii*) Is a formal group of organisation members who interact with one another to accomplish nonroutine organisational tasks. Members of any one task group can and often do come from various levels and segments of an organisation.

TASK IDENTITY

(*i*) The extent to which a task is composed of a single whole and identifiable piece of work.

(*ii*) A core job characteristic involving the degree to which the job allows the completion of a major identifiable piece of work, rather than just a fragment.

TASK LIST

A window that shows all the applications currently loaded in the main memory either running in foreground or background. This task list can be displayed by selecting the option "Switch to" from control menu or by pressing the ALT and TAB keys simultaneously.

TASK SIGNIFICANCE

A core job characteristic involving the extent to which the worker sees the job output as having an important impact on others.

TASK STRUCTURE

A factor in the *Fiedler Contingency Model* that refers to how structured a job is with regard to requirements, problem-solving alternatives, and feedback on how correctly the job has been accomplished.

TAVISTOCK INSTITUTE

The *Tavistock Institute of Human Relations* in North London is a research and consultancy organisation. It is known in particular for the development of socio-technical systems theory and its application to practical problems in industry, especially those resulting from the introduction of technical change.

TAX AUDIT

Scrutiny of books of accounts for purposes of taxation under the Income-tax Act, which stipulates audit of accounts of certain persons carrying on a business or engaged in a profession.

TAX AVOIDANCE

The management of financial matters so as to lower taxes as much as is legally possible.

TAX BASE

The value of assets or monies on which taxes are levied. Some of the more common task bases include, individual income, corporate income, real property (real estate), gifts, estates, and other property.

TAX CREDIT

A direct reduction of tax liability for income tax purposes, authorised by law to serve some broad economic, social, or political objective. Tax credits for plant construction or energy expenditures, or for conservation improvements are examples. Tax credits permit all or some percentage of the cost of such items to be deducted from the amount of tax which would otherwise be paid.

TAX-DEDUCTIBLE

Any business expense that can be deducted from income before the calculation of tax due.

TAX EVASION

The practice of evading or a reducing a the incidence of a tax in violation of the tax law of country.

TAX HAVEN

A country that provides tax advantages for companies incorporated under its laws.

TAX PLANNING

An arrangement of a person's financial position such that his tax liability is minimised.

TAX RETURN

A document containing details of an individual's income and expenses and his claims for personal reliefs that is used to assess his income tax.

TAX, *AD VALOREM*

A tax established according to the value or a portion of the value of thing that is taxed.

TAXABLE INCOME

Under tax law, either the "gross income" of business or the adjusted gross income of individuals, minus deductions and exemptions. It is the income against which tax rates are applied in order to compute ones tax obligation.

TAXATION

This includes computation of income tax as per tax laws and regulations, filling of returns and making tax payments. In recent times it also includes tax planning. Managers are concerned with taxation in three different ways:

(a) a business is often required to act as an unpaid collector of tax. Examples include deduction of PAY on employees' remuneration and collection of VAT charged to customers. If the business does not have an adequate system to cope with this collection, and to respond promptly to changes in tax law, then any failure to collect tax as required may result in the business becoming liable for the shortfall.

(b) the business may be liable for taxation on its own activities.

(c) changes in tax law may a influence on the operations of the market in which the business operates. For example, car manufacturers keep a careful watch on changes in the ways in which company car users are taxed.

TAX-EXEMPT BOND

A certificate sold by a tax-exempt organisation that pays interest of the bondholder. The bondholder is not required to pay taxes on the interest.

TAXI-CAB ADVERTISING

Advertising medium consisting of advertisement panels fitted to the nearside cab driver's door.

TAYLOR, FREDERICK W.

Founder of the scientific management movement. Born into a middle-class Pennsylvania family, he was prevented from going to college by poor eyesight and instead did an apprenticeship in the mechanical engineering industry. This led to an interest in the rationalisation of manual work and the development of time and motion study together with incentive payment systems. *Taylor* is also associated with the idea of functional foremanship, which involves separating out the technical and work preparation aspects of foremanship from the supervisory, and vesting them in different people. Though the idea of functional foremanship in the pure Taylor sense was not widely taken up, it has presaged changes in the organisation of production in the form of separate work study units, production control/scheduling departments, tool rooms, and the separate administration of piecework earnings.

TAYLORISM

A synonym for *Scientific Management,* or the linking of remuneration to output through a payment-by-results scheme.

TCD

Management technique of total cost approach to distribution.

TEAM

(*i*) A temporary or an ongoing task group whose members are charged with working together to identify problems, form a consensus about what should be done, and implement necessary actions in relation to a particular task or organisational area.

(*ii*) Is a group whose members influence one another toward the accomplishment of (an) organisational objective (S).

TEAM BUILDING

(*i*) *A traditional intervention focusing on work groups;* has been given renewed interest as organisations rediscover the power of team effort.

(*ii*) An intervention aimed at helping work groups become effective at task accomplishment.

TECHNICAL SKILLS

(*i*) Are skills involving the ability to apply specialised knowledge and expertise to work-related techniques and procedures.

(*ii*) Key management skills that reflect both an understanding of and a proficiency in a specialised field.

TECHNICAL VOCABULARY

Words used in specialised fields such as chemistry, engineering, medicine, and agriculture.

TECHNIK

German word that denotes the knowledge and skill relevant to manufacture, *i.e.,* the mix of TEAM engineering knowledge and craft skill. The idea of *Technik* serves as a rallying point for all those connected with manufacture, and sustains the status of the production function and related technical departments. There is no real equivalent in English, 'technology' lacking the folksy ring of Technik, and 'technique' being too general a word. The idea, however, is not exclusively Germany, with *Teknik* in Swedish and *Techniek* in Dutch, for example, expressing the same idea. In the late 1980s the word became very familiar in Britain through the Audi car advertisements slogan *Vorsprung durch Technik,* which may be translated as 'competitive advantage through superior engineering'.

TECHNOLOGICAL ELEMENT

The part of the mega-environment that reflects the current state of knowledge regarding the production of products and services.

TECHNOLOGICAL FACTORS

(*i*) Are any types of equipment or processes that assist organisation members is the performance of their jobs.

(*ii*) A type of forecasting aimed primarily at predicting long-term trends in technology and other important aspects of the environment; also called *Qualitative Forecasting*.

TECHNOLOGICAL INTERDEPENDENCE

The degree to which different parts of the organisation must exchange information and materials in order to perform their required activities.

TECHNOLOGICAL OBSOLESCENCE

The pattern of products becoming out of date because of technological improvements in competing products.

TECHNOLOGICAL PROGRESS

Quite frequently it refers to the construction of more and better instruments of production and to the utilisation for this purpose, of great share of the existing store of technical knowledge.

TECHNOLOGICAL TRANSFER

The transmission of technology from those who possess it to those who do not.

TECHNOLOGY

(*i*) An important concept that can have many definitions in specific instances but that generally refers to actions, physical and mental, that an individual performs upon some object, person, or problem to change it in some way.

(*ii*) Consists of any type of equipment or process that organisation members use in the performance of their work.

(*iii*) The knowledge, tools, equipment, and work techniques used by an organisation in delivering its product or service.

TECHNOLOGY TRANSFER

The transfer of a technology from an area in which it had been successfully applied to an area in which it has not yet been tried.

TECHNO-MARKETING SYNERGY

To overcome longer gestation periods in technology and its effect on marketing the forecasting, technology and marketing are brought together with use of computer to forecast introduction of new products. Uses technique such as *Delphi Time Scaling*.

TECHNOSTRUCTURAL ACTIVITIES

An intervention involving activities intended to improve work technology and/or organisation structure.

TELECOMMUNICATION CHANNEL

It is that part of communications network that connects the message source with the message receiver. It is a physical equipment which connects one location to another for the facilitating transmission and receipt of information.

TELECOMMUNICATIONS

Transmission of signals over long distances which includes not only data communications but also transmission of images and voices.

TELECOMMUTING

A form of working at home that is made possible by using computer technology to remain in touch with the office.

TELEMARKETING

Using the telephone as the primary means of communicating with prospective customers. Telemarketers usually use computers for order taking.

TELEPHONE

Studies of how managers actually spend their time in both Germany and the UK have shown that some 10% of time is spent on the telephone. Thus for the successful manager it is important to cultivate a good telephone technique, both in terms of manner on the telephone and recording key points afterwards.

TELEPHONE INTERVIEWING

An adoption of the interview technique used in survey research where face-to- face interviewing is not possible or advisable.

TELEVISION HOME SHOPPING

(*i*) A cable television shopping service in which consumers see a product on their home TV screens and place orders by telephone.

(*ii*) Direct response marketing using television as advertising medium. Orders phoned in and computer print-out supplied to advertiser.

TELEVISION STUDIO TESTS

Closed-circuit studio tests of commercial at TV studio, with depth interviews of specially recruited sample to measure comprehension of advertising message. As undertaken by *British Market Research Bureau.*

TELEWORKING

The application of telecommunications to benefit the home worker and to encourage other people to work from home.

TELLER

A bank employee or officer who actually handles money, receiving deposits and paying out withdrawals. In large banks there may be separate tellers for different transactions, such as paying, receiving, collecting notes, etc.

TEMPLATE

A device or a software program which is developed as standard sample product and enables the uniform product to be produced each time the template is used.

TEMPORAL RELATIONSHIP

Subjects or ideas arranged in a sequence in which time is an essential factor.

TENANCY

The status or act of being an occupant or holder of property or real estate; also, the interests of the occupant also the period of time of occupancy.

TENANT

A person or organisation occupying or having rights to a property or real estate.

TENDER

To offer money or something else of value in payment for goods or services or in payment of a debt money or something else of value.

TENOR

The implication, direction, or tone of a social or business interaction, or of a statement or act; a theme that continues throughout a social, business, or therapeutic interaction, communication, or transaction.

TERMINATION

Also, separation; the process of leaving a job, either voluntarily (in cases of resignation or retirement) or involuntarily.

TERMS OF TRADE

The relationship between the prices of exports and imports. It may be expressed as an index. This index is expressed as appropriation of the price index of exports to the price index of imports as follows:

$$= \frac{\text{Price Index of Exports}}{\text{Price Index of Inports}} \times 100$$

The price index of exports measures changes in the aggregate value of a representative selection of exports as compared with the corresponding value in a base year.

TEST MARKETING

A form of pilot study on a new product, where it is tried out in a limited area first in order to see whether it would be worth marketing more widely.

TEST, THEMATIC APPERCEPTION

A projective test in which the testee is asked to describe the situations portrayed in a series of rather ambiguous pictures.

TESTIMONIAL

A type of advertising in which a person, usually a well-known person, states that he or she owns, uses, or supports the product being advertised.

TESTING

A source of error in experimental studies that occurs when the performance of the subject changes because previous measurement of performance made the subject aware of the experiment.

TESTING

Is examining human resources for qualities relevant to performing available jobs.

TESTS

A test is a sample of an aspect of an individual's behaviour, performance or attitude. It also provides a systematic basis for comparing the behaviour, performance of attitude of two or more persons. Tests serve as a screening device and provide supplementary inputs in selection decisions.

TESTS, PROJECTIVE

Psychological tests to which the "right" answers are not predetermined and which, therefore, require the testee to project himself.

TEXT DATA

The sentences or phrases or paragraphs in some natural language used in document.

TEXT FILE

A file that contains only the letters, digits and symbols without any kind of formatting.

T-GROUP

A small group of people that meets, with a trainer, for the purpose of improving members' skill in interpersonal behaviour by talking and thinking.

THEME ADVERTISING

(1) Another term for above-the-line advertising.

(2) Advertising, normally of an above-the-line character.

THEORY OF REASONED ACTION

States that when a behaviour is a matter of choice, the best predictor of the behaviour is the person's intention to perform it.

THEORY X

Is a set of essentially negative assumptions about human nature.

THEORY X, Y AND Z

The 1950s and 1960s are an interesting time with regard to theories of motivation. The period was one of growth, prosperity and full employment, with the manufacturing sector still dominant over the tertiary sector and with a prevalence of semiskilled workers. In this situation the efficacy of purely financial incentives declined and there was a blossoming of studies and theories pointing up the importance of non-monetary incentives, known collectively as the neo-human relations movement. A central figure in this movement is the American academic, *Douglas McGregor*, whose book 'The Human Side of Enterprise' counterposed Theory X and Theory Y. Theory X is all that can be inferred from the scientific and classical management schools about the drives and behaviour of the employee: he is lazy, needs close supervision, and has no interest in his work; his output can be raised only by ergonomic improvements in the job process accompanied by mounting financial incentives. This old-style received wisdom is contrasted by *McGregor* with Theory Y in which people are viewed more positively: they are not basically lazy, they do want to work and will do so if they are treated right; people are able to develop, to take responsibility, to use initiative and to make decisions; people can be self-motivated and self-controlled and will work towards organisational goals if management create suitable conditions and opportunities. The neohuman relations movement in general emphasised social and status needs of employees, self-fulfilment and intrinsic satisfaction. *Theory Z;* The expression coined by *William Ouchi* of the University of California Graduate School of Management in his leading book of the same name (Theory Z, Addison-Wesley, Reading, Mass., 1981). It is part of the American response to the Japanese successes of the 1980s. Ouchi's view is that the focus of Western interest should be on Japanese management style and corporate culture, contrasting as they do with what is prevalent in the USA. Indeed Ouchi believes that if American companies are going to respond to the Japanese challenge they will have to combine the best of the two management traditions, taking from the Japanese their emphasis on the collective, group loyalty, co-operation and generalism. Part of the interest of Ouchi's ideas is that they are typical of the American response to Japanese economic hegemony in two ways. First, the USA, as the dominant economic power in the post World War two period, takes the Japanese challenge more seriously than, for instance, Britain, for whom Japan is just the most recent in a succession of countries whose economic achievements are to be admired. Second, it is interesting that American commentators generally put the emphasis on these cultural and stylistic aspects of Japanese management: this is not universally the case — the Dutch, for instance, put the emphasis on particular Japanese practices such as quality circles and JIT.

THEORY Y

Is a set of essentially positive assumptions about human nature.

THEORY Z

(*i*) A concept that combines positive aspects of American and Japanese management into a modified approach aimed at increasing U.S. Managerial effectiveness while remaining compatible with the norms and values of American society and culture.

(*ii*) Is the effectiveness dimension that implies that managers who use either theory X or Theory Y assumptions when dealing with people can be successful, depending on their situation.

THERAPY

Treatment intended to cure or alleviate a disordered condition.

THERBLIG

The smallest discreet human motion that can be identified in the performance of a task.

THERMAL PROCESS

In the thermography or heat transfer process, the document to be copied should be drawn, written or printed in a mineral-based ink or in pencil. Thus it will not copy ball pen inks, some coloured inks and spirit duplicates copy. By this method, the original document together with a sensitised paper, is fed into the machine, and is subjected to heat from an infra-red lamp. The infra-red rays are absorbed by the mineral based writing but are reflected from the plain areas on the original an impression is thus caused on the copy paper by heat transfer.

THESAURUS

A software program that provides meaning and alternative words for a given word.

THIRD-PARTY INTERVENTION

A technique concerned with helping individuals, groups, or departments resolve serious conflicts that may relate to specific work issues or may be caused by suboptimal interpersonal relations.

THIRD-PARTY SELLING

As in computer industry, manufacturer sells box to service company which adds software and sells complete package.

THREE-SHIFT SYSTEM

A system of shiftwork in which three shifts are worked in each period of 24 hours in most or all of each week. .

THREE-TWO-TWO SHIFT SYSTEM

Synonym for *Continental Shift System.*

THRESHOLD

In retailing, minimum number of customers per location and hinterland to justify existence of store.

THRESHOLD WORKER

A new employee who has not previously been employed.

THRUSTER

Manager (or organisation) which acts aggressively, is dynamic, positive and exploits opportunities.

TICKLER

Jargon for Reminder; A tickler file is maintained by some managers as a matter of style. Items may be entered into the file according to a specific date, time, or subject and accessed for use on the appropriate occasion.

TIME BUDGET

The preparation of a detailed timetable of work activities in order to help improve time management and efficiency.

TIME DIMENSION

Of a plan is the length of time the plan covers.

TIME IN LIEU

A period of time off work, usually taken at the employee discretion to make up for time worked over and above normal working hours, *i.e.*, exchange of time for the money that would have been paid for working an overtime rate.

TIME NOTE

Promissory note or similar document which specifies a date or dates of repayment.

TIME ORIENTATION

A concept that refers to the time horizon of decisions. Employees may have relatively short- or long-term orientations, depending on the nature of their tasks.

TIME RATE

A rate of payment for an individual's work based on the amount of time spent at work (Also known as a 'day rate' or 'timework rate').

TIME SERIES ANALYSIS METHOD

Is a method of predicting future sales levels by analysing the historical relationship in an organisation between sales and time.

TIME SERVED WORKER

Skilled craftsman or worker who has completed a formal apprenticeship.

TIME SPAN OF DISCRETION

The time between an employee doing something and having it checked by higher authority, or between a person making a decision and having it or its consequences reviewed by superiors. It is the invention of British industrial psychologist *Eliot Jacques,* who saw it as a criterion for classifying jobs and awarding differential payments. It is an important indicator of the demands and responsibility level of jobs, and a useful discriminator. It cannot, however, be used alone to characterise jobs, and it is vitiated in practice by the fact that, although the time span is held to be a property of the job, this is importantly affected at management level by the personality and strengths of particular job incumbents.

TIME STUDY

A method of determining the time necessary to perform a task. Procedure may involve timing the various elements (*e.g.,* very small components of the task such as picking up material, positioning it, or inserting it in the machine) with a stopwatch, totalling the number of times and adding "allowances" for such things as fatigue and personal time.

TIME TICKET

A report of time spent in performing a labour task usually in the form of a handwritten report or a punched card. Also known as *Job Ticket*

TIME TOKEN

Money whose face value is greater than the value of the material from which it is made.

TIME UTILITY

Economic utility created by making goods available when consumers want them.

TIME VALUE OF MONEY

The difference between the value of money on hand today and that of money to be received in the future. The difference is due to the interest or other return that money available now might be producing in the meantime.

TIME WAGE
The reward paid to labour by hour, day, month or year.

TIME WORKER
Work that is paid for by a time rate. (Also known as *Daywork*).

TIMELENGTH
Time of a commercial spot in television or radio.

TIME-SAVED BONUS SCHEME
Synonym for *Premium Bonus Scheme.*

TIME-SERIES METHODS
Methods of quantitative forecasting that use historical data to develop forecasts of the future.

TIME-SPAN OF DISCRETION
A term introduced to the work study area of ergonomics in the 1960s by the British industrial psychologist *Elliott Japues.* It is an attempt at equity in setting salary levels and differentials following a job evaluation. What is measured is the length of time during which someone has to exercise discretion, *i.e.,* personal judgement and responsibility in their job before requiring decision from superiors.

TIMING
The point in time that has been selected to initiate an organisational change method.

TITLE (OR CREDIT TITLE)
List of executives and performers in a television or film programme.

TOKENISM
(i) An action taken for its symbolic value as opposed to serious attempt at changing a given situation, *e.g.,* appointing alone woman to an all-male board of directors as an end in itself, *i.e.,* to show how open-minded and progressive the organisation is. (ii) Refers to being one of very few members of a group in an organisation.

TOLERANCE OF AMBIGUITY
The tendency to perceive ambiguous situations or events as desirable. In contrast, intolerance of ambiguity is the tendency to perceive ambiguous situations or events as sources of threat.

TOMMY SHOP
Formerly employer owned shop providing goods for employees in place of cash wages.

TONER
An ink in the form of dry power which is used in the cartridges of laser printer.

TONER CARTRIDGE
A hermetically sealed unit which contains the toner for laser printer.

TOOL SUBJECT
School subject thought of as valuable because of service to other subjects or to practical pursuits rather than be itself. Reading, writing, arithmetic and English are considered tool subject.

TOOLS OF FINANCIAL ANALYSIS
(a) Comparative financial statements;

(b) Common size statements;
(c) Trends percentages or ratios;
(d) Ratio analysis;
(e) Funds flow analysis; and
(f) Cash flow analysis.

TOP MANAGEMENT

Executive members of boards of directors or the layer of general management at the top of operating companies. At this level there is a need for strategic sense and for at least a leaven of cool, rational planners, as opposed to the energetic, intuitive wheeler-dealers who often predominate in middle management.

TOP MANAGERS

Managers at the very top levels of the hierarchy who are ultimately responsible for the entire organisation.

TOPICAL RELATIONSHIP

Subjects or ideas which fit together to make up a unified whole.

TOPICAL SENTENCE

A sentence in a paragraph which provides the subject to be discussed and developed.

TOPOGRAPHY

The geography, structure, or configuration of a surface problem, plan, or other natural or human creation or artifact.

TOTAL COST

Fixed costs plus variable cost.

TOTAL COST CONCEPT

In relation to physical distribution, all focus on the entire range of costs associated with a particular distribution method.

TOTAL-FACTOR PRODUCTIVITY

A productivity approach which measures organisational productivity by considering all the inputs involved in producing outputs.

TOTAL POWER

Is the entire amount of power an individual in an organisation possesses. It is made up of position power and personal power.

TOTAL PRODUCT

The wide range of tangible and intangible benefits that a buyer might gain from a product after purchasing it

TOTAL QUALITY ASSURANCE

A differentiation strategy which promises the customer's satisfaction with product quality.

TOTAL QUALITY MANAGEMENT (TQM)

(*i*) A quality control approach that emphasises organisationwide commitment, integration of quality improvement efforts with organisational goals, and inclusion of quality as a factor in performance appraisals.

(*ii*) A management principle aimed at instilling the idea of customer- driven quality throughout the organisation and managing all employees to that there will be continuous quality improvement.

(*iii*) Is the continuous process of involving all organisation members in ensuring that every activity related to the production of goods or services has an appropriate role in establishing product quality.

TOTAL REVENUE

Is all sales dollars accumulated from selling the goods or services produced by the organisation.

TOTTEN TRUST

A trust agreement in which a first person puts money into a bank account in his or her name as trustee for a second person or a non-profit organisation. The first person can take the money out at any time, but if he or she does not do so before dying, the money becomes the property of the second person or organisation.

TOUCH SCREEN

An input device that accepts the data when the finger is placed on it. It is a selecting device and allows the user to select the item out of those items only which appears on the screen.

TRACKING

The skill of an individual in making the necessary adjustment of hand and eye to follow an moving object in a visual display.

TRACTOR FEED

An electro-mechanical device fitted with printer. It transports continuous computer stationery paper for the print mechanism. It has pockets within which the paper with holes are fitted thereby providing the traction.

TRADE

Commerce, also, an occupation or job; also, to buy and sell, exchange or barter.

TRADE ADVERTISING

That aimed at distributors, suing media such as trade press, direct mail, exhibitions.

TRADE ASSOCIATIONS

Organisations that are composed of individuals or firms with common business concerns and that have environmental influence.

TRADE COUNCIL

In the UK most towns and districts have a 'trades council' representing local trade union branches. Trades councils act as local co-ordinators of trade union activity. They do not tend to be involved in direct negotiations, but are often accepted by both central and local government as sources of nominations of trade union representatives to public bodies. Most trades councils register with the Trades Union Congress, which exerts substantial influence on them. However, trades councils should not be regarded as TUC 'branches'.

TRADE DISCOUNT

A discount given by a seller to a buyer in a recognition of their bonafide activity in a common trade (*e.g.*, Builder's merchant sells materials to builders at a trade discount).

TRADEMARK

Any form of logo and/or wording which a company uses to identify its products or brands and distinguish them from their rivals like a copyright or a patent, the owner of a trademark which had been officially registered had the monopoly right to use it for a certain period of time.

TRADE PRESS

Journal, magazines or newspapers that cater for the interests of a particular trade or industry.

TRADE SHOW

A meeting or convention of members of a particular industry where business- to-business contacts are routinely made.

TRADE-CREDIT

Facilities by which firms who purchase industrial goods, or the intermediaries in any channel of distribution, are permitted to delay payment for goods they have bought.

TRADES UNION CONGRESS (TUC)

The TUC is a British association of trade unions, each of which retains its own independence. The TUC exercises influence rather than power over affiliated unions. Major functions of the TUC are to provide research and publicity services for the union movement as a whole, to formulate and articulate policies for the promotion of trade union interests, and to investigate and resolve disputes between member unions.

TRADITION DIRECTED

People who in trust act with their society mainly by following the rules and customers laid down in its traditions.

TRAILER

A special piece of data which indicates the end of input data.

TRAINEE

A person who is receiving training.

TRAINING

(*i*) Is the process of developing qualities in human resources that will enable them to be more productive.

(*ii*) Training is a learning experience in that it seeks a relatively permanent change in an individual that will improve his or her ability to perform on the job. We typically say training can involve the changing of skills, knowledge, attitudes, or social behaviour.

TRAINING AND DEVELOPMENT

A planned effort to facilitate employee learning of job-related behaviours in order to improve employee performance.

TRAINING NEEDS

Are the information or skill areas of an individual or group that require further development to increase the productivity of that individual or group.

TRAINING OFFICER

Takes central advisory and executive responsibility for implementing the training function.

TRAINING SCHEME

A series of activities planned to provide a specific type of training.

TRAINING SPECIFICATION

A detailed statement of what a trainee needs to learn based on a comparison between his job specification and his present level of ability, training or experience.

TRAINING TRANSFER

Extent to which effectiveness of training on a simulator or in training situation transfers to effectiveness on the job. This is also known as *Positive Transfer,* transfer of training or training benefit.

TRAINING WITHIN INDUSTRY PROGRAMMES (TWI)

A series of short training programs for first-line supervisors developed during World War II.

TRAIT APPROACH TO LEADERSHIP

Is an outdated view of leadership that sees the personal characteristics of an individual as the main determinants of how successful that individual could be as a leader.

TRAIT PERSONALITY THEORIES

Theories based on the premise that predispositions direct the behaviour of an individual in a consistent pattern.

TRAIT THEORY

Trait theory visualises personality as a reflection of certain traits of the individual. Even though there are many traits that are common to most people, there are many other traits that are unique to a person and are not shared by other individuals. On the basis of the trait theory, people can be described as aggressive, loyal, pleasant, flexible, humorous, sentimental, impulsive, cool and so on. Traits are the basic elements of personality and can be used to summarise behaviour. For example, if we saw people behaving in an extrovert and forceful manner in most situations, we could lable their personality as aggressive. Similarly, if a person is observed in different situations as letting someone else take the initiative in deciding what to do, we could describe his personality trait as "submissive". *Cattell* used groups of traits to describe the underlying structure of personality. He compiled a list of words that can be used to describe personality traits. He put these traits into two basic categories. These are the source traits and the surface traits. For example, stammering would be a surface trait resulting from the basic source trait of timidity. Some of the *Surface Traits* are: wise-foolish, sociable-seclusive, honest-dishonest and so on. Similarly, some of the *Source Trait* categories are: trustful-suspicious, forthright-shrewd, relaxed-tense, dominant-submissive, cheerfulness-depressed and so on.

TRAITS

Distinctive internal qualities or characteristics of an individual, such as physical characteristics, personality characteristics, skills and abilities, and social factors.

TRANSACTION

A business action or agreement usually involving a financial consideration; also a system, process, or procedure resulting in an exchange of information; any mechanical or human interaction.

TRANSACTION FILE

A file which contains the data related to certain transactions which is to be processed with master file. One transaction file contains the records related to one type of transactions only.

TRANSACTIONAL LEADERS

Leaders who motivate subordinates to perform at expected levels by helping them recognise task responsibilities, identify goals, acquire confidence about meeting desired performance levels, and understand how their needs and the rewards that they desire are linked to goal achievement.

TRANSACTIONAL LEADERSHIP

A leader who identifies what followers want or prefer and helps them achieve the level of performance that results in rewards that satisfy them.

TRANSACTION-PROCESSING SYSTEM (TPS)

A computer-based information system that executes and records the routine day-to-day transactions required to conduct an organisation's business.

TRANSFER

A transfer implies a lateral movement of an employee in the hierarchy of position with the same pay and status. Transfers may be either company- initiated or employee-initiated. A company may initiate a transfer to place employees in positions where

TRUCK WHOLESALER

A limited-service wholesaler that sells a limited line of items (often perishable goods) from a truck, thus providing immediate delivery. Also called *A Truck Jobber*.

TRUST

A term used in the early twentieth century for combinations of companies that resulted, or were expected to result, in quasi-monopoly. Also used of funds set up for specific purposes and managed by a group of trustees. For example, a company may set up a pension trust to provide money for the payment of pensions.

TRUST ACCOUNT

An account established by a depositor or trustee with a trust company. The depositor or trustee controls the trust account during his or her lifetime. After the donors death, the balance of the trust account is payable to the beneficiary(ies).

TRUST COMPANY

A corporation established and operated to perform the functions of a trustee. Most trust companies also engage in other banking and/ or financial business.

TRUST FUND

loney or property set aside in a trust set aside for a special purpose.

TURNAROUND

efensive strategy designed to reverse *gative trend and restore the nisation to appropriate levels of ability.

TURNKEY SYSTEM

A complete set of equipment and an installation agreement for it in which the vendor assumes all responsibilities for installation, including analysis of the buyer's needs, selection of the proper components, installation, maintenance, documentation, and training for all users of the hardware and operating software.

TURN-OVER

In finance, the number of times than assets are paid in full over a given time interval. For example, the turnover for accounts receivable is calculated by dividing the average balance of accounts receivable by the total billings of account for the same interval.

TURNOVER SALES REVENUE

The revenue from sales received by a company or individual in the course of business over a set period of time.

TURNOVER, EMPLOYEE

The percentage of the workforce who quit, get fired, or are otherwise separated from the payroll in given period.

TURNOVER, INVENTORY

The number of times total inventory is used up and replaced in the course of a year.

TVR (TELEVISION RATINGS)

A measure of coverage representing 1 per cent of a potential television audience. Calculated by using panel research information.

TWO-TIER OFFER

A takeover device in corporatae acquisitions and mergers in which a relatively high per-share price is paid for a controlling interest in a company targeted for acquisition, and a lesser per-share price is paid for the remaining shares.

TWO-WAY COMMUNICATION

The communication that results when the communication process explicitly includes feedback

TYING CONTRACT

An agreement tying the purchase of one product to the purchase of another. The buyer who wishes to purchase a certain product is required by the seller to purchase additional products, whether or not the buy wants to purchase those products.

TYPE (A) PERSONALITY

A set of personality characteristics that have been linked to a particular susceptibility to heart disease. These characteristics include being impatient, always rushing, trying to do too many things at once walking, talking and eating fast, being hard, driving at work, having few interests outside work and hiding feelings. Type (A) personality is always contrasted with type (B) personality.

TYPE (B) PERSONALITY

A set of personality characteristics that are the opposite of type (A) personality and therefore considered to be much less susceptible to heart disease. These characteristics include being causal about appointment, being a good listener, never feeling rushed, slow and deliberate in manner and speech, easygoing with many interests outside work and able to express feelings. Both (A) and (B) are esteem instances and people would generally fall somewhere between the two.

TYPEFACE

A style of forming the letters and digits designed for a specific purpose.

TYPEWRITER

It is the most commonly used machine in offices of all kinds, and requires hardly any introduction. It may be used not merely for neat and legible writing but also for obtaining a limited number of copies by the use of carbon paper.

U

U.S.A.

The world's largest economy and biggest market, the inventor of business schools and MBAs, and the source of most of the good quotes about business. Ironically, though most of the world's books about management have been written by Americans, they have not sought to offer an explicit picture of management in their own country, so we depend on the observations of foreigners with experience in the USA for a characterisation. Things which strike business visitors include:

- a strong marketing orientation;
- an attachment to the philosophy and apparatus of professional management;
- strong on target setting, monitoring and financial control;
- results oriented, but inclined to a short-term perspective;
- anti-trade union, and hostile to European notions of codetermination; and
- takes the Japanese very seriously.

Style and dress are generally informal by *European Standards.* Opinions differ on whether American management is genuinely (and effectively) more hardworking, or just puts in long hours and keeps up a charade of hyperactivity.

UDC

Universal Decimal Classification.

ULTIMATE CONSUMER

Person or persons who actually consume or use a product or service, as distinct from the shopper or buyer who may be no more than a purchasing agent, such as housewife.

ULTRAVIOLET LIGHT

Electro-magnetic radiation with wavelengths longer than the X-rays but shorter than those of visible light. These are used to erase the instructions from EPROM.

UNAIDED RECALL METHOD

Refers to the technique for assessing the effectiveness of advertisements in which an interviewer asks someone which advertisements he remembers having seen or heard.

UNCERTAINTY

An aspect of nonprogrammed decisions that is a condition in which the decision-maker must choose a course of action without complete knowledge of the consequences that will follow implementation.

UNCERTAINTY AVOIDANCE

(*i*) The degree to which people are comfortable with ambiguous situations and with the inability to predict future events with accuracy.

(ii) A cultural dimension in *Geert Hofstede's* framework for analysing societies that involves the extent to which members of a society feel uncomfortable with and try to avoid situations that they perceive as unstructured, unclear, or unpredictable.

UNCERTAINTY BEARING

Responsibility for risks which cannot be standardised and insured against.

UNCLAIMED WAGES

Wages earned but not claimed by employees, although cash is available to make the payment, Also, wage cheques not yet presented for payment.

UNCONSTITUTIONAL STRIKE

Strike called, with or without official trade union backing, in branch of agreed procedure or procedural agreement.

UNCONTROLLABLE COSTS

Those affecting a manager or management's budget and area of activity but outside his or its discretion and ability to affect.

UNCONTROLLABLE MEDIA

Media in which the PR practitioner has no control over what shall be published or broadcast.

UNCONTROLLABLE VARIABLE

A variable in a system which is not under the control of the managers of the system.

UNDER BOND

Also, in bond describing goods which are being stored in a bonded warehouse.

UNDERACHIEVER

A person who fails to meet the level of achievement expected of him. This term is sometimes used in the field of education to describe someone who doesn't try hard enough, *i.e.*, a person whose ability could take beyond her ambitions contrast with overachiever.

UNDERCONTROL

The granting of autonomy to an employee to such a point that the organisation loses its ability to direct the individual's efforts toward achieving organisational goals.

UNDERCUTTING-THE COMPETITION STRATEGY

A pricing strategy whereby an organisation sets prices at levels lower than those of competitors.

UNDERDEVELOPED COUNTRY

A country in which the standard of living is low and the economy is largely based on the land and agriculture.

UNDERDEVELOPMENT

Refers to the failure to utilise fully the potential economic output warranted by existing technological knowledge.

UNDEREMPLOYMENT

A situation in which people do not have enough work to do or are not being fully utilised in terms of their skill level.

UNDERFLOW

A condition occurring when the result of any arithmetic operation is a quantity to small to be stored in the available register or memory storage.

UNDERMANNING

A situation in which there are fewer people employed by an organisation than are necessary for the efficient performance of its work.

UNDER-POPULATION

Refers to a condition when the marginal product of labour is greater than the existing average output per head for the country as a whole.

UNDER-VALUE

Revaluation of assets to a level which is below their real worth.

UNDERWRITE

(*i*) To provide insurance for something.

(*ii*) To guarantee the purchase of shares in a flotation in the event that they are not all sold on the market. To person professional trained and specialising in the under-writing of insurance.

UNDERWRITING

In insurance, the selection, classification, evaluation, and assumption of risks according to their insurability; the process of evaluating data.

UNDERWRITING COMMISSION

Commission paid to someone who underwrites a public offer of securities.

UNDEVELOPED COUNTRY

A country in which the standard of living is low and the economy is largely based on the land and agriculture.

UNDIFFERENTIATED MARKETING

A marketing effort not targeted at a specific market segment but designed to appeal to a broad range of customers. This approach is appropriate in a market that lacks diversity of interest.

UNDO

A feature of most of software applications that allows the user to cancel his/her last action and go back one step. This is an important feature to cancel the actions of those commands which are executed by mistake.

UNEARNED INCOME

Income which does not arise from work of one sort or an other.

UNEARNED PREMIUM

That portion of a premium for which the protection of an insurance policy has not yet been given.

UNEMPLOYED PERSON

Refers to one who is seeking work of wages but is unable to find any suited to his capacities and under conditions which are reasonably judged by local standard.

UNEMPLOYMENT

The term generally used of people who, are able and willing to engage in paid employment but are unable to find any.

UNEMPLOYMENT BENEFIT

Payment which is made to a person available for employment to compensate for the fact that he is unable to obtain work and a regular income.

UNFAIR DISMISSAL

A dismissal which is judged to be unfair by a Tribunal. The case is usually brought against an employer by the individual concerned, supported by a Trade Union.

UNFAIR HOUSE (OR SHOP)

Where wages and/or working conditions are inferior to those in the industry or locality generally. A term originating in the printing industry.

UNFAIR LABOUR PRACTICE

US equivalent of an unfair industrial practice.

UNFAIR SALES PRACTICES ACTS

State laws that limit or prohibit the use of certain sales and marketing techniques; most commonly, laws that require that certain types of merchandise be sold at prescribed markups.

UNFORMAT

A DOS command to unformat the disk. This helps in recover the data from the disks which have been formatted accidentally.

UNFREEZING

Is the state in which individuals experience the ineffectiveness of their present mode of behaviour and become ready to learn new behaviours.

UNIFORM DELIVERED PRICING

A type of delivered pricing in which an organisation charges the same price for a given product in allocations.

UNILATERAL ARBITRATION

A situation in which one side in an industrial dispute decides unilaterally to go to an arbitration body to seek a solution to the problem.

UNILATERAL STRATEGIES

Strategies for introducing organisational change that do not allow for participation by subordinates.

UNINTERRUPTED POWER SUPPLY

A device fitted with battery that supplies power to a computer whom it is attached with for a limited time period say 20 minutes to that in case of power failure the work may not disturb.

UNION REFERENCE

Where a trade union or its representatives week to use a disputes procedure or a grievance procedure. Such a step by an employer is known as *An Employee Reference.*

UNIONS

Employee groups formed for the purpose of negotiating with management about conditions relating to their work.

UNIQUE SELLING POINT

In marketing, this term refers to the distinctive feature of a product that gives it a competitive advantage.

UNIQUE SELLING PROPOSITION (USP)

A unique characteristic of a product or brand identified by the marketer as the one on which to base a promotional campaign; often used in a product differentiation approach to promotion.

UNIQUE-PRODUCT PRODUCTION

These three systems of production and their principles are: The production of a unique product, each product is self-contained. Of course strictly speaking there is no such thing as manufacturing unique products. They are produced only by the artist. But building a battleship, a big turbine or a skyscraper comes close to turning out a unique product. So does the building of a house and in most cases, "batch production" in a job shop. Unique- product production has high costs for the individual product but great flexibility in the plant. Mass production "new style" has the ability to supply wants cheaply and within a wide and flexible range of products. But it requires much higher capital investment than unique-product production and a much higher level of continuous activity; it involves inventory risks and it needs a distributive organisation that can sell continuously rather than one that goes after a specialised individual.

UNIT AND SMALL-BATCH PRODUCTION

A type of technology in which products are custom-produced to meet customer specifications or they are made in small quantities primarily by craft specialists.

UNIT COST

The cost of one unit of production or of a single item. It is found but dividing the total costs by the number of units or items produced.

UNIT PRODUCTION

Making items in ones, as opposed to in batches or in long runs. Bespoke tailoring is an ideal type of unit production operation. Unit production usually puts a premium on a company's design capability and on work organisation flexibility. It implies a skilled workforce, together with supervisors who can show and help rather than control and order.

UNIT TRUST OF INDIA (UTI)

Established by the Government of India on 1st July, 1964 by an act of the Parliament, the main objectives of UTI are:

(*i*) to mobilise the small savings of the public through sale of unit schemes;

(*ii*) to invest these small savings in a wide range of securities;

(*iii*) to provide reasonable income with minimum risk and maximum of liquidity of investments to the unit-holders;

(*iv*) to cleanable small investors to take advantages of the skill and knowledge of the experts in the field of investments; and

(v) to facilitate growth and diversification of the economy through capital formation.

UNITY OF COMMAND

(*i*) In organisation theory, this is the principle that each member of an organisation should report to only one person.

(*ii*) Is the management principle that recommends that an individual have only one boss.

UNITY OF DIRECTION

One head and one plan for each segment of the organisation.

UNIVERSAL DESIGN THEORY

A point of view that states there is "one best way" to design an organisation.

UNIVERSAL PRODUCT CODE (UPC)

The array of black bars, readable by optical scanners, found on most products. The UPC permits computerisation of tasks such as check-out and compilation of sales volume information.

UNIVERSALITY OF MANAGEMENT

Means that the principles of management are applicable to all types of organisations and organisational levels.

UNIX

A Language of Computer.

UNLIMITED COMPANY

A company having no limit on the liability of its member is an unlimited company.

UNLISTED SECURITIES MARKETS (USM)

Set up in the UK in November 1980, the USM is a separate and distinct market within the Stock Exchange. The costs of access to the USM are much lower than those involved in obtaining a full listing on the Stock Exchange, and the requirements to be complied with the less onerous. Thus the USM gives the smaller, growing company easier access to the capital markets. Once a company is admitted to the USM, it is also easier to process to a full Stock Exchange listing.

UNLOADING

Disposing of goods in a market at a low or concessionary price.

UNMANNED MANUFACTURING

The technology of operating entire manufacturing facilities without the need for human operators (*e.g.* with the use of robots).

UNPAID WORK

Work carried out within the household for the benefit of its members, and difficult to assess in terms of national real income.

UNPRODUCTIVE LABOUR

In some accounting procedures, the same as indirect labour.

UNREALISED RENT

Rent, which the owner of a house property fails to recover from the tenant.

UNSKILLED WORK

Work that consists of simple manual operations that can be

learned in a short time and which requires the exercise of little or no independent judgment.

UNSKILLED WORKER

Someone who performs, or can only perform, unskilled work.

UNSUCCESSFUL COMMUNICATION

Refers to an interpersonal communication situation in which the information the source intends to share with the destination and the meaning the destination derives from the transmitted message are different.

UPGRADED TRAINING

Training to give supplementary skills and knowledge to increase versatility mobility of labour. Sometimes known as *Supplementary Training*.

UPGRADING

Improving something without making major changes. Especially, giving an employee more money and/or status and/or responsibility and usually a different title without significantly changing his job.

UPS

Uninterrupted power supply.

UPSTANDING WAGE

As guaranteed working wage.

UPWARD COMMUNICATION

(*i*) The vertical flow of communication from a lower level to one or more higher levels in the organisation.

(*ii*) Upward communication flows from individuals at lower levels of the organisation structure to those at higher levels. Among the most common upward communication flows are suggestion boxes, group meetings, and appeal or grievance procedures.

UPWARD ORGANISATIONAL COMMUNICATION

Is communication that flows from any point on an organisation chart upward to another point on the organisation chart.

USE

A command of dbase and is onwards versions which is used to open databases and to bring it into main memory.

USER

(*i*) An individual, other than an information system professional, who is engaged in the development and/or management of computer based information systems; also called *An End User*.

(*ii*) The buying-centre role played by the organisational member who will actually use the product.

USER DATABASE

Is a database developed by an individual manager or other user.

USANCE

Length of time allowed for payment of foreign bills of exchange; the period of time fixed by usage or custom for payments drawn in one country and payable in another.

UTILITY

A generic name given to the small independent software with miscellaneous applications. It includes disk managers, operating system adjuncts, file maintenance and handling programs.

UTILITY PROGRAM

A program provided to perform a task that is required by many programs. They may provide text editing, initiate execution of programs and perform other functions not directly related to the processing of data.

UTILITY THEORY

One of the decision theory techniques for calculating acceptable risk taking in business and project planning.

V

VACILLATING CUSTOMER

Customer unwilling, or unable, to determine own needs when presented with positive proposition.

VACUUM TUBE

An electronic device which consists of a glass tube to house electronic circuitry. The working of electronic circuitry depends on the vacuum within the tube. Vacuum tube are also known as *Valves* and were in use in *1960s*.

VALENCE

(*i*) A factor in expectancy theory that is our assessment of the anticipated value of various outcomes or rewards.

(*ii*) The strength of a person's preference for a particular outcome.

VALIDATION

The process of manually checking or testing the performance of a program.

VALIDITY

(*i*) The degree to which data used in a study or the results of a study are correct or true; the extent to which an observed situation reflects the true situation.

(*ii*) A concept underlying the use of various selection methods that concerns the degree to which a measure actually assesses the attribute that it is designed to measure.

VALS-2

A psychographic classification scheme that divides consumers into groupings according to values, attitudes, and lifestyles.

VALUE ADDED TAX

A method of taxing the value addition to inputs used in the production process.

VALUE ANALYSIS

A systematic analysis of each component of a product and of the operations performed on each to determine whether the value contributed by each is good enough to justify the cost.

VALUE ANALYSIS

Is a cost control and cost reduction technique that examines all the parts, materials, and functions of an operation.

VALUE SATISFACTION

Marketing term for the satisfaction or reasons that lead a consumer to purchase a particular product or service.

VALUE SURVEY

An instrument used to help an individual identify and clarify the priorities in his or her own value system. A typical value survey lists values and asks the survey taker to rank-order the values based on their importance to him or her.

VALUE-BASED CRITERIA

Some variables appear to have a linear value scale (more is always better than less) while others have a curvilinear scale (some optimum is desired, more or less both are to be avoided). The shape of the curves determines in part the trade-off relationships among assessment variable under conditions where simultaneous optimisation is not possible.

VALUES

(*i*) Are the global beliefs that guide one's actions and judgments across a variety of situations.

(*ii*) The guidelines and beliefs that a person uses when confronted with a situation in which a choice must be made.

VAN TESTING

Form of consumer panel using a mobile shop where product tests are conducted in different areas.

VARIABLE

A symbolic name assigned to a data item that will be used to store the data of any type. The value can vary throughout the program.

VARIABLE BUDGET

Also known as a *Flexible Budget;* is one that outlines the levels of resources to be allocated for each organisational activity according to the level of production within the organisation.

VARIABLE COST

The cost which tends to vary in direct proportion to changes in the volume of output or turnover.

VARIABLE COSTS

Are expenses that fluctuate with the number of products produced.

VARIABLE-INTERVAL SCHEDULE OF REINFORCEMENT

A type of partial reinforcement schedule based on a pattern in which a reinforcer is administered on a varying, or random, time schedule that averages out to a predetermined time frequency.

VARIABLE WORKING HOURS

Virtually as flexible working hours although sometimes used to describe a less formal system which allows employees even greater freedom of choice in working hours.

VARIABLE-RATIO SCHEDULE OF REINFORCEMENT

A type of partial reinforcement schedule based on a pattern in which a reinforcer is provided after a varying, or random, number of occurrences of the desired behaviour in such a way that the reinforcement pattern averages out to a predetermined ratio of occurrences per reinforcement.

VARIANCE RATIO

Refers to the ratio of one sample variance to another sample variance when both samples are taken from a norm population. The ratio is usually denoted by *F*.

VARIETY STORE

A store carrying a wide range of relatively inexpensive goods for the household.

VDU

Visual Display Unit.

VENDOR

The seller; but especially the seller of small items, *e.g.*, street newsvendor who sells newspaper.

VENDOR ANALYSIS

The rating of alternative suppliers on attributes such as product quality, reliability, delivery speed, and price.

VENDOR RATING

Classifying of distributors by volume of sales, with preferential trade terms for different grades of vendor.

VENDOR S LIEN

An unpaid seller's legal right to maintain possession of property until the purchase price has recovered.

VENTURE TEAM

A group of specialists in an organisation who operate in an entrepreneurial environment to develop a new business without being a closely controlled part of the organisation. The team independently develops, tests, and commercialises new products.

VENTURE TEAM

A group of two or more individuals who band together for the purpose of creating a new venture.

VERBAL APTITUDE OR INTELLIGENCE TESTS

Used in personnel selection etc. to test facility in the use of works in oral and written communication.

VERBAL COMMUNICATION

Is the sharing of information through words, either written or spoken.

VERIFICATION

Verifying the data.

VERSATILITY TRANSFERS

Such transfers are made to increase versatility of the employees from one job to another and one department to another. Transfers (or job rotations) are used as a devise to train the employees.

VERTICAL CHART

Most organisations use this type of chart which presents the different levels of organisation in the form of a pyramid with senior executive at the top of the chart and successive levels of management depicted vertically below that. Thus, lines of command proceed from top to bottom invertical lines.

VERTICAL COMMUNICATION

Communication that involves a message exchange between two or more levels of the organisational hierarchy.

VERTICAL CO-OPERATIVE PROMOTION

An approach whereby channel members at different levels jointly sponsor particular promotions.

VERTICAL COORDINATION

An aspect of organisation structure involving the linking of activities at the top of the organisation with those at the middle and lower levels in order to achieve organisational goals.

VERTICAL DIFFERENTIATION

The number of authority levels in an organisation. The more authority levels an organisation has, the more complex is the organisation.

VERTICAL DYAD LINKAGE APPROACH

A view that there is no such thing as consistent leader behaviour across subordinates. Each one-on-one relationship is unique.

VERTICAL INTEGRATION

A growth strategy that involves effecting growth through the production of inputs previously provided by suppliers or through the replacement of a customer role by disposing of one's own outputs.

VERTICAL INTEGRATION

The process whereby a company extends its business interests into other stages of production, or sales of its products. Though sometimes a company is able to do this for itself it is usually accomplished by some form of merger with, or takeover of, another firm concerned with a different stage of the same product, *e.g.*, a publisher may takeover a bookshop.

VERTICAL MARKET

Selling of a product or range of products restricted to one type or classification of market.

VERTICAL MARKETING SYSTEM

A vertical network of marketing establishments operating as a centrally coordinated distribution system. They may be linked by ownership, informal control, or contractual agreement.

VESTED MARKETING SYSTEM

As one of the chains or channels of distribution, consists of suppliers, coordinators, retailers, consumers instore or in-home.

VESTED RIGHT

A right entitled to government protection and belonging so absolutely and unconditionally to a person that it cannot be defeated by the act of any private person or organisation.

VESTING

The conveying of an irrevocable right to a benefit, usually after a specified number of years of continuous employment have been accmed within the same company; most prevalent in pension and profit-sharing plans.

VESTING DAY

Date public authority takes over the nationalised industry.

VICARIOUS LEARNING

A component of social learning theory involving our ability to learn new behaviours and/or assess their probable consequences by observing others.

VICARIOUS LIABILITY

The liability of an employer for the actions of employees while working under instructions.

VICE-PRESIDENT, EXECUTIVE

Generally the second in command to the president.

VICTIMISATION

The persistently unfair treatment of a worker, either by colleagues or employers.

VIDEO ADAPTER

The control circuitry for a monitor. This is the card which sends signals for display.

VIDEO CARD

The control interface card for visual display unit *i.e., Monitor*.

VIDEO MAGAZINE: PR MEDIUM

House Journal produced on video-cassette and supplied to organisation's locations for showing on television sets to employees.

VIDEO MEMORY

Video RAM; an area of RAM which is used exclusively by a monitor. It is updated as required by the CPU and in turn, it refreshes the screen image. Video RAM could be accessed directly only via assembly language programming.

VIDEO TELECONFERENCING

The holding of meetings with individuals in two or more locations by means of closed-circuit television.

VIDEOCASSETTE ADVERTISING

Commercials on home video-cassettes sold or hired out showing on domestic VCR's.

VIDEODISC OR VIDEODISK

Means of recording sound and vision on a disk like a small gramophone record, which can be played back on a special recorder and shown on a TV screen.

VIDEOPHONE

Marriage of telephone and television facilities so that caller and called can see each other.

VIGILANCE MEN

Trade union members who are responsible for reporting to their unions the emergence of any grievances or potential grievances at the workplace.

VIRTUAL

The cyber version of the real world.

VIRTUAL DRIVE

A portion of memory that is used as if it were a hard disk drive. These virtual drives are much faster than hard disks because computer can read information from memory much faster than information from hard disk. But contents of this drive losses when computer is switched off. This is also known as RAM *Drive*.

VIRTUAL MEMORY

A technique of operating system that uses swapping techniques to increase the apparent size of actual memory.

VIRUS

A destructive program that copies the destructive routines into the computer systems to make the computer malfunction or even to destroy all the programs of the computer by disrupting the operation of computer system. The program copies by itself on the other secondary storage media. So it spreads very fast from one system to another.

VISIBLE (OR VISIBLE TRANSACTION)

A sale, by a resident of goods (rather than services). For the buyer's country such a transaction is a Visible import; for the seller's country it is visible export'.

VISIBLE IMPORTS

Imports of physically visible goods appearing as payments in the current account of a country's balance of payments statement.

VISUAL

Drawing or illustration of an advertisement or other piece of promotional material, finished to an adequate standard for presentation to a client.

VISUAL ABILITIES TEST

Type of personnel selection test designed to test such visual abilities as acuity of sharpness of vision at various distances and the ability to perceive depth.

VISUAL ACUITY

Keenness of vision.

VISUAL DEFECT

An imperfection of vision.

VISUAL DISPLAY

The part of a computer that provides a visual display of its operations on a television-like screen.

VISUAL IMAGERY

A mental reconstruction of sensory experiences secured by means of vision.

VISUAL PERCEPTION TIME

The time it takes to 'read' a picture.

VISUALISATION OF ENTIRETY

The overall comprehension is valuable for it enables the manager to see important relationships gain a fuller understanding of each activity and appreciate the basis upon which managerial actions are supported. Isolation and confusion are reduced. Through planning a constructive identification with the problems and the enterprise as a whole is gained.

VITAL PERCEPTION TIME

The time it takes to 'read' a picture.

VITAL STATISTICS

Facts and figures relating to the essential matters of a company, person or economy.

VLSI

Abbreviation for *Very Large Scale Integration,* a fabrication technology in electronics which integrates more than 1000 gates on a single silicon chip.

VOCABULARY TEST

A sample of the words selected from a complete general dictionary presented for definition; the score is in index of the testee's total vocabulary.

VOCALISATION

Movement of lips, tongue, or vocal apparatus of the throat while reading silently.

VOCATIONAL GUIDANCE

Vocational guidance is a process of assisting the individual to choose an occupation, prepare for it, enter upon and progress on it. According to *John D. Cries*, "Vocational guidance is a facilitated process, a service rendered to the individual to aid him in choosing and adjusting to an occupation."

VOICE MAIL

A recording system that provides senders with the opportunity to leave messages for receivers by telephone.

VOLATILE MEMORY

This is a phrase used to specify the characteristic of primary memory or RAM. The word volatile implies that this memory will loss all its contents at once the power is turned off.

VOLITION

A state of decision or choice, the end condition of voluntary activity.

VOLUME

Any secondary storage medium. Each volume can be assigned a name or number.

VOLUME LABEL

All characters long name given to the volumes and is stored as an entry in directories.

VOLUNTARY CHAIN

A group of independent retailers linked to a wholesale supplier in a system instituted by the wholesaler.

VOLUNTARY GROUP

A number of retailers of similar goods who are associated with a single wholesaler and adopt a common policy or promotion.

VOLUNTARY MEMBERSHIP GROUP

In reference to an individual, a membership group to which the individual has chosen to belong.

VOLUNTARY REDUNDANCY

A situation in which an employee requests or agrees to redundancy usually in return for favourable terms of compensation.

VOLUNTARY UNEMPLOYMENT

A description given by Keynes to unemployment directly due to the withdrawal of their labour by a body of workers because they do not choose to work for less than certain areas reward.

VON NEUMANN, JOHN

A famous mathematician of *trinceton* who, in 1947, developed the concept of storing computer instructions in the internal memory of a computer. This concept is the basis of most of the computer operations.

VOUCHED

A receipt or a documentary evidence of an expenditure, which establishes the validity of a transaction.

VOUCHER

Any written document that serves as proof that money has been paid or received, such as a cancelled check, petty cash receipt, receipted bill etc.

VOUCHER INDEX

An alphabetical list, in card-index or carbon-copy form, of persons or firms that are payees of the company.

VOUCHER REGISTER

A journal or record, usually in columnar form for the entry of vouchers.

VOWEL INDEX

This is an improvement upon the book index. Under this type, the page of the index book reserved for each alphabet are divided into six sub-sections. Each sub-section is reserved for a vowel (A,E,I,0,U and Y).

VOWEL

An unconstructed letter sound made with open throat, mouth, teeth, and lips. These are vowels: a,e,i,o,u, and sometimes y.

VROOM'S EXPENTANCY THEORY OF MOTIVATION

The expectancy theory of work motivation has its roots in the cognitive concepts of pioneering psychologists *Kurt Lewin* and *Edward Tolmany* and in the choice behaviour and utility concepts from classical economic theory. However, the first to formulate an expectancy theory directly aimed at work motivation was *Victor Vroom.* Contrary to most critics, Vroom proposed his expectancy theory as an alternative to content models, which he felt were inadequate explanations of the complex process of work motivation. At least in academic circles, his theory has become a popular explanation for work motivation and continues to generate considerable research.

Fig. 4 briefly

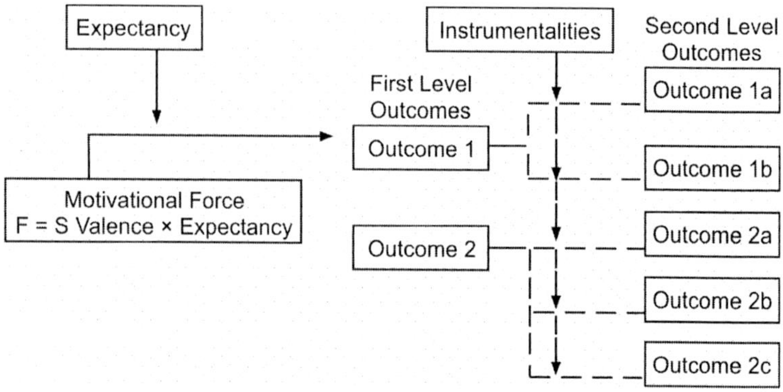

Fig. 4: Vroom's Expectancy or VIE, theory of work motivation.

summarises the Vroom model. As shown, the model is built around the concepts of valence, instrumentality, and expectancy, and is commonly called the VIE Theory. By valence, vroom means the strength of an individual's preference for a particular outcome. Other terms that might be used include value, incentive, attitude, and expected utility. In order for the valence to be positive, the person must prefer attaining the outcome to not attaining it. A valence of zero occurs when the individual is indifferent toward the outcome; the valence is negative when the individual prefers not attaining the outcome to attaining it. Another major input into the valence is the instrumentality of the first-level outcome in obtaining a desired second- level outcome. For example, a person would be motivated toward superior performance because of the desire to be promoted. The superior performance (first-level outcome) is seen as being instrumental in obtaining a promotion (second-level outcome).

VROOM-YETTON LEADERSHIP MODEL

A leadership model that specifies which leadership decision-making procedures are most effective in each of several different situations. Two of the proposed leadership styles are autocratic (AI and All); two are consultative (Cl and CII); and one is oriented toward joint (decisions) made by the leader and the group, GII).

VROOM-YETTON-JAGO (VYJ) MODEL OF LEADERSHIP

Is a modern view of leadership that suggests that successful leadership requires determining through a decision tree what style of leadership will produce decisions that are beneficial to the organisation and accepted and committed to by subordinates.

W

WPM.

The average number of words per minute which a person covers in reading a selection.

WAFER

A thin sheet of semi-conductive material from which microchips are manufactured.

WAGE

According to the Fair Wage Committee Report, "The living wage should enable the male earner to provide of himself and his family not merely the bare essentials of food, clothing and shelter, but also a measure of frugal comfort including education for children, protection against ill health, requirements of essential social needs and a measure of insurance against the more important misfortunes including old age." Wage is "a fair day's remuneration for a fair day's work," *i.e.*, standard performance. A wage incentive scheme is described as "a method of payment for work of an acceptable quality produced over and above a specified quantity or standard". Payment-by- Results (PBR) refers to a method which provides for the "direct linking of workers' earnings to a measure of their performance".

WAGE ADMINISTRATION

Activities concerned with fixing and sometimes, paying wages in an organisation.

WAGE AND SALARY ADMINISTRATIVE

Maintaining a logical salary and/or wage structure.

WAGE AND SALARY SURVEY

A survey of what other companies are paying for various jobs.

WAGE ASSIGNMENT

A voluntary transfer of earned wages to a third party to pay debts, but savings bonds, pay union dues, or execute other fiduciary actions.

WAGE COUNCILS

In the UK successive governments have set up wage councils for a number of individual industries. Generally these have been created for industries where there are a large number of employees making normal wage bargaining difficult. A wage council normally includes representatives of three groups: the employers, the unions and independent members appointed by the government. Currently the wage council system is under attack by critics who see it as leading to wage awards above market levels, with the consequence that workers are 'priced out' of jobs. Defenders of the system see it as protecting workers in industries, where union bargaining power is weak, from exploitation.

WAGE DRIFT

The gap between nationally negotiated wage rates and actual earnings which tend to be much higher.

WAGE RATE

The amount paid to the worker per hour or per normal working day or for performing a certain job.

WAGE SURVEY

After evaluation jobs are grouped or classified according to their worth, it is necessary to convert them to monetary values to determine the wages rates. To build up a competitive wage structure, it is necessary to know what are the rates prevailing for similar jobs in the same industry in the area.

WAGE-OFFER CURVE

A curve which shows the different amounts of hours of work which a worker will offer or work for different amounts of wage rates.

WAGE-PRICE GUIDEPOSTS

Conditions or standards set by the government in an effort to control the behaviour of wages and prices.

WAGES AND SALARIES

A term for remuneration paid to employees of a business or other organisation. Both are fixed by contract and are usually determined by a trade union or national agreement.

WAIT

A Dbase (and advanced versions) command. It makes the computer to pause the execution of program until the user presses any key. The key pressed is stored as a character string in a specified variable.

WAIT TIME

The time a job spends waiting to be moved or waiting to be worked on in the factory area. Also known as queue time.

WAN

Wide area network, the network which spreads over many far apart geographical sites.

WANTS

Desires which may not yet be apparent. They may be converted eventually into needs. New wants have to be anticipated by the marketer and satisfied with new products or services.

WAREHOUSE CLUB

A mass merchandise outlet in which only "members" are allowed to shop. Also called a Closed Door House.

WAREHOUSE RETAILER

A mass merchandiser that sells products from showrooms that double as storage places for stock.

WAREHOUSE-KEEPERS CERTIFICATE OR RECEIPT

A document issued by a warehousekeeper stating that

certain goods are held in his warehouse at the disposal of the person names. Such a certificate on receipt is not transferable, and the goods are not deliverable upon its production. It is simply an acknowledgment of having received certain goods.

WAREHOUSING

All the activities necessary for the holding and housing of goods between the time they are produced and the time of shipment to buyers.

WARRANTY

A guarantee that a product will perform in accordance with its specifications for at least a certain period after the date of sale, and that corrective action will be taken by or on behalf of the manufacturer should this not be so.

WASH SALE

A bogus transaction which is said to have taken place at an artificially high price in a commodity market used by a seller to boost prices.

WASTAGE

Proportion of employees, actual or predicted, leaving an employing organisation or type or category of employment.

WASTAGE RATE

Percentage of particular kinds of employee leaving an employing organisation during a particular period, usually a year.

WASTE CIRCULATION

Parts of a circulation which are of no value to the advertiser but which he nevertheless has to pay for in his campaign.

WASTING ASSETS

Assets whose economic value decreases as they are used because they cannot particularly be renewed or replaced, *e.g.*, coal-mines or oilfields.

WATER TRANSPORTATION

In relation to physical distribution, the use of ships, boat, or charges in the shipment of products.

WATER-OUT

Research problem or weakness that informants may be unable to sustain prolonged questioning, or may fail to respond to tests which place unrealistic demands on their ability to respond.

WAVER

An agreement attached to an insurance policy that exempts from coverage certain disabilities or injuries normally covered by the policy.

WAYBILL

The wealth of an individual can be defined as his stock of tangible or intangible assets which have a market value.

WEB PRESS

A press that prints on paper from a roll known as web.

WEBER'S LAW

For a salary structure to have uniform incentive value the salary levels should increase in geometric proportions.

WEIGHTED CHECKLIST

A rating system consisting of statements that describe the various types and levels of behaviour for a particular job. Each statement is weighted according to its importance.

WEIGHTED SAMPLE

Market research etc. term for a sample with a specific bias, rather than random sampling.

WELFARE

Public financial assistance to certain categories of poor persons.

WELFARE ARRANGEMENTS

'Welfare' arrangements for employees refer to those activities of the employers and the Government which are directed towards providing the employees with certain facilities, in addition to wages or salaries.

WELFARE CAPITALISM

The concept that workers will be discouraged from joining labour unions if employers create sufficiently favourable conditions.

WELFARE STATE

A social system based on the government's assumption of responsibility for providing unemployment compensation, medical care, old-age pensions, and income for families unable to participate in the productive process.

WELLNESS PROGRAMME

A programme that encourages improved health status and a healthful lifestyle through health education, exercise, nutrition, and health promotion.

WHARFINGER

A person who maintains a wharf at which goods are stored for compensation.

WHAT IF"ANALYSIS

Is the simulation of a business situation over and over again, using somewhat different data for selected decision areas.

WHEEL INDEX

In this system the cards are fitted in metal slits which are mounted on a hub fitted to a stand. When all the cards have been mounted on the hub it looks like a wheel and rotates like that.

WHEEL OF RETAILING

A theory positing that new forms of retail institutions enter the marketplace as low-status, low-margin, low-price operations and then gradually trade up, opening a market position for a new low-end retailer.

WHEEL PRINTER

A printer which has metal wheel with spokes having characters embossed on it for printing.

WHIP

A fast worker introduced by management as a pacesetter for other workers on a production line.

WHISTLE-BLOWER

An employee who reports a real or perceived wrongdoing under the control of his or her employer to those who may be able to take appropriate action.

WHISTLE-BLOWING

The process in which an employee, because of personal opinions, values, or ethical standards, concludes that an organisation needs to change its behaviour or practices and informs an outsider, by passing the organisation's authority system.

WHITE KNIGHT

Sometimes a company faced with a takeover bid that is difficult to resist. An alternative to simply fighting to stay independent is to look for a 'white knight,5 an alternative bidder whose aims are regarded as more compatible with those of the existing management.

WHITE PAPER

A document prepared by the Government on a given issue.

WHITE-COLLAR

Of, relating to, or performing clerical or supervisory work.

WHITE-COLLAR WORKER

Popular term for any member of staff who works in an office. The name derives from the practice of (men) wearing a white shirt to work (in the days when men wore white shirts with white collar). Usually contrasted with a blue collar worker.

WHOLESALE PRICE INDEX

A monthly published index showing changes in the wholesale price of selected items.

WHOLESALER

An organisation or individual that serves as a marketing intermediary by facilitating transfer of products and title to them. Wholesalers do not produce the product, consume it, or sell into ultimate consumers.

WHOLESALING

Acting as an intermediary or middleman between the production of goods and their retailing to the general public. It usually involves the stocking of relatively large quantities of goods for onward distribution.

WHOLLY OWNED SUBSIDIARY

An operation on foreign soil, by means of which organisations can conduct business internationally, that is totally owned and controlled by a company with headquarters outside the host country.

WIDE AREA NETWORKS

Networks through which end-user computing can be managed that provide communications among computers over long distances, usually through the facilities and services of public or private communications companies.

WIDGET

In general discussions on production and selling etc. a standard product, obviating the need to relate the instance to a particular product type.

WIDTH (OF A PRODUCT LINE)

The variety and diversity of products offered in a product line.

WIDTH OF PRODUCT MIX

The number of product lines within a product mix. Wide indicates diversity of product types; narrow indicates little diversity.

WILD CARD

A character used in operating system commands that is interpreted to have several meanings. One OS can have many wild cards. Like DOS have and ?. Wild cards are very productive tools but need to be used with care.

WILDCAT STRIKE

A local strike that does not have official trade union backing usually called without warning or at short notice.

WILDCAT STRIKE

A sudden or unexpected strike. Although both media and management often purport to be taken by surprise by strikes, many of them are loosely predictable in the sense of occurring at particular times of year (air traffic controllers strike in the summer, power workers in the winter) or in recognisable circumstances (annual pay bargaining). But in contrast, a wildcat strike is one than takes everyone by surprise.

WILL

A written document that provides for the distribution of the writer's property after his or her death.

WINCHESTER DISKETTE

A magnetic disk to store the data which is sealed as hard disk containing the access arms read/write head. This technology was developed by IBM and first introduced in 1973.

WINDFALL

An unanticipated sizable profit or other gain, such as unexpected inheritance, rise in stock prices, etc.

WINDFALL PROFIT

An unexpected profit usually arising from matter not directly connected with the activities of the lucky individual or organisation, *e.g.,* a bequest or a change in taxation. The original windfall consisted of apples blown of trees.

WINDING-UP

A process of closing the usual operations of a business unit and selling its assets to settle all its debts.

WINDOW-DRESSING

It refers to the practice of manipulating the current assets are current liabilities in a manner as to present a more favourable ratio than the actual one. Such manipulations can be carried out in the value of inventories and by recording in advance cash sales or outstanding liabilities for credit purchase of goods taken into closing stock. Also, they may be done by treating short-term obligations as long-term debts.

WINDOW-DRESSING SERVICE

Service provided by manufacturers who send windowdressers to their distributors and arrange window displays of their products.

WINDOWS

A software which was developed by Microsoft. It provides enhanced file handling features and has ability to load more than one program at a time. Initial version of windows required the system to have DOS loaded. But Windows 95 onwards version themselves are the complete Operating systems. They provide the graphical user interfaces and commands are present either as menu options or icons.

WINK

An interval of 0.0005 minute (0.03 second) employed in method study.

WINK COUNTER

A timing device, graduated in winks, which is photographed by a movie camera at the same time as the performance of a task for purposes of method study. A wink counter gives a digital display (c.f. microchronometer).

WINNING STREAK

The title of book by Walter Goldsmith and David Clutter back (Weidenfied and Nicolson, London, 1984) on the characteristics of top performing British companies and their leaders. A selfstyled British's equal to Peters and Waterman's In Search of Excellence; not as good as the American trail-blazer, but well worth reading.

WISH IMAGE

How company wishes to be seen by outsiders.

WITHHOLDING TAX

Federal, state, or local tax withheld by employers from the paychecks of their employees and paid directly to the taxing jurisdiction.

WIZZYWYG

Pronunciation of WYSIWYG.

WOMEN'S BUREAU

An agency concerned with promoting the welfare if wage-earning women, improving their work conditions, increasing their efficiency, advancing their opportunities for profitable employment and similar efforts.

WONDERLIC PERSONNEL TEST

General learning ability test that is particularly widely used by industry and business in the USA. Development in the 1960s, it is derived partly from the OTIS self-administering test of mental ability.

WORD ANALYSIS

Analysing of an unfamiliar word into known elements for the purpose of identification.

WORD PROCESSOR

An application package that can create, edit, manipulate and print text. Along with that they can also add graphics to the file. These packages have features like grammar and spelling checking, font setting, mail merging and are therefore widely used for preparing the documents like letters and reports.

WORD

A string of character that is considered as a unit. An ordered set of bits which could be accessed using the single read/write action.

WORK

Any kind of purposive activity whether paid or unpaid, full-time or part-time, formal or informal. With reference to an organisation it is used about the operations involved in a particular job or task.

WORK ADMINISTRATION

Personnel management helps in organising a system of adequate remuneration for the workers. Administration of all agreements, interpretation and application of their various terms are important responsibilities of the personnel manager.

WORK AGENDA

A management process element composed of a loosely connected set of tentative goals and tasks that a manager is attempting to accomplish.

WORK COUNCIL

A forum for joint consultation between employees and employers (or their representatives) in an organisation.

WORK ENVIRONMENT

Work environment is a condition in management that encourages and supports the most productive efforts of personnel' Before the days when economic development became a major concern of governments, and especially before the days when countries intervened in and actually engaged in economic activities, the need for specialized technological and other personnel in government service was not perceived as very great indeed; the number of such personnel were small. The status of specialized personnel was even more diminished than their numbers, in many countries. They were not prominent in policy-making or even decisive in programme formulation.

WORK EXPERIENCE

A period of time spent doing unpaid work in a workplace environment by young people about to leave school, as preparation for future employment.

WORK MEASUREMENT

An integral part of the work study process in which a variety of (subjective) methods like work sampling are used to fix a standard time for the acceptable performance of a given task by a trained worker.

WORK MEASUREMENT METHODS

Are operational tools that are used to establish labour standards.

WORK MODULE

An important characteristic of job redesign strategies that involves creating whole tasks so that the individual senses the completion of an entire job.

WORK METHODS ANALYSIS

Is an operational tool used to improve productivity and ensure the safety of workers.

WORK SAMPLING

A technique used in work measurement and work study for obtaining information about a particular job or task by the process of sampling (usually random sampling) from the work activities at various times rather than any continuous observation.

WORK SIMPLIFICATION

Concerned with simple techniques of analysing any aspects of work or system with the object of cutting out all unnecessary effort. May involve eliminating, combining, rearranging or simplifying work.

WORK SPECIALISATION

The degree to which the work necessary to achieve organisational goals is broken down into various jobs.

WORK STAFF

Office, supervisory or other white-collar workers whose occupations are closely involved with the manufacturing or production processes in a factory.

WORK STUDY

A set of techniques including work measurement which analyse a given area of work to see whether performance can be made more efficient and economical. It is based on the scientific management approach to the study of the organisation.

WORK TEAM

Is a task group used in organisations to achieve greater organisational flexibility or to cope with rapid growth.

WORK-TO-RULE

A form of industrial action short of a strike, where workers do not withdraw their labour but refuse and cooperation with their employers, beyond the explicitly contractual agreement made for them by their trade union. The net effect on the organisation is usually the same as a go-slow and they are often used together. One effect of these actions is to expose the degree to which the organisation in question depends upon the co-operation and goodwill of its employees.

WORKER-DIRECTOR

A representation of the workforce on the board of directors of an organisation. This is sometimes considered the ultimate in industrial democracy. It is extremely rare.

WORKFLOW

The arrangement of jobs in a particular sequence intended to help an organisation run smoothly and productively.

WORK-IN-PROCESS INVENTORY

The stock of items currently being transformed into a final product or service.

WORKPLACE LAYOUT

Space, facilities and conditions provided for a worker in the performance of a specified job.

WORKS COMMITTEE

Although there is no nationwide system of co-determination in Britain, and no legal requirement for companies to have a works council (see separate entry), many companies of their own volition have established some such employee representative or consultative body, for which works committee is the most common name. The essence of such a works committee is that it meets in a regular, scheduled way and not in response to a crisis. It is typically chaired by a production or general manager, and discuss issues of common interest. Unofficially such committees tend to be used as downward communication channels by management, more than as genuinely consultative bodies.

WORKSHEET

This is the another name for spreadsheets. Spreadsheets are used in the software systems like Quattro-pro, Excel,VPP.

WORKSTATION

The physical environment in which a job is done. It is used most often to refer to the location of a computer operator or word processor operator.

WORLD BRAND

A product that is widely distributed around the world with a single brand name common to all countries and recognised in all its markets.

WORLDWIDE INTEGRATION STRATEGY

A strategy aimed at developing relatively standardized products with global appeal, as well as rationalizing operations throughout the world; also called globalisation.

WORLDWIDE WEB

Is a segment of the Internet that allows managers to have an information location called a website available continually to internet users. Each website has a beginning page called a home page, and each home page generally has several supporting pages called branch pages that expand on the thoughts and ideas contained in the home page.

WRITE-OFF

To remove an item from a company's balance sheet for extraordinary reasons (*e.g.*, writing off, Preliminary Exp., Underwriting commission, Bad debts will never be recovered).

WRITING VOCABULARY

Words used and understood in ordinary writing.

WRITTEN DOWN VALUE

Value of an asset after depreciation has been taken into account. Written down value is virtually synonymous with net book amount.

X

X-EFFICIENCY

A situation in which a firms total costs are not minimised because the actual output from the given inputs is less than the maximum feasible level. This outcome is also termed a situation of technical inefficiency.

XENIX

An versatile, multi-user, multitasking, operating system developed by IBM. It is the name given by the company to UNIX operating system and market it as their product. Unix was originally developed by AT&T modified by Santa Cruz operations and University of California.

XENOPHON

Plato's contemporary, Xenophon, gives in his Cyclopaedia an account of the division of labour. He seems to appreciate the nature of private exchange: he distinguishes between the big cities in which division of labour is developed and the small cities in which it hardly exists.

XEROGRAHIC PRINTER

A page printer (*i.e.* a printer in which the character pattern is set for a whole page before printing) which uses principle of xerography.

XEROGRAPHY

This is a process of electrical photography and is based on the principle that like electrical charges repel each other whereas unlike charges attract each other. A copying camera which can enlarge or reduce the original is used to throw an image of the material to be copied on a plate with a positive electrical charge. A negatively charged power is then spread on the plate. The power adheres to the positively charged letters and lines on the plate. Then a sheet of paper which is positively charged is laid on the plate, removed and heated. As a result the powder on the paper fuses into the paper and forms the image or print. The Xerographic Copier — a model manufactured by Rank-Xerox Ltd. of the U.S.A. — can produce six prints per minute of any document or printed material. It is often possible to make up to eight copies from one exposure. The process can also be used for preparing master for offset-processes and direct process duplicators.

X-Y PLOTTER

Means data plotter.

Y

YARDAGE

Amount of space allocated to a brand on a supermarket shelf.

YARDSTICK

The rates charged by one business used as a measure for setting other rates.

YELLOW JOURNALISM

Sensationalised and exaggerated journalism.

YELLOW-DOG CONTRACT

An agreement to the effect that a new employee would refrain from joining a union, which employers fighting unionisation forced workers to sign.

YESTERDAY

Refers to previous period.

YOU APPROACH

Personalised form of copywriting which directs message at individual reader.

YOUNG PERSONS

Legislation re-advertising.

YOUNG-HELMOHOLTZ THEORY

Three-colour visions which assumes a three-colour mechanism of the retina which responds maximally to red, green and blue/violet respectively.

YOUTH TRAINING SCHEME (YTS)

A programme of work experience and education followed by 16-year old school-leavers in Britain, financed by government grants and administered by the manpower services commission.

YUPPIES (YOUNG, UPWARDLY MOBILE PROFESSIONAL)

A mildly derogatory reference to successful but status-conscious business (or other professional) people.

Z

ZAP

A command of dbase whose purpose is to destroy the records permanently from the storage.

Z-BUFFERING

A 3D computer graphics terms which removes the hidden lines and hidden surfaces.

Z-CHART

Known also as a graphic chart, it consists of three lines or curves which together look like the letter "Z". It is prepared to represent weekly, monthly or quarterly returns; cumulative totals of the figures for a particular period; and moving yearly totals of the figures. The line of weekly, monthly or quarterly figures indicates seasonal fluctuations, while the line showing the annual moving totals indicates the trend.

ZERO DEFECTS

The objective of a policy of total quality. It is to have every single item produced and delivered to the customer completely perfect as opposed to working within and acceptable range of quality and therefore, defectiveness.

ZERO TRANSMISSION LEVEL REFERENCE POINT

Arbitrarily chosen reference point in a circuit to which all relative transmission levels are referred.

ZERO-BASE BUDGETING

The use of budgets which start from a present base of zero and regard all future expenditure as being on new items rather than a continuation of existing ones. In practice this means that a budget has to be justified in full for each year of operation.

ZIP FILES

These are the file which are created when PKZIP-EXE program is applied on a file. These files have the extension ZIP. To use these files it is required to unzip the zipped files first using PKUNZIP-EXE program so that they come in their original form.

ZIP MODE

A mode of operation in which each input command represents an incremental deviation.

ZONE PRICING

A type of delivered pricing in which prices vary according to the number of geographic zones through which a product passes in moving from seller to buyer.

ZONING

The process by which local govern¬ments can designate the types of structures and activities that can be built and performed in a particular area. It is a complex legal process that is often affected by local politics.

ZOOM

A feature of graphic packages or spreadsheet packages which allows the user to magnifying a particular part of the graphics or spreadsheet. The term has been derived from photography/ (zoomed lens).